# Principles of International Finance and Open Economy Macroeconomics

# Principles of International Finance and Open Economy Macroeconomics
## Theories, Applications, and Policies

Cristina Terra
THEMA, Université de Cergy-Pontoise

ELSEVIER

AMSTERDAM • BOSTON • HEIDELBERG • LONDON
NEW YORK • OXFORD • PARIS • SAN DIEGO
SAN FRANCISCO • SINGAPORE • SYDNEY • TOKYO
Academic Press is an imprint of Elsevier

Academic Press is an imprint of Elsevier
125, London Wall, EC2Y 5AS.
525 B Street, Suite 1800, San Diego, CA 92101-4495, USA
225 Wyman Street, Waltham, MA 02451, USA
The Boulevard, Langford Lane, Kidlington, Oxford OX5 1GB, UK

**Notices**
Knowledge and best practice in this field are constantly changing. As new research and experience broaden our understanding, changes in research methods, professional practices, or medical treatment may become necessary.

Practitioners and researchers must always rely on their own experience and knowledge in evaluating and using any information, methods, compounds, or experiments described herein. In using such information or methods they should be mindful of their own safety and the safety of others, including parties for whom they have a professional responsibility.

To the fullest extent of the law, neither the Publisher nor the authors, contributors, or editors, assume any liability for any injury and/or damage to persons or property as a matter of products liability, negligence or otherwise, or from any use or operation of any methods, products, instructions, or ideas contained in the material herein.

**British Library Cataloguing-in-Publication Data**
A catalogue record for this book is available from the British Library

**Library of Congress Cataloging-in-Publication Data**
A catalog record for this book is available from the Library of Congress

For information on all Academic Press publications
visit our website at http://store.elsevier.com/

ISBN: 978-0-12-802297-9

Typeset by MPS Limited, Chennai, India
www.adi-mps.com

Printed and bound in the USA

Working together
to grow libraries in
developing countries

www.elsevier.com • www.bookaid.org

*Publisher*: Nikki Levy
*Acquisition Editor*: J. Scott Bentley
*Editorial Project Manager*: Susan Ikeda
*Production Project Manager*: Nicky Carter
*Designer*: Mark Rogers

# Contents

# PART IV  Crises and Exchange Rate Policy

# PART V

# Foreword

This is what international economy students and practitioners needed: A book on Open Economy Macroeconomics and International Finance with actual world examples. And the real world examples are from the developing world! What a treat. The book is well written. The analytical rigor is first rate, the reader can rest assure the mathematical models are consistent and can provide a solid basis to think about very important issues. The book covers countries balance of payments, their indebtedness, and its relationship with its current-account deficits, and also exchange rates—how they are determined and their fundamental role in economics. Having myself worked in this area for the past 20 years, I am happy to see that we are constantly evolving in our learning and understanding of the field. This book is an important contribution for that.

**Ilan Goldfajn**
*Pontifícia Universidade Católica, Rio de Janeiro*

# Preface

*Principles of International Finance and Open Economy Macroeconomics* grew out of international finance courses I taught in undergraduate and master programs over the past 20 years. It presents a macroeconomic framework for understanding and analyzing the global economy, emphasizing the perspectives of emerging economies and developing countries. It discusses the main theories of open economy macroeconomics and international finance, illustrating them with examples and actual cases, mostly related to developing countries.

The theories are built through a unified mathematical framework accessible to those with basic mathematical skills (basic calculus). With the focus on real world practical issues, the mathematical models serve as an analytical tool to help in organizing ideas and clarifying arguments. They make clear the assumptions and simplifications used to describe real economic situations. Moreover, mathematics ensures the logical precision of the argument and helps in understanding the connections among economic variables.

The book is aimed at upper division undergraduate and graduate level students. The format appeals to those who want to read single chapters as well as those who want to read the whole book. To this end, explanations are made step by step, focusing on economic intuition. More complicated mathematical passages are developed in appendices at the end of each chapter.

## How to Use This Book

As a guideline, the main material for a course can be found in Chapters 1, 2, 3, 4 (excluding Sections 4.3 and 4.4), 6, 7 (excluding Section 7.2), and 8 (excluding Section 8.4). These chapters contain the main models and issues concerning international macroeconomics and finance. Sections 4.3, 4.4, and 7.2 develop extensions to the basic model developed in the first sections of the respective chapters. Section 8.4 and Chapters 9–11 are more specialized or somewhat more advanced, and not essential for a basic course.

# Acknowledgments

Although academic work appears to be a solitary activity, it cannot be accomplished without the intellectual stimulation of interpersonal interactions. The lonely mind tends to always follow the same paths, while others take us out of our comfort zone, bringing light to new ways of reasoning. I am thankful for my students at Fundação Getulio Vargas, PUC-Rio, Université de Cergy-Pontoise, and ESSEC Business School, during these 20 years of teaching international macroeconomics. Their questions and comments were fundamental to the elaboration of this book. I also thank my colleagues of these institutions by the rich intellectual environment that taught me so much. I am sure that you, students and colleagues, will recognize your contribution in this book.

I thank FGV Projetos for financial support and Cesar Campos, its executive director, for his incentive, without which the project would not have materialized.

My special thanks to Rodrigo Soares de Abreu, doctoral student at EPGE/FGV, for his meticulous work in the construction of graphs, the preparation of the proposed exercises, as well as for his careful reading of the manuscript, which greatly contributed to eliminate inaccuracies and to enrich the text.

I am grateful to Mark Evans for the careful and competent translation of the book from its original version in Portuguese.

To be free to produce, the mind needs a quiet heart. I thank my parents, Hélio and Inês, for the love, support, and life example; my daughter, Tatiana, for enriching my life in so many dimensions; my stepchildren, Edmond and Ludmilla, for the joy; my sisters, Maria Inês, Carol, Bel, Elisa, Lis, Marisa, and Lulus; and my brothers, Bonomo, Gustavo, and Marco, for the safety net; my friends, for the support. I thank my husband, Thierry, for the affection and the complicity.

1

# Introduction

Reports on international finance always make the headlines. Industries complain that exchange rates are too appreciated. The American government accuses the Chinese of maintaining their exchange rates artificially depreciated while the Chinese deny it is the result of an active government policy. The debt crisis of the 1980s took Latin American countries into a decade-long struggle against astronomical inflation rates and government fiscal difficulties. It is even known as the region's *lost decade*. Now it is Europe that appears to be living its *lost decade*.

When is external debt excessive? How does one know if an exchange rate is overappreciated? What leads to an exchange rate crisis? Do variations in government spending affect the exchange rate? What is the relationship between fiscal deficit and current-account deficit? Which is better, a floating or fixed exchange rate regime? Should Greece abandon the Euro? This book intends to provide an analytical framework that allows the reader to understand how to deal with these and other important questions related to international economics from the macroeconomic point of view.

Macroeconomics and international finance are vast fields[1] and covering all questions, models, and applications pertinent to these two fields would be a "mission impossible." The objective for the choice of topics covered in this book is to provide a logical structure to aid in understanding and analyzing questions concerning exchange rates and balance of payments. Each chapter describes a facet of international finance, like pieces of a puzzle that, once put together, form a picture of international finance that allows one to appreciate the individual elements and their interactions. The idea is to help the reader in building their own conceptual framework, allowing them to form their own analysis and conclusions regarding issues related to macroeconomics and international finance. More important than understanding the crises in exchange rate that have already occurred, for example, is understanding how they function and what causes them, allowing one to analyze new international finance contexts that may come about in the future.

Each chapter presents economic situations that provide for the development of mathematical models to highlight the essence of the problem, understand how the economic variables interact, and illustrate the forces in play. These models are simple, presented in an

---

[1] *International macroeconomics* seeks to explain the interaction between macroeconomic variables, such as level of income, interest rates, and prices, while *international finance* focuses on the exchange of assets and currency between countries, that is, the monetary side of international economics.

intuitive manner, and have mathematical appendices that provide step-by-step explanations of how they work. Concrete examples show how the theory can be applied to real-world situations. The book presents graphs, using data easily found on the Internet, so that the reader can reproduce them for different countries or periods in order to perform their own analysis of situations of interest to them and which have not been covered in the book. The Annexes at the end of the book provide Internet addresses where the data used in the graphs can be found. The intent is to offer instruments for analysis and tools that can be used in concrete cases. Finally, exercises are given at the end of each chapter. Some are designed to consolidate the material presented while others propose questions that will require additional analysis.

## 1.1 Mathematical Modeling

Economic analysis is usually performed using mathematical models. It is important to emphasize that these are used as analytical instruments and not as an end in themselves. Mathematics can be considered a type of language where the mathematical model tells a story. But, why tell a story using mathematics and not English? Mathematics is a specific type of language with four characteristics that make it more attractive to use when dealing with economics.

First, each mathematical symbol, which corresponds to *words*, has a unique and precise definition. The same is not true for English. For example, the dictionary offers at least five different definitions for the word *symbol*.[2] Second, mathematics is a concise language. Once a term has been precisely defined, it can be represented by a symbol. A mathematical expression can represent an idea that would take an entire page to explain were it transcribed into English. Given its due proportion, the expression "a picture is worth a thousand words" can be applied in this case. Third, mathematical *grammar* is also very precise. In mathematics, there are strict rules regarding the relationships that can be made, or rather, about what can be expressed based on the initial definitions. There is no room for reading between the lines or for metaphors. It is really less charming than a discourse in English (there are those who may disagree) but when one desires a precise understanding of a concrete element, mathematics is best. Finally, mathematics is a universal language. Not everyone speaks English, but anyone who has been to school has studied math.

Due to these characteristics, when one tells a story in mathematics, it is told in such a way that each of its elements is precisely defined and the logical structure is strictly obeyed. Mathematics obliges the author of the story to express all the hypotheses used and the

---

[2] Definitions for "symbol," according to the *Merriam-Webster* online dictionary (http://www.merriam-webster .com/dictionary/symbol) are: 1. An authoritative summary of faith or doctrine; 2. Something that stands for or suggests something else by reason of relationship, association, convention, or accidental resemblance; especially: a visible sign of something invisible; 3. An arbitrary or conventional sign used in writing or printing relating to a particular field to represent operations, quantities, elements, relations, or qualities; 4. An object or act representing something in the unconscious mind that has been repressed; 5. An act, sound, or object having cultural significance and the capacity to excite or objectify a response.

*grammar* guarantees that there are no errors in logic. While it is true that the same story could be told in English, it is much more difficult to express with the same precision, and errors in logic are more easily made. Mathematics serves, therefore, as a tool to help mere mortals, such as myself, to make fewer mistakes.

Up to this point, I have only spoken regarding the advantages of using mathematics. After all, I must convince you that the analytical method presented in this book is the one best suited for its purpose: offer an analytical framework you can use to understand situations not covered in the book. I do not want to sell a pig in a poke: mathematics also has its limits. As is almost always true, its best quality is also is greatest liability. Given that it is very precise, mathematics does not capture all the nuances inherent to socioeconomic relations. Simplification is necessary to express the world in a mathematical model. This is where it becomes an art: how does one simplify in such a way as to make the model understandable while at the same time maintain the elements necessary to understand the problem?

If I throw a stone into the waters of Copacabana Beach in Rio de Janeiro, waves are created that, in principle, would reach Walvis Bay in Namibia. However, there is an ocean between Copacabana and Walvis Bay (both literally and figuratively) with currents and waves caused by other factors that make those waves created by my stone to be imperceptible in Africa (actually, well before reaching Africa). If, instead of my small stone, a large meteorite fell into the waters of Copacabana Beach, the impact would be felt in Walvis Bay. Just like waves in the ocean, markets and economies are interconnected. Buying grapes at the supermarket, in principle, could stimulate an increase in grape prices, which could lead people to eat more apples, given that grapes are more expensive. This could lead to greater apple imports, which could lead to a deficit in current account...and a crisis in balance of payments. Well, just as my small stone in the waters of Copacabana Beach will not cause a tsunami in Walvis Bay, I can buy grapes without worrying about causing an international crisis.

Of course, decisions in economic modeling are more subtle than the simple example given above. It is not always clear which variables are relevant. Actually, relevant variables can change over time, as will be seen in Chapter 9. Each new wave of exchange rate crises generates more literature, adding previously absent variables to the models. The first models developed in the 1980s did not consider foreign corporate debt, for example, which was essential to the development of the crises of the 1990s.

As George E.P. Box said, "essentially, all models are wrong, but some are useful." If on the one hand simplifications to an economic model make it unrealistic, on the other, not simplifying makes it impossible to understand what is occurring. Useful models are those that are able to discard what is really unimportant, but keep those elements essential for comprehension. A good model should be like a good map: it shows the trajectory from one point to another, identifies obstructions, topography, vegetation, and any other element important in reaching the destination. I present models that are useful, pointing out their limitations. The notations are uniform throughout the book and, whenever possible, the same model structure is used.

## 1.2 Book Structure

The first part of the book defines the object of our analysis. Given that macroeconomics and international finance deal with economic relations between countries, **Chapter 2** begins by describing the taxonomy of the international flow of goods and financial assets. The balance of payment registers the international transaction of goods, services, and financial assets between countries. In national accounts, we will see how the results of these transactions relate to the main macroeconomic aggregates. The main objective is to understand the relation between current-account balance and the evolution of the external debt of a country, and how private consumption and government expenses are associated to the current account.

The rate is a fundamental variable in international economics for it converts prices set in different currencies into a common currency. **Chapter 3** defines what an exchange rate is and how to assess its level, that is, what variables are relevant in determining if an exchange rate is appreciated or depreciated. An importer, for example, is interested in comparing the price of a product in their country with its price in another country. The exchange rate converts the two prices into a single currency, allowing comparison. Assessing the exchange rate depends, therefore, on the role of the exchange rate in comparing the purchasing power of the two currencies. However, for an individual who goes into debt in Chinese yuans, what matters is how much the exchange rate will change from the time they went into debt to when they pay it off. If the price of the Yuan goes up, the debt becomes more expensive. For the financial investor, what matters is the expectation of exchange rate variations.

**Part I** of the book describes and defines the variables and discusses the relationship between them. However, there is no discussion of causality. It is like a picture of the economic world but without defining if the horse is before the cart or the cart before the horse. The remainder of the book is dedicated to discussions of how the economy works.

**Part II** is dedicated to understanding how the main macroeconomic aggregates relate to foreign debt and the real exchange rate. **Chapter 4** shows how the current-account balance, which corresponds to the change in the country's net foreign liabilities, is the result of economic decisions regarding savings and investment. By means of the model presented in the chapter, it is possible to understand the source of benefits for a country in opening itself to the international financial market and what variables are relevant to assess if a given current-account level is desirable and/or sustainable.

Each current-account level is associated with a real exchange rate level, which, in turn, reflects the relative price of tradable and nontradable goods in the economy. As such, the trade balance is associated with level of the real exchange rate, which is covered in **Chapter 5**. We will see how economic variables, such as interest rates, fiscal policy, and terms of trade, affect the equilibrium real exchange rate. The analysis will show how an increase in international commodity prices in the last years caused an increase in services in Brazil, for example.

The notion of a real exchange rate is associated with the comparison of prices among countries by using the same currency. However, the variable published daily in the newspapers is the nominal exchange rate, or rather, how many Dollars are needed to buy one Euro, for example. Its interaction with the level of prices is what results in the real exchange rate. **Part III** covers the nominal exchange rate determiners. The analysis is divided into three chapters. **Chapter 6** considers the long-term exchange rate determiners, or rather, when prices are readjusted due to possible economic shocks. The focus is on the relationship between monetary policy and the exchange rate. **Chapter 7** studies the impact of these fiscal and monetary policies on the exchange rate and the level of short-term economic activity, or rather, before the complete adjustment of prices due to alterations in economic policy or other economic variables.

One common characteristic in Chapters 6 and 7 is that they consider international investors as being indifferent to assets from different countries. In practical terms, this means that a country never has a problem financing itself: all that is necessary is to equalize the return of its bonds to that of international bonds. This hypothesis would be reasonable in comparing American and Japanese bonds, for example, but is far from real when comparing an American bond with one from Greece. **Chapter 8** analyzes what happens when international investors are not indifferent when considering bonds from different countries. In this case, it is possible to understand, for example, the causes of the global imbalance seen during the first decade of the millennium, where the United States accumulated increasing current-account deficits which were financed in large part by Asian countries, China in particular.

With the aid of the analytical structure developed in Parts II and III, **Part IV** considers practical topics related to exchange rate policy. The exchange rate crises, which are the dark side of the international finance market, are considered in **Chapter 9**. The main characteristics of the exchange rate crises that have occurred over the last 30 years are studied and analytically modeled. **Chapter 10** describes the different exchange rate regimes adopted around the world as well as their economic implications. Finally, exchange rate economic policy is studied in **Chapter 11**. In it, the political motivations for a government's choice of an exchange rate policy are studied.

# Definitions

Part I, composed of two chapters, has the objective of defining the object of our study, which are the many variables related to international economic relations. We will begin, in Chapter 2, with a description of the macroeconomic variables that measure transactions between two economies, accounted for in the Balance of Payments by the international accounting system. We will describe how international transactions are divided, according to their nature, among the three Balance of Payments accounts: the Current Account, the Capital Account, and the Financial Account. We will show the relation between the Current Account balance and the country's external indebtedness and, by means of national accounts, its relation between aggregate savings and investments.

Different countries have, in general, different currencies so that economic transactions between them involve currency exchange. Therefore, exchange rates play a fundamental role in determining the costs and gains relative to both trade and financial transactions. This will be discussed in Chapter 3. Notions regarding nominal and real exchange rates are defined and parity conditions that regulate the international goods and assets markets are analyzed.

# 2

# How to Measure International Transactions

## CHAPTER OUTLINE

What economic variables should be analyzed to determine if there is risk of a balance of payments crisis; if the trajectory of foreign debt is sustainable; if the exchange rate is overvalued? Although an answer to each of these questions would require extensive study, based on an analysis of the economy and its relationship with other countries, let us begin by defining the object of our study. The balance of payments accounts for the transaction of goods, services, and assets between the residents of one country and those of the rest of the world. It is connected to the system of national accounts, which is a systematic structure for presenting the macroeconomic statistics of a country.

Sections 2.1 and 2.2 begin with a presentation of the basic structure of each of these accounting systems. Their objective is to identify the relevant statistics necessary to design an analytical framework of the macroeconomic situation of the country and its relation to the rest of the world. Section 2.3 discusses the idea of equilibrium in the balance of payments, and Section 2.4 maps the economic models presented in this book based on definitions presented in the previous sections.

Principles of International Finance and Open Economy Macroeconomics.
English translation © 2015 Elsevier Inc.

## 2.1 Balance of Payments

The balance of payments registers the transactions between the residents and nonresidents of a country for a specific period, usually a calendar year.[1] Accounting is done by means of a double-entry system: each transaction is a positive entry in one account and a negative entry in another, such that the sum of the entries is equal to zero.[2]

The balance of payments is divided into different accounts according to the nature of the transactions. There are three main accounts: **Current Account**, **Capital Account**, and **Financial Account**. The main difference between the current account and the others is that it deals with the flow impacting the period in question, while the capital and financial accounts deal with the accumulation of assets and liabilities in relation to the rest of the world. Table 2.1 presents the basic structure of the balance of payments, which I describe next.

### 2.1.1 Current Account

The Current Account registers the imports and exports of goods and services, as well as the payments of income, divided between the primary and secondary income balances.[3] Let us begin with the **trade of goods and services**. Goods are physical items that are produced and for which ownership can be established. Therefore, the imports and exports of goods represent the exchange of ownership of those goods between a resident and nonresident of a country.

**Services**, for their part, are the result of a productive activity that alters what is consumed, or that facilitates the exchange of goods and financial assets. In general, there is not anything physical that can be possessed. Some common examples are transportation and communication services, royalties, the liquefaction of natural gas, oil refinery, as well as other international activities that have grown with globalization, such as the packaging of goods, the assembly of electronics and clothes, and the transaction of goods that are transferred by Internet, such as software, among others.

The sale of a good or service by a resident of a country to a nonresident is an **export**, which is registered as a credit in the goods and services account, and is therefore a positive entry. Remembering that transactions are always registered using a double-entry in the balance of payments, the corresponding payment, be it a cash or credit transaction, appears

---

[1] For a detailed description of balance of payments, see the Sixth Edition of the IMF's *balance of payments and International Investment Position Manual* at http://www.imf.org/external/pubs/ft/bop/2007/bopman6.htm. At http://unstats.un.org/unsd/nationalaccount/sna.asp, a descriptive manual on the National Accounts can be found.

[2] In practice, however, this equality may not hold. The reason for the discrepancy is due to the data for credits and debits many times coming from different sources. The "Errors and Omissions" account is responsible for *closing* the balance.

[3] In the IMF 1993 *Manual for balance of payments,* there is no division between primary and secondary income. The division is made in the 2008 edition of the manual, which corresponds to the sixth edition.

**Table 2.1**   Balance of Payments

| Current Account | Credits (+) | Debits (−) |
|---|---|---|
| *Goods and Services* | | |
| Goods | Exports | Imports |
| Services | Sales | Purchases |
| *Primary Income* | Received | Sent |
| *Secondary Income* | Received | Sent |
| **Capital Account** | | |
| Capital transfers | Received | Sent |
| Acquisitions/disposals of nonproduced nonfinancial assets | Acquisition | Disposal |
| **Financial Account** | *Net incurrence of liabilities* (+) | *Net acquisition of assets* (−) |
| Direct Investment | By foreigners in the home country | By domestic residents abroad |
| Portfolio Investment | Sales of domestic assets | Purchases of foreign assets |
| Financial Derivatives | Sales of domestic assets | Purchases of foreign assets |
| Other Investment | Sales of domestic assets | Purchases of foreign assets |
| Reserve assets | Reduction | Increase |
| **Errors and Omissions** | | |
| **Total** | = | = |

as a debit on the financial account, as we will see shortly. If the export is considered a donation, that is, with no countering payment, it will appear as a debit on the secondary income balance in the current account, or in the capital account, as we will also see shortly.

An **import** is the purchase of a good or service from a nonresident by a resident. It constitutes a debit on the goods and services account, has a corresponding credit on the financial account, the balance of secondary income, or the capital account, and the same as in the case of the export.

Besides the transactions of goods and services, the current account registers the flow of income between residents and nonresidents. This income is classified as primary and secondary income. The **Primary income account** registers the payments to factors of production, the returns to financial assets, and the rent of natural resources. The income received is registered as a credit on this account, and includes salaries received by workers when employed by a company nonresident in the home country, with the workers still residing in country. It also includes dividends from multinational corporations, interest received from international loans, among others.[4] **Secondary income** corresponds to the redistribution of income by means of **current transfers**, such as donations from one government to

---

[4] The balance of primary income corresponds to the services factor in the balance of payments prior to 1993, and to the Balance of Income in the 1993 manual.

another or money an immigrant sends to his/her family.[5] Notice that there are two types of transfers: current, registered here, and capital, registered in the capital account. **Transfers of capital** occur when there is a transfer of ownership of an asset that is not currency. By exclusion, **current transfers** are those that are not transfers of capital. Examples of current transfers are international aid, personal transfers, such as lottery winnings, income tax paid by nonresidents, among others.

The current-account balance is the sum of the balances of the goods and services, primary income, and secondary income accounts. As we will see in Section 2.2, the balance of the primary income affects the national income, while the combination of primary and secondary income balances has an impact on the disposable national income. The transfers of capital do not affect the disposable income, and for such are not computed in the capital account (Box 2.1).

## 2.1.2 Capital Account

The **Capital Account** registers the acquisitions or disposal of **nonfinancial** and **nonproduced** assets.[6] This includes the exploitation of natural resources, such as mineral, forest, or airspace. Notice that to be registered on the capital account, there should be a change in the ownership of the right to exploit. If the use is temporary, the registration is made on the secondary income account of the current account. Also registered on the capital account are marketing assets transactions, such as brand names, trademarks, and contracts, that give exclusive rights over future goods and services, such as the amount paid by a foreign soccer club for a player.

Finally, the capital account includes transfers of capital between residents and nonresidents. Inheritance received, forgiveness of foreign debt between countries, or even the transfer of capital from a foreign government or international organization to finance an investment project, such as building roads, are included in this item.

An important difference between the current account and the capital account is that the latter is an accumulation account. It registers the accumulation of assets that have an impact on the future, while the current account deals with the flows relevant only to the current period. The financial account, which will be described next, is also an accumulation account that registers the transaction of financial assets. The capital and financial accounts explain the variations in international investment positions, which will be defined in Section 2.3.

## 2.1.3 Financial Account

The sum of the current account and capital accounts constitutes the economy's need of foreign financing. It represents the net debt accumulation (in the case of a deficit) or a credit (in the case of surplus) for a country in relation to the rest of the world. The role of the **Financial**

---

[5] The secondary income balance was denominated Current Transfers in the balance of payments prior to 2008.

[6] In contrast, the assets produced, that is, goods and services, are entered in the current account, while financial assets are entered in the financial account, which is described in the following section.

## BOX 2.1 CURRENT ACCOUNT AND TRADE BALANCE

Countries that make net primary and secondary income payments present a trade balance above that of the current account. In general, this is the case in countries that have external debt or that receive a large volume of Foreign Direct Investment (FDI), such as Brazil, for example. The country always made net primary and secondary income payments, since, as shown in Figure 2.1A, the

(A)

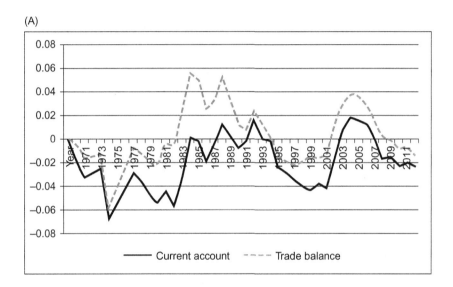

(B)

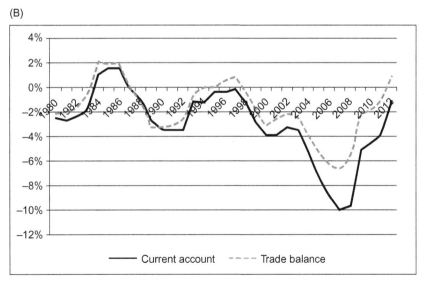

**Figure 2.1** Current account and trade balance (% of GDP). *The World Bank, Reference (1) on the Data List in the Appendix.*

*(Continued)*

BOX 2.1 (CONTINUED)

trade balance is always greater than that of the current account. This difference reached its apex at the beginning of the 1980s during the foreign debt crisis (which will be discussed in detail in Chapter 10).

This is also the case for Spain, as shown in Figure 2.1B. The international financial crisis at the end of the 2000s affected several European countries, including Spain, which suffered a significant increase in interest rates relative to its foreign debt. The result was a considerable increase in the primary income payment, which can be seen in the graph by the greater difference between the trade balance and the current-account balance.

There is an important difference between the external crisis in Latin America in the 1980s and the European in the 2000s. As we can see in the Brazil case, the Latin American countries had to generate a high trade surplus to pay for the servicing of external debt and obtain equilibrium in their current-account balance, being that they did not have credit in the international market to finance eventual deficits. The European countries in crisis at the end of the 2000s had the help of the European Union to finance their current-account deficits, as shown in the case of Spain in Figure 2.1B.

**Account** is to measure how loans are made, or how debt is financed, between residents and nonresidents. More precisely, the financial account registers the transactions between residents and nonresidents that involve **financial assets and liabilities**. A surplus in the financial account means an increase in net indebtedness between the country and the rest of the world.[7]

The entries on the financial account have as a counterpart the entries on the current account, the capital account, or even other items on the financial account. We saw that the export of a good, for example, is entered as a credit on the Goods and Services Account. The receipt of the value of the export is entered as a debit on the financial account, in the form of currency variation and deposits (if the payment is made in cash) or in trade credit (if the payment is financed).

The financial account registers all transactions of financial assets and liabilities, which are grouped into categories with characteristics similar either in nature, or in their economic motivations, or in their pattern of behavior. Transactions that imply an increase in assets are entered as negative and operations that correspond to an increase in foreign liability are entered as positive. The transactions are divided into direct investment, portfolio investment, financial derivatives, other investments, and reserve assets. We will now look at what each of these categories are.

**Direct investment** is that which results in the control, or significant degree of influence, of the management of a company resident in another country. It is associated with a long-term relationship that can involve additional contributions such as the transfer of technology,

---

[7] In the balance of payments manuals prior to 1993, this was called the Capital Account, *grosso modo*, which today is called the Financial Account. Due to this, economics textbooks still commonly use the term "Capital Account" to designate the variation of debt or credit of a country in relation to the rest of the world.

marketing, or management. The direct investment made by a resident American abroad is registered in the American balance of payments as a net acquisition of assets, while the direct investment by a foreigner in the United States constitutes a net incurrence of liabilities.

**Portfolio investments**, in turn, are transactions involving debt or equity securities, not including those referring to direct investment or reserve assets. Different from direct investment, in the case of portfolio investment, there is no influence in company management. It is associated with the financial market and offers liquidity and flexibility to the investor. Due to its characteristics, portfolio investment tends to be more volatile than direct investment. Its registry as assets and liabilities follows the same form as direct investment: the acquisition of foreign assets is registered as a net acquisition of assets, while the sale of domestic assets to nonresidents is registered as a net incurrence of liabilities.

Operations with **financial derivatives** deserve a separate grouping due to their nature as instruments by which risk is negotiated. In general, derivatives do not generate primary income, as is the case with other categories in the financial account.

The category of **other investments**, despite its name giving the impression that it is a *remainders* account, is actually an important category in the financial account. It involves operations of currency, deposits, trade, and credits. The payment in cash for an export performed appears in this account as a net acquisition of assets, or the trade credit for the importer is registered as a net incurrence of liabilities. Foreign debt also appears here: a loan made abroad by a domestic company, for example, appears as a net incurrence of liabilities in other investments. In summary, this category registers loans, currency transactions, and deposits made between residents and nonresidents, the allocation of special withdrawal rights from the International Monetary Fund (IMF), among others. In general, the purchase of a foreign asset is registered as negative on the financial account and corresponds as a loan to the rest of the world. Analogously, the sale of a domestic asset is entered as a positive and represents an obligation of the country to the rest of the world.

The **reserve assets** are foreign assets available to and under the control of monetary authorities. The assets registered as changes in reserves are the same as what appear in other categories of the financial account. The difference is that, when they belong to the monetary authorities, they are registered as reserve assets. As these assets belong to the monetary authorities, they can be used to cover financial needs in the balance of payments, intervene in the exchange rate market and other correlated objectives. Examples of these reserves are deposits, bonds, gold, foreign currency, and a reserve position with the IMF. The IMF suggests that the variations in reserve assets be registered in the financial account of the balance of payments. Some countries, however, opt for registering it in a separate account.

## 2.2 National Accounts

The balance of payments is part of the National Accounts system, which registers economic activity based on a standardized accounting system between nations. We will now see how transactions with the rest of the world relate to the main domestic macroeconomic aggregates, through the national accounts.

The main aggregate of national accounts is the **Gross Domestic Product** (GDP), which measures everything that is produced within the country's borders.[8] However, not all that is produced within the country belongs to the residents of that country. Consider, for example, the profit generated by a factory belonging to a multinational corporation. Production is done by means of a production factor, the capital, whose owners do not reside in the country. Therefore, the profit does not belong to the residents of that country. The **Gross National Income** (GNI), in turn, registers the value of all goods and services produced by production factors resident in the country. The difference between the two aggregates, GDP and GNI, corresponds to the net payment of income of the factors used in production but that are not residents in the country. As we saw in Section 2.1.1, the payment of income between residents and nonresidents is registered in the primary income account of the current account. Defining PI as the primary income balance, we have that:

$$\text{GNI} - \text{GDP} = \text{PI} \tag{2.1}$$

If the primary income balance is negative, that is, if the country makes net income payments, then the GDP is greater than the GNI.

The goods and services available for use in a country correspond to the sum of GDP ($Y$) and the import of goods and services ($M$). These goods and services can be used for private consumption ($C$), investment[9] ($I$), government consumption ($G$), or to be exported ($X$). This accounting can be represented by the equation:

$$Y + M = C + I + G + X$$

which can be rewritten as:

$$Y = C + I + G + \text{TB} \tag{2.2}$$

where TB is the trade balance, which is the balance of the goods and services account. Adding the primary income balance to both sides of Eq. (2.2) and using Eq. (2.1), we have that:

$$\underbrace{Y + \text{PI}}_{\text{GNI}} = C + I + G + \text{TB} + \text{PI} \tag{2.3}$$

Finally, adding the secondary income balance to both sides, we get:

$$\underbrace{\text{GNI} + \text{SI}}_{\text{Gross National Disposable Income}} = C + I + G + \underbrace{\text{TB} + \text{PI} + \text{SI}}_{\text{Current Account}}$$

---

[8] More precisely, the GDP registers all that is produced within national borders less the consumption of intermediate goods. Otherwise, the intermediate goods would be counted twice: in their production and again as part of the goods they were used as inputs.

[9] Investment here uses the economic definition: *gross fixed capital formation*, or the purchase of goods, such as machinery and equipment, that can be used in the production of other goods.

which we represent by:

$$Y^{\mathrm{d}} = C + I + G + \mathrm{CA} \tag{2.4}$$

where $Y^{\mathrm{d}}$ is the **Gross National Disposable Income**, defined as the GNI plus the secondary income balance. We have seen that secondary income includes items such as, for example, international aid or remittances by immigrants to their families. These incomes should therefore be added to what is available for consumption in the country. CA represents the current-account balance, which is, by definition, the sum of trade balance with the primary and secondary income balances: $\mathrm{CA} = \mathrm{TB} + \mathrm{PI} + \mathrm{SI}$.

Equation (2.4) represents the basic identity of national accounts. The left side of the equation is the total disposable income of domestic residents and the right side represents the uses for this income, which can be private consumption, investment, government consumption, or transactions with the rest of the world. We can write it as:

$$\underbrace{Y^{\mathrm{d}}}_{\text{Income}} - \underbrace{(C + I + G)}_{\text{Expenditures}} = \mathrm{CA} \tag{2.5}$$

which shows that when the current-account balance is positive, income is greater than expenditures in a country. In this case, the country can lend to the rest of the world. When the current-account balance is negative, the national income is less than expenditures and the country borrows from the rest of the world.

Another way to interpret Eq. (2.4) is by identifying private savings ($S^{\mathrm{p}}$) and government savings ($S^{\mathrm{g}}$) in the equation. To do this, we add and subtract taxes ($T$) on the left side of Eq. (2.5), thus obtaining:

$$
\begin{aligned}
(Y^{\mathrm{d}} - T - C) + (T - G) - I &= \mathrm{CA}, \\
S^{\mathrm{p}} + S^{\mathrm{g}} - I &= \mathrm{CA}.
\end{aligned}
\tag{2.6}
$$

According to the equation, a deficit in current account means that investment in the country is greater than savings. The equation also shows that a reduction of the account deficit has as a counterpart an increase in savings and/or a reduction in investment (Box 2.2).

It is important to emphasize that Eq. (2.6) is an accounting identity: it is true regardless of ideologies or viewpoints regarding how the economy functions. It defines the relation between economic variables, but does not indicate the causality between them. To know, for instance, what the impact will be of an increase in production on the current account or what type of economic policy to use to affect the current-account balance, one must understand the way the economy works, what the motivations are for the economic agents, and how the variables relate to each other.

What is the impact of economic shocks on the current account? Take, for example, a country that has a positive income shock, such as the discovery and exploitation of a new oil reserve. If the story were to end with this increase in GDP, Eq. (2.6) would tell us that there would be an increase in savings and, therefore, an increase in current-account balance.

---

**BOX 2.2 THE CHINESE EXCHANGE RATE**

During the 2000s, China was accused of maintaining its currency depreciated, generating trade surpluses and, consequently, very high current-account surpluses. Using Eq. (2.6), it becomes clear that the essence of the problem was an excess of savings in the economy: the over-depreciated currency was, actually, the result of high savings. According to what we will see in Chapter 5, the exchange rate is associated with the current account in such a way that the current-account surplus has as its counterpart a more depreciated currency. However, there is no way to alter the exchange rate by brute force to solve the problem. It is necessary to change the incentives for investment and savings for the economy to come to save less and invest more. Consequently, the surplus in current account will reduce and bring about a more appreciated exchange rate.

---

However, it is expected that, along with the increased income, the economic agents would decide to consume more. If all the additional income is consumed, there would be no change in the level of savings and the current-account balance would remain unaltered. Or rather, if it is known that more oil reserves will be exploited in the future, the population may decide to consume even more because they believe they will be even richer in the future, causing savings to fall along with the current-account balance. We can therefore see that the effects of a shock or a change in the economy depend on the reaction of the economic agents. Economic models try to represent individual incentives in order to capture the causalities among the variables. In Chapter 4, we will present a model that explains how variables such as the income level or international interest rates affect the current account, taking into consideration the behavior of individuals in response to changes in the economy.

One must remember that any economic model must obey the rules of the economy, among them the accounting identities of national accounts and balance of payments. In the next section, we will take a step in that direction by analyzing the conditions for equilibrium in balance of payments and the sustainability of current-account deficits. In this process, we will present some simplifying assumptions in order to study the topic. We will not develop an economic model, so to speak, since we will not analyze the behavior of individuals. We will only take the first step: simplify to better understand.

## 2.3  Balance of Payments Equilibrium

The double-entry system on which the balance of payments is built implies that a credit in one account always corresponds to a debit in another. Therefore, by construction, the sum of the balances in current account (CA), capital account (KA), and financial account (FA) is always equal to zero:

$$CA + KA + FA = 0. \tag{2.7}$$

As with Eq. (2.6) in national accounts, Eq. (2.7) is an accounting identity: it is always true by the form of registry accounting. The logic underlying to the grouping of different accounts facilitates the analysis of the balance of payments from an economic point of view. The equation can be written as:

$$CA = -KA - FA. \tag{2.8}$$

We have seen that the financial account balance corresponds to the variation of net indebtedness of a country. Take, for example, the case of a country with a current-account deficit. In this case, the country needs foreign financing, that is, in terms of Eq. (2.8), a surplus in the financial account: $FA > 0$.[10] If this country is already in debt, the amount of this surplus represents an increase in its foreign debt, or in the case of a net creditor country, the surplus in the financial account corresponds to a net reduction in loans by the country to the rest of the world. Therefore, the indebtedness of a country increases or its credit decreases, according to the case, when $CA < 0$.

It might be interesting to divide the balance of payments into the current account, which deals with the flows that only affect the current period, and the sum of the capital and financial accounts, which are accumulation accounts. We could even enter the reserve assets separately, since they are policy instruments available to the government. We would have then defined the financial-capital account, FKA, as a sum of the capital and financial balances, excluding registers of reserve assets, and defined $\Delta R$ as the variations in reserve assets. The balance of payments, in this way, would be written as:

$$CA + FKA = \Delta R, \tag{2.9}$$

that is, the variation of reserve assets corresponds to the sum of the balances in current account and financial-capital account.

Equation (2.9) shows that there is always a reduction in reserve assets when the deficit in current account is not compensated by a corresponding surplus in the capital and financial accounts, or rather, if there is insufficient external financing (Box 2.3).

---

**BOX 2.3 ARGENTINE CRISIS**

Based on Eq. (2.9), we can understand what happened in the 2001 Argentine crisis. The country had accumulated deficits in current account, which significantly increased as of 1998. According to the currency board regime,[a] in force in the country since 1991, the Argentine government would have to sell reserve assets when the capital inflow was insufficient to cover the deficit in current account to avoid the depreciation of the exchange rate. That actually happened when international investors began to question the sustainability of the Argentine situation and the inflow of capital through the financial account ceased to be sufficient. In 2001, the reduction of reserve assets reached almost 4% of GDP.

---

[a]In Chapter 10, we take a closer look at the functioning of the currency board regime.

---

[10] The capital account balance is effectively very small when compared to the balance in other accounts. To give one an idea, in the United States it is about 3100 times smaller than the current account balance.

What does it mean for the balance of payments to be in equilibrium? As Eq. (2.9) is always valid, given that it is an accounting identity, the simple fact that it is true does not define the balance of payments as being in equilibrium. We say the **balance of payments is in equilibrium when its composition can be sustained without intervention and without sudden shocks to the economy**. The condition of equilibrium can vary depending on domestic economic conditions and the international scenario.

Deficits in current account financed by foreign indebtedness can be sustainable and even desirable, as we will see in Chapter 4. Such was the case with Latin American countries in the 1970s. Low international interest rates and investment opportunities with high rates of return led to foreign indebtedness in these economies. Greece, Ireland, Portugal, and Spain lived this soap opera during the 2000s. The establishment of a single currency in Europe reduced the cost of foreign financing for these countries, which consequently took advantage of the opportunity.

In general, it could be desirable for a developing country to generate current-account deficits. If the rate of return for investment in the country is high, the country can use foreign financing, by means of current-account deficits, to invest more. The productive capability of the country will thereby increase and it can, in the future, increase its savings without reducing consumption, generating the surplus in current account necessary to pay its foreign debt. We could provide an analogy using the case of two individuals who go into debt. One of them borrows money to pay for continued education, while the other buys a new car for their pleasure. The education allows the individual to earn a better salary and, by this means, pay their debt without reducing consumption. For the one who bought the car, the debt does not contribute to an increase in income. Thus, to pay the debt, they must consume less in the future.

## 2.3.1 Sustainability of Current-Account Deficits

When are deficits in current account and the foreign debt resulting from them sustainable? To better understand this question, we must return to Eq. (2.4) and make some simple hypotheses.

The **Net International Investment Position** (NIIP) corresponds to the net international wealth of a country, or rather, the difference between the amount of foreign assets held by domestic residents and the amount of domestic assets held by foreigners. Let us designate $B_t$ as the NIIP at the beginning of period $t$. If the country is a net lender, we have that $B_t > 0$, while $B_t < 0$ describes the case of being a net borrower.

Suppose that the secondary income account is balanced, represented by $SI = 0$, which implies that $CA_t = TB_t + PI_t$.[11] Further, assume that the primary income account is restricted to interest paid on foreign debt (or received if the country is a net lender). Therefore, we have that $PI_t = i^*B_t$, where $i^*$ is the interest rate paid by the asset, which we will maintain constant for the sake of simplicity. Equation (2.5) can be therefore written as:

$$CA_t = Y_t + i^*B_t - (C_t + I_t + G_t). \tag{2.10}$$

---

[11] We will analyze the evolution of the trade balance and foreign indebtedness over time, reason being for subscript $t$ to be included: to follow the time.

To further simplify, we set the capital account balance as equal to zero. According to Eq. (2.8), we have:

$$CA_t = -FA_t.$$

Thus, when there is no change in the value of assets,[12] the current-account balance should correspond to the NIIP variation, as in[13]:

$$CA_t = B_{t+1} - B_t. \tag{2.11}$$

Combining Eqs. (2.10) and (2.11), we arrive at:

$$B_{t+1} - B_t = Y_t + i^*B_t - (C_t + I_t + G_t) \tag{2.12}$$

and, therefore:

$$-(1 + i^*)B_t = Y_t - (C_t + I_t + G_t) - B_{t+1}. \tag{2.13}$$

Using Eq. (2.13), we can compute $B_{t+1}$ as a function of $B_{t+2}$ and the macroeconomic variables for the period $t + 1$, and substitute the result in Eq. (2.13). Repeating this procedure indefinitely, as shown in the mathematical appendix, we arrive at:

$$-(1 + i^*)B_t = \sum_{s=t}^{\infty} \frac{Y_s - (C_s + I_s + G_s)}{(1+i^*)^{s-t}} - \lim_{s \to \infty} \frac{B_{s+1}}{(1+i^*)^{s-t}}.$$

We assume that the present value of the debt or credit of a country $(B_{s+1})$ in the indefinite future is zero, that is, $\lim_{s \to \infty} (B_{s+1}/(1+i^*)^{s-t}) = 0$, which is known as **transversality condition**. Economically, it makes no sense for this limit to have a value other than zero, for the following reason. Suppose that this value is strictly positive. This means that the country's credit would indefinitely grow at a rate greater than interest rates: the country would accumulate more and more wealth without taking advantage of it by increasing consumption. The country could reach a higher welfare level by consuming more and accumulating less credit with the rest of the world. On the other hand, the country could become well satisfied with a negative value for this limit, that is, an ever-growing debt at a rate greater than interest rates. The problem is that for it to have an explosive debt, another country would need to have an equally explosive credit, which we have seen would not happen.

Using Eq. (2.2), that says that the difference between GDP and expenditures is equal to the trade balance, we can write the previous equation as:

$$-(1 + i^*)B_t = \sum_{s=t}^{\infty} \frac{TB_s}{(1+i^*)^{s-t}}, \tag{2.14}$$

---

[12] In Chapter 8, we will see the relationship between the balance in current account and the NIIP when the value of assets can change over time, known as the valuation effect.

[13] Remember that the purchase of an asset is a negative entry on the financial account. As $B_t$ is defined as the net stock of assets, an increase in $B_t$ corresponds to a negative balance on the financial account.

which corresponds to the economy's intertemporal restriction of resources. It states that the amount of debt is equal to the present value of future trade balances. The country should generate deficits in current account in order to indebt itself, as indicated in Eq. (2.11), which it does by means of trade deficits. According to the restriction of resources in Eq. (2.14), at some time in the future the trade deficit should convert to surplus so that the debt does not become explosive. We can say that deficits in current account are sustainable when the generation of future trade surplus, to limit the foreign debt generated by them, can be made without abrupt shocks.

We have already argued that it may be desirable for a developing economy to generate foreign debt in order to invest domestically. What conditions are necessary for a debt strategy to be sustainable? There are three fundamental issues for the strategy to be a success.

First, the **counterpart of a deficit in current account should be an increase in the level of investment in the country, and not an increase in consumption**. Only an increase in investment will generate an increase in future productive capability in such a way as to generate the trade surplus necessary to pay the debt without reducing consumption. More precisely, since the generation of trade surplus is the result of an increase in production and/or a reduction in expenditures, as stipulated in Eq. (2.2), with greater economic growth the debt can be paid without reducing expenditures in the country (Box 2.4).

Second, **investment should be effective in increasing production capabilities, so that a higher level of investment would truly increase the rate of growth for a country**. An example of investments not resulting in an increase in production capacity in a country can be seen in Ghana, as described by Easterly (2001). During his mandate as president, Kwame Nkrumah implemented an ambitious project to build a hydroelectric power plant, which would be the base for an industrial complex where railroads would connect bauxite mines, aluminum smelters, and factories to produce aluminum and caustic soda. The idea was for these investments to generate ample externalities. The new lake formed by the reservoir would stimulate fishing activity, water transport, and irrigation for local farming. With the support of foreign financing, the Volta River was dammed and the hydroelectric plant and aluminum smelter were built. However, even though successful in terms of production, these projects did not generate the expected externalities: the fishing industry did not develop due to administrative conflicts; the bauxite mines, aluminum factories, and railroads to connect them never were built; sanitation problems such as worms and malaria plagued those who lived near the lake, reducing the productivity of local labor. Besides this, any plans for long-term development were hindered due to the instability generated by military coups and the successive changes in political leadership. We can therefore learn from this example that the mere investment in physical capital is not sufficient to stimulate the productive capability of a country.

The third problem is that **the inflow of capital should be stable during the investment period**. If debt repayment is required before an increase in the production capability of a country, that country will need to reduce spending in order to honor its foreign debt commitments. The country is therefore dependent on the evolution of the international environment. While international investors are willing to continue financing, the situation is sustainable. The problem is when the mood of the market changes. Equation (2.14) presupposes that there is no restriction in international credit, and that trade surpluses can be generated at any time

## BOX 2.4 ACCUMULATION OF FOREIGN DEBT AND GDP COMPOSITION

Let us look at the case of the Brazilian and Argentine foreign debt in the 1970s. Figures 2.2 and 2.3 show the decomposition of GDP in its components, according to Eq. (2.2).[a] We see that an increase in the Brazilian current-account deficit between 1970 and 1975 had an increase in investment as a counterpart, while private and government consumption remained roughly constant. In the case of Argentina, however, the deficit in current account during the same period was accompanied by a reduction in investment, an increase in private consumption, at first, and of public consumption in 1974−75. It is reasonable to say that the Brazilian trajectory was more consistent with the long-term sustainability of the foreign debt. It is interesting to notice that, in both countries, after the return of democracy in 1980, government spending jumped to a higher level, going from an average of 10% of GDP to 20% of GDP, while the levels of investment and private consumption fell.

As of the end of the 1990s, the United States began accumulating growing deficits in current account. Figure 2.4 shows that the increase in American current-account deficit had an increase in consumption as a counterpart, while investments remained between 17% and 20% of GDP. In other words, foreign debt was used to finance increasing levels of American consumption, similar to what happened in Argentina three decades before.

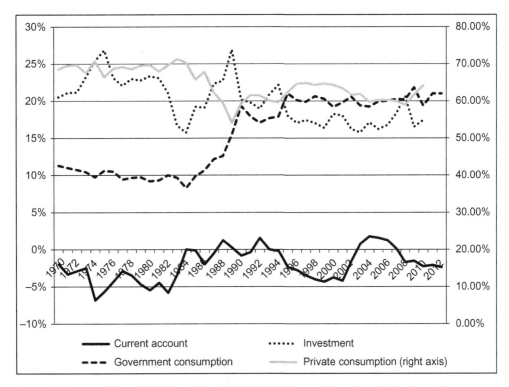

**Figure 2.2** Decomposition of GDP: Brazil (% of GDP). *IMF, Reference (2) on Data List in Appendix.*

(*Continued*)

BOX 2.4 (CONTINUED)

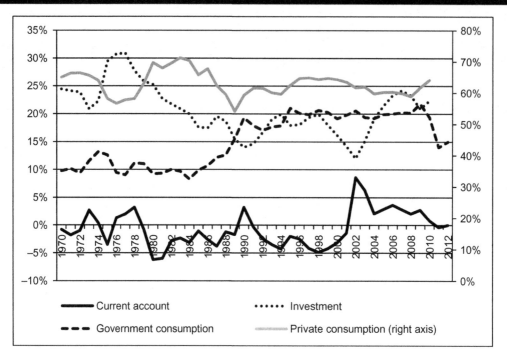

**Figure 2.3** Decomposition of GDP: Argentina (% of GDP). *IMF, Reference (2) on Data List in Appendix.*

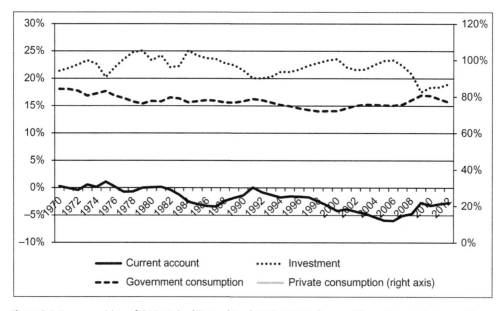

**Figure 2.4** Decomposition of GDP: United States (% of GDP). *IMF, Reference (2) on Data List in Appendix.*

[a]Notice that Figures 2.2 and 2.3 present the current account instead of the trade balance, as in the equation. This means that the four items in these figures do not add up to 1, but their sum corresponds to the income balance as a share of GDP. This is done since the current account indicates the change in foreign indebtedness, which is what is of interest to us here.

> **BOX 2.5 SUDDEN STOPS: LATIN AMERICA AND EUROPE**
>
> In the case of Latin American indebtedness in the 1970s, the problem began with the increase of the American interest rates at the beginning of the 1980s that came as part of the campaign to fight inflation. As the Latin American foreign debt had been taken under floating interest rates, the higher interest rates caused a significant increase in the service of the foreign debt. The need for foreign financing increased at the same time that available credit on the international markets was reducing. To avoid deficits in current account that could not be financed, these countries had to generate trade surplus in a short period of time. The result was a large currency depreciation, which represented reduced international purchasing power for the country, besides having important redistributive effects. As Rudiger Dornbusch said, "it is not speed that kills, it is the **sudden stop**."[a]
>
> In the European case, the crisis had its origin in the contraction of world credit caused by the 2008 American crisis. The scarcity of credit exposed the excessive indebtedness of several European countries, which came face to face with higher interest rates to compensate the perceived elevated risk, and with the difficulty of obtaining foreign financing. Different from the Latin American countries in their crises, the Europeans obtained financial aid from the European Union and were able to postpone the foreign adjustment.
>
> ───────────────
>
> [a]The term "sudden stop" came to designate abrupt reversals to the inflow of capital.

in the future, as long as the present value of trade balances is sufficient to pay the debt. In the real world, economies may find it difficult to find short-term foreign financing (Box 2.5).

The volatility of foreign financing depends, among other things, on the nature of the financing, or in other words, the composition of the country's external liabilities. Financing made by means of long-term debt instruments has the advantage of not requiring continued renewal. Short-term debt renders the economy more vulnerable. A crisis in the international credit market, for example, can cause a country not to be able to renew its credit, generating a balance of payments crisis. Portfolio investment is a sort of short-term financing, since it can leave the country at any time. Financing by means of direct foreign investment may be the most stable of all. When a company makes a direct investment in a country, it usually has a long-run perspective for this investment. Its yield, that is, the remittance of profits and dividends, depends on the performance of the economy. In this way, the interests of this type of investment are well aligned with economic interests of the country. Moreover, foreign investment brings new technologies that help increase the productivity of local businesses.[14]

Returning to our original question: what does it mean for the balance of payments to be in equilibrium? There is no single answer for this question. Our previous discussion indicates that the sustainability of the composition of current and financial accounts balances

---

[14] There is extensive literature on the impact of FDI on a local economy. Among the seminal articles in this literature, Rodriguez-Clare (1996) and Markusen and Venables (1999) theoretically analyze how FDI can contribute to development through intra- and inter-sectorial connections, while Aitken and Harrison (1999) use panel econometric models to measure the impact of DFI on productivity. Crespo and Fontoura (2007) present a review of the empirical literature on the impact of multinational corporations on the productivity of domestic firms.

depends, among other factors, on the conditions present in the international credit market, the perception of international investors in relation to a country's ability to pay, the composition of foreign financing, and the domestic use of foreign indebtedness or motivation for foreign savings, according to the case, may be among the answers. What appears to be true is that the accumulation of high deficits in current account tends to make the economy more vulnerable to shocks, both domestic and foreign.

## 2.4  Open Economy Models

To model an open economy, one must consider its transactions with the rest of the world. These transactions, as we have seen, are registered in the balance of payments. Based on Eq. (2.9), we can describe the balance of payments as the interaction between three markets: the goods and services market, represented by the current account, the assets market, by the financial-capital account, and the money market, by the reserve assets. The different open economy models provide for alternative simplifying hypotheses, depending on which of the market one intends to focus their analysis.

In the **intertemporal models of current-account adjustment**, which we will study in Part II of the book, the focus is on the interaction of the current-account balance with domestic aggregates, as established by Eq. (2.6). These models study the intertemporal decision of consumption by a representative individual, which determines savings over time. The decision for investment is also studied, so that the current-account deficits or surpluses can be analyzed as a result of these decisions.

The **monetary models**, as the name suggests, focus on the money market. By taking domestic and foreign assets as perfect substitutes, only one nonarbitrage condition guarantees balance in the asset market. These models are divided into two categories: those that assume that the prices of goods are flexible and those that consider prices as fixed. When prices are considered flexible, they automatically adjust, maintaining the goods market always in equilibrium. An important implication of this hypothesis is that changes in nominal exchange rate do not have an impact on the level of production or on the current-account balance, given that prices immediately adjust to compensate for the exchange rate changes. In fixed price models, the adjustment of prices to shocks is not immediate. The goods market can temporarily remain out of its long-run equilibrium, while prices gradually adjust. Monetary models with flexible prices are considered in Chapter 6, and those with fixed prices in Chapter 7.

Finally, the **models of portfolio diversification**, Chapter 8, focus on the assets market. This is the only class of models where domestic and foreign assets are not taken as perfect substitutes. The objective of the model is to better understand the choice between these two types of assets and how this choice is affected by different economic variables.

No model, by definition, is able to offer a complete explanation of functioning of the economy in all its complexity. The object of a model is to simplify the economy, suppressing lesser important elements in order to better understand the object of study. For this reason, using models should be done in moderation. One should consider if the simplification hypothesis for a model does not set aside crucial elements for the analysis that one desires to make. For example, if the objective is to study the impact of different exchange rate regimes on production, one should not use flexible price monetary models, given that they consider production to always be constant. On the other hand, these models are perfect to understand the relationship between exchange rate regimes and exchange rate volatility.

## Mathematical Appendix

Calculation to obtain Eq. (2.14)

Equation (2.13), reproduced here:

$$-(1 + i^*)B_t = Y_t - (C_t + I_t + G_t) - B_{t+1}$$

is valid for all time periods. Particularly, we can write that:

$$-(1 + i^*)B_{t+1} = Y_{t+1} - (C_{t+1} + I_{t+1} + G_{t+1}) - B_{t+2}$$

from which we obtain the value of $B_{t+1}$ as:

$$-B_{t+1} = \frac{Y_{t+1} - (C_{t+1} + I_{t+1} + G_{t+1}) - B_{t+2}}{(1 + i^*)}. \tag{2.15}$$

Substituting the value of $B_{t+1}$, described in Eq. (2.15), into Eq. (2.13), we have:

$$-(1 + i^*)B_t = Y_t - (C_t + I_t + G_t) + \frac{Y_{t+1} - (C_{t+1} + I_{t+1} + G_{t+1}) - B_{t+2}}{(1 + i^*)}$$

which can be rewritten as:

$$-(1 + i^*)B_t = \sum_{s=t}^{t+1} \frac{Y_s - (C_s + I_s + G_s)}{(1+i^*)^{s-t}} - \frac{B_{t+2}}{(1 + i^*)}. \tag{2.16}$$

We repeat the same procedure once again, writing Eq. (2.15) for $B_{t+2}$:

$$-B_{t+2} = \frac{Y_{t+2} - (C_{t+2} + I_{t+2} + G_{t+2}) - B_{t+3}}{(1 + i^*)}$$

and substitute it in Eq. (2.16). We obtain:

$$-(1 + i^*)B_t = \sum_{s=t}^{t+1} \frac{Y_s - (C_s + I_s + G_s)}{(1+i^*)^{s-t}} + \frac{(Y_{t+2} - (C_{t+2} + I_{t+2} + G_{t+2}) - B_{t+3}/(1 + i^*))}{(1 + i^*)}$$

which can be rewritten as:

$$-(1+i^*)B_t = \sum_{s=t}^{t+2} \frac{Y_s - (C_s + I_s + G_s)}{(1+i^*)^{s-t}} - \frac{B_{t+3}}{(1+i^*)^2}.$$

Repeating the procedure indefinitely, we arrive at:

$$-(1+i^*)B_t = \sum_{s=t}^{\infty} \frac{Y_s - (C_s + I_s + G_s)}{(1+i^*)^{s-t}} - \lim_{s \to \infty} \frac{B_{s+1}}{(1+i^*)^{s-t}}$$

which results in Eq. (2.14), where $\lim_{s \to \infty} (B_{s+1}/(1+i^*)^{s-t}) = 0$.

## 2.5 Exercises

### Exercise 1

A country performed, in a given year, the following transactions abroad. All payments were made in dollars.

1. Exports paid in cash: US$500 million
2. Imports paid in cash: US$400 million
3. Freight paid in cash abroad: US$200 million
4. Foreign investment in equipment: US$50 million
5. Donations received as merchandise: US$10 million
6. Loans received from foreign banks: US$200 million
7. Loan amortizations: US$50 million
8. Interest paid abroad: US$60 million

   Present the balance of payments, highlighting:

a. The trade surplus or deficit
b. The financial account balance
c. The net income sent abroad
d. The variation in reserve assets for the period

### Exercise 2

Suppose that, in a given year, Brazil performed the following foreign transactions:

1. A consortium of American banks lends Petrobrás US$50 million.
2. Brazil sends US$20 million in humanitarian aid to Somalia.
3. The Brazil Central Bank authorizes interest payments of US$10 million to an American bank. At the same time, it is able to refinance interest payments of US$20 million due this year.

4. Brazilian workers living in the United States send the equivalent of US$100 million to their families living in Brazil.
5. Brazil imports oil from Iran for the amount of US$500 million, paid in cash.
6. A Brazilian company invests the equivalent of US$20 million to build a factory in Argentina.
7. A Spanish tour agency pays a Brazilian hotel chain US$10 million for lodging services provided to Spanish tourists.
8. A German automobile manufacturer purchases a shipment of steel from Brazil for the FOB amount of US$200 million.
9. The subsidiary of a French company invests the equivalent of US$50 million in Brazil.

Present the balance of payments, highlighting:

a. The trade surplus or deficit
b. The financial account balance
c. The net income sent abroad
d. The variation in reserve assets for the period

## Exercise 3

Before the 2008 global economic crisis, one of the most serious economic problems in the American economy was that of the twin deficits, an expression used to represent a situation in which the country simultaneously had a current-account deficit and fiscal deficit. Based on the national account identities, show and explain how these deficits are related.

## Exercise 4

Suppose that countries A and B are economically similar, being different only by the fact that country A has a high level of foreign debt, while country B is a net foreign creditor. In which of these countries will GDP be less than GNI and in which will it be greater? Justify your answer.

## Exercise 5

Consider an economy, that we will call Balanced, which always maintains a current-account balance equal to zero. Between years 1 and 2, government expenditures in consumption and investment increased, while private expenditures in consumption and investment remained constant. What could be said regarding Balanced's economic GDP? Justify your answer.

## Exercise 6

Consider a country, that we will call Debtor, has a negative NIIP and adopts a policy to achieve surplus in the trade balance sufficient to pay only a small but constant portion of the debt each period. The remainder of the debt is rolled over. In other words, suppose the country adopts the following rule for its trade balance: $TB_s = -\xi r B_s$, $0 < \xi < 1$.

**a.** Using the current-account identity and the definition of trade balance, show that, under this policy, the NIIP follows the following equation: $B_{s+1} = [1 + (1 - \xi)r]B_s$.

**b.** Show that the intertemporal budget restriction is satisfied by any $\xi > 0$.

## Exercise 7

Derive the mathematical condition that represents a necessary condition for the debt/GDP relationship for a determined economy to remain constant.

## Exercise 8

The relation of foreign debt/GDP of country Indebted is 60%, given that the greatest part is sovereign debt (i.e., it represents government obligations with foreign investors). Given that the foreign investors are concerned about a possible *default* by the Indebted government, the interest rate on the debt is 10%. Assume that product growth for Indebted is only 1% and that the capital-account balance is equal to zero.

**a.** Compute the current-account balance Indebted needs to maintain the debt/GDP ratio constant.

**b.** The deficit in current account for Indebted is 6.8% of GDP. Calculate the lack in current resources and interpret the result.

# The Foreign Exchange Market

The **nominal exchange rate** is the price for foreign currency. When we say that the exchange rate for the dollar in relation to the euro is 1.3, it means that one must pay US$1.30 to buy €1.00. Yet, if the exchange rate is merely a price, why do we talk about it so much? Why are books written about the exchange rate and not the price of bananas? A book about the price of bananas might interest a banana producer, but it would never make the bestseller list. The exchange rate, on the other hand, interests all importers, exporters, international investors, tourists and, well, all those who trade goods, financial assets or services with other countries. The exchange rate is an important price as it is a reference for doing business with the rest of the world. The first section of this chapter will define what the nominal exchange rate is, the meaning of exchange rate appreciation and depreciation, as well as some characteristics of the exchange rate market.

One of the first relationships we learn about in an economics course is that the price of a good affects the individual producer and consumer incentives: the higher the price, the greater the enticement for the producer to produce and sell their good, and the lower the motivation for consumers to buy. Also, the interaction between supply and demand determines the market price of a product: an excess of supply triggers a reduction in price, while excess in demand results in a price increase. We can think of the exchange rate the same way. The balance of payments registers the supply and demand for foreign currency since it registers all transactions with the rest of the world. More specifically, the credits registered on the balance of payments represent the supply of foreign currency, while the debits indicate the demand for foreign currency.

How does the exchange rate affect the supply and demand for foreign currency? The exchange rate between the Kazakhstan tenge and the Nepal rupee was about 1.80 in August 2014. Was the rupee cheap or expensive for the Kazakhs? With no more information, it is impossible to answer this question. If a Kazakh is interested in taking a vacation in Nepal, they will want to know what the purchasing power of their tenge is in Nepal. They will compare prices in Nepal, converted into tenges by the exchange rate, with the prices in Kazakhstan to decide if they will visit Nepal or just appreciate the beautiful scenery in their home country. In other words, if our interest is to consume goods and services in another country, we compare prices in the two countries by converting them into the same currency by using the exchange rate.

On the other hand, if a Nepalese is thinking about investing their savings in Kazakh financial assets, they will exchange their rupees for tenges in order to purchase the Kazakh assets. Later, when the assets mature, the Nepalese will convert the tenges earned with the assets back into rupees. They will not be interested in comparing the purchasing power of their currency in Kazakhstan, but in the interest rate on the Kazakh assets and the exchange rate variation between when they make their investment and redeem it.

We see, then, that the relevant variables that interact with the exchange rate to determine supply and demand for foreign currency depend on the nature of the transaction that generates the demand or the supply, more specifically, if the purchase or sale of foreign currency has its origin in the transaction of goods and services or in a financial assets transaction. The distinction between the two main accounts in the balance of payments, the current account and the financial account, refers exactly to this dimension: the current account registers transactions involving goods and services, while the financial account registers the purchase and sale of financial assets. The relation between the exchange rate and supply and demand of foreign currency for transactions involving goods and services is studied in Section 3.2, while Section 3.3 will cover transactions involving financial assets.

## 3.1 The Nominal Exchange Rate

**The exchange rate is the price relative to two currencies**. When we compare the dollar to the euro, for example, we could, in principle, define the exchange rate in one of two ways.

A dollar/euro exchange rate of 1.3 means that one would pay US\$1.30 to buy €1. We represent this rate as $S_{USD/EUR}$. Alternatively, we could say that the euro/dollar exchange is 0.77, that is, € 0.77 euros are required to purchase US\$1. This rate is $S_{EUR/USD}$. Clearly, the two definitions should establish the same exchange rate between the two currencies, namely:

$$S_{USD/EUR} = \frac{1}{S_{EUR/USD}}$$

To avoid confusion when speaking about exchange rate, **a convention was established to always quote the exchange rate as the price of the foreign currency in terms of the domestic currency.**[1] Therefore, the European newspapers always present the price of other currencies in terms of the euro; in other words, they show how many euros are needed to purchase one unit of a foreign currency. This rate is called the nominal exchange rate, opposed to the real exchange rate, which measures the purchasing power of a currency as defined in the following section.

## 3.1.1 What Does Exchange Rate Changes Mean?

An increase in the price of a foreign currency means that the domestic currency is worth less. We say, then, that there has been an **exchange rate depreciation** or a **depreciation of the domestic currency**. Analogously, a reduction in the price of foreign currency implies a higher value for the domestic currency, which constitutes an **exchange rate appreciation** or an **appreciation of domestic currency**. Using the convention to measure the exchange rate as the price of foreign currency, the depreciation is associated with an increase in exchange rate and the appreciation, to a reduction. So as to not risk misunderstanding, it is preferable to use the terms appreciation and depreciation, instead of speaking of increases and decreases of the exchange rate.

## 3.1.2 What Determines the Exchange Rate?

A large part of currency transactions are performed by commercial banks, but can also be done by central banks, private agencies, or even companies. When GAP exports clothes to Europe, for instance, the importer deposits payment in euros in the bank (of its country), which converts the euros into dollars to transfer them into the GAP account in the United States. If an European purchases a book from Amazon.com with their credit card, they pay in euros and the bank transfers the corresponding amount in

---

[1] Traditionally, the exchange rate is defined as the rate between domestic currency and foreign currency for all countries, except the United States. The origin of this tradition is in the unique role of the United States in the Bretton Woods system. According to the world monetary agreement set out by the system, gold had its price fixed in dollars, while all other currencies maintained their parity fixed in relation to the dollar (see Chapter 6, Box 6.1). Due to the unique position held by the dollar in the system, the practice was adopted to define the exchange rate as the currency of other countries in relation to the dollar, and not the opposite.

dollars to Amazon.com. An American who wants to spend their vacation in India generally goes to a commercial bank or a currency exchange bureau to buy rupees. In principle, they could buy rupees directly from Boeing, for example, which would have this currency as a result of exporting aircraft to India. As it would be complicated to arrange this type of meeting, financial institutions serve to intermediate the parts. Besides that, there are generally legal restrictions on currency exchange, such as who has the right to transact foreign currency and under what conditions.

The exchange rate is the price that balances the supply and demand for foreign currency in the exchange rate market, as is the case for prices in any market. Suppose there is an excess supply of foreign currency. As the balance of payments registers all transactions between countries, an excess supply of foreign currency would be reflected in a surplus in the balance of payments. With an excess of foreign currency in the market, its price tends to fall, that is, there is an exchange rate appreciation. The appreciation of domestic currency, on the one hand, would make imports cheaper and, on the other, reduce the income from exports as measured in domestic currency. Exports contract and imports increase, which reduces the surplus in the balance of payments and, consequently, the excess supply of foreign currency. The nominal exchange rate is then the rate compatible with equilibrium in the balance of payments. Who sets the exchange rate? The same "agent" that sets the price of bananas: the market.

### 3.1.3 Can the Government Choose the Exchange Rate?

The government can intervene directly in the exchange rate market, buying and selling foreign currency, and affect its price. Government transactions in foreign currency are synthesized in the international reserves account, as we saw in Section 2.1.3. Through them, the government acts as an additional agent that supplies or demands foreign currency. Suppose the government wants to maintain an appreciated exchange rate, namely, a rate that results in a deficit in the balance of payments. Since there is an excess demand for foreign currency at that rate, the government must sell international reserves to prevent exchange rate depreciation. In terms of Eq. (2.9), this means there is a deficit in the sum of the current and capital-financial accounts, which has as a counterpart a reduction in government international reserves. Clearly, to maintain an appreciated exchange rate, the government needs a sufficiently large stock of international reserves. As the stock of reserves cannot be infinite, it is not possible to maintain an appreciated exchange rate indefinitely.

The government can also indirectly affect the exchange rate by using economic policies to stimulate private agents to increase or decrease their demand for foreign currency. For example, a contractionary monetary policy that increases domestic interest rates causes domestic financial assets to be more attractive to foreign investors. This leads to an inflow of financial capital, which constitutes an increase in the supply of foreign currency, causing an exchange rate appreciation.

In brief, **the government can choose the exchange rate level in the same way it can choose the price of bananas: by supplying eventual excesses in demand or buying eventual excesses in supply at the chosen price, or offering incentives to producers and consumers to alter their patterns of supply and demand.**

It is important to emphasize that government influence over the exchange rate is limited. In the long run, the exchange tends to an equilibrium level compatible with the economy's intertemporal constraint of resources, as represented by Eq. (2.14). This constraint establishes that for an indebted country, for example, the present value of the flow of trade balances should be positive. Since higher trade balances are associated with a more depreciated exchange rate, as we will see in Chapter 5, the exchange rate cannot be maintained artificially appreciated indefinitely.

## 3.1.4 But, There Are Many Currencies…

Up until now we have spoken about domestic and foreign currencies, as if there were only one other currency for reference. Actually, even though there are 164 currencies in the world,[2] each country transacts with only a limited number. For example, since Argentina is an important trade partner with Brazil, it is easy to find financial institutions in Brazil with pesos available to exchange for reais, or that are willing to exchange reais for pesos. However, if a Brazilian wishes to spend their vacation in Nepal, they may find it difficult to find someone in Brazil with Nepalese rupees for sale. The solution is to use a third currency, in international circulation, to intermediate. This way, the tourist going to Nepal purchases dollars in their home country to exchange for rupees upon arriving in Nepal. In this case, the dollar acts as a **vehicle currency**. The main vehicle currencies are the dollar, euro, yen, and sterling pound. In short, **countries usually negotiate in the currency of their main trade partners and currencies commonly used in the world, which are used as currency vehicles.**

## 3.1.5 Nonarbitrage Condition

The international exchange rate market is composed of many agents ready to take advantage of any eventual possibility for arbitrage, which is a transaction that takes advantage of price differences in order to profit. Suppose that the exchange rate between the dollar and euro is different for France and the United States. More specifically, let us assume $S_{EUR/USD}^{FR} > 1/S_{USD/EUR}^{US}$, where $S_{EUR/USD}^{FR}$ represents the price of dollars in France and $S_{USD/EUR}^{US}$ the price of euros in the United States. This inequality means that the dollar is worth more in terms of euros in France than in the United States. A bank with agencies in both countries could transfer US\$1 from the United States to France, and with this dollar it would buy $S_{EUR/USD}^{FR}$ euros. Next, it would transfer the euros to the United States and exchange them for $S_{EUR/USD}^{FR} \times S_{USD/EUR}^{US}$ dollars. Given the previous inequality, we have that

---

[2] The International Organization for Standardization publishes an official list of codes for current currencies in a standardized norm known as ISO 4217. Its 2012 publication lists 164 currencies in circulation, including Special Drawing Rights (SDR) emitted by the IMF. A representative list can be found in Annex I at the end of the book.

$S^{FR}_{EUR/USD} \times S^{US}_{USD/EUR} > 1$, that is, the bank would end the transaction with more dollars than with what it began. This arbitrage performed by many agents causes an increase in the supply of dollars in France, which pressures its price to decrease, appreciating the euro in France. At the same time, the supply of euros in the United States increases, also pressuring down its price, which appreciates the dollar in the United States. In equilibrium, these rates become equal, i.e., $S^{FR}_{EUR/USD} = 1/S^{US}_{USD/EUR}$. This is the nonarbitrage condition that should hold true between exchange rates.

The nonarbitrage condition should also hold true when involving three currencies, so that no profit is obtained by indirect transactions. The exchange rate between the Brazilian real and the Argentine peso should be equal to the indirect exchange rate when going through the dollar, namely, exchanging reais for dollars and then dollars for pesos, i.e.:

$$S_{BRL/ARG} = S_{BRL/USD} \times S_{USD/ARG} = \frac{S_{BRL/USD}}{S_{ARG/USD}} \tag{3.1}$$

The nonarbitrage condition for nominal exchange rate, according to Eq. (3.1), makes the diffusion of information regarding exchange rates much easier since it is not necessary to know the exchange rate between each pair or currencies. All that is needed is the relation of the currency to a reference currency, such as the dollar, and the bilateral exchange rates can be calculated based on Eq. (3.1) (Box 3.1).

## 3.2 The Goods and Services Market: The Real Exchange Rate

Let us return to the Kazakh interested in purchasing Nepalese goods or services. What does the exchange rate of 1.8 mean to them? What matters to the consumer is the purchasing power of their currency in the two countries. They compare the purchasing power of tenges in Kazakhstan to their purchasing power in Nepal. Given that goods in Nepal are priced in rupees, they need to be converted to tenges by means of the exchange rate. I chose Kazakhstan and Nepal as an example to make it clear that the value of the nominal exchange rate in and of itself does not tell us much, given that I believe my readers do not have *a priori* information regarding the relative purchasing power of the currencies of these two countries. (Actually, even in the improbable case of having Kazakh or Nepalese readers, they possibly do not have much intuition regarding the purchasing power between their currencies since there is not much trade between the two countries.[3])

---

[3] According to the Trade Export and Promotion Centre of Nepal, the value of total bilateral trade between Nepal and Kazakhstan in 2010 amounted to NRS9,951,000.00, about US$136,315.07, which represented 0.0022% of all international trade by Nepal and 0.00013% of trade by Kazakhstan.

## BOX 3.1 EVOLUTION OF THE NOMINAL EXCHANGE RATE

Figure 3.1 shows the evolution of local currency/dollar exchange rates between 1990 and 2011 for six emerging countries: the BRICs (Brazil, Russia, India and China), Argentina, and South Korea. We can observe some interesting movement.

In Argentina, the nominal exchange rate was fixed with respect to the dollar at 1 peso to 1 dollar when the currency board was in force between 1991 and 2001.[a] The regime established total convertibility between dollars and pesos. It was possible to hold bank accounts in dollars, the dollar was used as a means of exchange and the government guaranteed the exchange rate of 1 between

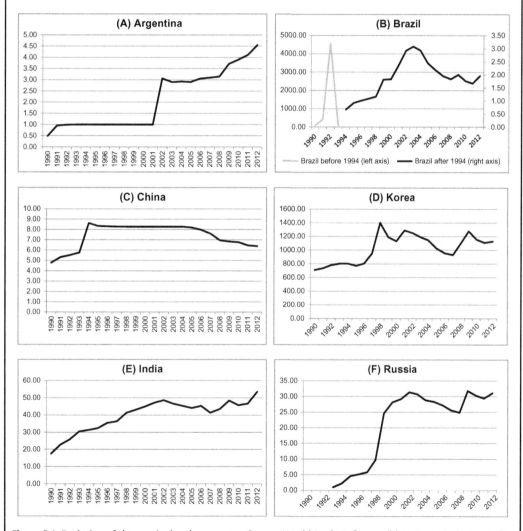

**Figure 3.1** Evolution of the nominal exchange rates. *Source: World Bank, Reference (3) on Data List in Appendix.*

*(Continued)*

the two currencies. The country accumulated deficits in the balance of payments, especially toward the end of the regime. Being more precise, there were deficits in the sum of the current account with the capital-financial account, which was financed by reducing the government international reserves (see Chapter 2, Eq. (2.9)). As could be expected, with the end of the currency board regime, the exchange rate depreciated to a level compatible with equilibrium in the balance of payments, that is, to balance the sum of the current and capital-financial accounts. The exchange rate remained at about 3 until 2008, when it went through a new depreciation process.

The evolution of the exchange rate in Brazil between 1990 and 1994 is quite impressive: it jumped from near 70 in 1990 to about 400 in 1991, surpassing 4500 in 1992. In the following section, we will see how these movements are associated with the high inflation present in Brazil during that period. Between 1994 and 2010, there were significant movements in the exchange rate, but in a more "normal" order of magnitude.

It is interesting to notice that there was similar movement in the exchange rates of India, South Korea, and Russia. The currencies of India and Russia continually depreciated until 2002, just as had happened in Brazil. For South Korea, the most accentuated depreciation occurred between 1994 and 1998. The currencies of Brazil, India, Russia, and South Korea appreciated between 2003 and 2007, depreciated between 2008 and 2009, and had a new appreciation between 2009 and 2010.

The Chinese yuan had a considerably different trajectory from the other countries in the group. The yuan depreciated between 1990 and 1994. The exchange rate was fixed at 8.28 from 1997 to 2005. As of 2006, it appreciated, reaching the level of 6.4 in 2012. The Chinese exchange rate has been the subject of heated debates in international economic policy. In the eyes of the North American government, the Chinese exchange rate appreciation has been excessively timid, giving the Chinese a significant advantage in bilateral trade between these countries.

---

[a]A description of exchange regimes is given in Chapter 10.

The **real exchange rate**, $Q$, measures the relative price of goods between the two countries and is formally defined as:

$$Q \equiv \frac{SP^*}{P}, \tag{3.2}$$

where $P$ is the price index in the domestic country and $P^*$ the price index in the foreign country (Box 3.2). An increase in the real exchange rate means that foreign goods are more expensive in relation to domestic goods. In other words, the purchasing power of the domestic currency decreases, which represents a **depreciation of the real exchange rate**. Analogously, a reduction in the real exchange rate, as defined in Eq. (3.2), denotes an increase in purchasing power of the domestic currency, which corresponds to an **appreciation of the real exchange rate**.

The real exchange rate is a measure of the incentive our Kazakh has to purchase local goods or to import them from Nepal. The more appreciated the Kazakhi real exchange rate is, the greater the incentive for the Kazakh to purchase Nepalese goods, since they are

---

**BOX 3.2 PRICE INDEX**

The price index is the price for one unit of a basket, or set, of goods. It is a weighted average of the goods prices, where the price of each good is weighted according to its share in the basket. There are price indices for different baskets of goods. For computing the real exchange rates, two price indexes are more commonly used: the consumer and the producer price indices. In the consumer price index, the weight of each good in the composition of the index corresponds to the average consumption of the good as a share of total consumption, while in the producer price index, the weights of the goods are relative to their share in production.

---

relatively cheaper than local goods. Imports from Nepal increase and exports decrease, leading to a smaller trade balance between Kazakhstan and Nepal. Kazakhstan, however, does not trade only with Nepal. Actually, it trades very little with Nepal.[4] We can calculate the real exchange rate between Kazakhstan and all its trade partners and, just as with Nepal, the more appreciated the real exchange rate with each of them, the smaller the trade balance will be. Given that the total trade balance for the country is the sum of the bilateral balances, a more useful measure is a multilateral exchange rate, which is a weighted average of the bilateral real exchange rates, taking into consideration the trade share of each partner in the country's total trade. This measure is the **real effective exchange rate** (REER), or the **multilateral exchange rate**, defined as:

$$Q^F \equiv \prod_{i \in I} \left( \frac{S^i P^i}{P} \right)^{w^i},\tag{3.3}$$

where $Q^F$ is the real effective exchange rate, $P^i$ is the price index in country $i$, and $I$ is the set of countries with which the domestic country trades. $w^i$ is the trade share of country $i$ in the home country's total trade, defined as $w^i \equiv (X^i + M^i) / \sum_{j \in I} (X^j + M^j)$, where $X^i$ and $M^i$ are imports and exports between the home country and country $i$. Notice that the weight of the bilateral real exchange rate is higher for the more important trade partners.

Summarizing, we can say that an appreciated real effective exchange rate is associated with a smaller trade balance, while for a depreciated real effective exchange rate the trade balance is higher. What is the equilibrium value of the real exchange rate? Let us take a look.

## 3.2.1 The Law of One Price and Purchasing Power Parity

Imagine an extreme case where there are neither transportation costs nor any trade barriers. In this case, the nonarbitrage condition should hold true and the price of a good should be

---

[4] See footnote 3.

the same in both countries, when measured in the same currency. This would be the **Law of One Price**:

$$SP_b^* = Pb, \tag{3.4}$$

where $P_b$ and $P_b^*$ is the price of good $b$ in the domestic and foreign country, respectively.

For the same basket of goods, that is, if the price index is calculated in exactly the same way in the countries, and if there are no international trade costs for any good, the purchasing power of the currency in both countries should be identical. This condition is known as **Absolute Purchasing Power Parity** (Absolute PPP), described as:

$$\frac{SP^*}{P} = 1 = Q = Q^F, \tag{3.5}$$

that is, the real exchange rate as defined by Eq. (3.2) is always constant and equal to 1. Given that all bilateral real exchange rates are equal to 1, their weighted average, i.e., the real effective exchange rate, is equal to 1. In this case, people would be indifferent when purchasing either domestic or foreign goods.

Intuitively, a real exchange rate greater than 1, for example, would lead all consumers from both countries to purchase only goods from the domestic country, which would cause an increase in domestic prices, and this rise in prices would only end when the real exchange rate returned to 1. In this perfect arbitrage of goods prices, the real exchange rate is equal to 1 and compatible with any level of current account balance. The trade balance would be that which would bring equilibrium to the balance of payments, such as the result of the intertemporal current account model presented in Chapter 4, for example.

The PPP is a very old idea in economics, the term being coined in 1918 by Gustav Cassel.[5] However, it is based on very strong hypotheses, which are not verified in practice.[6] The PPP is frequently violated: prices are not equal between countries. As can be attested, at the moment I write this book, by the hoard of Brazilians spending their vacations in Argentina due to cheaper prices there. (It is possible that while you read this book, the Brazilian real has been depreciated in relation to the Argentine peso and it is the Argentinians who are invading the Brazilian beaches, as has happened in the past.)

One reason that is always raised for the violation of absolute PPP is the fact that transportation costs are not null, as well as the existence, very often, of trade barriers. The Internet has created some goods for which transportation costs are really zero. When one buys software or an e-book, for example, they can be instantly downloaded from the Internet with no additional cost. However, this is not the case for most products. Realistically, with costs associated with international trade, there can be a difference in price between the two countries,

---

[5] The article referred to is Cassel (1918).
[6] In a review of the literature, Sarno and Taylor (2002) discuss motives for the invalidity of the PPP.

so long as this difference is not higher than transportation costs. More precisely, we can say that, for good $b$:

$$\frac{1}{1+\tau} \leq \frac{SP_b^*}{P_b} \leq 1+\tau,$$

where $\tau > 0$ represents the cost associated with international trade, which can be either the transportation cost or costs related to trade barriers. Trade costs limit the possibility of arbitrage when prices differ. Consequently, the higher the transportation costs, more distant purchasing power parity is between the two currencies. In general, we can then say that:

$$\frac{1}{1+\tau} \leq Q^F \leq 1+\tau. \tag{3.6}$$

There are goods that simply cannot be transported. One cannot transport land, for example. There are other goods for which transportation costs are so high in relation to price that they are not worth transporting. A classic example is a haircut. In principle, it is possible for a French hair stylist to fly to New York to cut a person's hair. However, the cost of the imported haircut would be so high when compared to a local haircut that there would be no demand. (Unless, of course, there is some eccentric millionaire who brings their French hair stylist to periodically style their hair, but that is another story.) These goods are referred to as nontradable. There is no limit for price differences in nontradable goods between countries, therefore making impossible the arbitrage of their prices by means of international trade. The fact that the goods baskets contain these types of goods could be a reason for the PPP not being valid.

There are also differentiated goods. The German automobile is not exactly like the French or the American, and consumers have different preferences in regards to different types of automobiles. The person who prefers German automobiles, because they are more powerful, will continue to purchase them even if they cost more than the American, for example. The idea is that there are goods that are substitutable between themselves—all automobiles have the same function—but that are not perfect substitutes given that automobiles manufactured by different companies have their own characteristics. Hence, the price of these goods can be different, and this difference affects their relative demand. These goods are therefore called **differentiated goods**. The more expensive the German automobile is in relation to the American, the smaller its demand. However, within certain limits, the demand for the more expensive German automobile will not be zero because fans of the German cars will continue to buy them. When one compares the production baskets of different countries, the existence of differentiated goods could be another reason for the nonvalidity of the purchasing power parity, even for tradable goods.

Finally, the price indexes used in empirical work are not always computed the same in different countries. The consumer price index, for example, is computed according to the aggregate consumption basket of the country. If goods are consumed in different proportions in different countries, the composition of the index will not be the same. The divergence in relation to the PPP could simply refer to the fact that the comparison is being made between very different baskets of goods.[7]

Summarizing, **the existence of nontradable and differentiated goods causes that the prices of goods and services to not be identical between countries when measured by the same currency. Also, possible differences in the composition of the price indexes cause differences in the aggregate purchasing power between countries**.

Nevertheless, even if restrictions to trade prevent perfect arbitrage, it happens to some degree. Even if the real exchange rate is not equal to 1, as purchasing power parity foresees, it should be at a level compatible with equilibrium in the economy. Changes in the real exchange rate impact the trade balance. Consequently, each level of real exchange rate is associated with a trade balance value. The equilibrium value of the real exchange rate will be that which generates equilibrium in the current account, as will be seen in Chapter 5. This level depends on variables that affect the equilibrium level of the current account or that affect the relationship between the real exchange rate and the current account, such as the relative productivity between tradable and nontradable sectors, the terms of trade, government expenditures, the level of indebtedness of a country, among others.

When the real exchange rate is at its equilibrium level, and the variables that determine this level remain constant, the **relative purchasing power parity** (Relative PPP) should hold true. According to it, changes in the nominal exchange rate should follow changes in the relative prices in such a way that the real exchange rate remains at its constant equilibrium level. Computing the natural logarithm of Eq. (3.2), to then totally differentiate the equation as developed in the mathematical appendix, we arrive at:[8]

$$\dot{s}(t) = \pi(t) - \pi^*(t) \tag{3.7}$$

where $\dot{s}(t) \equiv d \ln S(t)/dt = (dS(t)/dt)/S(t)$ is the percentage rate of change of the nominal exchange rate at period $t$, $\pi(t) \equiv (dp(t)/dt)/p(t)$ and $\pi^*(t) \equiv (dp^*(t)/dt)/p(t)$ are the rates of domestic and foreign inflation, measured as the percentage rate of change of the price index.

The relative PPP implies an ever-constant real exchange rate, but not necessarily equal to 1. In other words, the absolute PPP (Eq. (3.5)) implies relative parity (Eq. (3.7)), but the contrary is not necessarily true. The relative purchasing power parity is, therefore, a milder version of the absolute PPP.

The absolute PPP cannot be empirically verified: there are substantial deviations of PPP in the short run. In relation to the relative PPP, it appears to be valid in the long run. In other words, the nominal exchange rate tends to follow the inflation differential between countries. Empirical literature, however, finds deviations from the relative PPP for extended time

---

[7] Using alternative price indexes, Terra and Vahia (2008) found major evidence of PPP for price indexes with a greater proportion of tradable goods and which composition is more similar between countries.

[8] Notice that now we indicate the variables as a function of time. In Chapter 2, time was indicated as a subscript of the variable, as praxis when treating time as a discrete variable. Here, on the other hand, we treat time as a continuous variable, reason for which it appears in parenthesis, indicating that the variable in question is a function of time.

periods. The estimates point toward a convergence rate of up to 10% per year, which appears to be excessively slow.[9] Several explanations have been recently explored, among them, changes in the equilibrium real exchange rate over time. We will take up this point again in Chapter 4 (Box 3.3).

---

### BOX 3.3 EMPIRICAL EVIDENCE OF PURCHASING POWER PARITY

Figure 3.2 shows the evolution of consumer price indices, all measured in dollars, for a group of emerging markets (BRICs: Brazil, Russia, India, and China). Figure 3.3 presents the indices for a group of developed countries (Germany, Canada, the United States, France, and the United Kingdom). The year 1994 was chosen as the base year for the indices in order to make a comparison of their evolution between 1994 and 2010 easier.[a] It is interesting to note that changes in the ratio between prices and the nominal exchange rate in Figure 3.2 are significantly smaller than the changes in the nominal exchange rate in Figure 3.1. This shows that price changes tend to follow exchange changes, as relative PPP proposes.

Equation (3.7) also indicates that changes in domestic prices measured in foreign currency should follow changes in international prices, i.e., $\pi(t) - \dot{s}(t) = \pi^*(t)$. In fact, the price series measured in

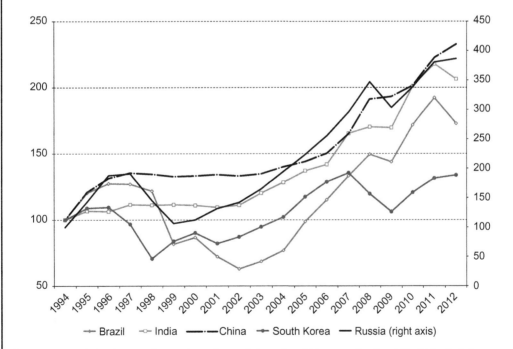

**Figure 3.2** P/S relation in emerging markets. *Source: International Monetary Fund and World Bank, References (2) and (3) on Data List in Appendix.*

---

*(Continued)*

[9] Rogoff (1996) and Taylor and Taylor (2004) discuss the empirical evidence related to the PPP.

**BOX 3.3 (CONTINUED)**

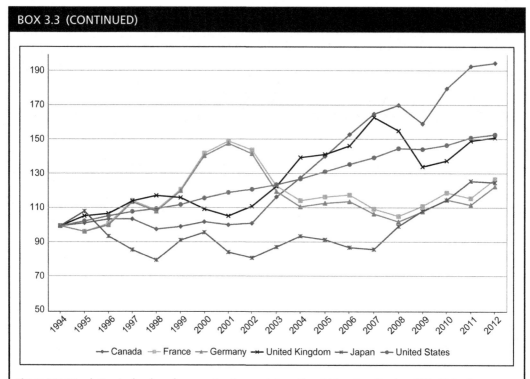

**Figure 3.3** P/S relation in developed economies. *Source: International Monetary Fund and World Bank, References (2) and (3) on Data List in Appendix.*

dollars in the developing countries in Figure 3.2 have a growing tendency, just as the index of American prices presented in Figure 3.3. Between 1997 and 1999, prices measured in dollars in Brazil and Russia fell. This can be explained by the large exchange rate depreciation occurring in those countries during the period caused by crises in the balance of payments. The prices in all developing countries presented in the graph fell soon after the 2008 crisis, with the tendency to rise returning as of 2009.

Curiously, the price indices for the developed countries present more diverging paths. Germany and France have had the same currency since 2002, even though the euro had been used in financial transactions since 1999. Also, the nominal exchange rate between these two countries was practically constant before the single currency. The price levels of these two countries, when measured in dollars, increased significantly in the years preceding the implementation of the euro, and then decreased between 2003 and 2008. They have had an upward tendency over the more recent period.

Prices in Canada and United Kingdom followed similar paths, with an increasing tendency over time, following, roughly, American inflation. Japan is a different case. The country experienced deflation in the 1990s, which lasted until 2007, when prices began increasing.

---

[a]This means that the indexes were built in a way such that $(P/S) = 100$ for all countries in 1994. What we observe in the graphs, therefore, are variations of this ratio in relation to 1994.

## 3.3 The Assets Market: Interest Rate Parity Conditions

In the previous section, we saw the relationship between the exchange rate and the supply and demand for foreign currency, applied to the international trade of goods and services. We will now study the relation between exchange rate and the trade of financial assets between countries.

Consider the case of a person or company residing in Germany with a given amount of wealth to save for the future. They consider buying either a German or an American financial asset. In general, there are three basic characteristics of an asset that matters to an investor: its return, its liquidity, and the associated risk. To begin, let us compare the return of the two assets. For the German asset, its return is the embedded interest rate, which we will denote $i_t$. By investing €1 in the German asset, the individual earns $€(1 + i_t)$ for the next period.[10]

For the American asset, computing its return is a little more complex, given that we must measure the return in euros to be able to compare it to the yield of the German asset. With €1 in hand, the first step is to buy dollars in order to purchase the American asset, which is traded in that currency. With €1, one buys US$ $(1/S_t)$, where $S_t$ is the nominal exchange rate of the euro in relation to the dollar. In the next period, the asset yields an American interest rate, which is represented by $i_t^*$, giving a total of US$ $(1/S_t)(1 + i_t^*)$. This amount should be converted back into euros. To guard against currency risk, the investor must, at the time they purchase the asset, buy euros in the future exchange rate market to convert the return back into euros at the time of redemption. In this way, in the next period the individual will have $€ (_tF_{t+1}/S_t)(1 + i_t^*)$, where $_tF_{t+1}$ is the exchange rate in the future market contracted in period $t$ for period $t + 1$. The following schematic summarizes the transaction.

$$€1 \xrightarrow{\text{converts}} US\$\frac{1}{S_t} \xrightarrow{\text{invests}} US\$\frac{1}{S_t}(1 + i_t^*) \xrightarrow{\text{converts back}} €\frac{_tF_{t+1}}{S_t}(1 + i_t^*)$$

The difference in returns between the two assets, DIFF, is therefore:

$$\text{DIFF} \equiv (1 + i_t) - \frac{_tF_{t+1}}{S_t}(1 + i_t^*). \tag{3.8}$$

The return differential in Eq. (3.8) is one of the criteria used by investors to decide which asset to purchase. The American and German assets can also differ in relation to their liquidity or the risk associated with them, which are the other two criteria used. In this way, the higher the relative return of the American asset, the higher its attractiveness will be in relation to the German, and, consequently, the higher its demand will be.

If, however, the German and American assets in question differ neither in relation to risk[11] nor liquidity, the only difference between them is their return. In this case, we say the two assets

---

[10] Here, we return to use discreet time, with the subscript indicating the moment in which the variable is evaluated.

[11] The precise condition is that the risk between the two assets should be perfectly positively correlated. If the risk is not perfectly positively correlated, the investors, in general risk averse, will prefer to diversify their assets portfolio. In other words, considerations regarding risk may continue affecting preferences in relation to assets, even if the risk associated with them is the same.

are perfect substitutes. The relevant aspect is the relative return of the assets, and the individual will invest in that asset with the higher return. If there is free capital mobility between the countries, a difference in the assets returns will lead investors to allocate all available wealth to invest in the asset with the higher return. Clearly, the possibility of this type of arbitrage cannot occur in equilibrium. Hence, the return differential in Eq. (3.8) should equal zero.

### 3.3.1 Carry Trade

To understand the mechanism that does not allow the existence of this type of arbitrage, suppose an American asset has a higher return than a German. All investors would want to buy American assets. Even more, they would have an incentive to borrow money in Germany in order to buy American assets, and make a gain from this operation. This type of operation is known as **carry trade**. There would be an excess demand for American assets accompanied by an excess indebtedness by international investors in Germany. The price of American assets would increase, reducing their yield. Analogously, the excess supply of German assets would increase their return. This process would occur until the return of both assets was the same, when measured in the same currency. In this way, with the free capital mobility and assets being perfect substitutes, which occurs when we consider the same risk and liquidity, the nonarbitrage condition implies the same return for German and American assets:

$$\frac{{}_tF_{t+1}}{S_t}(1 + i_t^*) = (1 + i_t).$$

### 3.3.2 Covered Interest Rate Parity

Reorganizing the previous equation, we have the **covered interest rate parity condition**:

$$\frac{{}_tF_{t+1}}{S_t} = \frac{1 + i_t}{1 + i_t^*}. \tag{3.9}$$

This parity condition is called *covered* since it is covered for the exchange rate risk. It is commonly written in log, so we take the natural logarithm from the covered interest rate parity, Eq. (3.9), to get:

$$_tf_{t+1} - s_t = i_t - i_t^*, \tag{3.10}$$

where $s \equiv \ln(S)$, $f \equiv \ln(F)$, and $i \equiv \ln(1 + i)$.

It is interesting to note that, for an investor, it is not the exchange rate that matters, but its variation over time. A change in the exchange rate between the time of buying and selling a foreign asset alters its value in domestic currency. If a large exchange rate depreciation is expected in the foreign country, for example, the interest rate offered on the asset must be high enough to compensate the loss caused by currency depreciation.

There are two crucial assumptions for the covered interest rate parity to hold true: free capital mobility and the perfect substitutability of assets. When there are restrictions to the international flow of capital, the arbitrage between the potential different returns cannot be made and, therefore, the interest rate parity may not be satisfied.

### 3.3.3 Risk Premium

Even if there is perfect mobility of capital, there can be differences in return between assets if they are not perfect substitutes. The differences in their return reflect differences in their relative attractiveness. An asset could have less liquidity, for example, making it less attractive. Their return would have to be relatively higher in equilibrium to render it equally attractive when compared to other assets with higher liquidity. The sovereign risk associated with the emitting country could be another factor that renders the assets different. There are credit risk evaluation agencies, such as Standard & Poor's (S&P) and Moody's, the two most well known, that attribute credit risk ratings to countries, companies, and banks. In this case, countries with a higher credit risk should supply a higher yield on their assets to compensate investors for the risk incurred. The term **risk premium** refers to this increase in return associated with the ability to pay of the issuer of the asset. The covered interest rate parity, taking into account the sovereign risk, can be written as:

$$i_t - i_t^* - [_tf_{t+1} - s_t] = \phi_t^s, \tag{3.11}$$

where $\phi_t^s$ represents the sovereign risk premium. The left side of Eq. (3.11) corresponds to the covered interest differential in Eq. (3.8) (in log), which should be equal to the sovereign risk in the case that there is capital mobility and the only difference between the assets is the sovereign risk associated with them (Box 3.4).

In general, the interest rate should respond to the risk associated with the asset in order to maintain its attractiveness. Consider the case of Europe in the 2000s. During the European financial crisis, in January 2012, S&P's lowered the long-term ratings on sovereign debt for nine European Union countries. Cyprus, Italy, Portugal, and Spain had their ratings lowered two levels. The Portuguese debt reached the category of *junk bond*.[12] The countries of Malta, Slovakia, Slovenia, Austria, and France had their ratings cut one degree, given that the last two countries were downgraded from their "AAA" rating, the best given by the agency. S&P maintained the long-term *ratings* for Belgium, Estonia, Finland, Germany, Ireland, Luxemburg, and the Netherlands, but stated that these economies now had a negative trend. Moody's also lowered their ratings for Italy, Portugal, Spain, Slovenia, and Malta and decided to give a negative trend to the "AAA" ratings for France, the United Kingdom, and Austria.

The market reaction was immediate. In the case of Italy, the interest rate on 10-year bonds passed 7%, the highest level reached since the Asian crisis of 1997/98. In Portugal, the situation was even more dramatic, with the interest rate on 10-year bonds being negotiated

---

[12] *Junk bonds* are high risk assets, with a low risk classification and generally with a high return, in case of payment.

## BOX 3.4 RISK PREMIUM

**BRAZIL–UNITED STATES**

Let us look at the data. Figure 3.4A shows the evolution of the covered interest differential between Brazilian and American government bonds, i.e., $i_t - i_t^* - [_t f_{t+1} - s_t]$, during the 2000s. We see that the return on Brazilian bonds was higher than that of the American in practically all months in the series. The most impressive movement was the significant increase in the relative return on

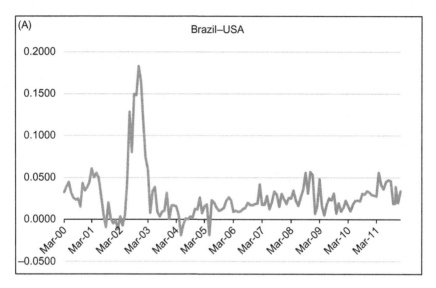

**Figure 3.4** Deviations in covered interest parity. *Sources: (A) Central Bank of Brazil and the Federal Reserve Bank, References (1) and (5) on Data List in Appendix; (B) Eurostat and OECD, References (3) and (4) on Data List in Appendix.*

(Continued)

---

**BOX 3.4 (CONTINUED)**

Brazilian government bonds at the end of 2002, at the time of the Fernando Henrique Cardoso to Luiz Inácio Lula da Silva government transition. Fernando Henrique Cardoso, who governed Brazil from 1995 to 2002, was responsible for price stabilization, ending a long period of extraordinary inflation rates. His commitment to an austere monetary policy was widely known. In general, the government sought the development of strong institutions to create a stable economic environment. In October 2002, Lula was elected president, but would only be sworn in on January 1, 2003. In his past marked by opposition, Lula always repudiated the austere Fernando Henrique monetary policy and was an outspoken critic of the economic policies and institutional changes implemented up to that time. There was nothing more natural, therefore, for there to be a great deal of uncertainty in relation to the direction economic policy would take under the new government, including in relation to fulfilling contracts and maintaining the openness of the financial account of the balance of payments. This uncertainty led to a substantial increase in the covered interest differential at the end of 2002, which is explained by the increase in sovereign risk for that period.

**UNITED STATES–EUROPE**

In Figure 3.4B, we have the interest differential between the average return on European governments bonds and American ones. We see that the difference in returns is at times positive and at others, negative. In other words, there is not a sustained difference indicating a continued difference in risk between the countries. Moreover, the differentials are much smaller than in Figure 3.4A, which compares American bonds to Brazilian, that is, a developed country compared to an emerging market.

---

at over 15%. In Spain, the interest rate on bonds with the same maturity increased from 6% to a peak of 7%, a lower jump explained by the fact that most investors already anticipated the negative credit evaluation. In France, the reaction of the 10-year interest rate was smaller, increasing to about 3.5%, but was lowered in the following weeks due to government announcements reinforcing its commitment to fiscal stability in the country.

## 3.3.4 Uncovered Interest Rate Parity

Investors on the international financial market can, as an alternative, opt to arbiter between the return of two assets without resorting to the future exchange rate market, that is, they assimilate the exchange rate risk and only trade currencies at the time they make the conversion between them. In this case, the nonarbitrage condition is given by:

$$\frac{E(S_{t+1})}{S_t} = \frac{1 + i_t}{1 + i_t^*},\qquad(3.12)$$

which is known as the **uncovered interest rate parity** condition. The term *uncovered* refers to the fact that the transaction is not covered for the currency risk. Taking the logarithm of the uncovered interest rate parity in Eq. (3.12), we have that:

$$E(S_{t+1}) - s_t = i_t - i_t^*,\qquad(3.13)$$

where $E(s_{t+1}) \equiv \ln E(S_{t+1})$.

If there is no exchange rate risk premium, be it due to lack of uncertainty with respect to the exchange rate level in the future or because investors are risk neutral, the exchange rate depreciation reflected in the future market should be equal to the actual expected exchange rate depreciation, that is:

$$_t f_{t+1} - s_t = E(s_{t+1}) - s_t. \tag{3.14}$$

If the condition of Eq. (3.14) verifies, the covered and uncovered interest rate parities are equivalent, i.e., both Eqs. (3.9) and (3.12) hold true simultaneously.

We can say that if the covered interest rate parity is verified, then there is perfect capital mobility between countries and the assets are perfect substitutes. If the covered parity is verified but the uncovered not, then Eq. (3.14) is not true. There is uncertainty with respect to the exchange rate in the future and the agents are not neutral to currency risk so that there is a risk premium. The exchange rate change in the future market incorporates a risk premium, so that:

$$_t f_{t+1} - s_t = E(s_{t+1}) - s_t + \phi_t^c, \tag{3.15}$$

where $\phi_t^c$ is the currency risk premium. Therefore, the version of interest rate parity in Eq. (3.13) that takes into account the currency risk can be written as:

$$i_t - i_t^* - [E(s_{t+1}) - s_t] = \phi_t^c, \tag{3.16}$$

that is, the return of the domestic assets may be different than that of the foreign, and this difference corresponds to the currency risk premium. The left side of Eq. (3.16) represents the uncovered interest rate differential.

Empirical validity of the uncovered interest rate parity is harder to verify, given that data on expectations for the future exchange rate is needed. To circumvent this difficulty, the actual value of the exchange rate is commonly used as a *proxy* for the exchange rate expectation. It is based on the assumption that, if expectations are rational, there should be no persistent errors in them. In other words, on average the exchange rate forecasts should be correct, and the forecast error should be equal to zero in expected value. We can represent this assumption as:

$$E(s_{t+1}) = s_{t+1} + \mu_{t+1}, \tag{3.17}$$

where $\mu_{t+1}$ is the expectation error for the exchange rate in period $t+1$. Substituting the expected exchange rate into Eq. (3.16), we have that:

$$i_t - i_t^* - [s_{t+1} - s_t] = \phi_t^c + \mu_{t+1}. \tag{3.18}$$

Equation (3.18) shows that the uncovered interest differential can be explained by the currency risk premium and by the error in exchange rate expectation. With rational expectations, the expected error is equal to zero:

$$E(\mu_{t+1}) = 0.$$

If this is true, on average the uncovered interest differential should be equal to the currency risk premium.

In practice, data analysis reveals relatively persistent deviations from interest rate parity. In this case, there are possible gains from arbitrage for the individuals who can indebt themselves in a country where the interest rate is low and invest in assets where the return is higher, that is, they practice *carry trade*.[13] Faced with such a situation, one may wonder why carry trade is not done in an extent large enough to impact assets prices and exhaust those gains, as the theory predicts. A possible answer lies in the possibility of an abrupt depreciation of the currency where the resources are invested in relation to where the loan is taken. Such a depreciation would increase the value of the debt and, if it is large enough, even bring about a loss for the carry trader. To illustrate such a situation, in Box 3.5 I compare the yield of Swiss and French bonds at the beginning of the 2000s.

---

**BOX 3.5 THE RISK OF CARRY TRADE**

Let us examine the evolution of interest rates on bonds with a 1-year maturity issued in Switzerland and France, as well as the exchange rate path between the countries since the beginning of 2000.

As a starting point, consider the case of an investor who seeks to exploit arbitrage gains by borrowing Fr100 in January 2000 in Switzerland to invest in French government bonds. The blue area of Figure 3.5B represents the evolution of uncovered interest rate deviation of its parity, as defined by the left side of Eq. (3.18). We see that, in the first years, this investment results in loss since the deviations in uncovered interest rate parity were negative. Figure 3.5A shows that, in spite of the interest rate in France always being higher than that in Switzerland, the depreciation of the euro in relation to the Swiss franc more than compensated the difference between the interest rates, causing the operation to generate a loss.

As of the end of 2001, the uncovered interest rate differential was taken by the appreciation of the euro, which resulted in a positive interest differential up to the beginning of 2007. The gains between 2002 and 2004 compensated the losses from the beginning of the decade, as can be seen by the red line in Figure 3.5B, which represents the gains accumulated by the investor who set up their position at the beginning of 2000. The possibility of arbitrage gains with the higher interest rate differential must have attracted other individuals, who possibly set up investments similar to our fictitious investor at some time when gains were favorable. However, in 2008 the situation changed abruptly. The beginning of the world economic crisis resulted in a mass rush to secure assets, which led to a strong depreciation of the euro in relation to the franc. At this time, the investor, who had initially invested in 2000, saw a reduction in accumulated gains, while those who had decided to exploit the arbitrage gains months before the crisis suffered heavy losses. Therefore, risk of loss due to abrupt variations in exchange rates renders investors reticent to take advantage of positive interest rate differentials. In terms of Eq. (3.18), this is captured by a positive exchange rate risk premium $\phi^c$.

*(Continued)*

---

[13] Bacchetta (2013) reviews the main explanations for the observed deviations in interest rate parity.

**BOX 3.5 (CONTINUED)**

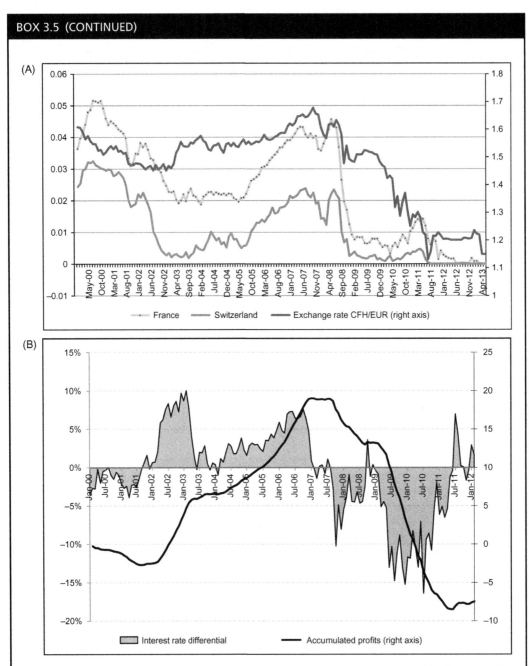

**Figure 3.5** Interest differential and potential arbitrage: (A) interest and exchange rates and (B) deviations of the uncovered interest rate parity and arbitrage gains. (For interpretation of the references to color in the text, the reader is referred to the web version of this book.) *Source: Eurostat and World Bank, References (3) and (4) on Data List in Appendix.*

## 3.3.5 The Peso Problem

According to Eq. (3.18), the two interest rates should be equal when there is a fixed exchange rate regime between the two countries, given that, in this case, there are no exchange rate depreciations. In a fixed exchange rate regime, however, there can be an expectation of exchange rate depreciation if there is any uncertainty in regards to maintaining the regime.

To understand what this means in terms of the uncovered interest rate differential, suppose that agents attribute probability $\lambda$ to the maintenance of the fixed regime, where the exchange rate is maintained at level $\bar{s}$. If the fixed exchange rate regime is abandoned, we assume that the exchange rate jumps to $\hat{s} > \bar{s}$. We can then write the expected exchange rate as:

$$E(s_{t+1}) = \lambda \bar{s} + (1 - \lambda)\hat{s}. \tag{3.19}$$

Substituting the expected value from Eq. (3.19) into Eq. (3.17) for the period in which the regime is maintained, that is, when $s_{t+1} = \bar{s}$, we have that:

$$\mu_{t+1} = (1 - \lambda)(\hat{s} - \bar{s}) > 0.$$

Hence, there are persistent and biased expectation errors. This simple example shows that, even when expectations are perfectly rational, there can be persistent errors in exchange rate expectations when there is a probability of regime change. This is called the **peso problem**.[14]

The expectation of exchange rate depreciation causes the right side of the interest rate differential equation (3.18) to be positive, leading to an increase in domestic interest rates in relation to international. Moreover, the lower the confidence in the fixed exchange rate regime (in our notation, lower $\lambda$), the higher the expected exchange rate depreciation. Consequently, the higher domestic interest rate should be to maintain the attractiveness of domestic assets to investors (Box 3.6).

---

**BOX 3.6 THE PESO PROBLEM IN ARGENTINA**

The peso problem can be seen in the Argentina example. Between 1991 and 2002, Argentina adhered to a currency board regime, where the Argentine peso exchange rate in relation to the dollar was fixed. The interest rate differential between the two countries, however, changed considerably over the period, as can been seen in Figure 3.6. In the first years of the regime, the interest rate differential between Argentina and the United States was high, which can be explained by the lack of credibility at the onset of the regime. The currency board regime was instituted as a means for

*(Continued)*

---

[14] The peso problem received its name for being identified the first time in relation to the Mexican peso in the 1970s, as originally mentioned by Rogoff (1977).

**BOX 3.6 (CONTINUED)**

the Argentine government to end the chronic inflation it had been facing. It is reasonable to think that, at the beginning, economic agents were skeptical as to the ability of the government to maintain this economic policy. There was a period of calm during the second half of the 1990s, when interest rates were very close. As of the end of 1999, when external shocks put in check the possibility of maintaining the regime, Argentine interest rates again began distancing themselves from the American. Near the end of the regime, Argentine interest rates had an astonishing increase, reaching the level of 91.2%, while the American interest rates were at 3.39%.

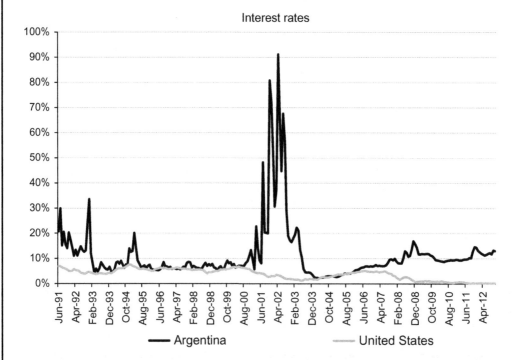

**Figure 3.6** Interest rates evolution: Argentina and the United States. *Source: Federal Reserve Bank and Banco Central de La República Argentina, References (5) and (6) on Data List in Appendix.*

# Mathematical Appendix

## Deriving the Relationship Between Exchange Rate Variation and Inflation

Using the natural logarithm from the definition of real exchange rate in Eq. (3.2), which we repeat here as subscript $t$ to indicate time:

$$Q_t = \frac{S_t P_t^*}{P_t}$$

we obtain:

$$\ln Q_t = \ln S_t + \ln P_t^* - \ln P_t.$$

Taking the derivative of the above equation with respect to time, we have:

$$\frac{d \ln Q_t}{dt} = \frac{d \ln S_t}{dt} + \frac{d \ln P_t^*}{dt} - \frac{d \ln P_t}{dt},$$

which can be written as:

$$\frac{dQ_t/dt}{Q_t} = \frac{dS_t/dt}{S_t} + \frac{dP_t^*/dt}{P_t^*} - \frac{dP_t/dt}{P_t}. \tag{3.20}$$

When the real exchange rate is at its equilibrium level, it should not change, i.e., $(dQ_t/dt)/Q_t = 0$. Incorporating this information into Eq. (3.20), we arrive at:

$$0 = \dot{s}_t + \dot{p}_t^* - \dot{p}_t \Leftrightarrow \dot{s}_t = \dot{p}_t - \dot{p}_t^*.$$

Finally, defining $\dot{s}_t \equiv (ds_t/dt)/s_t$, the above equation can be written as:

$$\dot{s}_t = \pi_t - \pi_t^*.$$

# 3.4 Exercises

## Exercise 1

Suppose the nominal interest rate on a 1-year US bond is 5% and the nominal interest rate in Mexico for a bond of the same maturity is 10%. The current exchange rate in the spot exchange rate market is 2.5 peso$/US$.

**a.** If the uncovered interest rate parity is valid and the expected exchange rate for the next year is 2.4 peso$/US$, which of the two investments is more interesting to an American investor?

**b.** If the covered interest rate parity is valid, what should be the nominal exchange rate on the future dollar contract with a 1-year term?

## Exercise 2

Suppose that the 3-month interest rate on English bonds is 10%. The rate of return for the US bonds of the same maturity is 6%. The *spot* exchange rate between the dollar and pound is 2 US$/pound.

**a.** With free financial capital mobility between the two countries, and the bonds from the two countries being perfect substitutes, what should be the expected depreciation for the dollar? Explain the economic intuition for your answer.

**b.** Suppose the exchange rate for the future pound contract is 1.99 US$/pound. Is it possible for a North American investor to exploit an arbitrage opportunity?

## Exercise 3

Suppose the Mexican government imposes a tax rate of $t\%$ on the profitability of Mexican bonds as well as on gains received from exchange rate operations. How will this situation affect the uncovered exchange rate parity equation?

## Exercise 4

A country imposes an import tariff, represented by $\tau$, with $\tau \in (0.1)$. Suppose that the currency in this country is the peso and that the international currency accepted for transactions is the pataca.

**a.** How does the imposition of this tariff affect the real exchange rate between the peso and the pataca in the short term, that is, with fixed prices? What is the long-term effect of this measure after eventual price adjustments?
**b.** How will the imposition of the tariff affect the nominal exchange rate in the short term? What is the long-term effect?

## Exercise 5

Consider two bonds, one of them Spanish, denominated in euros (€), and the other denominated in Chilean pesos ($), a Chilean bond. Assume both bonds have a 1-year maturity and that they are negotiated with discount, in other words, they pay a determined value per maturity and have a current price equal to a fraction of the amount paid at maturity. The current exchange rate is $S = 2.5$ $/€. The face value of the Chilean bond is $1,000.00, while the face value of the Spanish bond is €1,000.00. The market price for the Chilean bond on date $t$ is $956,00 and the market price for the Spanish bond is €945,00.

**a.** What is the nominal interest rate for each of the bonds?
**b.** Find the expected exchange rate at bond maturity that is compatible with the uncovered interest rate parity.
**c.** If you expect there will be a short-term appreciation of the Chilean peso against the euro, which of the bonds should you buy?
**d.** Suppose you are a Chilean investor who is considering exchanging pesos for euros to purchase the Spanish bond. One year later the exchange rate will be $S = 2.3$ $/€. What is the rate of return measured in pesos? Compare to the rate of return you would have received by investing in Chilean bonds.
**e.** Are the differences in returns obtained in the previous question compatible with the uncovered interest rate parity? Explain your answer.

## Exercise 6

$\pi_{EUR}^e$ is the inflation expected in the Eurozone between period $t$ and period $t+1$, and $\pi_{UK}^e$ the inflation expected in the United Kingdom during the same period. $S_t$ is the nominal exchange rate of the euro with respect to the pound (€/£) for period $t$ and $E(S_{t+1})$ is the nominal exchange rate expected for the next period. Assuming that the purchase power parity is valid, answer the following items.

**a.** If $\pi_{EUR}^e$ rises in relation to $\pi_{UK}^e$, what should occur with the expected depreciation of the euro?

**b.** What is the impact on the real interest rate differential, $i_{EUR} - i_{UK}$?

**c.** How would your answer change for the previous item if the purchasing power parity was not valid?

## Exercise 7

Russia and China both produce two goods: cellular telephones, a tradable good designated as $T$, and haircuts, a nontradable good designated as $N$. Each good is produced in competitive markets in a single process. Workers receive the marginal productivity for their labor. Suppose there are no trade costs for cellular phones, while for haircuts they are prohibitively high. The rate for per hour work is $w$ rubles in Russian and $w^*$ yuans in China. $S$ represents the nominal exchange rate defined in terms of rubles per yuan. Suppose that in one hour of work a Russian laborer is able to produce $y_T = 30$ telephones, while the Chinese produces $y_T^* = 15$ telephones per hour. In both countries, one worker is able to produce only one haircut per hour. Suppose the price of a cellular phone is 1 ruble.

**a.** If $S = 0.5$, what is the price of the cellular telephone in yuans?

**b.** What would be the hourly wage in Russia, assuming that the labor market is competitive, so that workers receive as salary the value of their productivity? What would be the hourly wage in China in yuans?

**c.** What would be the price of haircuts in each country?

**d.** Suppose that cellular telephone productivity in China doubles. What would happen to the price of haircuts in China? What would happen to the real exchange rate between Russia and China?

## Exercise 8

Consider a small, open economy that decides to establish parity between their currency and the dollar, but where the greater part their international trade is done with Europe.

**a.** Consider a short-term horizon, where prices for goods do not vary. If the dollar depreciates in relation to the euro, what happens to the trade of this economy with countries that have adopted the euro as their currency?

**b.** Continuing the assumption of dollar depreciation, how should the financial account balance for this country change? What happens if international investors are not willing to invest in this country? How should their central bank act to avoid losing the parity with the dollar?

**c.** Assume that, even though the dollar parity remains stable, investors believe the exchange policy of this country is not credible. What monetary policy should be adopted so that exchange rate parity is maintained in face of the credibility problem? Explain the mechanism associated with you answer.

## Exercise 9

Suppose that the Russian economy maintains trade relations only with countries in the Eurozone and China, and that 80% of Russian trade is with the Eurozone and the remaining 20% with China. Suppose also that the following data for 2012 and 2013 is true:

|                          | 2012  | 2013  |
|--------------------------|-------|-------|
| Exchange rate ₽/€        | 24.30 | 24.00 |
| Exchange rate ₽/¥        | 4.90  | 5.20  |
| Price index in Russia    | 100   | 107   |
| Price index in Eurozone  | 100   | 102   |
| Price index in China     | 100   | 103   |

**a.** What was the depreciation/appreciation of the ruble (₽) with respect to the euro (€), in real terms, between 2012 and 2013? And of the ruble (₽) with respect to the yuan?

**b.** Is purchasing power parity, in its absolute version, true for Russia, the United States, and China? And the purchasing power parity in its relative version?

**c.** Calculate the real effective exchange rate for Russia in 2012 and 2013. What was the depreciation/appreciation of the real effective exchange rate between 2012 and 2013?

**d.** Assume the uncovered interest rate parity is valid, that the exchange rates observed in 2013 correspond to expectations formed in 2012, and that the fixed income assets in each country are denominated in their own currency. What should be the respected relation of the nominal interest rate between Russia, the Eurozone, and China for assets with similar characteristics?

## Exercise 10

In the 1970s, the Mexican government tied the exchange rate of the peso to the North American dollar. During the same period, short-term Mexican interest rates, those defined by their central bank, were significantly higher than those in the United States.

**a.** In this situation, what is the expectation of financial market participants in relation to the peso/dollar exchange rate in the future?

**b.** If financial market participants believe that probability $p$ exists for peso depreciation, show that there is a persistent error in the forecast of the future exchange rate.

## Exercise 11

Suppose that you are an operator who works in an investment bank and you need to close on a strategy based on the future market of the yen for the next 3 months. You know that a Japanese government bond with a 3-month maturity is being negotiated at a rate of 0.004% and that the rate for Canadian bonds with the same maturity is 2.811%. The spot exchange rate between the Canadian dollar and the American dollar is 1.5054 C$/US$. The exchange rate between the yen and the American dollar is 118 ¥/US$. Suppose that the future exchange rate for 3 months is 1.2032 C$/US$. Calculate the future exchange rate between the yen and the American dollar for 3 months.

# Current Account and Real Exchange Rate

In Chapter 2, we saw that the current-account balance corresponds to the variation of the net international investment position of a country, that is, the variation of its debt or net credit with the rest of the world. This corresponds to the difference between the aggregate savings and investment for the country. This part of the book analyzes the current-account determinants, as well as the real exchange rate associated to it, by means of a study of the savings and investment decisions by the economic agents.

Savings and investment are studied in Chapter 4, which will allow us to analyze how the current-account balance adjusts itself to the changes in domestic and international scenarios. Chapter 5 will focus on the real exchange rate. In an economy where there are tradable and nontradable goods, the real exchange rate is related to the relative price between tradables and nontradables. In this context, we will show that each current-account level is associated with a value for the real exchange rate. The real exchange rate equilibrium is therefore deduced as that which is suitable to the optimum current-account balance studied in Chapter 4. We analyze the relation between the real exchange rate equilibrium and domestic economic variables, such as productivity and public expenditures, and international variables, such as the international interest rate and terms of trade.

# What Is the Optimum Current-Account Level?

**CHAPTER OUTLINE**

Is it better to have a current-account deficit or surplus? How does an income shock, such as a change in international export prices, affect the current-account balance of a country? As we saw in Section 2.2, the current-account balance corresponds to the difference between the aggregated savings and investment in a country. Therefore, the answer to this and other similar questions depends on the investment and savings decisions made by individuals, and how these decisions are affected by economic shocks. **The intertemporal model of current-account adjustment does exactly that it studies the optimum choices for savings and investment in a country, and the current account is the result of these choices**.

Principles of International Finance and Open Economy Macroeconomics.
English translation © 2015 Elsevier Inc.

There are several reasons for saving: avoiding changes in consumption over time, investing, and guarding against uncertainties in relation to income or the need for future consumption, among others. In the first version of the model that we will see, in Section 4.1, for an economy with no government and, in Section 4.3, with a government, the focus will be on the savings generated with the objective of smoothing consumption over time. Intuitively, when the consumer knows that their income will change, they save during the periods when they are relatively better off in order to consume in the periods when they have relatively less. In the second version, presented in Section 4.4, the decision to invest is added. Savings in this case will have two objectives: smooth consumption and invest to increase the production capacity in the future. Section 4.5 discusses the capacity of the model to explain concrete facts as well as some extensions.

## 4.1 Basic Hypotheses

As always in economic models, some simplifying hypotheses are made. We assume that **there is only one good** in the economy. The existence of more than one good would generate the problem of deciding allocation of consumption among the many goods, which is not the focus of this chapter. This one good can be interpreted as the consumption basket composed of all goods consumed.

In this model **there are only two periods**, which can be interpreted as the present and the future. The same model can be developed for an infinite number of periods.[1] Given that the intuitive results from the model do not change when more periods are included, we will work with the simplest model.

We will study the case of **a small, open economy**. A small economy, in international economics, means that it does not have the ability to influence international prices. In other words, the amount a country imports or exports does not affect the prices of goods traded on the international market, and the amount it borrows from or lends to the rest of the world does not affect international interest rates. It is possible that an economy can be *small* in some markets and *large* in others. Chile, for example, is a large country in the copper market, since it is a large world producer, but small in other goods markets.

In relation to the credit market, we assume that the country is not only small, that is, its market activity does not influence the international interest rates, but that **it can freely borrow at a constant interest rate**. This is certainly a strong hypothesis. One does not need to be a very perceptive analyst to notice that when a country's debt begins to accelerate, the cost of indebtedness increases, even for a small country, due to the increase in risk associated with its debt. This does mean that the model is useless, but that one must be clear regarding the model's limitations for the situations in which it can be used. It is an adequate model to analyze situations where the variations in a country's debt or credit with the rest of the world are of a relatively moderate magnitude, such that it does not affect the interest rate under which it transacts on the international credit market.

Finally, we will work with an economy where there is no uncertainty. Including uncertainty adds another factor for choosing saving, without the other motives for saving

---

[1] The two-period model presented here follows the one by Obstfeld and Rogoff (1996), in Chapter 1. Chapter 2 in their book develops the model for an infinite number of periods.

disappearing.[2] In other words, even with uncertainty, consumers will continue saving to smooth consumption and to invest.

## 4.2 Consumption Smoothing

Let us first consider an economy where there is neither production nor investment and where each consumer receives an endowment of goods each period. Abstracting the decision to invest, which will be introduced in Section 4.4, we can focus on the decision to save in the economy. In this first version of the model, we assume that there is no government.

The evolution of economic variables is studied based on decisions made by **a representative consumer, who chooses how much to consume each period, subject to a budget constraint**. The preferences of consumer $i$ between present consumption ($c_1^i$) and future consumption ($c_2^i$) can be represented by the following **intertemporal utility function**:

$$U_1^i \equiv u(c_1^i) + \beta u(c_2^i), \tag{4.1}$$

where the intertemporal discount factor $\beta$, $0 < \beta < 1$, measures the degree of consumer "patience." The greater $\beta$ is, the more the consumer values future consumption and, therefore, the more patient they are. We assume that the consumer always prefers to consume larger quantities, but the more they consume, less is the utility increment with the additional consumption. Mathematically, this translates into function $u(\cdot)$ increasing and strictly concave: $u'(\cdot) > 0$ and $u''(\cdot) < 0$.[3]

The utility function in Eq. (4.1) can be represented in the two-dimensional space ($c_1^i, c_2^i$) by indifference curves, where each of them groups the possible combination of present and future consumption that give the consumer the same utility. The curves in Figure 4.1 are an example of a map of indifference curves. The consumer obtains the same utility $U_1$ in points A and B, for example, that represent two combinations of consumption in periods 1 and 2. The farther from the origin, the higher the utility represented by the indifference curve. The negative slope of the indifference curves indicates the substitutability between present and future consumption: the consumer can have the same utility with less present consumption, if future consumption is higher, as in points A and B. In point A, the present consumption is lower than in B, $c_{1,A}^i < c_{1,B}^i$, but future consumption is higher in A in relation to B, $c_{2,A}^i < c_{2,B}^i$. The value of this slope is denominated the **marginal rate of substitution**, being defined, in absolute value, as[4]

---

[2] For the extension of the model to include uncertainty in an infinite-period setting, see Chapter 2 of Obstfeld and Rogoff (1996).

[3] Additionally, we assume that utility is zero when consumption is null, $u(0) = 0$, that the utility increment tends to infinity when approaching null consumption, and tends to zero when consumption goes to infinity, expressed as $u'(0) \rightarrow \infty$ and $\lim_{C \rightarrow \infty} u'(C) = 0$. These assumptions, named Inada conditions, guarantee the choice of positive quantities of consumption for each period.

[4] To derive the marginal rate of substitution, we apply the implicit function theorem to the utility function evaluated at a given level of utility, i.e., taking $U_1^i = u(c_1^i) + u(c_2^i) = \overline{u}$, where $\overline{u}$ is a constant. Therefore,

$$\left. \frac{dc_2^i}{dc_1^i} \right]_{U_1^i = \overline{u}} = -\frac{\partial U_1^i / \partial c_1^i}{\partial U_1^i / \partial c_2^i} = -\frac{u'(c_1^i)}{\beta u'(c_2^i)}.$$

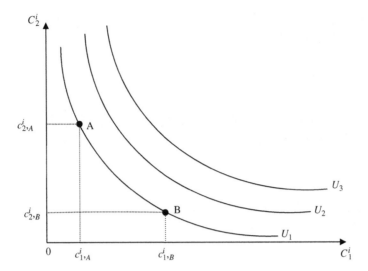

**Figure 4.1** Map of indifference curves.

$$|\text{TMS}| \equiv \left| \frac{dc_2^i}{dc_1^i} \right|_{U_i = \bar{u}} = \frac{u'(c_1^i)}{\beta u'(c_2^i)}. \tag{4.2}$$

The consumer is subject to an **intertemporal budget constraint**. We assume that for each period $t$ they receive endowment $y_t^i$ of the good, and can then lend or borrow from the international credit market at interest rate $r$. To simplify, we will consider the good as the numeraire, so that its price is always equal to 1. The budget constraint establishes that the present value of consumption should be equal to the present value of their income (Box 4.1) and can be written as

$$c_1^i + \frac{c_2^i}{1+r} = y_1^i + \frac{y_2^i}{1+r}. \tag{4.3}$$

The straight line in Figure 4.2 represents the budget constraint. Its slope indicates the rate at which the consumer can exchange present consumption for future consumption,

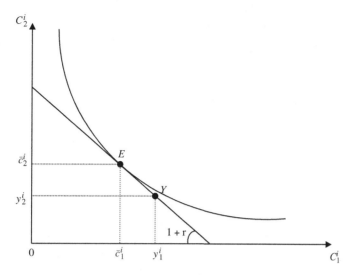

**Figure 4.2** The consumer's problem.

**BOX 4.2 PRESENT VALUE**

*Present value* is the value today of values to be available in the future. Intertemporal money transfer is possible through the financial market: one may bring money from the future to the present by borrowing in the financial market, at the cost of the interest rate. Hence, to compute the present value of the stream of consumption, for instance, we add to the value of consumption in period 1, the consumption in period 2 discounted by the interest rate that would have to be paid to transfer that value to the present time.

which corresponds to the rate by which income can be transferred between periods. In this way, budget constraint is a straight line with slope $-(1+r)$ in space $(c_1^i, c_2^i)$ (Box 4.2). Point $Y = (y_1^i, y_2^i)$ in the figure represents the consumer endowment. Given that the consumer can always choose to consume exactly their endowment, the budget constraint must go through this point.

The consumer chooses the amount to consume during each period so as to maximize its utility, as represented by Eq. (4.1), subject to budget constraint in Eq. (4.3). To algebraically solve the consumer's problem, notice that, according to budget constraint, the decision to consume in the present determines what will be consumed in the future. More precisely, budget constraint states that

$$c_2^i = (1+r)(y_1^i - c_1^i) + y_2^i. \tag{4.4}$$

Substituting future consumption defined in Eq. (4.4) in the utility function in Eq. (4.1), the consumer's problem can be rewritten as

$$\max_{c_1^i} u(c_1^i) + \beta u((1 + r)(y_1^i - c_1^i) + y_2^i),$$

where the consumer chooses present consumption $c_1^i$. The first-order condition[5] for a level of consumption that maximizes utility is

$$u'(c_1^i) = (1 + r)\beta u'(c_2^i), \tag{4.5}$$

in which $c_2^i$ is given by Eq. (4.4).

Equation (4.5) is known as the Euler equation. It determines that, at the optimum point, the consumer cannot increase their utility by reallocating consumption between periods. Intuitively, by consuming one unit less in the present, the total utility for the consumer reduces in $u'(c_1^i)$. This amount is saved, rendering $(1 + r)$, so that, in the future, the consumer can consume $(1 + r)$ additional units of the good,[6] which increases the total utility in $(1 + r)\beta u'(c_2^i)$. When the condition of Eq. (4.5) is satisfied, these two values are exactly the same.

The Euler equation can also be written as

$$\frac{u'(c_1^i)}{\beta u'(c_2^i)} = 1 + r. \tag{4.6}$$

The left side of equality of Eq. (4.6) is the slope of the indifference curve, as defined by Eq. (4.2), while the right side is the slope of the budget constraint, interpreted as the relative price of consumption between the two periods. Consequently, **the consumer maximizes their utility, subject to the budget constraint, when the marginal rate of substitution of consumption between the two periods is equal to its relative price**.

In terms of Figure 4.2, the consumer's problem consists in choosing a point on the budget constraint belonging to an indifference curve that is farthest from the origin. This point is that where an indifference curve passes tangent to the budget constraint, i.e., with the same slope. Therefore, point E represents the allocation of consumption between present consumption and future consumption that maximizes the consumer intertemporal utility. It is easy to see that, at any other point of the budget constraint, the indifference curves are closer to the origin, therefore representing less utility than that which passes through point E.

Notice that access to the international credit market allows the value of consumption for reach period to be different from the endowment of product available to the consumer. This

---

[5] The first-order condition for the maximization problem of a function with one variable establishes that the derivative of the objective function with respect to the choice variable should be equal to zero at the maximum local point.

[6] Notice that, according to this reasoning, $1 + r$ can be interpreted as the price of consumption in period 2 relative to consumption in period 1.

can be observed in Figure 4.2 by the fact that the endowment vector $(y_1^i, y_2^i)$ is different than the consumption vector $(\bar{c}_1^i, \bar{c}_2^i)$.

To know the value of consumption for each period, it is necessary to define the functional form for function $u(\cdot)$, as well as the value of intertemporal preference factor $\beta$ and the interest rate $r$. In order to advance in the analysis without knowing the functional form for $u(\cdot)$, we assume that $\beta = 1/(1 + r)$. In this case, the Euler equation (4.5) becomes $u'(c_1^i) = u'(c_2^i)$, which, given the strict concavity of the utility function, implies that

$$c_1^i = c_2^i \equiv \bar{c}^i. \tag{4.7}$$

Therefore, **when subjective intertemporal discount factor $\beta$ is equal to the credit market discount factor $1/(1 + r)$, the consumer does not want changes in consumption over time.** We can therefore say that the consumer performs perfect **consumption smoothing**.

Substituting the condition of Eq. (4.7) into the budget constraint in Eq. (4.4), we find that

$$\bar{c}^i = \frac{(1 + r)y_1^i + y_2^i}{2 + r}, \tag{4.8}$$

which defines the level of consumption for each consumer for each period. The endowment and consumption aggregates will be the sum of the endowment and consumption of all consumers in the economy.

Given that individual heterogeneity is not of interest to our analysis, we assume that all individuals are identical and have the same product endowment for each period. To simplify the notation, we also assume that the population is formed by a continuum of individuals in the interval $[0, 1]$. With these hypotheses, both the endowment and the consumption aggregates, $Y$ and $C$, will be equal to their individual values, i.e., $Y = y^i$ and $C = c^i$ (Box 4.3). With these hypotheses, we have that Eq. (4.8) presents the aggregate consumption as

$$\bar{C} = \frac{(1 + r)Y_1 + Y_2}{2 + r}, \quad \text{when } \beta = \frac{1}{1 + r}. \tag{4.9}$$

It is important to remember that this is a small country in the international credit market; in other words, its decision to lend or borrow does not alter the international interest rate $r$. Any excess supply or demand for credit within the country generated by this interest rate is

---

**BOX 4.3 ECONOMIC VARIABLES: FROM INDIVIDUAL TO AGGREGATE**

Here is the trick commonly used to transform individual variables into aggregate variables in economic models. We assume all individuals are identical, and that there is an infinite number of them indexed over the interval $[0, 1]$. Let us take income as an example. By definition, aggregate income is the sum of the income of all individuals in the economy, or, mathematically, under our assumptions: $Y = \int_{i=0}^{1} y^i di$. Since each individual $i$ receives the same endowment $y^i = y$, we can write aggregate income as $Y = \int_{i=0}^{1} y \, di = y \int_{i=0}^{1} di = y$. The same logic can be used to compute all aggregate variables that are identical for all individuals.

balanced by transactions with the rest of the world: by foreign debt or credit. Therefore, individuals can maintain the same level of consumption in the present and in the future, even if their endowment is different between periods.

## 4.2.1 Current Account

The national accounts identity represented by Eq. (2.10) can be written as

$$CA_t = Y_t + rB_t - C_t, \tag{4.10}$$

remembering that in our economy we are assuming that, for the time being, there is neither government nor investment in physical capital accumulation. The endowment of the economy $Y_t$ corresponds to the gross domestic product. These are goods produced in the country, or received as endowment as in this model, but that do not necessarily belong to the national residents, as in the case where the country is indebted and pays the service of its foreign debt. $B_t$ is the Net International Investment Position[7] (NIIP), which can be positive or negative, depending on if the country is a net creditor or debtor with respect to other countries, so that $rB_t$ represents the net investment income of the country.

Notice that, in the case of an economy with no physical capital as the one we are considering here, the current-account balance depends only on the decision to save, on the right side of the equation. When savings are positive, the current-account balance is positive and the country lends to the rest of the world. When savings are negative, the country borrows.

Given the aggregate endowments in the two periods, $Y_1$ and $Y_2$, Eq. (4.9) establishes the aggregate consumption for each period in the case where $\beta = 1/(1 + r)$. Inserting this information into Eq. (4.10), we can compute the current-account balance in each period:

$$CA_1 = \frac{Y_1 - Y_2}{2 + r} + rB_1, \tag{4.11a}$$

$$CA_2 = \frac{(1 + r)(Y_2 - Y_1)}{2 + r} + rB_2. \tag{4.11b}$$

According to the balance of payments, the current and financial account balances should be equal, and the latter corresponds to the variation in the value of net foreign assets in the country, that is, the net international investment position, as established in Eq. (2.11): $CA_t = B_{t+1} - B_t$.

We assume that, in the first period, the country carries over no debt or loans,[8] that is, $B_1 = 0$, and at the end of the second period, the country ends up with no debt or loans: $B_3 = 0$.[9] Incorporating these assumptions into Eq. (2.11), we arrive at

---

[7] One should remember that *investment*, in this context, refers to investment in financial capital.

[8] Note that this assumption is implicit in the budget constraint of Eq. (4.3). If the consumer had a stock of foreign assets (positive or negative) in the first period, the right side of Eq. (4.3) should include the receipt (or payment as the case may be) for the debt service.

[9] The assumption that $B_3 = 0$ corresponds to the transversality condition described in Section 2.3, for the case where time runs indefinitely. The intuition for this condition is found in the section regarding the sustainability of deficits in current account in Chapter 2, in the derivation to arrive at Eq. (2.14).

$$CA_1 = B_2 - B_1 = B_2, \tag{4.12a}$$

$$CA_2 = B_3 - B_2 = -B_2, \tag{4.12b}$$

and, therefore

$$CA_1 = -CA_2.$$

In other words, a deficit in current account in the first period should be compensated with a surplus in the second period for the economy to honor its foreign commitments.

Combining Eqs. (4.10) and (4.12a), and using the assumption that $B_1 = 0$, we have that

$$CA_1 = Y_1 - C_1 = B_2. \tag{4.13}$$

Equation (4.13) shows that, given there was no initial debt, the current-account balance is simply the difference between income and consumption in the economy, which corresponds to first period savings. When consumption is greater than income, the current-account balance will be negative and the country will accumulate a debt in the absolute value of $|B_2|$.

We also have from Eq. (4.11a) that

$$CA_1 = \frac{Y_1 - Y_2}{2 + r} = -CA_2. \tag{4.14}$$

Equation (4.14) shows how a country smooths its aggregate consumption by means of the international financial market. The current account is other than zero when income is different across periods. When the future income is higher than the present, $Y_2 > Y_1$, the country goes into debt to consume more in the present and, with a greater future income, pays its debt. On the other hand, if its future income is less than the present, it saves in the present to be able to consume more than its income in the future. In this way, the country is able to smooth its aggregate consumption by transferring income between the periods.

Figure 4.3A illustrates the case of a borrower country, and Figure 4.3B the case of a lender country. Under the assumption that $\beta = 1/(1 + r)$, aggregate consumption is equal in both periods, which means the consumption vector is situated at the point of the resources constraint of the economy that crosses the 45-degree ray coming from the origin. In the case of the borrower country in Figure 4.3A, the country's endowment is lower in the first than in the second period, $Y_1 < Y_2$. The country borrows in the first period, when it is relatively poorer, and pays the debt in the second, when it is relatively richer. The distance between $Y_1$ and $\overline{C}_1$ is the amount of contracted debt, which corresponds to the deficit in current account in the first period. Given the assumption that the initial NIIP is zero ($B_1 = 0$), the current-account balance is the trade balance in the first period. For the lender country in Figure 4.3B, the income in the first period is greater than in the second, $Y_1 > Y_2$. The credit of the country with the rest of the world is the distance between $Y_1$ and $\overline{C}_1$, which corresponds to the trade surplus.

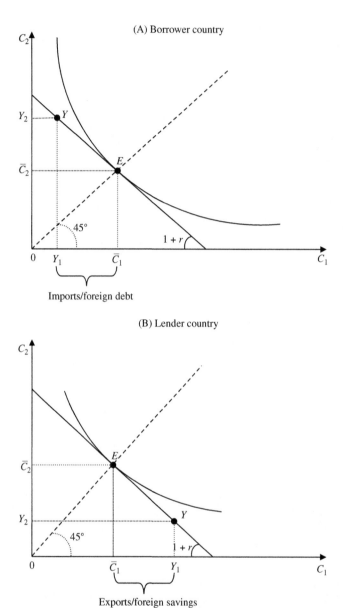

**Figure 4.3** Current account: lender country versus borrower country.

We see that, in order to have external debt or credit, it is not only necessary to have access to the international financial market but also to the international goods market. The country that borrows, consumes more than it produces, the difference being supplied by the import of goods. The country that lends produces more than it consumes, exporting the excess in production.

**Is it better to have a current-account deficit or surplus?** From what we have seen until now, **the evolution of income in a country over time is an important factor in answering this question**. For a developing country that is growing fast, the best strategy is to go into debt in the present. In the future, the country will have a higher income and be able to pay its debt without reducing its level of consumption. For a country that has attained a high level of development and is growing at lesser rates, the best strategy is to save so as to live from their return in the future.

## 4.3 Comparing with a Closed Economy

To understand the benefit generated by the possibility of participating in international goods and credit markets, let us see what the economic allocation would be if the economy were in autarky. When the country cannot trade financial assets or goods with the rest of the world, consumption cannot be intertemporally reallocated, so that in each period the country can only consume that which it produces. In the terms of our model, this means that $C_1 = Y_1$ and $C_2 = Y_2$. The consumers cannot transfer income between periods at the international interest rate, given that they do not have access to the international credit market. They do have access to the domestic financial market, which interest rates are those that balance the supply and demand for credit.

As in an open economy, the consumer chooses present and future consumption in such a way as to maximize its utility (Eq. (4.1)), subject to a budget constraint. The budget constraint in a closed economy can be represented by Eq. (4.3), with the difference that the interest rate is not the international rate, but the domestic rate, which we will denominate as $r^A$. The intertemporal allocation of consumption is determined based on the Euler equation as in Eq. (4.6), with autarky interest rate $r^A$ substituting the international interest rate.

### 4.3.1 Equilibrium Interest Rate in a Closed Economy

What is the equilibrium interest rate in a closed economy? Given that the individuals in our economy are identical, the only way to have either aggregate debt or savings is for each of the individuals to consume exactly their endowment each period. Therefore, the equilibrium interest rate in a closed economy is that which encourages each one to choose to consume their endowment each period. Substituting condition $C_1 = Y_1$ and $C_2 = Y_2$ into the Euler equation (4.6), we have that the interest rate in autarky is the one that satisfies equation:

$$\frac{u'(Y_1)}{\beta u'(Y_2)} = 1 + r^A.$$

Figure 4.4A and B compares the equilibrium in autarky to the possible equilibria in an open economy, that is, when the country is either a borrower or lender. Notice that the interest rate in autarky corresponds to the slope of the indifference curve that goes through the endowment point of the economy.

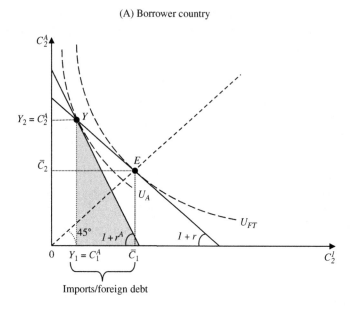

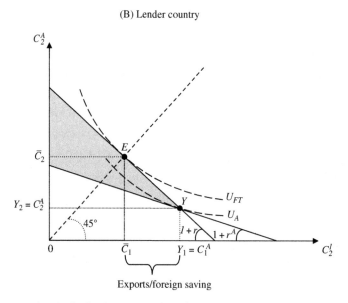

**Figure 4.4** Current account in autarky: lender country versus borrower country.

We begin with a comparison of the international interest rate with the interest rate in autarky for a borrower country. Observing Figure 4.4A, we see that for a country opting to borrow when it has access to international markets, the slope of the indifference curve that passes through the endowment point is higher than the international interest rate. Therefore, for this country, the current interest rate in autarky is higher than the international interest rate: $r^A > r$.

The intuition for this comparison between the two interest rates is as follows: since consumers would choose to borrow in the first period if they had access to the international capitals market, they should face a higher cost to do so, that is, a higher interest rate, to choose not to borrow while in autarky. Looking at it from a different angle, a higher interest rate would make current consumption more expensive in relation to future consumption. Hence, in autarky, present consumption is relatively more expensive and future consumption relatively less expensive, when comparing with the rest of the world. This means that the country is relatively less abundant in present output in relation to future output; therefore it is willing to trade future consumption for present consumption with the rest of the world. When open to trade, this country *imports* present consumption and *exports* future consumption.

For a lender country, in Figure 4.4B, interest rate in autarky is lower than the international interest rate. The intuition is analogous. A creditor country is relatively abundant in present output compared to the rest of the world and, therefore, *exports* present consumption and *imports* future consumption.

Summarizing, **the interest rate in autarky would be higher than the international interest rate for a borrower country and lower for a lender country**.

## 4.3.2 Benefiting from Access to International Markets

Countries trade goods and assets among themselves, and, in a crisis, make an effort to fulfill their international obligations so as to not be ostracized from these markets. This is a sign that countries benefit from access to international markets. In this model, we can measure the gain obtained from trade and financial openness by comparing the utility level an economy in autarky attains to that of an open economy.[10] In terms of Figure 4.4A and B, the benefit of openness is proportional to the distance between the indifference curve $U_A$ that crosses the endowment point, which corresponds to consumption in autarky, and the indifference curve $U_{FT}$ that crosses the point of consumption in an open economy.

The first interesting observation regarding the gain from openness is related to the first question in this chapter: Is it better to have a current-account deficit or surplus? Comparing the gain from openness for a borrower country (Figure 4.4A) to the gain for a lender country (Figure 4.4B), it is clear that **both borrowers and lenders benefit from access to international markets**. The gain from openness captured by this model results from the fact that it

---

[10] Being more precise, social welfare can be measured as a weighted average of the utility attained by each individual in an economy. In the model in question, as the individuals are identical, social welfare coincides with the utility of the representative individual.

allows the country to smooth consumption between periods, thanks to access to international markets.

Another interesting point is that the **gain from openness is greater, the greater the difference between the international interest rate and the domestic rate under autarky**. Notice that access to the international market promotes an expansion of the set of consumption possibilities biased in favor of the period where consumption is relatively limited in the country. That is, for the country that goes into debt, the expansion favors greater possibilities for present consumption, while for the country that lends, consumption expands in the direction of future consumption. The greater the difference in interest rates, the greater the (biased) expansion of the consumption possibilities, therefore greater the level of welfare that can be reached by the country. The gray areas in Figure 4.4A and B represent the expansion of consumption possibilities here described.

The other side of the coin is the current-account balance: the greater the difference between interest rates, the greater the current-account balance will be in absolute value, i.e., greater the deficit for borrowers and greater the surplus for lenders. Therefore, **countries that either borrow more or lend more are those that would be most harmed if they did not have access to international markets**. Intuition is clear if one compares the extreme case of a country where the interest rate in autarky is exactly equal to the international interest rate. Whether open or closed, this country will always consume its endowment each period. The current account would be balanced in the open economy and the welfare level would be exactly the same with either an open or closed economy. When the interest rate in autarky is different from the international rate, the current-account balance is other than zero and the country achieves a higher indifference curve with trade.

## 4.4 How Economic Shocks Affect the Current Account

The current-account balances of countries oscillate between deficits and surpluses over time. These movements are generally responses to economic shocks or changes. The increase in current-account balances of commodities exporting countries in the first half of the 2000s, for example, is generally attributed to the increase in the relative price of commodities, which represented an improvement in the terms of trade for those countries (Box 4.4). Even though simple, this model allows us to predict the impact of some relevant variables on the current-account balance. I propose three variables: (i) an increase in international interest rates, (ii) a higher value attributed to future consumption, and (iii) a positive shock to income.

---

**BOX 4.4 TERMS OF TRADE**

*Terms of Trade* is the relative price of goods exported and imported. An increase in terms of trade means that the average price of exports increases in relation to the average price of imports, which, all else being equal, would lead to an increase in the trade balance for the country.

## 4.4.1 Increase in International Interest Rates

The international interest rate can be interpreted as the relative price between present and future consumption. An increase in international interest rates causes present consumption to be relatively more expensive. By the Euler equation (4.6), we see that **a higher international interest rate encourages individuals to reduce present consumption relative to future consumption.**[11] This is the so-called **substitution effect** of the interest rate on consumption.

There is a second effect denoted **income effect**. As the name suggests, this effect captures the impact of the interest rate on the country's income. This effect is different for borrowers and lenders. For a borrower country, an increase in interest rates means an increase in the cost of its debt, which translates in a reduction of disposable income for consumption. In the case of a lender country, a higher interest rate increases the revenue received with its credit, representing, therefore, an increase in disposable income. **The income effect from an increase in interest rate implies a rise in consumption for lender countries and a reduction for borrower countries.**

For an indebted country, both the income effect and the substitution effect resultant from an increase in interest rates cause a decrease in present consumption. Consequently, there is a reduction in the current-account deficit in the first period, which is measured as the difference between consumption and income. The indebtedness, therefore, decreases. The situation is less evident for the lender country. The income effect and the substitution effect have opposite effects on consumption in the first period, and, in principle, it is impossible to say if it increases or decreases. The current-account surplus for the lender country increases if the substitution effect is stronger than the income effect, and reduces if in the opposite case.

Notice that the result would be the inverse in the case of a reduction in international interest rates. The substitution effect would imply an increase in present consumption for both types of countries, while the income effect would increase present consumption for a borrower country and decrease consumption for a lender country. In this way, the deficit in current account would increase for the borrower country and the impact on current-account surplus for the lender country would be uncertain.

However, we can make more precise forecasts in the case described in Section 4.1 of an economy with no initial debt or credit, from a starting point where the international interest rate is equal to the intertemporal discount rate, $\beta = 1/(1+r)$, that is, under complete consumption smoothing. The impact of a marginal increase in interest rates on consumption can be measured by taking the derivative of consumption, in Eq. (4.9), with respect to the interest rate, which results in

$$\frac{\partial \overline{C}}{\partial r} = \frac{Y_1 - Y_2}{(2+r)^2}. \tag{4.15}$$

---

[11] Since the utility function is strictly concave, i.e., $u''(\cdot) < 0$, for the value of ratio $(u'(C_1)/\beta u'(C_2))$ to increase, the ratio $(C_1/C_2)$ should decrease.

The derivative indicates that the impact of the interest rate on consumption is positive if present income is greater than future income, i.e., for a lender country, while it is negative if to the contrary. Therefore, for the lender country, the income effect from a higher interest rate outweighs the substitution effect, leading to an increase in consumption for the first period and a reduction in current-account balance. For the borrower country, as always, both the income effect and the substitution effect lead to a reduction in consumption in the first period, consequently reducing the current-account deficit.

## 4.4.2 Higher Value Attributed to Future Consumption

Life expectancy has been increasing worldwide. When people expect to live longer, it is natural for them to attribute more value to future consumption since they believe there is a greater possibility of being alive to consume. In our model, this phenomenon can be captured by an increase of the intertemporal discount factor $\beta$. Attributing a greater value to future consumption, individuals will prefer higher future consumption in relation to the present. In terms of our model, the slope of the indifference curve $(u'(C_1)/\beta u'(C_2))$ reduces with the increase of $\beta$. For a given international interest rate, the Euler equation (4.6) will then be satisfied with a smaller $(C_1/C_2)$ ratio. The reduced present consumption will have a positive impact on current account. In this way, a borrower country will reduce its level of indebtedness, while a lender country will increase the amount it lends to the rest of the world.

## 4.4.3 Positive Shock to Income

The increase in the price of agricultural products in the 2000s, for example, represented an improvement in the terms of trade for countries that exported these products, such as Australia, Argentina, and Brazil, which translated into an increase in purchasing power for these countries. The international financial crisis, in turn, caused a recession in some countries and smaller growth in others. Shocks, such as these that affect the disposable income in countries, occur frequently. What is the impact of such shocks on the current account?

To answer this question, let us take the intertemporal model, assuming that $\beta = 1/(1 + r)$, which implies the same level of consumption for the two periods, as described in Eq. (4.9). Let us further assume that, initially, $Y_1 = Y_2 = Y$, that is, output is the same in both periods. As consumption is also equal in both periods, we have that $\overline{C} = Y$, and the current account will be balanced in both periods: there will be no foreign borrowing. In this scenario, now suppose there is a positive shock to the first period output, but that it will return to its original level in the future. Such a shock corresponds, for example, to a temporary improvement in terms of trade. In terms of the model, the endowment for each period becomes $Y_1 = Y' > Y = Y_2$.

Substituting this new output path into the equation that determines current account (Eq. (4.14)), we obtain:

$$CA_1 = \frac{Y' - Y}{2 + r} > 0.$$

The current account in the first period becomes positive. Before the output shock, the country did not need to resort to international financial markets to achieve the optimum consumption path because it had a constant income over time, which allowed it to completely smooth consumption. With the positive output shock in the first period, the country income increases, but is no longer constant over time. It saves a portion of the additional income from the first period to be able to also consume more in the future and thereby smooth consumption.

What would happen if the increase in output were permanent? This could represent the case of an increase in productivity, for example, that increases the economy's production not only in the present but also the future. In this case, the output of the economy continues to be the same each period, only at a higher level: $Y_1 = Y_2 = Y'$. The current account, in Eq. (4.14), continues balanced as in the beginning. With the increase of income being the same for both periods, the country smooths consumption by totally consuming the additional income each period. There is no need to save part of the additional income.

The conclusion we can make from the exercise is that **permanent income shocks do not alter the current-account balance, while positive temporary shocks increase it.**

## 4.5 Adding Government

Government is added in a very simple manner: it collects taxes from consumers and uses them for public expenditures. We also assume that the government can lend or borrow each period at the same interest rate $r$. The government intertemporal budget constraint is analogous with that of the private sector and can be written as

$$G_1 + \frac{G_2}{1+r} = T_1 + \frac{T_2}{1+r}, \tag{4.16}$$

where $G_t$ and $T_t$ correspond to expenditures and taxes for period $t$, respectively.

The consumer budget constraint changes since they now pay taxes. The budget constraint establishes that the present value of consumption should be equal to the present value of disposable income, i.e.,

$$C_1 + \frac{C_2}{1+r} = Y_1 - T_1 + \frac{Y_2 - T_2}{1+r}.$$

Substituting the government balanced budget condition (Eq. (4.16)) into the previous equation, we get

$$C_1 + \frac{C_2}{1+r} = Y_1 - G_1 + \frac{Y_2 - G_2}{1+r}. \tag{4.17}$$

Comparing this budget constraint (Eq. (4.17)) with the budget constraint for the economy with no government (Eq. (4.3)), we see that the inclusion of government does not change the rate of substitution between present consumption and future consumption: the slope of the consumer budget constraint remains unaltered. The only difference is that the set of available consumption baskets described by the new consumer budget constraint is smaller, given that the consumer disposable income becomes $Y_1 - G_1 + (Y_2 - G_2)/(1 + r)$, instead of $Y_1 + Y_2/(1 + r)$. Graphically, the budget constraint of the economy with a government is represented by a straight line closer to the origin than when there is no government.

The consumer's problem is solved in the same fashion as in Section 4.1.[12] The consumption path, with the presence of government and assuming $\beta = 1/(1 + r)$, will be

$$C_1 = C_2 = \overline{C} = \frac{(1 + r)(Y_1 - G_1) + (Y_2 - G_2)}{2 + r}. \tag{4.18}$$

Notice that the chosen level of consumption depends on the amount of government expenditures, which is equal to taxes paid. For a given present value, how expenditures or taxes are spread over time does not affect the choice of private consumption.

Let us now see what the current account balance will be with the presence of government. The national accounts identity establishes that the current-account balance is equal to

$$CA_t = Y_t + rB_t - C_t - G_t. \tag{4.19}$$

Taking $B_1 = 0$, as we did previously, and substituting the consumption level described by Eq. (4.18) into the current account in Eq. (4.19), and using the government budget constraint in Eq. (4.16), we arrive at

$$CA_1 = \frac{(Y_1 - Y_2) - (G_1 - G_2)}{2 + r}. \tag{4.20}$$

An interesting result is that government expenditures that are equal between periods do not affect the current-account balance which would be in place in the case there were no government, as can be verified by comparing the current-account balance with government (Eq. (4.20)) with the equation where there is no government (Eq. (4.14)). The reason for this result is the following: according to Eq. (4.18), when government spending is equal between periods, the reduction in private consumption each period is exactly equal to government expenditure. Hence, private consumption is substituted by government consumption, so that aggregate expenditure is the same as in the case with no government.

---

[12] Notice that we adopted the simplifying assumption that public expenditure does not affect the indifference map. This does not necessarily mean that government spending does not affect utility. We can assume that, for example, the utility obtained from government expenditures is added to the level of utility obtained with private consumption, i.e., $V_1^i \equiv u(C_1^i) + \beta u(C_2^i) + H(G_1, G_2)$, where $H(\cdot)$ is an increasing function. The indifference map for the utility function $V_1^i$ is identical to that of function $U_1^i$ defined in Eq. (4.1), differing only with respect to the level of utility represented by each indifference curve.

On the other hand, if government spends relatively more in the first period in relation to the second, the current-account balance for the first period will be lower with government than without. The reduction in private consumption is equal to a weighted average of government expenditures in both periods, which is smaller than government spending in the first period when $G_1 > G_2$. In this way, in the first period, the reduction of private consumption does not totally compensate government consumption. The total expenditures for the economy increases leading to a smaller current-account balance.

Analogously, when government spends more in the second period than in the first, the presence of government causes an increase in current-account balance in the first period. Summarizing, **government will affect the current-account balance as long as it alters relative aggregate expenditures between the two periods**.

## 4.6 The Model with Production and Investment

We saw, in Eq. (2.6), that the current-account balance depends on the aggregate saving and investment in the economy. In this section, we will add the decision to invest to that of saving, which we analyzed in the previous sections.

Output is now the result of production, using the stock of capital available in the economy. We assume that the larger the capital stock, the greater the amount produced. Besides, the increment in production becomes smaller as a larger quantity of capital is used. In mathematical terms, the production function is represented by[13]

$$Y_t = F(K_t), \tag{4.21}$$

which is increasing, $F'(\cdot) > 0$, but with decreasing returns to scale, that is, the production function is concave, $F''(\cdot) < 0$, where $K_t$ is the capital stock. We assume that output is null when the stock of capital is equal to zero, $F(0) = 0$.[14]

The capital stock is the result of investment made over time. More specifically, the only good in this economy may be transformed into capital through investment. There is no cost associated to this transformation, but it takes time: investment made in one period produces capital for the following period. We assume there is no depreciation of capital, so that capital accumulation is equal to investment, i.e.,

$$K_{t+1} - K_t = I_t. \tag{4.22}$$

---

[13] In Box 4.3, we saw that the aggregate variables correspond to the representative consumer variables when we assume that the population is formed by a *continuum* of identical individuals in interval [0, 1]. To simplify, from this point on we will refer directly to the aggregate variables.

[14] In a more general formulation, we can say that production uses the stocks of capital and labor in the economy based on a production function such as $G(K_t, I_t)$, with constant return on scale. As population evolution does not interest us here, we assume that the stock of labor is constant, $L_t = \overline{L}$. Hence, $Y_t = G(K_t, \overline{L})$, and we define $F(K_t) \equiv G(K_t, \overline{L})$. Given that the stock of labor is constant, the increase of the capital stock has a less than proportional impact on output. We therefore have the concavity of function $F(\cdot)$.

Our representative consumer chooses how much to consume each period in order to maximize the utility, represented by Eq. (4.1). The budget constraint, however, is now a little different since there is production and investment. The new budget constraint is

$$C_1 + I_1 + \frac{C_2 + I_2}{1 + r} = Y_1 + \frac{Y_2}{1 + r}, \tag{4.23}$$

where the left side of the equation corresponds to the present value of consumption and investment in both periods, while the right side represents the present value of disposable income. The output in each of the periods is produced according to Eq. (4.21), and the stock of capital depends on investment, as in Eq. (4.22).

Summarizing, the consumer chooses consumption and investment in both periods, $C_1$, $I_1$, $C_2$, and $I_2$, so as to maximize their utility, described by the function in Eq. (4.1), subject to the budget constraint in Eq. (4.23), and the restrictions regarding production established in Eqs. (4.21) and (4.22).

To find the solution to the consumer problem, we will make some simplifications. According to the investment equation (4.22), the capital stock in the second period is given by

$$K_2 = I_1 + K_1. \tag{4.24}$$

Therefore, production in periods 1 and 2 can be written as

$$Y_1 = F(K_1) \text{ and } Y_2 = F(I_1 + K_1). \tag{4.25}$$

Since there are only two periods in our world, it does not make sense to leave positive capital stock for a third period, which does not exist. Therefore, the consumer must "disinvest" all they can in the last period, i.e.,

$$K_3 = 0 \text{ and } I_2 = -K_2 = -(I_1 + K_1), \tag{4.26}$$

where we use Eq. (4.24) for the last equality.[15] Substituting these relations into the budget constraint (Eq. (4.23)), we can write it as

$$C_1 + I_1 + \frac{C_2 - (I_1 + K_1)}{1 + r} = F(K_1) + \frac{F(I_1 + K_1)}{1 + r},$$

where $K_1$ is an endowment, while $C_1$, $I_1$, and $C_2$ are consumer choices. Now we proceed in the same way as in Section 4.1, writing the second period consumption as a function of the other variables:

$$C_2 = (1 + r)[F(K_1) - C_1 - I_1] + F(I_1 + K_1) + I_1 + K_1,$$

---

[15] The real world will not end any time soon, or at least we do not know if or when it will end. In a world without expiration date, the correspondent of result $K_3 = 0$ would be a type of transversality condition $\lim_{t \to \infty} (K_t/(1+r)^t) = 0$, which states that the present value of the capital stock when time tends to infinity is equal to zero. In other words, the capital stock cannot grow at a rate greater than the interest rate.

and substitute the result into the utility function. We arrive at

$$U_1 = u(C_1) + \beta\{u[(1 + r)[F(K_1) - C_1 - I_1] + F(I_1 + K_1) + I_1 + K_1]\}. \tag{4.27}$$

With these simplifications, the consumer problem boils down to the maximization of function (4.27), choosing $C_1$ and $I_1$. To find the maximum point, we take the derivative of the objective function, $U_1$, with respect to the choice variables, $C_1$ and $I_1$, and make it equal zero. From the derivative with respect to $C_1$, we obtain

$$u'(C_1) = (1 + r)\beta u'(C_2), \tag{4.28}$$

which is the same Euler equation we had found in the more simple model, where there was no investment. Therefore, the inclusion of production and investment did not in any way alter incentives for the decision between consumption and saving.

Taking the derivative of the utility with respect to $I_1$ and equaling zero, we arrive at

$$F'(K_2) = r, \tag{4.29}$$

which says that the marginal productivity of capital is equal to the interest rate at the optimum point. The marginal productivity of capital is the return on the investment in physical capital, while the interest rate is the return on financial capital. If the return on physical capital were, for example, greater than the return on financial capital, it would be worth the while to borrow money to invest in more physical capital. The higher capital stock in the second period would reduce its return (remember that the production function has decreasing returns to scale), which would bring the return on physical capital closer to that of financial capital. The individual remains indifferent to these two types of investment when the two rates are equal. In this way, the optimum level of investment in physical capital is that which makes productivity of capital equal to the interest rate.

With the first-order conditions in Eqs. (4.28) and (4.29), the definitions in Eqs. (4.24) and (4.25), and the budget constraint in Eq. (4.23), it is possible to derive the values of $C_1$, $I_1$, $C_2$, and $I_2$ (and $K_2$).

Equations (4.28) and (4.29) show that the decision to consume between periods does not depend on the decision to invest. The incentives for the individual to save or not, as the case may be, to smooth consumption is not affected by the amount they decide to invest. It is clear that the level of investment will affect the level of consumption in both periods, given that the income available to consume depends on second period production, and this, in turn, depends on the level of investment. However, the allocation of consumption across periods is not affected by investment.

## 4.6.1 Graphic Representation

To better understand the intuition for the relationship between the decisions to consume and to invest, let us construct a graphic analysis of the problem. We will begin by determining the resources constraint for the country. In the case of an endowment economy such as in Section 4.1, the constraint is limited to the endowment point. With production and investment, it becomes possible to transfer output between periods. To understand the construction of this restriction, we rewrite the budget constraint (Eq. (4.23)) as

$$C_1 + \frac{C_2}{1+r} = Y_1 - I_1 + \frac{Y_2 - I_2}{1+r}. \tag{4.30}$$

We see that the amount of resources available for consumption is the present value of output for each period subtracted from investment. Therefore, in order to maximize the utility from consumption, the investment decision should maximize the available resources represented on the right side of Eq. (4.30).

We begin by determining the possible combinations of $Y_1 - I_1$ and $Y_2 - I_2$ for the economy, taking into consideration the production function (Eq. (4.21)) and the capital accumulation (Eq. (4.22)). Defining $R_t \equiv Y_t - I_t$ and using the equalities in Eq. (4.25), we have that

$$I_1 = F(K_1) - R_1 \quad \text{and} \tag{4.31}$$

$$F(I_1 + K_1) = R_2 + I_2. \tag{4.32}$$

Using the fact that in the second period all existent capital is disinvested, as established in Eq. (4.26), Eq. (4.32) can be written as

$$F(K_1 + I_1) = R_2 - (K_1 + I_1).$$

Finally, substituting investment in the first period as defined in Eq. (4.31) into the preceding equation, we obtain the resources constraint for the economy:

$$R_2 = F(K_1 + F(K_1) - R_1) + F(K_1) - R_1 + K_1. \tag{4.33}$$

Equation (4.33) establishes the trade-off between present consumption and future consumption in the country, from the domestic point of view. In other words, if the country could not trade goods or financial assets with the rest of the world, this would be the consumption possibilities constraint, and $R_t$ would be the amount consumed each period. This restriction is linear in $R_1$. The slope of the curve is

$$\frac{dR_2}{dC_1} = -(1 + F'(K_2)) \tag{4.34}$$

and its concavity

$$\frac{d^2 C_2}{(dC_1)^2} = F''(K_2) < 0.$$

Restated, the resources constraint is decreasing and concave, as represented by curve RR in Figure 4.5. When the country avails all its resources in the first period, without investing anything for consumption in the second period, the amount of available resources in the first period will be $F(K_1) + K_1$ and 0 in the second period. This is the point on the RR curve that intercepts the horizontal axis. On the other hand, if the country invests all its production, without leaving any resources available in the first period, it will have $F(K_1 + F(K_1)) + F(K_1) + K_1$ resources available in the second period, which is the point of the RR curve that intercepts the vertical axis.

The individual chooses the point on the resources constraint RR that offers the greatest availability of resources $R_1 + (R_2)/(1 + r)$. The latter can be represented on the graph by a straight line with slope $-(1 + r)$, which height indicates the value of resource availability. The point on RR constraint that maximizes the availability of resources is the one through which passes the line of resource availability farthest from the origin. Point A in Figure 4.5 corresponds to the optimum choice of domestic resources allocation between the two periods. It is the tangency point between the curve and the line, given by

$$-(1 + F'(K_2)) = -(1 + r),$$

which is equivalent to the first-order condition for maximization represented by Eq. (4.29).

The intuition for the result is as follows. Equation (4.33) represents the amount of resources the country can transfer from one period to another by means of domestic production and investment. However, with access to the international credit market, the country can exchange present consumption for future consumption at international interest rates,

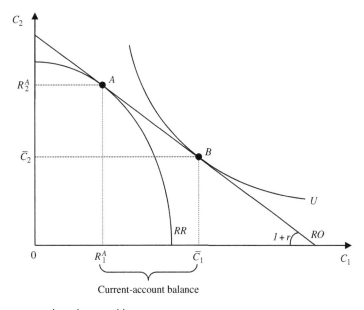

**Figure 4.5** The consumer and producer problems.

which is the slope of budget constraint, represented by Eq. (4.23). The country chooses, essentially, between transferring resources between periods by means of internal production or by means of the international credit market. At the optimum point, the rate of exchange between the two forms should be the same.

Notice that the coordinates of point A correspond to the difference between production and investment for each period, which, according to the national accounts identity (Eq. (2.10)), corresponds to consumption added to the current-account balance and the net payment to factors of production, as in

$$Y_t - I_t = C_t + CA_t - rB_t. \tag{4.35}$$

The consumer could consume at point A. In fact, if there was no international trade, nor access to foreign credit, and if this was the allocation of resources between the two periods, then consumption should be exactly at this point. The consumer, however, can lend or borrow (exporting or importing the corresponding amount of goods) at the interest rate $r$. Their budget constraint, represented by Eq. (4.23) is a straight line with slope $-(1 + r)$, passing through point A of the resources constraint. The consumer will choose their consumption in the two periods under this budget constraint in such a way as to obtain the greatest level of utility possible, i.e., the point belonging to an indifference curve that is farthest from the origin. Therefore, the point where an indifference curve passes tangent to the budget constraint, represented in Figure 4.5 by point B. This tangency point satisfies the Euler equation (4.28).

Given that point A is the difference between production and investment and that point B is consumption, according to Eq. (4.35) the horizontal distance between the two points corresponds to the current-account balance in the first period (remembering that $B_1 = 0$). The economy represented in Figure 4.5 has a negative current-account balance in the first period.

## 4.6.2 The Relation Between Investment and Savings

By means of the graph, it is easier to understand the relation between the decisions to invest and save. The decision to invest is made by taking into account the productivity of capital and the international interest rate, as in the first-order condition in Eq. (4.29), and determines the chosen point on the resources constraint of the economy.

The consumer budget constraint passes through the chosen point on the resources constraint, having the international interest rate as its slope. In this way, the decision to invest affects the height of the budget constraint, but not its slope. In other words, investment affects the level of disposable income, but not the relative incentives between present consumption and future consumption.

This result is due, basically, to two characteristics of the model: (i) the individual has free, unlimited access to the international financial market at a constant interest rate $r$ and (ii) there is free trade of the only good that is consumed or invested. The free access to the financial market guarantees that the amount they decide to save does not affect the interest rate at which the investment is financed. Free trade of all goods (in our case there is only one good) guarantees that the amount they decide to consume or invest does not affect the relative price of goods. The decisions to invest and save are governed by different motives, summarized in the first-order conditions (Eqs. (4.28) and (4.29)), and differences between the two aggregates are compensated by international loans.

## 4.7 The Model and the World

This model can explain the current account surplus observed in countries exporting agricultural products and raw materials at the beginning of the 2000s. There was a significant increase in the relative price of these goods, which represented an improvement in the terms of trade for exporting countries. If the terms of trade are expected to eventually return to their original level, or at least that commodities prices do not remain as high in the future, part of the increase in income should be saved so that consumption can also be higher in the future. The current account surplus is, therefore, explained by the smoothing of consumption described by the model.

Let us consider Chile, Norway, and Brazil, countries where commodities represent 87%, 80%, and 53%, respectively, of exports. In these countries, an increase in commodities prices is clearly associated with an improvement in the terms of trade. Figure 4.6 presents the evolution of the current-account balance as a percentage of GDP in the three countries, as well as the Commodity Research Bureau (CRB) commodities aggregate index.[16] As we can see in this figure, the price of commodities more than doubled between 2001 and 2004, while the current-account balance increased in the three countries under consideration. Summarizing, given that a large part of the export sector in these countries is linked to the behavior of commodities, the increase of the price related to these products can be interpreted as a positive income shock, which resulted in an improvement in current account, or rather, an accumulation of foreign savings.

The same reasoning can be used to explain the surplus in current account seen in oil-exporting countries. In 2001, the price for a barrel of oil measured by the OPEC (Organisation of Petroleum Exporting Countries) basket was US$23.12.[17] In 2008, the price of the commodity rose to US$94.45, which represented an increase of 309%. In this same period, the current-account balance in Saudi Arabia, the largest oil exporter in the world, went from 5.1% GDP to 23.4%. The same behavior was seen in the other countries where oil was a large part of their exports. In Iran, the current-account balance rose from 5.2% GDP in 2001 to 10.5% in 2007, and in the United Arab Emirates, the balance rose from 2.5% GDP in 2002 to 15.3% in 2007. This movement was partially reversed after the 2008 crisis, when the basket price for oil fell 35%. The increase in oil prices drove the process of an accumulation of foreign savings for the large oil exporters.

---

[16] The CRB is an aggregate index of prices for the main commodities traded on international markets. It is compiled by the Commodity Research Bureau/Jeffrey Reutters.

[17] The OPEC basket price for oil corresponds to the average price for oil exported by countries that compose the group. The relation of prices for OPEC oil can be found at: http://www.opec.org.

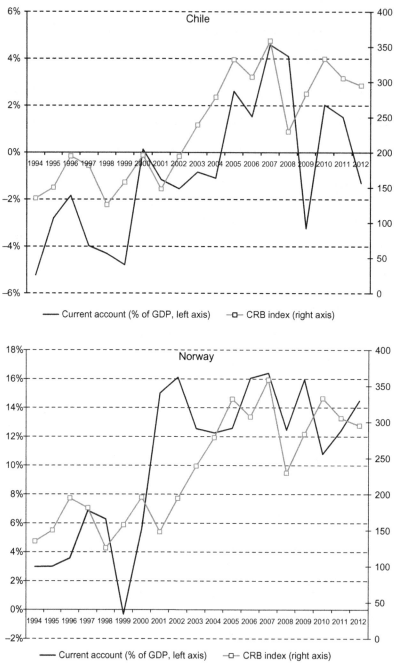

**Figure 4.6** Current account and CRB index. *Source: IMF and Thomson Reuters, References (2) and (9), respectively, on Data List in Appendix*

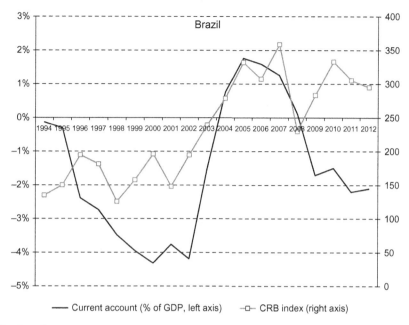

**Figure 4.6** (Continued)

Countries such as Japan, Germany, and Switzerland presented surpluses in current account that, at least in part, can be explained by the fact that these countries have an aging population. In general, an aging population in a country is due to an increase in life expectancy and/or a fall in birthrates. In most advanced economies, the fall in birthrates is what is mainly responsible for the aging population. In 2010, 6% of Japan's population was 80 or over. According to projections made by the United Nations,[18] this number will rise to 12.9% in 2050 and will reach 13.9% by 2100. In Germany, this percentage will rise from 5.2% in 2010 to 13.5% in 2050, will have a slight reduction in 2100 to 12.6%. With respect to Switzerland, the number of elderly in the population will rise from 4.9% in 2010 to 12.8% in 2050, and rise even farther to 13.9% in 2100.

On the one hand, the aging of the population leads individuals to attribute a greater weight to future consumption in their utility functions, which is represented on the model by the rate of intertemporal discount $\beta$. As we said in Section 4.1, an increase in this rate stimulates savings. On the other hand, the aging of the population also means a reduction in future active population, and therefore a reduction in production. In terms of the model, this is captured as a negative income shock in the future, which also stimulates savings. An increase in savings increases the current-account balance, as established by Eq. (2.6).

---

[18] Projections published in the report: World Population Prospects—2010 Revision, available at: http://esa.un .org/wpp/unpp/panel_population.htm.

Finally, the intertemporal model gives an explanation for the deficits in current account in Latin American countries in the 1970s, as discussed in Section 2.3. These countries invested in industrialization, where return on investment was generally high. They opted to increase their rates of investment by resorting to foreign debt, which is in accordance to the optimum trajectory for indebtedness foreseen by this model. What the model did not foresee, in this case, was neither the increase in international interest rates nor the reduction in the availability of foreign credit at the beginning of the 1980s, which led to a foreign debt crisis. But that is another story...

## 4.7.1 The Voracity Effect

An increase in commodities prices has a positive effect on the current account, as previously described, as a result of the optimum decision to invest and save over time. In practice, however, this is not always true. Tornell and Lane (1999) show that a positive shock can actually have a negative impact on the current account of an economy with a weak legal-political institutional infrastructure and powerful organized groups. The pressure for redistribution can be so high that, in the end, there is a higher than proportional increase in fiscal redistribution after a positive income shock. In other words, the expenditures generated to attend the demands for redistribution are greater than the increase in income received from the increase in commodities prices, for example. Therefore, weak institutions can cause the increase in commodities prices to produce deterioration in the current-account balance, different than what would be optimum from the point of view of maximization of intertemporal welfare.

In an empirical study for the period ranging between 1970 and 2007, Arezki and Brückner (2012) noticed that booms in commodities prices increased the current-account balance as predicted by the intertemporal model of the current account, but only in countries with ethnically homogeneous populations. In ethnically polarized countries, there was deterioration in current account after a commodities price increase. The ethnic polarity would be associated to the existence of few strong, opposing pressure groups, which confirmed what Tornell and Lane (1999) foresaw.

## 4.7.2 The Feldstein–Horioka Puzzle

We can find a large number of examples where changes in the economic scenario caused changes in the flow of foreign debt or credit that can be understood in light of the intertemporal model. Besides specific predictions in relation to the impact of shocks, the model delivers the strong result that the decisions to save and invest are independent, as discussed in the previous section. Feldstein and Horioka (1980) tested to see if saving and investment are correlated for a group of 16 countries of the Organisation for Economic Cooperation and Development (OECD) between 1960 and 1974. The correlation between the two variables is not only positive but is close to 1: saving and investment seem to walk hand in hand. The interpretation given by the two authors is that there was not sufficient capital mobility in the world, given that, as discussed at the end of Section 4.4, the independence between saving and investing decisions is only possible for an economy with access to international credit markets facing an exogenous interest rate. Clearly, in a closed economy one should save domestically in order to invest.

The findings by Feldstein and Horioka, which became known as the Feldstein–Horioka Puzzle, have generated a huge amount of literature trying to explain it, and which is still being written. This literature is divided into two strands: an empirical, which has difficulty accepting the puzzle and investigates alternative data and methods to try to produce the correlation (or rather, its lack) presented by the theory; and another that accepts the positive correlation between savings and investment and seeks a theoretical explanation for it. I will not even try to summarize the literature here since it is not within the scope of this book to do so. I will stick to describing and commenting on one of the explanations proposed for the puzzle, which I believe to be especially relevant today.

### 4.7.2.1 Portfolio Diversification

The intertemporal model of the current account presented here does not take into account the risks associated with investment in physical capital. The inclusion of uncertainty on the return of investment, as done in more elaborate versions of the model,[19] does not alter the basic result of independence between saving and investment. This uncertainty would simply add an additional reason for saving. However, in the real world there is uncertainty not only in relation to the return on domestic investment but also in relation to international loans. The ultimate destination of savings, wherever one decides to save, is the financing of investment projects. Consequently, when loans are made to another country, they ultimately end up as investment in foreign physical capital. In the same way that there is uncertainty in relation to return on domestic capital, there should be uncertainty in relation to return on foreign capital. Finance theory and popular wisdom teach us that, in a world of uncertainty, one should not put all one's eggs in one basket. Technically, investors should maintain a diversified portfolio. Optimum portfolio diversification can be established precisely, according to estimates of the expected return and the risk associated to each asset available for investment. It is based on this idea that Kraay and Ventura (2000) explain the Feldstein–Horioka Puzzle.[20]

How does optimum portfolio diversification change the predictions of the intertemporal current-account model? The intertemporal model says that a positive and temporary income shock induces greater savings, while investment remains unaltered. The result is an increase in the current-account balance. Looking at it from another angle, the intertemporal model says that every increase in savings is "saved" in foreign assets. Kraay and Ventura (2000) argue that, in an uncertain world, the additional savings should be diversified, according to the optimum portfolio diversification while taking into consideration the underlying risks associated with domestic assets and foreign assets and their rates of return.

---

[19] See, for example, Obstfeld and Rogoff (1996).

[20] I would like to remind that this is neither the first nor last explanation for the puzzle. The importance for this explanation is in the fact that it emphasizes portfolio diversification to explain the evolution of current account and its relation to the exchange rate.

In practical terms, this means the following. A lender country on the international market divides its wealth between domestic and foreign assets: it invests a share smaller than 1 of its wealth in domestic assets. When this country has additional savings, it should follow the same standard and invest a portion in domestic assets and another in foreign, according to the optimum diversification of its assets portfolio. In this way, the increase in savings leads to an increase in domestic investment, with a final result of an increase in the current-account balance.

The more interesting case is that of the borrower country. For this country, in the choice of portfolio diversification, the portion of wealth invested in domestic assets is greater than 1. When the country savings increases, it should, as always, allocate them according to its optimal portfolio diversification. In this case, it should invest a portion greater than 1 of additional savings in domestic capital. As a result, the increase in investment is greater than the increase in savings, which causes a reduction in current account! Summarizing, **a temporary positive income shock leads to an increase in current-account balance in lender countries, while it causes a reduction in current-account balance in borrower countries**.

In a more recent study, Tille and van Wincoop (2010) show that this prevision by Kraay and Ventura (2000) is true under two hypotheses. First, the return on capital should be constant. In terms of the intertemporal model presented previously, this means a constant marginal productivity of capital, which implies a production function linear in capital: $F''(K_t) = 0$. Second, the capital flow should occur in only one direction, in other words, there is no simultaneous inflow and outflow of capital. This second condition goes against the pattern of recent evolution of capital flow. There has been a rapid increase in asset stock in the portfolio of countries as of the 1970s, especially after 1990.[21] The stock of assets is much greater than the observed net flows and can be equal to multiples of GDP for the country. Nevertheless, the more realistic model economy developed by Tille and van Wincoop (2010) still predicts the empirical regularities captured by Kraay and Ventura (2000).

### 4.7.3 Global Current-Account Imbalances

Between 1997 and 2008, the world economy experienced an unprecedented situation. The United States, the richest country in the world, accumulated increasing current account deficits, reaching 6% of GDP in 2006. The deficit in current account had as its counterpart a significant deterioration of public accounts, a situation known as **twin deficits**. The financial imbalance in the American economy resulted in elevated dependence on foreign financing from countries with current-account surpluses, which was guaranteed while there was a low perception of the risk of US insolvency. That the credit risk of the American government was considered low was a consensus among participants in the sovereign debt market. However, the American government debt trajectory as well as the current-account balance gave signs of unsustainability in the long run.

The counterpart of the American deficit was, basically, a surplus in oil-exporting countries and Asian economies, especially China. Therefore, there was a growing US deficit with the

---

[21] See Lane and Milesi-Ferretti (2001b, 2007).

rest of the world, financed primarily by Asian savings. This scenario was perplexing, since, according to the intertemporal current-account model, the international flow of capital should go from wealthy countries to poorer countries. More precisely, the flow of capital should go from countries with a greater growth perspective to countries with lower growth. Even though the American economy had presented high growth rates, with an average of 2.8% in the period, it was lower than that of China, where the average growth in the period was 9.9%.

The intertemporal current-account model studied in this chapter does not seem to be able to explain the global imbalances of the 2000s. An important hypothesis implicit in the intertemporal model is that assets are equal between countries, that is, the interest rate is the same for all countries.[22] To be more precise, in the version studied here, the hypothesis is even stronger: the country can lend or borrow at an exogenous and constant interest rate. The fact that the bonds are not identical between countries has been pointed out as a fundamental element in generating these imbalances.

We can list at least three reasons for the increase in current-account balance for oil exporter countries and Asian countries. First, several currency crises devastated developing countries during the 1990s, causing significant economic losses with a series of social consequences. The governments of some of these countries, such as South Korea, opted to accumulate international reserves, with the idea of reducing their exposure to crises. Second, oil exporters and raw material exporters experienced a significant improvement in their terms of trade, which led to surpluses in current account, as previously discussed. Finally, precarious retirement and social security systems led the population to increase their savings, such as in China, which is a country with rapid growth and an aging population.

These three reasons required secure, long-term financial products. This is where the fact of bonds not being equal between countries comes into the picture: emerging developing countries do not have this type of asset available. The United States, on the other hand, had a "comparative advantage" in long-term assets, even more so in that they were denominated in dollars, which is the currency most used in international transactions. The American deficit in current account would have been, therefore, the counterpart to the "global savings glut."[23] Hence, in order to understand these events, it is necessary to provide a model where assets are not perfect substitutes, which will be studied in Chapter 8.

## 4.8 Exercises

### Exercise 1

Consider a small, open economy where there is one good and one representative individual who lives for two periods. In this simplified economy, there is neither government nor

---

[22] More precisely, the return from financial assets is the same between countries. Given that in the model there is no exchange rate, an equal return translates into the same interest rate. Reread Section 3.3 for more details on the meaning of equal return between financial assets when there are different currencies and the exchange rate between them that can change over time.

[23] This explanation for global imbalances is explored by Caballero et al. (2008) and Mendoza et al. (2009).

production. Each period the individual receives an endowment of the good, $Y_t$, and chooses how much to consume, $C_t$, so as to maximize its utility $U_1$, represented by

$$U_1 = \ln(C_1) + \beta \ln(C_2),$$

where $\beta$ is the intertemporal discount rate.

In the first period, the difference between what they consume and their endowment is their savings or debt, which in the second period will either be redeemed or paid, depending on the case. As such, the consumer should satisfy the following budget constraint:

$$C_1 + \frac{C_2}{1+r} = Y_1 + \frac{Y_2}{1+r},$$

where $r$ is the real interest rate. Assume that $\beta = 1/(1+r) = 0.75$.

**a.** Assume that $Y_1 = Y_2 = 100$. Calculate the value of consumption and the value of the current account for each period.

**b.** Assume there is a negative product shock in the first period, so that the endowment becomes $Y_1 = 80$ and $Y_2 = 100$. What are the new values of consumption? What is the new current account in the two periods? Interpret the results.

**c.** Now suppose that the negative product shock affects both periods, i.e., $Y_1 = Y_2 = 80$. What are the quantities consumed and the current account in this case? Interpret the results.

## Exercise 2

With respect to the sustainability of deficits in current account, answer the following:

**a.** Intertemporal models for determining current account say that it may be desirable for a developing country to accumulate deficits in current transactions. What conditions should be met for this trajectory to be beneficial to the country?

**b.** However, history has shown us that maintaining elevated deficits in current account can lead a country into serious balance of payment crises, with high costs in terms of welfare. Keeping this fact in mind, a country, initially being under full employment and presenting an elevated deficit in current account, desires to implement an economic policy with the objective of reducing the probability of suffering a balance of payments crisis. Without altering the levels of consumption and investment, what would be the best economic policy to be implemented in the country? Why?

## Exercise 3

Consider the model of an open economy with two periods, with only one good and with no investment. The representative consumer preferences for this economy are represented by the utility function:

$$U_1 = \sqrt{C_1} + \beta\sqrt{C_2},$$

where, as is usual, $C_t$ represents consumption for period $t$ and parameter $\beta$ is the intertemporal discount factor. Assume that $r^* = 0.10$ and that $\beta = 1/(1 + r^*)$. The representative consumer possesses net wealth in the initial period of $(1 + r)B_1 = 1$, besides receiving an endowment of 5 units of goods during period 1, and 10 units in period 2. There is perfect capital mobility.

a. Compute the consumption in equilibrium for both periods, and the trade balance and the current-account balance for the first period.
b. Now assume that the government imposes a capital control, where it is required that the net international investment position at the end of period 1 is not negative, i.e., $B_2 \geq 0$. Find the equilibrium value of the domestic interest rate for periods 1 and 2, the trade balance and the current-account balance for period 1.
c. Evaluate the impact of the capital controls on welfare. In a more specific way, find the utility level for the representative agent under capital control and compare with the level of utility obtained when capital controls do not exist.

   Now consider that the country experiences an increase in endowment for period 1, which becomes $Y_1 = 9$, while the endowment for period 2 remains unchanged.
d. Considering the case of free mobility of capital between countries, compute the effect of this product shock on the equilibrium consumption for periods 1 and 2, the trade balance and the current-account balance.
e. Now consider a situation with capital controls as described in item (b). Is there any change in the behavior of the representative consumer?

## Exercise 4

Consider a small, open economy with two periods where there is only one consumer good for each period. The representative agent preferences are represented by

$$U_1 = \ln(C_1) + \beta \ln(C_2),$$

where $C_t$ represents consumption for period $t$ and intertemporal discount factor $\beta$ is equal to 0.91. The representative consumer has access to the international financial market, where they can freely lend or borrow at interest rate $r^* = 10\%$. The beginning net international investment position is equal to zero, i.e., $B_1 = 0$.

   The good consumed is produced using capital as input, according to the following production function:

$$Y_t = \sqrt{K_t},$$

where $Y_t$ represents production for period $t$ and $K_t$ the stock of capital. In the first period, each individual receives an endowment of 10 units of capital. Assume that the capital completely depreciates from one period to the next so that the stock of capital in the second period corresponds to the investment made in the first period: $K_2 = I_1$.

a. Write the maximization problem for the representative consumer and find the optimum consumption levels for both periods.

b. Find the optimum level of savings for the economy, as well as the current-account balance for the first period.

c. Now, consider that an increase in capital productivity occurs. More specifically, assume that, as a result of technological improvement, the production function becomes $Y_t = 2\sqrt{K_t}$. Find the new equilibrium levels for savings and investment and the current-account balance for the first period. Compare your new results with those obtained in the previous items and provide an economic intuition for the differences discovered.

## Exercise 5

Consider an endowment economy that exists for two periods. Assume that the representative individual preferences are represented by the following utility function:

$$U_1 = \sqrt{C_1} + \beta\sqrt{C_2}$$

where $C_1$ and $C_2$ represent consumption for periods 1 and 2, respectively. In each period, this individual receives an endowment of 10 units of the only consumer good in this economy. The individual begins with no financial assets, i.e., $B_1^p = 0$, and can lend or borrow at market interest rate $r = 10\%$.

The individual pays *lump-sum* taxes to the government each period, represented by $T_1$ and $T_2$, respectively. The government does not have any type of financial debt or asset at the beginning of the first period, i.e., $B_1^g = 0$. In period 1, the government collects taxes and consumes one unit of consumer good, i.e., $G_1 = 1$. In period 2, the government repeats the same procedure, collecting taxes and consuming $G_2 = 1$. As with the representative agent, the government has access to the financial markets. Assume, moreover, that $\beta = (1/1 + r)$.

a. Find the equilibrium values for consumption, trade balance, and current account for each of the two periods.

b. Assume that $T_1 = 0$. Find the value of $T_2$. What is the value of public and private savings in each of the two periods?

c. Assume now that $T_1$ goes from zero to one, while government expenditures remain unaltered. How does this change in taxes affect the current account and fiscal deficit in period 1? Explain your answer.

d. Assume that the government begins to consume two units of consumer goods in the first period ($G_1 = 2$) and that it also doubles the tax burden in the first period, i.e., $T_1 = 2$. What is the impact of these changes on the current account for period 1? Present an economic intuition for your answer.

**e.** Alternatively, suppose government expenditure increase permanently, i.e., $G_1 = G_2 = 2$. What is the reaction of the current account in period 1? Compare your result with that obtained in the previous items.

## Exercise 6

Consider a two-period intertemporal model, where the representative agent has a utility function given by

$$U_1 = \frac{C_1^{1-\sigma}}{1-\sigma} + \beta \frac{C_2^{1-\sigma}}{1-\sigma},$$

where $C_t$ in consumption for the period $t$, $\sigma > 0$ is the preference parameter, and $\beta \in (0,1)$ is the intertemporal discount rate. In period $t \in \{1,2\}$, this individual receives an exogenous flow of income $Y_t$. There is a financial market that remunerates savings at the rate of $r$. The interest rate charges on debt are also given as $r$.

**a.** Write and interpret the intertemporal budget constraint for the agent. Illustrate this constraint with a graph, along with the map of the indifference curves of the representative agent.

**b.** Derive the first-order condition for the consumer's problem. Obtain the Euler equation and present its economic interpretation.

**c.** Obtain the intertemporal elasticity of substitution for the representative consumer. [*Hint:* The mathematical expression for the elasticity of substitution is given by $\eta = (d(c_1/c_2)/d\text{TMS})(\text{TMS}/(c_1/c_2))$, where TMS is the marginal rate of substitution.]

## Exercise 7

Consider a small, open economy, with a single good and a representative individual who lives for two periods. In this economy, there is a government that has a balanced budget. There is no production and the individual receives an endowment of goods, $Y_t$. They choose how much to consume each period in such a way as to maximize its utility, represented by

$$U_1 = C_1^{\alpha} + \beta C_2^{1-\alpha},$$

where $C_t$ represents consumption by the individual in period $t$, $\beta \in (0,1)$ and $\alpha \in (0,1)$. In the first period, the difference between their available income and endowment is their savings or debt, which will either be redeemed or paid in the second period, depending on the case. Therefore, the consumer must satisfy a budget constraint at the time they make their choices to consume. The assets or debts in this economy are remunerated by the real interest rate $r$, which we assume to be constant over time and is equal to the international interest rate. Moreover, assume that $\beta = (1/1+r)$.

a. Based on the national accounts identities, show the intertemporal budget constraint this individual faces. Interpret the equation.
b. Compute the amount consumed and the level of the current account each period. Under what assumptions should the individual save during the first period? In what situation should they borrow?
c. Assume that $Y_1 = Y_2$. What is the value of the current account in each period? How does this compare with the autarky equilibrium? Interpret the results.
d. Now assume that the representative agent in this economy has become more patient, giving more value to future consumption, so that $\beta' = 2\beta$ is the new intertemporal discount rate. How does this new equilibrium compare with the previous exercise? Interpret the result.
e. Assume that there has been an exogenous increase in international interest rates, so that $r' = 2r$, where $r'$ is the value of international interest rates and that the intertemporal discount rate remains as before, $\beta$. What are the new values for consumption and current account? Interpret the result.

## Exercise 8

Consider a small economy where the individuals live for two periods and receive an exogenous endowment for each period, $Y_t$. Under autarky, the aggregate offer is equal to the aggregate product for each period, i.e., $Y_t = C_t$ for all of $t$, where $C_t$ represents aggregate consumption. Besides this, assume that the utility function for the representative consumer is given by

$$U_1 = \frac{C_1^{1-\sigma}}{1-\sigma} + \beta \frac{C_2^{1-\sigma}}{1-\sigma},$$

where $\beta \in (0, 1)$ represents the intertemporal discount rate. Let $B_t$ be the net stock of assets inherited from period $t - 1$ and assume that $B_1 = B_3 = 0$.

a. Calculate the equilibrium interest under autarky, denoted by $r^A$, and illustrate the intertemporal budget constraint for the representative agent in a diagram with first period consumption shown on the horizontal axis and consumption in the second period shown on the vertical axis.
b. How do changes in $Y_1$ and $Y_2$ affect the equilibrium interest rates in autarky? What is the effect of a marginal change on intertemporal discount rate $\beta$?
c. Use a graph to illustrate the effect of changes in $Y_1$, $Y_2$, and $\beta$ on the equilibrium interest rates in autarky.
d. Now suppose that this small economy has been open to the international goods and credit market since the beginning of period 1. Under what conditions will the current account for period one be positive?

## Exercise 9

The world economy is formed by two countries, foreign and home, which exist for two periods. Each individual in each country receives an exogenous, perishable endowment of goods for each period, $Y_t^c$, with $t \in \{1, 2\}$ and $c = \{H, F\}$. Superscript $H$ denotes variables associated with the domestic economy, while superscript $F$ denotes variables associated with the foreign economy. This is an endowment economy where there is neither production nor capital accumulation. The net exports for each economy in period $t$ is given by $NX_t^c$, and where, in equilibrium, the net exports of one country should correspond to the net imports of the other, i.e., $NX_t^H + NX_t^F = 0$ should be true.

The utility function for consumers in each economy is given by

$$U_1^c = \ln(C_1^c) + \beta \ln(C_2^c),$$

where $C_t^c$ represents consumption of country $c$ in period $t$ and $\beta \in (0, 1)$ represents the intertemporal discount rate. Let $B_t^c$ represent the net international investment position for each economy and assume that $B_1^H = B_3^H = B_1^F = B_3^F = 0$.

a. Compute the interest rate equilibrium under autarky for each of the countries, denoted by $r^{A,H}$ and $r^{A,F}$.
b. Find the international interest rate when there is the free trade of goods and services between the countries, denoted by $r$, and show that it remains between the values of autarky interest rates $r^{A,H}$ and $r^{A,F}$.
c. Show that the country with an autarky interest rate lower than the world interest rates will have a surplus in current account in period 1, while the country with interest rates above the international rate will run a deficit.
d. How does an increase in $Y_2^F$ affect the utility of the representative consumer in the domestic economy? What conclusions can you draw?

## Exercise 10

Consider a closed economy that exists for two periods with a production function given by

$$Y_t = K_t^\alpha L_t^{1-\alpha},$$

where $\alpha \in (0, 1)$, $K_t$ is the capital endowment and $L_t$ is the labor endowment for the economy for period $t$. Assume that the labor endowment is equal to the size of the population in this economy, which we will assume is equal to 1 for each period. Further assume that the economy receives a capital stock of $K_1 > 0$ in period 1, and the capital depreciates in such a way as that capital stock in period 2 is given by $K_2 = K_1 + I_1$, where $I_1$ represents investment in period 1.

Representative agent preferences in this economy are represented by the following utility function:

$$U_1 = \ln(C_1) + \beta \ln(C_2).$$

**a.** Derive the production possibilities frontier in the economy, assuming that $K_3 = 0$.
**b.** Illustrate by means of a graph the production possibilities frontier obtained in item (a). How does the concavity of the curve change with variations in $\alpha$?
**c.** How does the existence of a government that consumes positive quantities of product in period 2 affect the production possibilities frontier of the representative agent?
**d.** Compute the interest rates in autarky in the case where $\alpha = 1$.
**e.** Illustrate the equilibrium in autarky by means of a graph that relates savings and investment.

## Exercise 11

Consider a small, open economy where there is the accumulation of capital and production. Production in the domestic economy is given by means of function:

$$Y_t = A_t K_t^\alpha.$$

There is total depreciation of capital from one period to the next, such that $K_{t+1} = I_t$, and each individual receives an initial endowment of capital in the first period, $K_1 > 0$, so that production is exogenous at $t = 1$. Besides this, assume that $B_1 = B_3 = 0$. The utility function for the representative agent is given by

$$U_1 = \ln(C_1) + \beta \ln(C_2),$$

where $\beta \in (0, 1)$ represents the intertemporal discount rate and $C_t$ is consumption in period $t$.

**a.** Obtain the savings of the domestic economy in period 1, denoted by $S_1$, in function of $Y_1$, $Y_2$, $K_1$, $K_2$, and $r$.
**b.** Given interest rate $r$, determine the optimum level of capital in the second period, $K_2$, consistent with the maximization of the utility of the representative individual, and the respective level of investment. Show that investment in the economy, represented by $I_1$, is a negative function of interest rates.
**c.** Using the optimum choice of $K_2$ determined in item (b), and the corresponding production $Y_2$, compute domestic savings as a function of interest rates $r$, i.e., $S_1(r)$. Show that $S_1(r)$ is a positive function of interest rates.

**d.** Illustrate the autarky equilibrium in the domestic economy on a graph with savings and investment represented on the vertical axis and interest rates on the horizontal axis.

**e.** Assume the world is composed of only a domestic economy and a foreign economy, and that all is symmetrical to the domestic economy, with the exception of the intertemporal discount rate. Assume that $\beta > \beta^*$, where $\beta^*$ is the intertemporal discount rate in the foreign economy. Find the current-account balance for the domestic economy and for the foreign economy.

**f.** Illustrate on a graph the equilibrium obtained in the previous item.

## Exercise 12

Consider a small, open economy that exits for two periods and that has an endowment $Y_t$ for each period of the only existing good. Furthermore, assume that such endowments are compatible with the current-account equilibrium. In the short term, the stock of capital in the economy cannot be adjusted, such that a sudden increase in immigration to this economy temporarily reduces *per capita* capital and, consequently, the *per capita* income in the economy. This can be modeled as a fall in $Y_1$, with $Y_2$ remaining constant. What should happen to the current account in this country if there is an increase in migratory flow?

## Exercise 13

Consider a small open economy that exists for two periods and that possesses an initial stock of assets $B_1 < 0$, i.e., that there is indebtedness inherited from a period before the initial. The stock of assets at the end of the first period is given by $B_2 - B_1 = rB_1 + Y_1 - C_1$. Assume that the relation $\beta(1 + r) = 1$ is valid. The endowment for the first period is given by $Y_1$ and the endowment for the second period is equal to zero.

**a.** Present the intertemporal budget constraint and the conditions that establish the optimum levels for consumption and investment.

**b.** What would be the effect of a reduction in debt (a reduction in $|B_1|$) on the present value of income in the country? What would be the impact on consumption and current account in the first period?

## Exercise 14

Determine if the following statements are correct, incorrect, or uncertain. Justify your answer.

**a.** In a situation where a country chooses to go into debt, such deterioration in its welfare would occur that it is not beneficial for it to go into debt. In other words, Thomas Fuller was correct when he said, "Debt is the worst poverty."

**b.** According to the intertemporal current-account determination models, it is desirable for an emerging country to accumulate deficits in current account.

**c.** Consider a country that, initially, is at full employment and presents a large current account deficit. If this country desires to implement an economic policy with the objective of reducing the probability of undergoing a balance of payment crisis, it will, necessarily, need to alter its level of consumption and investment.

# 5

The Equilibrium Real Exchange Rate

In Chapter 3, we saw that if all goods were tradable at no cost, international trade would arbitrage away any price differences between countries, causing prices to be the same in all countries when measured in the same currency. This is not what the data shows, however. The real exchange rate, measured as the price ratio between two countries, does change over time. This variation is not just a short-term phenomenon, which leads us to believe that there are changes in the equilibrium level of the real exchange rate. In this chapter, we will study the variables that affect this equilibrium value.

The real exchange rate is defined as the ratio between the aggregate prices of goods from two countries, measured in the same currency, as established in Eq. (3.2). Prices in the two countries can only diverge if there are barriers to the trade of goods between them, for if not, trade would arbitrage a way the possible differences in prices so that, in equilibrium, the prices would always be the same in both countries. Barriers to international trade can be legal, such as tariffs or import quotas, or physical barriers associated with transportation costs. Barriers that increase the cost of the international trade of goods, but that are not sufficiently large to impede trade, allow for a difference in prices between countries, but only within the limit established by the transaction cost. There are, however, goods whose transport cost is so high in relation to price that international trade becomes impossible. The classic example is that of the hairdresser services.

This chapter expands the intertemporal current-account model presented in Chapter 4, dividing goods into two extreme types: on one end we have tradable goods, whose transportation cost we assume to be zero, and at the other those nontradable goods for which international trade is impossible. In this way, the real exchange rate can vary with the changes in the relative price of nontradable goods between countries.

We begin by deriving the relation between the real exchange rate and the relative price of nontradable goods in Section 5.1. To derive the equilibrium price of nontradable goods, Section 5.2 adds a sector of nontradable goods to the intertemporal model of current account determination studied in Chapter 4. Finally, the last section investigates the impact of a number of economic variables on the equilibrium real exchange rate.

## 5.1 The Real Exchange Rate and the Price of Nontradable Goods

The real exchange rate, which we will denote RER, is the ratio of price indexes between two countries, measured in the same currency, as defined in Eq. (3.2), which is as follows:

$$Q \equiv \frac{SP^*}{P},$$

where $Q$ is the real exchange rate, $S$ is the nominal exchange rate, and $P$ and $P^*$ are the domestic and foreign price indexes, respectively.

Let us use the consumer price index to measure it. This index is computed as a geometric average of prices, using the share of each good in total expenses as weights. Assuming that there are only two goods in the economy, tradable and nontradable, and that $\alpha$ is the share of nontradable expenses, the consumer price index will be

$$P = p_N^\alpha p_T^{1-\alpha}, \tag{5.1}$$

where $p_N$ and $p_T$ are the prices of nontradable and tradable goods, respectively. If consumers from both countries have the same preferences, the price index for the foreign country will be computed using the same formula.

By the RER definition, we then have that

$$Q = \frac{S(p_N^*)^\alpha (p_T^*)^{1-\alpha}}{p_N^\alpha p_T^{1-\alpha}},$$

where $P_N^*$ and $P_T^*$ are the prices in the foreign country. The previous equation can be rewritten as

$$Q = \frac{Sp_T^* \left(\frac{p_N^*}{p_T^*}\right)^\alpha}{p_T \left(\frac{p_N}{p_N}\right)^\alpha}.$$

The price of tradable goods should be the same in both countries if there is no barrier or cost associated with their trade, therefore $Sp_T^* = p_T$. In this case, the RER is a function of the ratio of the relative prices of nontradables in both countries:

$$Q = \left(\frac{p_N^*/p_T^*}{p_N/p_T}\right)^\alpha. \tag{5.2}$$

Equation (5.2) makes it clear that, to understand what determines the RER, it is necessary to understand how the relative nontradable goods prices are determined.

Notice that the individual trajectory of prices for each type of good is not important in this model: the relevant variable is the relative price among the goods. Hence, to simplify the notation without loss of generality, we assume that the price of the tradable goods is constant and equal to 1, $p_T = Sp_T^* = 1$, so that

$$Q = \left(\frac{Sp_N^*}{p_N}\right)^\alpha. \tag{5.3}$$

Therefore, **the variables that affect the real exchange rate are those that determine the relative price of nontradable goods in both countries**.

We assume that the price of nontradable goods in the foreign country, $p_N^*$, is exogenous, that is, it is determined in the foreign country and its value is not affected by the domestic resident's consumption and production decisions. The model developed in the following section analyzes the variables that affect the relative prices of nontradables in the domestic country, $p_N$. An increase in this price causes a reduction in the RER, according to Eq. (5.3). In other words, **an increase in the relative price of nontradable goods in the domestic country represents an appreciation of the real exchange rate**. Analogously, **a reduction in the relative price of nontradables means a real exchange rate depreciation**. To simplify, I will take S = 1, and refer to increases in the prices of nontradables $p_N$ as RER appreciations, and reductions of $p_N$ as depreciations.

### 5.1.1 How to Determine the Real Exchange Rate

We begin with the intertemporal current-account model where the evolution in current-account balances is motivated by consumption smoothing, similar to the model developed in Section 4.1. In that model, we assumed that there was only one good to be consumed, transacted without cost between countries, or that could even be transformed into capital for production by means of investment (in the extended version of Section 4.2). The model showed how consumption smoothing explained the current-account balance. However, that model is not adequate to analyze RER changes, since, with only one good freely traded, there are no RER changes: the RER is always equal to one. In order to adapt the model to take into account RER variations, we add two elements to it.

First, we assume that there is a nontradable good in the economy, besides the tradable good with no trading costs. The existence of nontradables allows the RER to change, since the prices of these goods can be different between countries. Second, we assume that producers choose how much to produce of each type of good, given a global resources constraint. This choice is introduced into the model to capture the important RER function of providing incentives to the allocation of production resources between the tradable and nontradable sectors in the economy.

Notice that in this model we do not cover the question of investment. Even if the presence of investment brought additional elements to the analysis, the more relevant issues from the practical point of view can be covered without investment, with the advantage of having a simpler and more easily understood model.

## 5.2 Production, Consumption, and Equilibrium

As in Chapter 4, we will here consider a small, open economy, in a world with two periods, and a population formed by a continuum of identical individuals uniformly distributed in the interval [0,1]. We also assume that there are two types of goods in this economy: tradables and nontradables. For each period, each individual receives an endowment of inputs and chooses how much to produce of each type of good, given the production technology. The chosen production determines the income that they have for each period to either consume or save. We begin with a description of the production decision in the economy.

### 5.2.1 Production

In the intertemporal current-account model in Section 4.1, the consumers receive an endowment of the single good each period. Now they receive an endowment of inputs and choose, given the available technologies, how much to produce of each of the two types of existing goods. Assuming that the resources are used in an efficient way, i.e., there is no waste; the possibilities of production choices between the two goods can be represented by a **production possibilities frontier** (PPF), which we will represent by Eq. (5.4)[1]:

$$\left[\left(\frac{T}{a_{\mathrm{T}}}\right)^{\rho}+\left(\frac{N}{a_{\mathrm{N}}}\right)^{\rho}\right]^{\frac{1}{\rho}}=\overline{Y}, \quad \text{for } \rho > 0, \tag{5.4}$$

where $T$ and $N$ represent the amount of tradable and nontradable goods produced, respectively.[2] $\overline{Y}$ represents the endowment of production resources that the individuals receive each period. The greater $\overline{Y}$ is, the greater the total quantity of the two goods that can be produced. Parameters $a_{\mathrm{T}}$ and $a_{\mathrm{N}}$ capture the productivity of each of the two sectors. The greater $a_{\mathrm{T}}$, for example, the more tradable goods one can produce for the same amount of resources. Finally, $\rho$ is a parameter related to the elasticity of transformation between the two goods.[3]

The curve of Figure 5.1 represents the PPF from Eq. (5.4). It is natural to assume that, given that production is efficient, it is necessary to reduce production of one good in order to increase production of the other. This is captured by the fact that the PPF is a decreasing curve, as shown in the figure. Going from point A to point B, the production of tradable goods decreases ($T^A > T^B$) so that the production of nontradable goods can increase ($N^A < N^B$). The points of the curve that touch the axes are the points where the economy specializes in the production of one of the goods. In this case, the total quantity produced is $a_i\overline{Y}$ where $i = T$ or $N$, depending on if the good produced is tradable or not. The role of $a_i$ is clearer as sector productivity and that of $\overline{Y}$ as the restriction to global production: the more $\overline{Y}$ increases, the PPF uniformly distances from the origin, while as $a_i$ increases for one of the sectors, there is an expansion in PPF biased in favor of that sector.

The slope of the curve, denoted the **marginal rate of transformation**, indicates how much more of the tradable good can be produced when one unit less of the nontradable good is produced. It is given by

$$\left.\frac{\mathrm{d}T}{\mathrm{d}N}\right|_{\overline{Y}}=-\left(\frac{a_{\mathrm{T}}}{a_{\mathrm{N}}}\right)^{\rho}\left(\frac{N}{T}\right)^{\rho-1}. \tag{5.5}$$

---

[1] From the quantity of production factors and the production function for each sector, we can derive the PPF for the economy. I chose to start directly from a functional form for the PPF, given that we are not interested in the allocation of inputs between the sectors.

[2] Our hypotheses regarding population distribution causes that the values for individual variables be identical to the aggregate values (see Chapter 4, Footnote 9). As a shortcut, we will directly use the aggregate variables in the description of the individual production and consumption decisions. Moreover, we have omitted the time subscript whenever possible in order to simplify the notation.

[3] Actually, Eq. (5.4) is often used in economics exactly because it presents constant transformation elasticity, and this elasticity, in this formulation, is equal to $\frac{1}{\rho-1}$. This type of function is called a *Constant Elasticity of Transformation* (CET) function.

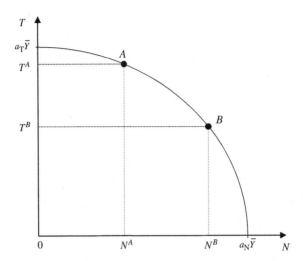

**Figure 5.1** Production possibilities frontier.

This slope will be greater, in absolute value, the greater $\frac{a_T}{a_N}$ is, which is proportional to the relative productivity of the two sectors. Moreover, the more an economy specializes in tradable goods, the smaller the slope of the production possibilities frontier: in other words, the smaller the increment of tradable goods when there is more specialization in the production of these goods.

The producer should choose the allocation of resources between the two sectors, i.e., a point on the production possibilities frontier. Economic models, in general, assume that producers seek to maximize their profit, and it will be no different here. Given that resources $\overline{Y}$ are an endowment received by the producer, the production cost is null. Therefore, maximizing profit corresponds to the maximization of global revenue resulting from the sale of the two types of goods produced. The aggregate income corresponds to the GDP for the country, which is represented by Eq. (5.6):

$$Y = T + p_N N, \tag{5.6}$$

where we take the tradable good as numeraire, i.e., $P_T = 1$.

The producer chooses the allocation of production between the two types of goods so as to maximize the aggregate income, constrained by their production capability as defined by the production possibilities frontier. The solution to this problem, described in detail in the Mathematical Appendix presented at the end of this chapter, can be described graphically.

In Figure 5.2, the set of production pairs $(N, T)$ that result in the same GDP level, that satisfy Eq. (5.6) for a given GDP, can be represented iso-GDP lines. Since on the graph the quantity of tradable goods is represented on the vertical axis, the iso-GDP lines have a slope

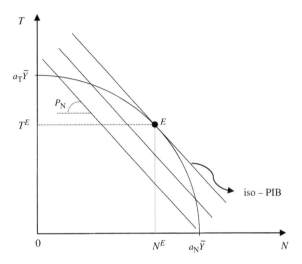

**Figure 5.2** Solution to the producer problem.

equal to $-p_N$. The farther from the origin, the higher the GDP represented by the iso-GDP line. Therefore, the producer will choose the point on the production possibilities frontier belonging to the iso-GDP that is farthest from the origin. This will be the point the iso-GDP is tangent to the PPF, i.e., the point where the two functions have the same slope. Therefore, using Eq. (5.5), the optimum choice for the producer is the allocation $(N, T)$ that satisfies equation:

$$p_N = \left(\frac{a_T}{a_N}\right)^\rho \left(\frac{N}{T}\right)^{\rho-1},$$

which is represented by point E on the figure.

With the above equation and the PPF in Eq. (5.4), we can obtain the supply functions for both goods:

$$T = \overline{Y} \left(\frac{a_T^\rho}{\prod(p_N)}\right)^{\frac{1}{\rho-1}}, \tag{5.7a}$$

$$N = \overline{Y} \left(\frac{p_N a_N^\rho}{\prod(p_N)}\right)^{\frac{1}{\rho-1}}, \tag{5.7b}$$

where function $\prod(p_N)$ is defined by

$$\prod(p_N) = \left[a_T^{\frac{\rho}{\rho-1}} + (p_N a_T)^{\frac{\rho}{\rho-1}}\right]^{\frac{\rho-1}{\rho}}. \tag{5.8}$$

Some interesting relations can be inferred from supply functions (5.7a) and (5.7b). First, the production of both goods increases when there is an increase in available resources $\overline{Y}$ or an increase in total productivity factor, which is captured in this model by a simultaneous and proportional increase of $a_N$ and $a_T$. On the other hand, an increase in productivity only in the tradable sector increases production only in this sector, while it reduces that in the nontradable sector.[4] Finally, a rise in the price of nontradable goods, $p_N$, increases their supply, and reduces that of tradable goods.

Substituting the chosen production for the two sectors (Eqs. (5.7a) and (5.7b)) into the GDP equation (Eq. (5.6)), we obtain the economy GDP:

$$Y = \overline{Y}\left[a_T^{\frac{\rho}{\rho-1}} + (p_N a_T)^{\frac{\rho}{\rho-1}}\right]^{\frac{\rho-1}{\rho}} = \overline{Y}\prod(p_N), \tag{5.9}$$

where $\prod(p_N)$ is defined in Eq. (5.8).

The GDP described by Eq. (5.9) determines the income available to the consumer to either save or spend each period. We include the time subscript since it will be necessary for what comes next. In principle, the amount of available resources $\overline{Y}$ and the productivity parameters $a_i$ may change over time. Given that $\prod(p_N)$ defined in Eq. (5.8) depends on the productivity parameters, it may also vary over time.

## 5.2.2 Consumption

Our consumer has two choices to make: how much to save each period and how to allocate expenditures between the consumption of tradable and nontradable goods. The consumer preferences continue to be represented by a utility function like Eq. (4.1). In Chapter 4, I argued that the single good could be interpreted as representing a basket of goods. That is exactly what we do here: now $C$ corresponds to a consumption basket that includes the two types of goods in the economy.

To simplify the analysis, assume that function $u(\cdot)$ is a logarithmic function, i.e.,

$$u(C_t) = \ln(C_t),$$

such that the utility function becomes

$$U_1 = \ln C_1 + \beta \ln C_2. \tag{5.10}$$

The composition of the consumption basket $C_t$ reflects consumer preferences in relation to the two types of goods, and we assume that they are represented by a Cobb–Douglas function:

$$C_t = C_{Tt}^{1-\alpha} C_{Nt}^{\alpha}, \tag{5.11}$$

---

[4] This second effect is due to the impact of $a_T$ on $\Pi(p_N)$.

where $C_{Tt}$ and $C_{Nt}$ correspond to consumed quantities of tradable and nontradable goods, respectively. $\alpha \in (0,1)$ is a parameter of the utility function that determines the share of expenditures spent on nontradable goods, as we will see in Eq. (5.18) further ahead. We will also see that this functional form for preferences yields the consumer price index in Eq. (5.1).

Notice that, by using a utility function that is separable in time, namely, the function (5.10) is the sum of the utility in each period, the choice of the composition of the consumption basket does not have an intertemporal effect. In other words, the allocation of expenditures between the two goods does not affect the decision for intertemporal allocation of consumption. This property is very convenient, for it allows us to separate the decision to consume into two decisions: (i) how to allocate consumption between the two periods and (ii) how to allocate total consumption for the period between the two goods.

The consumer budget constraint is given by

$$P_1 C_1 + \frac{P_2 C_2}{1 + i^*} = Y_1 + \frac{Y_2}{1 + i^*}, \tag{5.12}$$

where consumption basket $C_t$ is in Eq. (5.11) and $P_t$ is the price of one unit of consumption basket $C_t$, that is, it is the consumer price index in period $t$. The formula for this price index depends on consumer preferences, and will be derived farther ahead. $i^*$ is the international interest rate[5] and $Y_t$ represents the income for each period, which corresponds to the GDP described in Eq. (5.9). Notice that, as the GDP is already defined in nominal terms, the variable that represents it does not need to be multiplied by a price index.

It is interesting to note that, now, the price index can change from one period to another: only one of the goods can be used as numeraire (in this case, the numeraire is the tradable good), while the price of the other good can change over time.

**Let us solve the consumer problem splitting it into two choices: (i) the intertemporal choice, where they choose how much to save each period and (ii) the intratemporal choice, which corresponds to the allocation of expenditures between the two goods, i.e., the composition of the consumption basket.**

### 5.2.2.1 Intertemporal Consumption Allocation

The choice to save or spend results from the maximization of the utility function (Eq. (5.10)) subject to the budget constraint (Eq. (5.12)), where the choice variables are $C_1$ and $C_2$. Analogous to the problem with only one good, solved in Chapter 4, the optimum choice

---

[5] Notice that now, differently from the setting in Chapter 4, interest rate $i^*$ can differ from the real interest rate when the price index changes across periods. In Chapter 4, there was only one good and it was used as numeraire, that is, its price was always equal to one. It was therefore possible to use the real interest rate in place of the nominal since the two rates were always equal. Here, we include a nontradable good, hence relative prices can change over time, causing shifts in the price index. When this happens, the nominal interest rate differs from the real.

occurs when the marginal rate of substitution across periods is equal to the relative price, as described in Eq. (4.6), which, under the new assumptions, becomes

$$\frac{C_2}{\beta C_1} = \frac{P_1(1 + i^*)}{P_2},$$

where we use $\frac{d \ln C_t}{dC_t} = \frac{1}{C_t}$. With this equation and the budget constraint in Eq. (5.12), we obtain consumption for each period, as described in detail in the Mathematical Appendix at the end of the chapter:

$$P_1 C_2 = \frac{1}{1 + \beta} \left[ Y_1 + \frac{Y_2}{1 + i^*} \right]$$

and

$$P_2 C_2 = \frac{(1 + i^*)\beta}{1 + \beta} \left[ Y_1 + \frac{Y_2}{1 + i^*} \right].$$

We have total expenditures smoothing when $\beta(1 + i^*) = 1$. In this case, the optimum expenditure for each period is given by[6]

$$P_1 C_1 = P_2 C_2 = \frac{(1 + i^*)Y_1 + Y_2}{2 + i^*}. \tag{5.13}$$

### 5.2.2.2 Current Account

Equation (2.10), which defines the current-account balance based on national accounts, is now

$$CA_t = Y_t + i^* B_t - P_t C_t. \tag{5.14}$$

Assuming, as we did with the intertemporal model in Chapter 4, that the economy begins and ends with no debt or credit with the rest of the world, $B_1 = B_3 = 0$, we have that $CA_1 = -CA_2$. Substituting in Eq. (5.14) the optimum expenditure in the case of total smoothing, established in Eq. (5.13), we have that the current account for each year is given by

$$CA_1 = \frac{Y_1 - Y_2}{2 + i^*} = -CA_2. \tag{5.15}$$

According to Eq. (5.15), **a country borrows in the first period if it expects a higher GDP in the second period and lends in the opposite case.**

---

[6] The same expenditure value for both periods is the result of the assumption that $\beta(1 + i^*) = 1$. We adopt this assumption to simplify the resolution of the model and the interpretation of its results.

It is interesting to note that the equations that determine current account here are exactly equal to those derived for the case with only tradable goods in Eq. (4.11), if in that equation we use the nominal international interest rate, instead of making the substitution for the real domestic interest rate.[7] Concerning the savings decision between the two models, the only difference in the present model is in the fact that the price of the consumption basket can change across periods. The assumption that $\beta(1 + i^*) = 1$, combined to the logarithmic utility function, implies the same expenditures value in both periods, so that the results in terms of aggregate savings are the same for both models.

### 5.2.2.3 Allocation of Consumption Between Tradable and Nontradable Goods

Once expenditure $P_t C_t$ is chosen for each period, the consumer decides its allocation between the two types of goods so as to maximize their utility. More specifically, the consumer maximizes their consumption basket, $C_t = C_{Tt}^{1-\alpha} C_{Nt}^{\alpha}$, subject to the constraint that expenses with tradable and nontradable goods cannot exceed the total expenditure chosen for the period. Mathematically, this budget constraint is represented by

$$C_{Tt} + p_{Nt} C_{Nt} = P_t C_t. \tag{5.16}$$

In a way analogous to the intertemporal choice, in the optimum choice for expenditure allocation between the two types of goods, the marginal rate of substitution should be equal to the relative price, i.e.,

$$\frac{(1 - \alpha) C_{Tt}}{\alpha C_{Nt}} = p_{Nt},$$

which can be written as

$$\frac{C_{Tt}}{C_{Nt}} = \left(\frac{\alpha}{1 - \alpha}\right) p_{Nt} \tag{5.17}$$

and shows that an increase in the relative price of nontradable goods increases the relative consumption of tradable goods.

Combining the relation (5.17) to the budget constraint (5.16), as shown in the Mathematical Appendix at the end of the chapter, we have the demand functions for each of the goods as a function of the total expenditure:

$$C_{Tt} = (1 - \alpha) P_t C_t \text{ and} \tag{5.18a}$$

$$p_{Nt} C_{Nt} = \alpha P_t C_t. \tag{5.18b}$$

---

[7] Footnote 5 in Chapter 4 explains why the nominal international interest rate is equal to the real domestic interest rate when prices are constant.

### 5.2.2.4 The Amount Consumed of Each Good

Finally, we can join the result of the two consumer decisions, the intertemporal and intratemporal, to determine how much of each good will be consumed in each period in the case $(1 + i^*)\beta = 1$. Substituting the optimum expenditure decision (Eq. (5.13)) into the consumption allocation decision for each period (Eq. (5.18)), we have that

$$C_{Tt} = (1 - \alpha) \left[ \frac{(1 + i^*)Y_1 + Y_2}{2 + i^*} \right] \tag{5.19a}$$

and

$$p_{Nt} C_{Nt} = \alpha \left[ \frac{(1 + i^*)Y_1 + Y_2}{2 + i^*} \right] \tag{5.19b}$$

where GDP $Y_t$ is given by Eq. (5.9).

It is interesting to note that the assumption that $(1 + i^*)\beta = 1$ implies a constant expenditure over time. Given that the consumer consumes a constant share of their income on each good, spending on each good is also constant over time.

## 5.2.3 The Equilibrium Price

In equilibrium, the production of nontradable goods should be equal to consumption given that, by definition, these goods cannot be exported. The equilibrium price for nontradable goods, therefore, should be that which makes their demand equal to their supply, expressed as

$$N_t = C_{Nt}$$
$$\Downarrow$$
$$N_t = \frac{\alpha}{p_{Nt}} \left[ \frac{(1 + i^*)Y_1 + Y_2}{2 + i^*} \right] \cdot \tag{5.20}$$

Notice that, as described in Eq. (5.6), the GDP corresponds to the total value of production: $Y_t = T_t + p_{Nt}N_t$. According to Eq. (5.19b), the value of nontradable consumption is equal in both periods, consequently, their production value should also be equal. The equation for equilibrium in the nontradable market can therefore be written as[8]

$$N_t = \frac{\alpha}{P_{Nt}} \left[ p_{Nt}N_t + \frac{(1 + i^*)T_1 + T_2}{2 + i^*} \right]$$

which results in

$$p_{Nt} = \left( \frac{\alpha}{1 - \alpha} \right) \left[ \frac{(1 + i^*)T_1 + T_2}{N_t(2 + i^*)} \right], \tag{5.21}$$

[8] The Mathematical Appendix shows how we arrive at Eq. (5.21).

where the quantities produced, $T_t$ and $N_t$, are given by Eqs. (5.7a) and (5.7b), repeated here:

$$T = \overline{Y}\left(\frac{a_T^\rho}{\prod(p_N)}\right)^{\frac{1}{\rho-1}} \text{ and } N = \overline{Y}\left(\frac{p_N a_N^\rho}{\prod(p_N)}\right)^{\frac{1}{\rho-1}}, \tag{5.22}$$

where $\prod(p_N)$ is defined in Eq. (5.8).

Equation (5.21) establishes a set of two equations, one for each period, based on which it is possible to determine the price of nontradable goods for each period. It is not possible to obtain a closed solution, that is, we cannot write the price for each period as a function of the model parameters due to the nonlinearity of the supply functions in relation to price. Nevertheless, allowing for some simplifications, it is possible to come to some quite interesting conclusions in relation to the impact of the exogenous variables on the equilibrium price, as we will see in Section 5.3.

### 5.2.3.1 Equilibrium Price in Autarky

The equilibrium price in autarky will be a relevant reference to analyze the impact of certain variables on the real exchange rate. In autarky, by definition, there is no international trade of goods or assets. The representative individual, therefore, can neither borrow nor lend, and spends each period all their income by consuming tradable and nontradable goods produced domestically. Therefore, using Eq. (5.9), which defines the income for each period, we have that $P_t C_t = \overline{Y}_t \prod_t(p_{Nt})$. The autarky version of nontradable goods market equilibrium is given by[9]

$$N_t = \frac{\alpha}{p_{Nt}}\left[\overline{Y}_t \prod_t(p_{Nt})\right],$$

which results in a nontradables price determined by

$$p_{Nt}^A = \left(\frac{a_{Tt}}{a_{Nt}}\right)\left(\frac{\alpha}{1-\alpha}\right)^{\frac{\rho-1}{\rho}}, \tag{5.23}$$

where $p_{Nt}^A$ is the price of the nontradables in autarky.

Notice that the price in autarky is a function of the following parameters: (i) the productivity parameters, $a_T$ and $a_N$, (ii) the parameter concerning the preferences between tradable and nontradable goods, $\alpha$, and (iii) the parameter regarding the transformation elasticity between the two goods, $\rho$. The relative income between the two periods does not affect this price, given that, with a closed economy, it is not possible to transfer income between the periods.

---

[9] Details for this calculation are in the Mathematical Appendix.

### 5.2.4 Price Index and Real Exchange Rate

The consumer price index is a weighted average of the prices of consumption goods, where the weight attributed to the price of each good corresponds to its share in the total expenditures. With Cobb–Douglas preferences, represented in Eq. (5.11), the consumer spends a share $(1 - \alpha)$ of their expenditures on tradable goods and a share $\alpha$ on nontradable goods, according to Eq. (5.18). Therefore, the choice of the Cobb–Douglas function to represent the preference between goods generates a price index as defined in Eq. (5.1). Taking the tradable good as numeraire, $p_{Tt} = 1 \ \forall \ t$, the price index is given by

$$P_t = p_{Nt}^{\alpha}, \tag{5.24}$$

and the real exchange rate can be represented by Eq. (5.3), here repeated for $S = 1$:

$$Q = \left( \frac{p_N^*}{p_N} \right)^{\alpha}.$$

Therefore, **the equilibrium price of nontradable goods determines the real equilibrium exchange rate.**

### 5.2.5 The Real Exchange Rate and the Current Account

The relationship between the RER and the current account helps understand how the equilibrium real exchange rate responds to shocks or changes in other economic variables. The current-account balance is the sum of the income and the trade balances. Following the simplification employed since Chapter 4, we assume that the income balance is composed only of the payment and receipt of interest by the net international investment position. Using the definition of trade balance as the difference between GDP and the aggregate expenditures,[10] the current account in Eq. (5.14) can be written as

$$CA_t = i^* B_t + TB_t, \tag{5.25}$$

where $TB_t$ is the trade balance of the country.

The trade balance, in turn, is the difference between the total production and consumption of tradable goods. In this model with no government or investment, the total expenditure is reduced to private consumption. Thus, we can say that

$$TB_t = T_t - C_{Tt}.$$

On the one hand, the supply of tradables $T_t$ is a decreasing function of the price of nontradables $p_{Nt}$, as established in Eq. (5.7a). On the other hand, the consumption of tradables

---

[10] See Eq. (2.2).

$C_{Tt}$ increases with the price of nontradable goods, as we saw in Eq. (5.17). Hence, the relative price of nontradable goods has a negative impact on the trade balance:

$$\text{TB}_t(p_{Nt}) = T_t(p_{Nt}) - C_{Tt}(p_{Nt}), \tag{5.26}$$

where

$$\frac{\partial \text{TBC}_t(p_{Nt})}{\partial p_{Nt}} < 0, \quad \text{since} \quad \frac{\partial T_t(p_{Nt})}{\partial p_{Nt}} < 0 \text{ and } \frac{\partial C_{Tt}(p_{Nt})}{\partial p_{Nt}} > 0.$$

It is important to emphasize that Eq. (5.26) establishes the trade balance as a function of the **relative** price of nontradable goods. In the equation, only $p_N$ appears as an argument, but, if we had not assumed that a nominal exchange rate constant and equal to 1 ($S = 1$), the arguments of supply and demand would be in $p_N/S$. Consequently, a depreciation of the nominal exchange rate, that is, an increase in $S$, would cause a reduction in relative price to the nontradable good, leading to a trade balance increase, according to Eq. (5.26).

Given that the trade balance is part of the current account as indicated in Eq. (5.25), we then have that the current account is also a decreasing function of the nontradable price:

$$\frac{\partial CA_t(p_{Nt})}{\partial p_{Nt}} < 0. \tag{5.27}$$

Finally, Eq. (5.3) establishes a negative relation between the RER and the domestic price of nontradables: a higher price for nontradables means a more appreciated RER. Therefore, **a smaller current-account balance is associated with a higher price for nontradables, which means an appreciated real exchange rate**.

**The equilibrium real exchange rate can be interpreted as the rate that generates an optimum balance in current account. It can change, basically, in two ways. First, if the optimum level of current account changes.** Thus, variables that affect the optimum current-account balance, as those studied in Chapter 4, will also have an impact on the equilibrium RER. **Second, the equilibrium RER can change if there are changes in the relation between the current-account balance and the relative price of nontradables**, i.e., if there is a change in the function $\text{TB}_t(p_{Nt})$. This can occur if there is, for example, a productivity shock in the economy. The next section analyzes how some of these variables affect the current account.

# 5.3  How Does the Real Exchange Rate Respond to Shocks?

## 5.3.1  Income Shock

We begin with an intuition. The impact of income shocks on current account was analyzed in Chapter 4. We saw that permanent income shocks do not have an impact on current account, while a temporary positive shock would have a positive impact on current account. Given this result, and the negative relation between the RER and the relative price of nontradables as previously discussed, it would be expected that a permanent income shock would not affect the equilibrium RER, while a temporary increase in income should cause a depreciation of the RER. Let us see what the model tells us.

To simplify, we begin with a balanced current account. To this end, we assume that the economic parameters are the same for both periods, including the restriction of global resources, $\overline{Y}_1 = \overline{Y}_2 = \overline{Y}$. According to Eq. (5.15), this assumption guarantees, effectively, a balance in current account in both periods. Production is the same for both periods, as well as the equilibrium price of nontradable goods. Substituting the supply functions (5.22) in the equilibrium price equation for nontradable goods (5.21), and using the fact that the parameters are the same for both periods, we find that the price of nontradables is defined by the same Eq. (5.23) of the autarky price.

We want to capture an income shock that increases the productive capacity of the economy, but without altering the relative productivity between the two sectors. In the model, such a shock can be captured by an increase in the endowment of resources $\overline{Y}_t$. If the shock is permanent, it is easy to verify that the equation that determines equilibrium RER remains unaltered, and continues to be defined by Eq. (5.23).

We now see what happens when the positive income shock is temporary. Assume that there is an increase in income during the first period, but that it returns to its original level in the second period, such that $\overline{Y}_1 = \overline{Y}' > \overline{Y} = \overline{Y}_2$.

Computing the price of nontradable goods for each period based on Eq. (5.21), using the supply equation (5.22) and the equilibrium price in autarky (5.23), we have that[11]

$$p_{N1}^{\frac{\rho}{\rho-1}} = (p_N^A)^{\frac{\rho}{\rho-1}} \left\{ \frac{(1+i^*) + \left[ \frac{\overline{Y}_2}{\overline{Y}_1} \left( \prod (p_{N1}) \over \prod (p_{N2}) \right)^{\frac{1}{\rho-1}} \right]}{2 + i^*} \right\} \quad \text{and} \tag{5.28}$$

$$p_{N2}^{\frac{\rho}{\rho-1}} = (p_N^A)^{\frac{\rho}{\rho-1}} \left\{ \frac{1 + (1+i^*) + \left[ \frac{\overline{Y}_1}{\overline{Y}_2} \left( \prod (p_{N2}) \over \prod (p_{N1}) \right)^{\frac{1}{\rho-1}} \right]}{2 + i^*} \right\}. \tag{5.29}$$

We combine Eqs. (5.28) and (5.29) to get

$$\frac{p_{N1}^{\rho} / \prod (p_{N1})}{p_{N2}^{\rho} / \prod (p_{N2})} = \left( \frac{\overline{Y}_2}{\overline{Y}_1} \right)^{\rho - 1}. \tag{5.30}$$

Given that $\overline{Y}_1 > \overline{Y}_2$ and $\rho > 1$, the right side of Eq. (5.30) is less than one. Consequently, for the equation to be satisfied, it is necessary that $p_{N1}^{\rho} / \prod (p_{N1}) < p_{N2}^{\rho} / \prod (p_{N2})$, which is only possible when $p_{N1} < p_{N2}$, given that the ratio $p_{Nt}^{\rho} / \prod (p_{Nt})$ is increasing in $p_{Nt}$. Therefore

$$p_{N1} < p_{N2} \Leftrightarrow \overline{Y}_1 > \overline{Y}_2. \tag{5.31}$$

---

[11] The details of the calculation are in the Mathematical Appendix.

This means that the **RER is more depreciated in the period when the country has a positive income shock and appreciated when income returns to its original level**. The intuition for the result from the nontradable market viewpoint follows. Access to the international credit market allows consumers to smooth their consumption. If the relative price of nontradables was the same for both periods, there would be an excess supply of these goods in the first period, when the economy has relatively more production resources. A smaller price for nontradable goods in the first period would simultaneously cause a bias in production against these goods and an increase in their demand, balancing the market.

On the tradables market, the cheapening of nontradables would cause a reduction in demand for tradables and an increase in their supply. The excess supply of tradable goods is then exported. We can conclude that the depreciation of the real exchange rate is a mechanism that allows the internal equilibrium of an economy that goes through a period of excess of resources. This "leaking" of supply is accompanied by an increase in the current-account balance.

The result is in keeping with our initial intuition: a permanent income shock does not affect the optimum current-account level, thus the equilibrium RER remains unaltered; whereas a temporary positive income shock leads to an increase in current-account balance, accompanied by a depreciation of the real exchange rate.

We can also use Eq. (5.30) to analyze the case of a country that undergoes a temporary negative shock. In this case, the country has fewer resources in the first period in relation to the second, $\overline{Y}_1 < \overline{Y}_2$, which causes the right side of the equation to be greater than one. Therefore, the exchange rate is more appreciated in the first period, and the country accumulates a deficit in current account. In the following period, when the country pays its debt, the current-account balance will be positive and the exchange, devalued.

## 5.3.2 Impact of an Exogenous Reduction in Financial Flows

Throughout this chapter, we have assumed that the country has unlimited access to the international credit market. We know, however, that this is not true. The results discussed here are valid for situations where the country's choice to borrow is not large enough to affect the interest rate it pays on its debt and does not attain the limit in relation to the amount other countries are willing to lend. There are situations, however, that even when the country is within the debt limits, an external shock reduces the inflow of capital to the country. We can therefore ask what the impact of an exogenous reduction in capital flow will be on the real exchange. Clearly, this question only makes sense for a net receiver of financial capital, namely, a country that presents a deficit in current account. In the terms of our model, it concerns the first period for a country where $\overline{Y}_1 < \overline{Y}_2$.

Intuitively, a reduction in the capital flow requires an increase in current-account balance. As we say in Eq. (5.27), a higher trade balance is associated with a lower price of nontradable goods, which means a more depreciated RER. Let us see how this can be illustrated in the model equations.

Using Eq. (5.30) to substitute the expression $\left(\frac{\overline{Y}_2}{\overline{Y}_1}\right)\left(\frac{\prod(p_{N2})}{\prod(p_{N1})}\right)^{\frac{1}{\rho-1}}$ by $\left(\frac{p_{N1}}{p_{N2}}\right)^{\frac{\rho}{\rho-1}}$ in Eq. (5.28), we can write $P_{N1}$ as[12]

$$p_{N1} = p_N^A \left\{ \frac{1+i^* + \left(\frac{p_{N1}}{p_{N2}}\right)^{\frac{\rho-1}{\rho}}}{2+i^*} \right\}^{\frac{\rho-1}{\rho}}, \tag{5.32}$$

where $p_N^A$ is the price of nontradables in autarky, defined by Eq. (5.23). For a country that borrows in the first period, we have that $\frac{p_{N1}}{p_{N2}} > 1$, according to what is established by inequality (5.31). Therefore, $p_{N1} > p_N^A$, i.e., **the real exchange rate for a country that borrows is more appreciated than the exchange that would be in force in autarky**.

Returning to our question: What is the impact of an exogenous reduction of capital flow? In an extreme case of a total stop of capital flow, the price of nontradables would go to its value in autarky, which entails a depreciation of the real exchange rate. When the capital flow just decreases, without stopping completely, there will be a depreciation of the real exchange, even if in a relatively smaller magnitude. Consequently, **an exogenous reduction in the flow of capital results in a depreciation of the RER**.

## 5.3.3 Increase in International Interest Rates

Another interesting exercise is to investigate the impact of an increase in international interest rates on the real exchange. Once again, let us begin with the intuition, with the impact of the interest rate on the equilibrium current-account balance as our starting point. In Section 4.2, we saw that the interest rate affects consumption by means of two distinct effects: a substitution effect and an income effect. A higher interest rate makes present consumption relatively more expensive, which stimulates consumers to save more. This is the substitution effect, which has a positive effect on the current account in the first period.

The income effect is related to the impact of the interest rate on the payment or receipt of income associated to the net international investment position. For a net borrower, the increase in interest rate means an increase in the net payment to foreign creditors. With a smaller disposable income, consumption falls. Since the substitution effect also leads to a reduction in consumption, the final result is a reduction in the current-account balance. Given the negative relation between current account and the relative price of nontradables, and the positive relation between the latter and the RER, the result will be **a depreciation of the real exchange in face of an increase in international interest rates for indebted countries**.

In the case of a net lender, the income received from its international credit increases with the interest rate, leading to an increase in consumption. As the income and the substitution effects lead in opposite directions, in principle it would not be possible to know if aggregate consumption would increase or decrease with a higher international interest rate.

---

[12] For details, see the Mathematical Appendix.

However, we will show that, with complete consumption smoothing, the income effect surpasses the substitution effect, entailing an increase in the current account balance. Consequently, the **increase in interest rates would lead to an appreciation of the RER for international creditor countries**.

In terms of the model, to compute the impact of interest rates on the price of nontradables, we take the derivative of the nontradables price with respect to the interest rate using Eq. (5.32) to get:

$$\frac{\partial p_{N1}}{\partial i^*} = p_{N1}^{-\frac{1}{\rho-1}} (p_N^A)^{\frac{\rho}{\rho-1}} \left(\frac{\rho-1}{\rho}\right) \left(\frac{1-(p_{N1}/p_{N2})^{\frac{\rho}{\rho-1}}}{(2+i^*)^2} + \frac{\frac{\partial}{\partial i^*}\left[(p_{N1}/p_{N2})^{\frac{\rho}{\rho-1}}\right]}{(2+i^*)}\right), \tag{5.33}$$

where the second term of the expression between parenthesis is equal to[13]

$$\frac{\partial}{\partial i^*}\left[(p_{N1}/p_{N2})^{\frac{\rho}{\rho-1}}\right] = \left(\frac{\rho}{\rho-1}\right) \left(\frac{p_{N1}}{p_{N2}}\right)^{\frac{\rho}{\rho-1}} \left(\frac{\partial p_{N1}/\partial i^*}{p_{N1}} - \frac{\partial p_{N2}/\partial i^*}{p_{N2}}\right). \tag{5.34}$$

Substituting Eq. (5.34) into Eq. (5.33), using Eq. (5.32), and reorganizing the equation, we obtain that

$$(1+i^*)\frac{\partial p_{N1}/\partial i^*}{p_{N1}} + \left(\frac{p_{N1}}{p_{N2}}\right)^{\frac{\rho}{\rho-1}} \left(\frac{\partial p_{N2}/\partial i^*}{p_{N2}}\right) = \left(\frac{\rho-1}{\rho}\right) \left(\frac{1-(p_{N1}/p_{N2})^{\frac{\rho}{\rho-1}}}{2+i^*}\right). \tag{5.35}$$

Equation (5.35) shows that a linear function of the sum of the derivative of the nontradables price with respect to the interest rate in each of the periods has the sign of the expression $1 - (p_{N1}/p_{N2})^{\frac{\rho}{\rho-1}}$. We also know that, based on Eq. (5.30), $\frac{\partial p_{N1}}{\partial i^*}$ and $\frac{\partial p_{N2}}{\partial i^*}$ have the same sign.[14] With this result, we can state that the impact of interest rates on the RER is positive or negative, depending on the sign of the term $1 - (p_{N1}/p_{N2})^{\frac{\rho}{\rho-1}}$.

We saw in the result (5.31) that the expression $(p_{N1}/p_{N2})^{\frac{\rho}{\rho-1}}$ is greater than 1 when $\overline{Y}_1 < \overline{Y}_2$, i.e., for a borrower country. In this case, the right side of Eq. (5.35) is negative, which implies a more depreciated exchange rate when the international interest rate increases.

The intuition from the point of view of nontradable goods market follows. For an indebted country, an increase in interest rates represents a reduction in disposable income since the service on the foreign debt increases. With a smaller disposable income, individuals consume fewer units of all goods, particularly nontradables. At the same relative price of nontradables, there would be an excess supply of these goods. Their price decreases in order to destimulate production in that sector and balance the market. The consequent RER

---

[13] The computation of these derivatives is in the Mathematical Appendix.

[14] Taking the derivative of Eq. (5.30) with respect to the interest rate, we have

$$\frac{\partial (p_{N1}^\rho/\Pi(p_{N1}))}{\partial p_{N1}} \frac{\partial p_{N1}}{\partial i^*} = \left(\frac{\overline{Y}_2}{\overline{Y}_1}\right)^{\rho-1} \left(\frac{\partial (p_{N2}^\rho/\Pi(p_{N2}))}{\partial p_{N2}} \frac{\partial p_{N2}}{\partial i^*}\right).$$

Therefore, $\frac{\partial p_{N1}}{\partial i^*}$ and $\frac{\partial p_{N2}}{\partial i^*}$ have the same sign, given that $\frac{\partial (p_{Nt}^\rho/\Pi(p_{Nt}))}{\partial p_{Nt}} > 0$.

depreciation also destimulates imports, reducing the "leaking" of demand. The experience of Latin American countries in the early 1980s, as discussed in Box 2.5, is one such example. The increase in US interest rates in the early 1980s led to large real exchange rate devaluations among the highly indebted countries in the region.

The result is exactly the opposite for a lending country. This type of country has $\overline{Y}_1 > \overline{Y}_2$, and the expression $(p_{N1}/p_{N2})^{\frac{\rho}{\rho-1}}$ becomes less than 1. The right side of Eq. (5.35) becomes positive, which means that an increase in interest rates represents an increase in disposable income, and consequently an increase in consumption. The increase in nontradable prices sends an incentive for the productive sector, which increases the offer of this good.

## 5.3.4 The Impact of Government Spending

Government spending is commonly pointed out as an important variable in determining the equilibrium RER. Let us include government spending in the model, but, before beginning the algebraic solution, let us look at the intuition for the impact of government on the RER.

In Section 4.3, we saw how government spending affects the optimum current-account level. Different levels of government spending across periods have an impact on the aggregate expenditures: higher public spending in the first period in relation to the second, for example, reduces the current-account balance in the first period. Given the negative relation between the current account and the RER, government spending affects the equilibrium RER by means of its impact on the current-account balance, which we will denote the **government spending intertemporal effect**. Notice that public spending only has an effect on the RER by the intertemporal effect if they are different between periods, so as to alter the relative disposable income. A permanent change in spending does not cause this intertemporal effect.

There is, however, an additional channel by which the government affects the real exchange rate, which is associated with the composition of public spending between tradable and nontradable goods. The relative price of nontradable goods is determined by the equilibrium between the supply and demand of these goods. On the one hand, government spending reduces private consumption given that the taxes imposed to finance them reduce consumer disposable income. On the other, public consumption is added to aggregate expenditures. Intuitively, public spending will have an effect on the real exchange when its composition between the two types of goods differs from the composition of private spending. We call this impact the **government spending composition effect**. It is interesting to note that this effect does not relate to changes in the optimum current-account level, as in cases seen up until now. It is associated to the fact that public spending can change the relation between the price of nontradables and the trade balance, i.e., the shape of function $TB_t(p_{Nt})$ indicated in Eq. (5.26). More specifically, government spending can affect the relationship between price and demand $C_{Tt}(p_{Nt})$, as we will see further ahead.

Now, let us introduce government spending into the model. We denote $G_t$ as the value of aggregate government spending and $T_t$ as the value of taxes. Assuming that the government maintains a balanced budget between periods, its budget constraint is the same as described by Eq. (4.16).

The consumer, in turn, chooses the intertemporal consumption allocation so as to maximize its utility as represented in Eq. (5.13),[15] subject to a budget constraint, as in Eq. (4.17). Solving the problem of intertemporal consumption allocation, it is easy to verify that, in the case where $(1 + i^*)\beta = 1$, the private expenditure in each period is given by

$$P_1 C_1 = P_2 C_2 = \frac{(1 + i^*)(Y_1 - G_1) + (Y_2 - G_2)}{2 + i^*},$$

(5.36)

where the current-account balance in the first period corresponds to

$$CA_1 = \frac{(Y_1 - Y_2) - (G_1 - G_2)}{2 + i^*}.$$

(5.37)

It is interesting to note that this current-account balance is equal to that resulting from the model with no nontradable goods, described in Eq. (4.20). This equation captures the **intertemporal impact of public spending**.

Another important element regarding the impact of government spending on the exchange rate is its composition between tradable and nontradable goods. Assume that a share $\alpha^g$ of the aggregate government spending $G_t$ is allocated on nontradable goods, so that

$$G_{Tt} = (1 - \alpha^g)G_t$$

and

$$G_{Nt} = \frac{\alpha^g G_t}{p_{Nt}},$$

where $G_{Tt}$ and $G_{Nt}$ represent the amount of tradable and nontradable goods consumed by the government.

The equilibrium condition in the market of nontradable goods should now include government expenditures with this type of good, as in

$$N_t = C_{Nt} + G_{Nt}$$
$$\Downarrow$$
$$N_t = \frac{\alpha}{p_{Nt}} \left[ \frac{(1 + i^*)(Y_1 - G_1) + (Y_2 - G_2)}{2 + i^*} \right] + \frac{\alpha^g G_t}{p_{Nt}},$$

(5.38)

---

[15] Notice that we did not include government spending in the utility function. This does not necessarily mean that public spending does not have an effect on welfare. We would obtain the same results in terms of consumer choices if we introduced government spending as an additive term in the utility function (5.10). The fundamental hypothesis that we make here is that spending does not have an impact on the choices related to private consumption.

which can be written as

$$N_t = \frac{\alpha}{p_{Nt}}\left[\frac{(1+i^*)Y_1 + Y_2}{2+i^*}\right] - \frac{\alpha}{p_{Nt}}\left[\frac{(1+i^*)G_1 + G_2}{2+i^*}\right] + \frac{\alpha^g G_t}{p_{Nt}}. \qquad (5.39)$$

**The intertemporal and the composition effects of public spending are captured in Eq. (5.39): the intertemporal effect results from the differences in the level of aggregate spending between the two periods, while the composition proceeds from the difference of the composition of government and private expenditures.** Notice that if the expenditures are equal between the two periods, $G_1 = G_2$, and if the portion spent by the government on nontradables is the same as in the private sector, $\alpha^g = \alpha$, the two effects are canceled and Eq. (5.39) is transformed into Eq. (5.20) which determines the price of nontradables in the absence of government.

### 5.3.4.1 The Intertemporal Effect of Government Spending

To understand the intertemporal effect, we will consider the composition of government spending as the same as the private sector, i.e., $\alpha^g = \alpha$, and see the impact of different spending across periods. Equation (5.39) for each period can be written as

$$p_{N1} = \frac{\alpha}{N_1}\left[\frac{(1+i^*)Y_1 + Y_2}{2+i^*}\right] + \frac{\alpha}{N_1}\left[\frac{G_1 - G_2}{2+i^*}\right],$$

$$p_{N2} = \frac{\alpha}{N_2}\left[\frac{(1+i^*)Y_1 + Y_2}{2+i^*}\right] - \frac{\alpha}{N_2}\left[\frac{(1+i^*)(G_1 - G_2)}{2+i^*}\right].$$

The first term of these two expressions corresponds to the nontradable market equilibrium equation when there is no government, such as in Eq. (5.20). Consequently, the sign of the second term indicates whether the equilibrium price of nonnegotiables will be greater or lesser than when in an economy with no government. **More precisely, relatively higher public spending in the first period leads to an appreciation of the real exchange in the first period and a depreciation in the second.**

Intuitively, relatively higher spending in the first period causes a reduction in the current-account balance, and smaller current-account balances are associated with a more appreciated RER. Analogously, reduced public spending in the second period leads to an increase in the current-account balance for that period, resulting in a depreciated real exchange rate.

### 5.3.4.2 The Composition Effect of Government Spending

Now, let us do an inverse exercise: we will maintain government spending constant between the periods, $G \equiv G_1 = G_2$, and allow its composition to differ from that of the private sector, $\alpha^g \neq \alpha$. Equation (5.39) therefore becomes

$$p_{Nt} = \frac{\alpha}{N1}\left[\frac{(1+i^*)Y_1 + Y_2}{2+i^*}\right] + \frac{(\alpha^g - \alpha)G}{N_t}.$$

As in the intertemporal effect, the first term of the previous equation is identical to the price equation without government (5.20). The impact of government depends on the sign in the second term of the equation.

**In general, governments spend a larger share on nontradables than the private sector**, given that an important part of government spending is with education and health, which are usually nontradable. In this case, with $\alpha^g > \alpha$, the second term is negative, which indicates that **government spending causes an appreciation of the real exchange rate**.

The intuition for the result is the following: to spend, the government must tax the private sector, reducing disposable income for private consumption. When the government spends relatively more on nontradables than the private sector, the reduction in consumption of nontradables by the private sector is less than the increase in consumption for this type of good by government. Thus, government spending causes an increase in the aggregate demand for nontradable goods, leading to an increase in their price.

**Summarizing, an increase in government spending tends to appreciate the real exchange, both by its intertemporal effect and by the composition effect, when a greater portion of public spending is on nontradable goods.**

## 5.3.5 Differences in Productivity: The Balassa–Samuelson Effect

A common explanation for changes in equilibrium RER is based on the differences in productivity between countries. This is the famous **Balassa–Samuelson effect, which states that the RER tends to appreciate when there is an increase in the tradable sector productivity in relation to the nontradable sector of a country in relation to the rest of the world**.

This is one more case where the equilibrium RER varies due to a change in the relationship between the current account and the RER. On the one hand, an increase in productivity that is not the same across sectors alters the supply functions. In particular, the supply of tradable goods as a function of relative prices, $T_t(P_{Nt})$, changes, modifying, thereby, the trade balance function $TB_t(P_{Nt})$, and, consequently, the current account as a function of the relative price of nontradables $CA_t(P_{Nt})$. On the other hand, when there is also an increase in productivity in the foreign country, its relative price of nontradables changes. According to Eq. (5.3), a variation in the price of nontradables in the foreign country changes the relationship between the RER and this price in the domestic country.

To understand the Balassa–Samuelson effect by means of our model, we assume that all economic parameters are the same in both periods, as well as the resources endowment $\overline{Y}_1 = \overline{Y}_2$. As we previously showed in the analysis of an income shock, in equilibrium, the relative price of nontradable goods is the same as the one in autarky, as defined by Eq. (5.23).[16]

---

[16] In this case, the country neither lends nor borrows by its own choice since income is constant over time. In this way, the equilibrium price of nontradables comes to be the same as the price in. Notice, however, that a temporary income shock would affect the relative price of nontradables with an open economy, as we saw before, while in autarky the price would remain the same, regardless of the relative income between periods.

Assuming that the economic parameters are also equal across periods in the foreign country, and assuming, as we did before, that preferences are equal between the two countries, Eq. (5.23) results in

$$Q = \left(\frac{a_T^*/a_N^*}{a_T/a_N}\right)^{\alpha}. \tag{5.40}$$

We want to know how variations in productivity in the two sectors and in the two countries affect the equilibrium RER. A quite simple means to do the calculation based on Eq. (5.40) is by taking the natural logarithm from both sides of the equation and, next, totally differentiate the equation, taking the coefficient $\alpha$ as constant, as done in the Mathematical Appendix. We arrive at

$$\dot{Q} = \alpha[(\dot{a}_T^* - \dot{a}_N^*) - (\dot{a}_T - \dot{a}_N)], \tag{5.41}$$

where

$$\dot{x} \equiv \frac{dx}{x}.$$

Equation (5.41) concludes that

$$\dot{Q} < 0 \Leftrightarrow \dot{a}_T - \dot{a}_N > \dot{a}_T^* - \dot{a}_N^*. \tag{5.42}$$

In other words, **there is an appreciation of the real exchange when the increase in productivity for the tradable sector in relation to the nontradable is greater in the home country in relation to the foreign country** (Box 5.1).

## 5.3.6 Terms of Trade

The *terms of trade* is measured by the ratio between the prices of exported and imported goods. **An increase, or an improvement, in the terms of trade, therefore, means that there has been an increase in the average price of exported products in relation to imported**. To study the effect of the terms of trade, it is necessary to distinguish the tradable goods between those that are exported and those that are imported. We will then have three goods in the economy: exportables, importables, and nontradables. The production possibilities frontier becomes[17]

$$\left[\left(\frac{X}{a_X}\right)^{\rho} + \left(\frac{M}{a_M}\right)^{\rho} + \left(\frac{N}{a_N}\right)^{\rho}\right]^{\frac{1}{\rho}} = \overline{Y}.$$

[17] Notice that, on this production possibilities frontier, the elasticity of transformation between any two of the three types of goods is constant and equal to the elasticity of transformation between tradables and nontradables in Eq. (5.4).

---

**BOX 5.1 DUTCH DISEASE**

The exploration of new natural resources can be captured in this model as a simultaneous increase of the resources endowment $\overline{Y}$ and of the productivity of the tradable goods sector $a_T$, given that the new natural resources represent greater global production, but that is biased in favor of tradable goods. According to the inequality indicated in Eq. (5.42), the increase in relative productivity of the tradable sector causes an appreciation of the RER.

We can think of tradable goods as a basket of goods that not only includes natural resources but also manufactured goods. The appreciation of the exchange rate caused by the exploration of new natural resources discourages the production of tradables in general, among them manufactured goods. Consequently, **the exploration of natural resources can lead to the deindustrialization of a country in a phenomenon known as the *Dutch Disease*.** The term was coined in reference to the industrial decline in the Dutch economy after the discovery of large natural gas reserves in the country at the end of the 1950s.

---

Solving the producer problem of GDP maximization, subject to the production possibilities frontier in the previous equation, we have that the supply of each of the goods can be written as[18]

$$X = \overline{Y}\left(\frac{p_X a_T^{\rho}}{\prod(p_N)}\right)^{\frac{1}{\rho-1}}, \quad M = \overline{Y}\left(\frac{a_T^{\rho}}{\prod(p_N)}\right)^{\frac{1}{\rho-1}}, \quad N = \overline{Y}\left(\frac{p_N a_N^{\rho}}{\prod(p_N)}\right)^{\frac{1}{\rho-1}},$$  (5.43)

where $\overline{\prod}(p_N) \equiv \left[(p_X a_N)^{\frac{\rho}{\rho-1}} + a_T^{\frac{\rho}{\rho-1}} + (p_N a_N)^{\frac{\rho}{\rho-1}}\right]^{\frac{\rho-1}{\rho}}$, and $p_X$ is the price of exportable goods. Notice that we take the price of the importable good as being equal to one, so that $p_X$ corresponds to the term of trade, that is, the price of the exportable good in relation to the importable.

The equilibrium price of the nontradables, which was given by Eq. (5.21), is now determined by

$$p_{Nt} = \left(\frac{\alpha}{1-\alpha}\right)\left[\frac{(1+i^*)(p_X X_1 + M_1) + (p_X X_2 + M_2)}{N_t(2+i^*)}\right],$$

where we assume that the price of exportable goods is the same for both periods. Using the supply functions (5.43), the previous equation can be written as

$$p_{Nt} = p_N = \frac{\left[(p_X a_N)^{\frac{\rho}{\rho-1}} + (a_M)^{\frac{\rho-1}{\rho}}\right]^{\frac{\rho-1}{\rho}}}{a_N}\left(\frac{\alpha}{1-\alpha}\right)^{\frac{\rho-1}{\rho}},$$  (5.44)

assuming that the production possibilities frontier parameters do not change over time, as we did in the previous section.

---

[18] The solution to this optimization problem is analogous to that solved in Section 5.2 and will be covered later in the exercises given for the chapter.

To simplify the analysis, let us assume there are only two countries: the home country and the foreign. The consumer preferences are identical in the two countries, but they differ in relation to the production possibilities frontier parameters. More specifically, they differ in the productivity parameters.

In the foreign country, the price of nontradables is given by

$$
p_N^* = \frac{\left[(p_X a)^{\frac{\rho}{\rho-1}} + (a_M^*)^{\frac{\rho-1}{\rho}}\right]^{\frac{\rho-1}{\rho}}}{a_N^*} \left(\frac{\alpha}{1-\alpha}\right)^{\frac{\rho-1}{\rho}}.
\tag{5.45}
$$

Notice that in the foreign country, good X is imported, and good M is exported. For the home country to export good X and import good M, it needs to have a comparative advantage in the production of good X: its production of X should be relatively greater than the production of M in relation to the foreign country.[19] Stated differently, it is necessary that

$$
\frac{a_X}{a_M} > \frac{a_X^*}{a_M^*}.
\tag{5.46}
$$

As we will see, this relation is essential to identify the effect of terms of trade variations on the RER.

Substituting the prices of nontradables in the two countries, Eqs. (5.44) and (5.45), into the RER equation (5.3), we have that[20]

$$
\begin{aligned}
Q &= \left[\frac{(p_X a_X^*)^{\frac{\rho}{\rho-1}} + (a_M^*)^{\frac{\rho-1}{\rho}}}{(p_X a_X)^{\frac{\rho}{\rho-1}} + (a_M)^{\frac{\rho-1}{\rho}}}\right]^{\frac{\rho-1}{\rho}} \frac{a_N}{a_N^*} \\
&= \left[\frac{(p_X a_X^*)^{\frac{\rho}{\rho-1}} + 1}{(p_X a_X)^{\frac{\rho}{\rho-1}} + 1}\right]^{\frac{\rho-1}{\rho}} \frac{a_M a_N}{a_M^* a_N^*}
\end{aligned}
\tag{5.47}
$$

It is easy to verify that, given the inequality (5.46), **a permanent increase in the terms of trade, $p_X$, causes an appreciation of the RER**: $\frac{\partial Q}{\partial x} < 0$. Intuitively, an improvement in the terms of trade means, *grosso modo*, an increase in the real income for the country. A greater

---

[19] This statement is true under the assumption that consumer preferences are equal in both countries.

[20] To be more precise, the price index now includes three goods, and can be written as $P = p_N^\alpha p_X^{\alpha_X}$, where $\alpha_X$ is the share of expenditures spent on exportable goods. The RER will then be $Q = \frac{p_N^{*\alpha} p_X^{\alpha_X}}{p_N^\alpha p_X^{\alpha_X}} = \left(\frac{p_N^*}{p_N}\right)^\alpha$, where we assume that $S = 1$.

income implies more consumption, therefore an increase in the relative price of nontradables to rebalance the market of this good.

Notice that, since we assume the relative price of exportable goods is the same for both periods, the increase in the terms of trade is also the same for both periods. This assumption causes the terms of trade variation to not affect the relative disposable income between the two periods, so that it does not have an impact on the current-account balance. The exchange rate appreciation occurs because the terms of trade alter the relation between the current-account balance and the real exchange rate. **More specifically, improvement in the terms of trade causes an increase in the trade balance for a given RER. Therefore, to maintain the trade balance and, consequently, a constant current account, there should be an appreciation of the RER.**

Temporary changes in the terms of trade would, therefore, have an additional impact on the equilibrium current-account level. An improvement in the terms of trade represents an increase in domestic purchasing power. If the improvement is temporary, the effect on the current account is equivalent to a positive and temporary income shock (see Section 4.2): it causes an increase in the current-account balance. Greater current-account balances are associated with a more depreciated exchange, in this way mitigating the appreciation resulting from the direct impact on relative prices captured by Eq. (5.47) (Box 5.2).

---

### BOX 5.2 EMPIRICAL STUDIES ON EQUILIBRIUM REAL EXCHANGE RATES

There is extensive and evolving empirical literature on the estimation of equilibrium exchange rates (EERs), which has generated several new creative acronyms. Among the different empirical approaches, there are CHEERs (capital enhanced EERs), ITMEERs (intermediate term model based EERs), BEERs (behavioral EERs), FEERS (fundamental EERs), DEERs (desired EERs), APEERs (theoretical permanent EERs), and PEERs (permanent EERs), whose description can be found in MacDonald (2000) and Driver and Westaway (2005). The models differ basically on the exchange rate definition they use, the time frame they envisage, and the way they model the dynamics.

CHEERs and ITMEERs focus on nominal exchange rate estimations. Both methods consider the financial dimension, which involves combining the purchasing power parity to the uncovered interest parity. ITMEERs add fundamentals to the estimation, such as the economic variables discussed in this chapter, to capture expected future movements in real exchange rates. BEER estimations focus on effective real exchange rates, using interest rate differentials and economic fundamentals as explanatory variables. Theoretically, they are based on the uncovered interest parity condition, where economic fundamentals are used to control for expectations of RER changes. All three of them, CHEERs, ITMEERs, and BEERs, are more closely related to short-term equilibrium.

FEERs and DEERs, on their turn, have a more medium-term perspective. They do not estimate equilibrium RER directly. They concentrate on estimating either complete macroeconomic models or simply current accounts, resulting in a RER consistent with medium term equilibria. APEERs and PEERs also focus on RER, but they are concerned with medium to long run equilibrium values.

# Mathematical Appendix

**Computing the marginal rate of transformation in** Eq. (5.5): The marginal rate of transformation between $N$ in $T$ is defined as how much more of tradable goods can be manufactured, when producing one unit less of nontradables, satisfying the economic resources restriction. In mathematical terms, we can write it as $\frac{dT}{dN}\big|_{\overline{Y}}$, that is, the derivative of $T$ with respect to $N$, under the restriction of remaining in the production possibilities frontier. To calculate it, we use the implicit function theorem in Eq. (5.4):

$$\frac{dT}{dN}\bigg|_{\overline{Y}} = -\frac{\partial \overline{Y}/\partial N}{\partial \overline{Y}/\partial T}$$

$$= -\frac{\dfrac{1}{\rho}\left[\left(\dfrac{T}{a_T}\right)^\rho + \left(\dfrac{N}{a_N}\right)^\rho\right]^{\frac{1}{\rho}-1}\left(\dfrac{\rho}{a_N^\rho}\right)N^{\rho-1}}{\dfrac{1}{\rho}\left[\left(\dfrac{T}{a_T}\right)^\rho + \left(\dfrac{N}{a_N}\right)^\rho\right]^{\frac{1}{\rho}-1}\left(\dfrac{\rho}{a_T^\rho}\right)T^{\rho-1}},$$

which simplified becomes

$$\frac{dT}{dN}\bigg|_{\overline{Y}} = -\frac{a_T^\rho T^{\rho-1}}{a_N^\rho N^{\rho-1}} = -\left(\frac{a_T}{a_N}\right)^\rho \left(\frac{N}{T}\right)^{\rho-1}.$$

**Solution to the Producer Problem**: The producer problem optimization can be written as follows:

$$\text{Max } Y_{\{T,N\}} = T + p_N N$$

$$\text{subject to: } \overline{Y} = \left[\left(\frac{T}{a_T}\right)^\rho + \left(\frac{N}{a_N}\right)^\rho\right]^{\frac{1}{\rho}}.$$

To solve the problem we write the lagrangian function as

$$\mathcal{L} = T + p_N N - \lambda\left\{\left[\left(\frac{T}{a_T}\right)^\rho + \left(\frac{N}{a_N}\right)^\rho\right]^{\frac{1}{\rho}} - \overline{Y}\right\},$$

where $\lambda$ is the lagrangian multiplier. The point of maximum is that for which the derivatives of the lagrangian function with respect to the choice variables, $T$ and $N$, and the lagrangian multiplier, $\lambda$, are equal to zero. The first-order conditions for maximization are, therefore:

$$[T]\colon \frac{\partial \mathcal{L}}{\partial T} = 0 \Rightarrow 1 - \lambda\left[\left(\frac{T}{a_T}\right)^\rho + \left(\frac{N}{a_N}\right)^\rho\right]^{\frac{1}{\rho}-1}\left(\frac{T}{a_T}\right)^{\rho-1}\frac{1}{a_T} = 0 \Rightarrow$$

$$\lambda = a_T^\rho T^{1-\rho}\overline{Y}^{\rho-1} \text{ or } T = \overline{Y}\left(\frac{a_T^\rho}{\lambda}\right)^{\frac{1}{\rho-1}}$$

(5.48)

$$[N]: \frac{\partial \mathcal{L}}{\partial N} = 0 \Rightarrow p_N - \lambda \left[ \left( \frac{T}{a_T} \right)^\rho + \left( \frac{N}{a_N} \right)^\rho \right]^{\frac{1}{\rho} - 1} \left( \frac{N}{a_N} \right)^{\rho - 1} \frac{1}{a_N} = 0 \Rightarrow$$

(5.49)

$$\lambda = p_N a_N^\rho N^{1-\rho} \overline{Y}^{\rho-1} \quad \text{or} \quad N = \overline{Y} \left( \frac{p_N a_N^\rho}{\lambda} \right)^{\frac{1}{\rho-1}}$$

$$[\lambda]: \frac{\partial \mathcal{L}}{\partial \lambda} = 0 \Rightarrow \left[ \left( \frac{T}{a_T} \right)^\rho + \left( \frac{N}{a_N} \right)^\rho \right]^{\frac{1}{\rho}} - \overline{Y} = 0 \Rightarrow$$

(5.50)

$$\left[ \left( \frac{T}{a_T} \right)^\rho + \left( \frac{N}{a_N} \right)^\rho \right]^{\frac{1}{\rho}} = \overline{Y}.$$

Notice that by combining Eqs. (5.48) and (5.49), we have that, as in the graphic solution, the slope of the production possibilities frontier is equal to the relative price of goods:

$$\frac{a_N^\rho T^{\rho-1}}{a_T^\rho N^{\rho-1}} = p_N.$$

However, to algebraically solve the problem, it is easier to follow another path. Equations (5.48) and (5.49) define $T$ and $N$ as a function of $\lambda$. Substituting these functions into Eq. (5.50), we find the value of $\lambda$, which is equal to

$$\lambda = \left[ a_T^{\frac{\rho}{\rho-1}} + (p_N a_N)^{\frac{\rho}{\rho-1}} \right]^{\frac{\rho}{\rho-1}} \equiv \Pi(p_N).$$

(5.51a)

Substituting Eq. (5.48) into Eqs. (5.48) and (5.49), we obtain the following supply functions:

$$T = \overline{Y} \left( \frac{a_T^\rho}{\Pi(p_N)} \right)^{\frac{1}{\rho-1}} \quad \text{and}$$

(5.51b)

$$N = \overline{Y} \left( \frac{p_N a_N^\rho}{\Pi(p_N)} \right)^{\frac{1}{\rho-1}}.$$

(5.51c)

**Solution to the Consumer Intertemporal Problem**: The representative consumer chooses how much to consume each period so as to maximize its utility, subject to budget constraint, as in

$$\text{Max } U_{i[C_1, C_2]} = \ln(C_1) + \beta \ln(C_2)$$

$$\text{subject to: } P_1 C_1 + \frac{P_2 C_2}{1 + i^*} = Y_1 + \frac{Y_2}{1 + i^*}$$

We write the lagrangian function for this problem as

$$\mathcal{L} = \ln C_1 + \beta \ln C_2 - \lambda \left\{ P_1 C_1 + \frac{P_2 C_2}{1 + i^*} - \left( Y_1 + \frac{Y_2}{1 + i^*} \right) \right\},$$

where $\lambda$ is the lagrangian multiplier. The first-order conditions associated to the maximization of the lagrangian function are given by

$$[C_1]: \frac{\partial \mathcal{L}}{\partial C_1} = 0 \Rightarrow u'(C_1) - \lambda P_1 = 0 \Rightarrow$$

$$\lambda = \frac{u'(C_1)}{P_1} \tag{5.52}$$

$$[C_2]: \frac{\partial \mathcal{L}}{\partial C_2} = 0 \Rightarrow \beta u'(C_2) - \frac{\lambda P_2}{1 + i^*} = 0 \Rightarrow$$

$$\lambda = \frac{\beta u'(C_2)(1 + i^*)}{P_2} \tag{5.53}$$

$$[\lambda]: \frac{\partial \mathcal{L}}{\partial \lambda} = 0 \Rightarrow Y_1 + \frac{Y_2}{1 + i^*} - P_1 C_1 - \frac{P_2 C_2}{1 + i^*} = 0 \Rightarrow$$

$$P_1 C_1 + \frac{P_2 C_2}{1 + i^*} = Y_1 + \frac{Y_2}{1 + i^*}. \tag{5.54}$$

Combining Eqs. (5.52) and (5.53), we obtain the Euler equation:

$$u'(C_1) = \frac{P_1}{P_2}(1 + i^*)\beta u'(C_2), \tag{5.55}$$

where the only difference in relation to the corresponding condition in Eq. (4.5) is that now we take into consideration possible price variations across periods.

Computing the derivatives $u'(C_1)$, we have that

$$P_1 C_1 = \frac{P_2 C_2}{(1 + i^*)\beta}. \tag{5.56}$$

Substituting into the budget constraint, we obtain

$$\frac{P_2 C_2}{(1 + i^*)\beta} + P_2 C_2 = Y_1 + \frac{Y_2}{1 + i^*},$$

which, by rearranging the terms, results in

$$P_2 C_2 = \frac{(1 + i^*)\beta}{1 + \beta}\left[Y_1 + \frac{Y_2}{1 + i^*}\right].$$

Substituting this result into Eq. (5.56), we have that

$$P_1 C_1 = \frac{1}{1 + \beta}\left[Y_1 + \frac{Y_2}{1 + i^*}\right].$$

Finally, assuming that $(1 + i)\beta = 1$, the expenditure will be equal in both periods:

$$P_1 C_1 = P_2 C_2 = \frac{(1 + i^*)Y_1 + Y_2}{2 + i^*}. \tag{5.57}$$

**Solution to the Consumer Intratemporal Problem**: The problem of the intratemporal allocation of consumption between tradable and nontradable goods can be mathematically represented as

$$\text{Max } C_{t\{C_1, C_2\}} = C_{Tt}^{1-\alpha} C_{Nt}^{\alpha}$$

$$\text{subject to: } C_{Tt} + p_{Nt} C_{Nt} = P_t C_t.$$

To solve this problem, we write the lagrangian function for each $t, t = \{1, 2\}$:

$$\mathcal{L}_t = C_{Tt}^{1-\alpha} C_{Nt}^{\alpha} - \mu_t\{C_{Tt} + p_{Nt} C_{Nt} - P_t C_t\},$$

where $\mu_t$ is the lagrangian multiplier associated with the budget constraint. The first-order conditions for maximization are given by

$$[C_{Tt}]: \frac{\partial \mathcal{L}}{\partial C_{Tt}} = 0 \Rightarrow (1 - \alpha) C_{Tt}^{1-\alpha} C_{Nt}^{\alpha} - \mu_t = 0 \Rightarrow$$

$$(1 - \alpha) \left(\frac{C_{Nt}}{C_{Tt}}\right)^{\alpha} = \mu_t, \tag{5.58}$$

$$[C_{Nt}]: \frac{\partial \mathcal{L}}{\partial C_{Nt}} = 0 \Rightarrow \alpha C_{Tt}^{1-\alpha} C_{Nt}^{\alpha} - \mu_t p_{Nt} = 0 \Rightarrow$$

$$\alpha \left(\frac{C_{Nt}}{C_{Tt}}\right)^{1-\alpha} = \mu_t p_{Nt}, \tag{5.59}$$

$$[\mu_t]: \frac{\partial \mathcal{L}}{\partial \mu_t} = 0 \Rightarrow C_{Tt} + p_{Nt} C_{Nt} - P_t C_t = 0 \Rightarrow$$

$$C_{Tt} + p_{Nt} C_{Nt} = P_t C_t. \tag{5.60}$$

Combining Eqs. (5.58) and (5.59), we obtain the following contemporaneous relation between $C_{Tt}$ and $C_{Nt}$:

$$C_{Tt} = \left(\frac{\alpha}{1 - \alpha}\right) p_{Nt} C_{Nt}. \tag{5.61}$$

Finally, substituting Eq. (5.61) into the budget constraint (5.60), we obtain the final demands for tradable and nontradable goods in period $t$:

$$C_{Tt} = (1 - \alpha) P_t C_t \text{ and} \tag{5.62}$$

$$p_{Nt} C_{Nt} = \alpha P_t C_t. \tag{5.63}$$

**Development of** Eq. (5.21): Based on the market equilibrium condition of nontradable goods, $N_t = C_{Nt}$, and taking into account that the value of production is constant in the two periods $N_1 = N_2 = N$, we have

$$N = \frac{\alpha}{p_{Nt}}\left[\frac{(1+i^*)Y_1 + Y_2}{2+i^*}\right] \Rightarrow N = \frac{\alpha}{p_{Nt}}\left[\frac{(1+i^*)(T_1 + p_{Nt}N) + T_2 + p_{Nt}N}{2+i^*}\right] \Rightarrow$$

$$N = \frac{\alpha}{p_{Nt}}\left[p_{Nt}N + \frac{(1+i^*)T_1 + T_2}{2+i^*}\right].$$

Solving for $p_{Nt}$, we have that

$$N_t p_{Nt} - \alpha p_{Nt}N = \alpha\left[\frac{(1+i^*)T_1 + T_2}{2+i^*}\right] \Rightarrow p_{Nt} = \frac{\alpha}{N_t(1-\alpha)}\left[\frac{(1+i^*)T_1 + T_2}{2+i^*}\right].$$

**Development of** Eq. (5.23): In autarky, the total expenditure of individuals should be equal to the total income, i.e., $P_t C_t = \overline{Y}_t \prod_t(p_{Nt})$. In this way, the demand for the nontradable good will be given by $C_{Nt} = \frac{\alpha}{p_{Nt}}P_t C_t \Rightarrow C_{Nt} = \frac{\alpha}{p_{Nt}}\overline{Y}_t\prod_t(p_{Nt})$. The market equilibrium condition for the nontradable good will be given as $N_t = C_{Nt} = \frac{\alpha}{p_{Nt}}\overline{Y}_t\prod_t(p_{Nt})$. Substituting the value of $N_t$ with Eq. (5.7b), we have that

$$\overline{Y}_t = \left(\frac{p_{Nt}^A a_N^\rho}{\prod_t(p_{Nt}^A)}\right)^{\frac{1}{1-\rho}} = \overline{Y}_t\prod_t(p_{Nt}^A)\frac{\alpha}{p_{Nt}^A} \Rightarrow p_{Nt}^A = \left[a_N^{\frac{1}{\rho-1}}\alpha(\prod_t(p_{Nt}^A))^{\frac{\rho}{\rho-1}}\right]^{\frac{\rho}{\rho-1}} \Rightarrow$$

$$p_{Nt}^A = \frac{1}{a_N}a_N^{\frac{\rho}{\rho-1}}\prod_t(p_{Nt}^A).$$

Substituting $\Pi(p_N)$ as defined by Eq. (5.8), we have that

$$p_{Nt}^A = \frac{1}{a_N}a_N^{\frac{\rho}{\rho-1}}\left[a_T^{\frac{\rho}{\rho-1}} + (p_{Nt}^A a_N)^{\frac{\rho}{\rho-1}}\right]^{\frac{\rho}{\rho-1}} \Rightarrow p_{Nt}^A = \frac{1}{a_N}\left\{\alpha\left[a_T^{\frac{\rho}{\rho-1}} + (p_{Nt}^A a_N)^{\frac{\rho}{\rho-1}}\right]\right\}^{\frac{\rho}{\rho-1}} \Rightarrow$$

$$(a_N p_{Nt}^A)^{\frac{\rho}{\rho-1}}(1-\alpha) = \alpha a_T^{\frac{\rho}{\rho-1}} \Rightarrow p_{Nt}^A = \left(\frac{a_{Tt}}{a_{Nt}}\right)\left(\frac{\alpha}{1-\alpha}\right)^{\frac{\rho-1}{\rho}}.$$

**Development of** Eq. (5.28): Substituting Eqs. (5.7a) and (5.7b) into Eq. (5.21), we obtain

$$p_{N1} = \left(\frac{\alpha}{1-\alpha}\right)\left[\frac{(1+i^*)\overline{Y}_1\left(\frac{a_T^\rho}{\prod_1(p_{N1})}\right)^{\frac{1}{\rho-1}} + \overline{Y}_2\left(\frac{a_T^\rho}{\prod_2(p_{N2})}\right)^{\frac{1}{\rho-1}}}{\overline{Y}_1\left(\frac{p_{N1}a_N^\rho}{\prod_1(p_{N1})}\right)^{\frac{1}{\rho-1}}(2+i^*)}\right] \Rightarrow$$

$$p_{N1}^{\frac{\rho}{\rho-1}} = \left(\frac{\alpha}{1-\alpha}\right)\left(\frac{a_T}{a_N}\right)^{\frac{\rho}{\rho-1}}\left[\frac{(1+i^*)\overline{Y}_1\left(\frac{1}{\prod_1(p_{N1})}\right)^{\frac{1}{\rho-1}} + \overline{Y}_2\left(\frac{1}{\prod_2(p_{N2})}\right)^{\frac{1}{\rho-1}}}{\overline{Y}_1\left(\frac{1}{\prod_1(p_{N1})}\right)^{\frac{1}{\rho-1}}(2+i^*)}\right] \Rightarrow$$

$$p_{N1}^{\frac{\rho}{\rho-1}} = \left(\frac{\alpha}{1-\alpha}\right)\left(\frac{a_T}{a_N}\right)^{\frac{\rho}{\rho-1}}\left[\frac{(1+i^*)}{(2+i^*)} + \frac{1}{(2+i^*)}\left(\frac{\overline{Y}_1}{\overline{Y}_2}\right)\left(\frac{\prod_1(p_{N1})}{\prod_2(p_{N2})}\right)^{\frac{1}{\rho-1}}\right] \Rightarrow$$

$$p_{N1}^{\frac{\rho}{\rho-1}} = \left(\frac{\alpha}{1-\alpha}\right)\left(\frac{a_T}{a_N}\right)^{\frac{\rho}{\rho-1}}\left\{\frac{(1+i^*) + \left(\frac{\overline{Y}_1}{\overline{Y}_2}\right)\left(\frac{\prod_1(p_{N1})}{\prod_2(p_{N2})}\right)^{\frac{1}{\rho-1}}}{(2+i^*)}\right\}.$$

**Development of** Eq. (5.29): Adopting the analogous procedure as used in the development of Eq. (5.28), we have

$$p_{N2} = \left(\frac{\alpha}{1-\alpha}\right)\left[\frac{(1+i^*)\overline{Y}_1\left(\frac{a_T^\rho}{\prod_1(p_{N1})}\right)^{\frac{1}{\rho-1}} + \overline{Y}_2\left(\frac{a_T^\rho}{\prod_2(p_{N2})}\right)^{\frac{1}{\rho-1}}}{\overline{Y}_2\left(\frac{p_{N2}a_N^\rho}{\prod_2(p_{N2})}\right)^{\frac{1}{\rho-1}}(2+i^*)}\right] \Rightarrow$$

$$p_{N2}^{\frac{\rho}{\rho-1}} = \left(\frac{\alpha}{1-\alpha}\right)\left(\frac{a_T}{a_N}\right)^{\frac{\rho}{\rho-1}}\left\{\frac{(1+i^*)\left[\left(\frac{\overline{Y}_1}{\overline{Y}_2}\right)\left(\frac{\Pi(p_{N2})}{\Pi(p_{N1})}\right)^{\frac{1}{\rho-1}}\right] + 1}{(2+i^*)}\right\}.$$

**Development of** Eq. (5.32): From Eq. (5.30), we have that

$$\left(\frac{p_{N1}}{p_{N2}}\right)^{\frac{\rho}{\rho-1}} = \left(\frac{\overline{Y}_2}{\overline{Y}_1}\right)\left(\frac{\prod_1(p_{N1})}{\prod_2(p_{N2})}\right)^{\frac{1}{\rho-1}}.$$

Substituting the previous equation into Eq. (5.28), we arrive at

$$p_{N1}^{\frac{\rho}{\rho-1}} = \left(\frac{\alpha}{1-\alpha}\right)\left(\frac{a_T}{a_N}\right)^{\frac{\rho}{\rho-1}}\left\{\frac{(1+i^*) + \left(\frac{p_{N1}}{p_{N2}}\right)^{\frac{\rho}{\rho-1}}}{(2+i^*)}\right\}.$$

Equation (5.23) can be rewritten as

$$(p_{N1}^A)^{\frac{\rho}{\rho-1}} = \left(\frac{a_T}{a_N}\right)^{\frac{\rho}{\rho-1}} \left(\frac{\alpha}{1-\alpha}\right),$$

which we substitute into the previous equation to get

$$p_{N1}^{\frac{\rho}{\rho-1}} = (p_{N1}^A)^{\frac{\rho}{\rho-1}} \left\{ \frac{1+i^* + \left(\frac{p_{N1}}{p_{N2}}\right)^{\frac{\rho}{\rho-1}}}{2+i^*} \right\}.$$

**Development of** Eq. (5.33): Taking the derivative of Eq. (5.32) with respect to $i^*$, we obtain

$$\frac{\partial p_{N1}}{\partial i^*} = p_N^A \left(\frac{\rho}{\rho-1}\right) \left\{ \left(\frac{1+i^*}{2+i^*}\right) + \frac{(p_{N1}/p_{N2})^{\frac{\rho}{\rho-1}}}{2+i^*} \right\}^{-\frac{1}{\rho}} \left\{ \left[ \frac{(2+i^*) - (1+i^*)}{(2+i^*)^2} \right. \right.$$

$$\left. \left. + \frac{\frac{\partial}{\partial i^*}\left[(p_{N1}/p_{N2})^{\frac{\rho}{\rho-1}}\right](2+i^*) - (p_{N1}/p_{N2})^{\frac{\rho}{\rho-1}}}{(2+i^*)^2} \right] \right\}.$$

But, notice that Eq. (5.32) can be written as

$$p_{N1}^{-\frac{1}{\rho-1}} = (p_N^A)^{-\frac{1}{\rho-1}} \left\{ \frac{1+i^* + \left(\frac{p_{N1}}{p_{N2}}\right)^{\frac{\rho}{\rho-1}}}{2+i^*} \right\}^{\frac{1}{\rho}}.$$

Multiplying both sides of the previous equation by $(p_N^A)^{\frac{1}{\rho-1}}$ we arrive at

$$(p_N^A)^{\frac{1}{\rho-1}} p_{N1}^{-\frac{1}{\rho-1}} = \left\{ \frac{1+i^* + \left(\frac{p_{N1}}{p_{N2}}\right)^{\frac{\rho}{\rho-1}}}{2+i^*} \right\}^{-\frac{1}{\rho}}.$$

Substituting this expression in the main equation, we obtain

$$\frac{\partial p_{N1}}{\partial i^*} = p_{N1}^{-\frac{1}{\rho-1}}(p_N^A)^{\frac{\rho}{\rho-1}}\left(\frac{\rho}{\rho-1}\right)\left(\frac{1-(p_{N1}/p_{N2})^{\frac{\rho}{\rho-1}}}{(2+i^*)^2} + \frac{\frac{\partial}{\partial i^*}\left[(p_{N1}/p_{N2})^{\frac{\rho}{\rho-1}}\right]}{2+i^*}\right).$$

**Development of** Eq. (5.34): Deriving the quotient $p_{N1}/p_{N2}$ with respect to $i^*$, we obtain

$$\frac{\partial}{\partial i^*}\left[(p_{N1}/p_{N2})^{\frac{-\rho}{\rho-1}}\right] = \left(\frac{\rho}{\rho-1}\right)\left(\frac{p_{N1}}{p_{N2}}\right)^{\frac{1}{\rho-1}}\left(\frac{\frac{\partial p_{N1}}{\partial i^*}p_{N2} - p_{N1}\frac{\partial p_{N2}}{\partial i^*}}{(p_{N2})^2}\right)$$

$$= \left(\frac{\rho}{\rho-1}\right)\left(\frac{p_{N1}}{p_{N2}}\right)^{\frac{1}{\rho-1}}\left(\frac{\frac{\partial p_{N1}}{\partial i^*}}{p_{N2}} - \frac{p_{N1}\frac{\partial p_{N2}}{\partial i^*}}{(p_{N2})^2}\right) \Rightarrow$$

$$\frac{\partial}{\partial i^*}\left[(p_{N1}/p_{N2})^{\frac{-\rho}{\rho-1}}\right] = \left(\frac{\rho}{\rho-1}\right)\left(\frac{p_{N1}}{p_{N2}}\right)^{\frac{1}{\rho-1}}\left(\frac{p_{N1}}{p_{N2}}\right)\left(\frac{\frac{\partial p_{N1}}{\partial i^*}}{p_{N2}} - \frac{\frac{\partial p_{N2}}{\partial i^*}}{p_{N2}}\right) \Rightarrow$$

$$\frac{\partial}{\partial i^*}\left[(p_{N1}/p_{N2})^{\frac{-\rho}{\rho-1}}\right] = \left(\frac{\rho}{\rho-1}\right)\left(\frac{p_{N1}}{p_{N2}}\right)^{\frac{\rho}{\rho-1}}\left(\frac{\partial p_{N1}/\partial i^*}{p_{N1}} - \frac{\partial p_{N2}/\partial i^*}{p_{N2}}\right) \Rightarrow$$

**Development of** Eq. (5.35): Substituting Eq. (5.34) in Eq. (5.33), we arrive at

$$\frac{\partial p_{N1}}{\partial i^*} = p_{N1}^{-\frac{1}{\rho-1}}(p_N^A)^{\frac{1}{\rho-1}}\left(\frac{\rho}{\rho-1}\right)\left(\frac{1-(p_{N1}/p_{N2})^{\frac{\rho}{\rho-1}}}{(2+i^*)^2} + \frac{\left(\frac{\rho}{\rho-1}\right)\left(\frac{p_{N1}}{p_{N2}}\right)^{\frac{\rho}{\rho-1}}\left(\frac{\partial p_{N1}/\partial i^*}{p_{N1}} - \frac{\partial p_{N2}/\partial i^*}{p_{N2}}\right)}{2+i^*}\right).$$

Per Eq. (5.32), we obtain

$$\frac{\partial p_{N1}}{\partial i^*} = p_{N1}^{-\frac{1}{\rho-1}}(p_N^A)^{\frac{1}{\rho-1}}\left\{\frac{2+i^*}{(1+i^*) + \left(\frac{p_{N1}}{p_{N2}}\right)^{\frac{\rho}{\rho-1}}}\right\}\left(\frac{\rho}{\rho-1}\right)$$

$$\left(\frac{1-(p_{N1}/p_{N2})^{\frac{\rho}{\rho-1}}}{(2+i^*)^2} + \frac{\left(\frac{\rho}{\rho-1}\right)\left(\frac{p_{N1}}{p_{N2}}\right)^{\frac{\rho}{\rho-1}}\left(\frac{\partial p_{N1}/\partial i^*}{p_{N1}} - \frac{\partial p_{N2}/\partial i^*}{p_{N2}}\right)}{2+i^*}\right)$$

$$\frac{\partial p_{N1}}{\partial i^*} = \left\{ \frac{1}{(1+i^*) + \left(\frac{p_{N1}}{p_{N2}}\right)^{\frac{\rho}{\rho-1}}} \right\} \left(\frac{\rho}{\rho-1}\right) \left[\frac{1 - (p_{N1}/p_{N2})^{\frac{\rho}{\rho-1}}}{(2+i^*)^2}\right]$$

$$+ \left\{ \frac{1}{(1+i^*) + \left(\frac{p_{N1}}{p_{N2}}\right)^{\frac{\rho}{\rho-1}}} \right\} \left(\frac{p_{N1}}{p_{N2}}\right)^{\frac{\rho}{\rho-1}} \left(\frac{\partial p_{N1}/\partial i^*}{p_{N1}} - \frac{\partial p_{N2}/\partial i^*}{p_{N2}}\right) \Rightarrow$$

$$\frac{\partial p_{N1}}{\partial i^*} = \left[\left((1+i^*) + \left(\frac{p_{N1}}{p_{N2}}\right)^{\frac{\rho}{\rho-1}}\right) - \left(\frac{p_{N1}}{p_{N2}}\right)^{\frac{\rho}{\rho-1}}\right] = \left(\frac{\rho}{\rho-1}\right)\left[\frac{1 - (p_{N1}/p_{N2})^{\frac{\rho}{\rho-1}}}{(2+i^*)^2}\right] - \left(\frac{p_{N1}}{p_{N2}}\right)^{\frac{\rho}{\rho-1}} \frac{\partial p_{N2}/\partial i^*}{p_{N2}} \Rightarrow$$

$$(1+i^*)\frac{\partial p_{N1}/\partial i^*}{p_{N1}} + \left(\frac{p_{N1}}{p_{N2}}\right)^{\frac{\rho}{\rho-1}} \frac{\partial p_{N2}/\partial i^*}{p_{N2}} = \left(\frac{\rho}{\rho-1}\right)\left(\frac{1 - (p_{N1}/p_{N2})^{\frac{\rho}{\rho-1}}}{2+i^*}\right).$$

**Computing** Eq. (5.41):
Based on Eq. (5.40), repeated here:

$$Q = \left(\frac{a_T^*/a_N^*}{a_T/a_N}\right)^a,$$

we arrive at Eq. (5.41) in the following way. Taking the natural logarithm of the equation above, we get

$$\ln Q = \alpha[(\ln a_T^* - \ln a_N^*) - (\ln a_T - \ln a_N)].$$

Totally differentiating this equation, we arrive at

$$\frac{d \ln Q}{dQ} dQ = \alpha\left[\left(\frac{d \ln a_T^*}{d a_T^*} da_T^* - \frac{d \ln a_N^*}{d a_N^*} d a_N^*\right) - \left(\frac{d \ln a_T}{d a_T} d a_T - \frac{d \ln a_N}{d a_N} d a_N\right)\right],$$

which, using the fact that $\frac{d \ln X}{dX} = \frac{1}{X}$ for any variable $X$, can be written as

$$\frac{dQ}{Q} = \alpha\left[\left(\frac{da_T^*}{a_T^*} - \frac{da_N^*}{a_N^*}\right) - \left(\frac{da_T}{a_T} - \frac{da_N}{a_N}\right)\right].$$

We therefore arrive at Eq. (5.41), using the notation $\dot{x} \equiv \frac{dx}{x}$.

## 5.4 Exercises

### Exercise 1

Consider a small, open economy that exists for two periods. This economy has a representative agent who, in the first period, receives an endowment of 6 units of a tradable good ($Y_1^T$) and 9 units of a nontradable good ($Y_1^N$). In the second period, this agent receives 13.2 units of the tradable good and 9 units of the nontradable. At the beginning of period 1, the agent possesses neither credit nor debt, so that the net international investment position is $B_0 = 0$. This country has access to the international financial market, where the current interest rate is $i^* = 10\%$. The representative agent's preferences are given by

$$U(C_1^T, C_1^N, C_2^T, C_2^N) = \ln(C_1^T) + \ln(C_1^N) + \ln(C_2^T) + \ln(C_1^N),$$

where $C_t^T$ and $C_t^N$ represent the consumption of tradable and nontradable goods in period $t$, respectively, while $p_{Tt}$ and $p_{Nt}$ represent their prices.

**a.** Find the demand for tradable and nontradable goods in periods 1 and 2.
**b.** Find the net international investment position for period 1 ($B_1^*$).
**c.** For period 2, obtain the equilibrium current-account balance and the relative price of tradable goods in terms of the nontradable. Intuitively explain why $p_{Nt}$ changes over time.
**d.** Let the consumer price index, $P_t$, be defined as $P_t = \sqrt{p_{Tt}p_{Nt}}$. Similarly, let the consumer price index for a foreign economy be $P_t^* = \sqrt{p_{Tt}^*p_{Nt}^*}$, where the superscript $*$ represents the foreign variables. Nominal foreign prices are denominated in terms of the foreign currency. Assume that the purchasing power parity of tradable goods is valid. Finally, find the real interest rate between periods 1 and 2 that makes the relative price of nontradables in terms of tradables equal to 1 in both periods.

### Exercise 2

Consider an economic environment where there are two economies, a domestic and a foreign. Assume that the price levels in the domestic economy are given by $P = P_N^\alpha P_T^{1-\alpha}$, where $P_T$ represents the price of tradables and $P_N$ the price of nontradable goods. The price level in the foreign economy is given by $P^*$, where $P^* = P_N^{*\beta} P_T^{*1-\beta}$. In relation to the price indexes, we have that $\alpha, \beta \in (0, 1)$. The real exchange rate, designated by RER, is defined as $\text{RER} \equiv \frac{SP^*}{P}$, where S is the nominal exchange rate in terms of the domestic currency necessary to purchase one unit of foreign currency.

**a.** Show that, if the Law of One Price is valid for tradable goods and if the ratio $\frac{P_N^*}{P_T^*}$ is approximately constant, then changes in the real exchange rate are for the most part explained by changes in the ratio $\frac{P_N}{P_T}$. If the foreign economy is significantly developed, do you think it is reasonable to consider the hypothesis that $\frac{P_N^*}{P_T^*}$ is approximately constant? Explain your answer.

**b.** Present a brief summary of the Balassa–Samuelson model, listing the main hypotheses used.

**c.** Explain how changes in the terms of trade affect the equilibrium real exchange rate.

**d.** Throughout the 2000s, the real exchange rate in the Brazilian economy appreciated significantly in relation to the American dollar. Using your answers to the previous items, explain the movement of the Brazilian real exchange rate. Will this appreciation be permanent?

**e.** In which of the following situations would you expect the Brazilian real exchange rate to present the greatest appreciation: When measured based on the Consumer Price Index or when measured by the Producer Price Index?

## Exercise 3

Consider the same model as in the previous exercise, with domestic and foreign price indexes given by $P = P_N^\alpha P_T^{1-\alpha}$ and $P^* = P_N^{*\beta} P_T^{*1-\beta}$, respectively, and with $\alpha, \beta \in (0, 1)$. Now assume that consumers in the domestic economy spend fraction $\gamma$ of their total expenditures on domestically produced, tradable goods, represented by H, and a share, $1 - \gamma$, on tradable goods produced abroad, which are represented by F. In the foreign economy, there is an analogous behavior, with a fraction of spending on tradable goods produced in the domestic economy, designated as $\gamma^*$ Using a Cobb–Douglas type function, the price index for tradable goods will be given as $P_T = P_H^\gamma P_F^{*1-\gamma}$ and $P^* = P_H^{\gamma^*} P_F^{*1-\gamma^*}$.

**a.** Define the real exchange rate of tradable goods as $RER_T \equiv \frac{SP_T^*}{P_T}$.

**b.** Based on the Law of One Price, what is the expected relation between the prices of goods H and F?

**c.** Use the ratios $\frac{SP_F^*}{P_F}$ and $\frac{SP_H^*}{P_H}$ to identify the real exchange rate determiners for the tradable goods.

**d.** Qualify the following statements as either true or false and justify your answer.

   **1.** If the Law of One Price is valid, then the real exchange rate will be equal to 1.

   **2.** If the Law of One Price is valid, then the real exchange rate for tradable goods $RER_T$ will be equal to 1.

## Exercise 4

There are two economies, one domestic and the other foreign. There are two types of goods: tradable and nontradable. Assume that the foreign economy consumes only tradable goods. The domestic economy, however, consumes both tradable and nontradable goods. The nontradable goods answer for 50% of the consumption basket of the domestic economy. The production function for tradable goods is identical in both countries, given by

$$Y_T = a_T L_T,$$

where $Y_T$ is the amount produced of the tradable good, $L_T$ is the amount of labor employed in the productive process, and $a_T > 0$ is the parameter that measures the productivity of the tradable goods sector. The production function of the nontradables is given by

$$Y_N = a_N L_N,$$

where $Y_N$ is the quantity of the nontradable good produced, $L_N$ is the amount of labor employed in the productive process, and $a_N > 0$ is a parameter that measures the level of productivity in the nontradable goods sector.

Both the product and the factors markets are perfectly competitive and labor is fully mobile within each economy, but does not possess international mobility.

a. Assuming that the Law of One Price for the tradable goods segment is valid, derive the expression for the real exchange rate between the foreign and domestic economies, as a function of the relative productivity between the two sectors.
b. Assume that both $a_T$ and $a_N$ grow at a rate of 3%. What will be the real exchange rate growth rate? Is the relative Power of Purchase Parity valid? Is the absolute Power of Purchase Parity valid? Explain your answers.
c. Now assume that $a_T$ grows at a rate of 4% and that $a_N$ grows at a rate of 3%. What will be the real exchange rate growth rate? Will the Power of Purchase Parity, in its relative or absolute version, be valid? Explain your answers.

## Exercise 5

Consider a small, open economy where there are two types of goods: tradables, represented by T, and nontradables, represented by N. The representative consumer preferences in this economy are given by

$$U(c_T, c_N) = c_T^\alpha c_N^{1-\alpha},$$

where $c_T$ represents the domestic consumption of tradable goods and $c_N$ represents the consumption of nontradables. In this economy, both tradables and nontradables are produced with the following technologies:

$$Y_T = A_T K_T^{\rho_T} L_T^{1-\rho_T} \quad \text{with } \rho_T \in (0,1)$$

$$Y_N = A_N K_N^{\rho_N} L_N^{1-\rho_N} \quad \text{with } \rho_N \in (0,1),$$

where $Y_i, K_i, L_i$ represent the amount produced of good $i$, $i = T, N$, while $K_i, L_i$ represent, respectively, the amount of capital and labor used as supplies. Assume that factor $K$ possesses total international mobility, while factor $L$ cannot be transferred from one country to another. However, these two factors possess total mobility between the sectors where goods $T$ and $N$ are produced. Assume that this economy is small, so that the real interest rate of

$i^* \geq 0$ is a given and that the international market determines the price of the tradable good. To simplify, assume that good $T$ is the numeraire, so that $p_T = 1$.

**a.** Considering the utility function of the representative consumer, explain why $P = P_T^\alpha P_N^{1-\alpha} = P_N^{1-\alpha}$ is an adequate price index for the economy.

**b.** What is the share of income the representative individual spends on tradable goods? What is the portion spent on nontradable goods?

**c.** Assuming the Law of One Price for the segment of tradable goods, obtain an expression for the real exchange rate between the foreign economy and the domestic economy, as a function of the relative productivity between the two sectors.

**d.** Applying a condition of zero profit in the sector that produces nontradable goods, calculate the price $p_N$ as a function of $a_T, a_N$. Evaluate the result when $\rho_T = \rho_N$.

**e.** How does the increase in productivity affect the price index $P$? In other words, what is the sensitivity of $P$ in relation to $a_T$ and $a_N$.

**f.** How does an increase in the interest rate $i^*$ affect the price index $P$?

## Exercise 6

The real exchange rate of the economy is defined as $RER_t \equiv \frac{S_t P_t^*}{P_t}$, where $S_t$ represents the nominal exchange rate, $P_t^*$ the international price index, and $P_t$ the domestic price index. Explain how the real exchange rate changes in the following situations:

**a.** The government increases public spending.

**b.** A natural catastrophe devastates production in the rest of the world.

**c.** A technological shock increases domestic economic productivity in relation to the rest of the world.

**d.** Under what conditions would the real exchange rate be invariant in relation to the events cited in items (a) and (b)?

## Exercise 7

Consider a world where there are two countries, denominated A and B, which have trade relations, in an economic environment identical to that presented in Section 5.3. In each country, tradable goods are classified as either exported or imported. The production structures for both countries are identical, differing only in their parameters, which are presented by the superscript i, $i \in \{A, B\}$. As such, $K^i$ represents variable $K$ in country i. The structure of household preferences is identical in both countries, differing only in the parameters that are also identified by the superscript i, $i \in \{A, B\}$.

**a.** Solve the producer optimization problem in country $i$, obtaining the supply of the exported good, the imported good, and the nontradable good.

**b.** Find the price of the nontradable good, assuming that the production function parameters do not alter over time. Obtain the real exchange rate.

**c.** For country $A$ to be a net exporter of good $X$ it is necessary that condition $\frac{a_X^A}{a_M^A} > \frac{a_X^B}{a_M^B}$ is valid. Present an economic interpretation for this condition.

**d.** Assume that $\frac{a_X^A}{a_M^A} > \frac{a_X^B}{a_M^B}$ is valid, what happens when there is an increase in the terms of trade? Analytically justify your answer and present an economic intuition for the result.

## Exercise 8

Based on the content presented in this chapter, answer what the following items request:

**a.** Comment on the statement: "an increase in productivity causes the real exchange rate to appreciate."

**b.** What hypotheses must be satisfied for the real exchange rate parity to be verified?

# Determination of the Nominal Exchange Rate

The focus of Part III is the nominal exchange rate. Being the price of foreign money, the exchange rate is influenced by the supply and demand conditions of international transactions, which are those that require money conversion to be fulfilled. To know how the nominal exchange rate is determined, it is necessary to understand how the goods, assets, and money markets work, for they are the ones that influence the exchange rate. In Chapter 3, we saw the importance of the relationship between the nominal exchange rate level and prices in the trade of goods, and between expectations of exchange rate variations and the interest rates on assets transactions. In particular, the money market exerts a fundamental role since it affects both prices and interest rates. This part of the book presents alternative models to determine the nominal exchange rate.

## Why Different Models?

A model is always a simplification of reality: we simplify in order to better understand. One crucial question in building a model is to decide where to simplify. The simplification cannot eliminate elements that are important in understanding the situation in question. Therefore, it depends on what one wants to understand about reality. Therefore, the existence of different exchange rate models. Each of them seeks to understand different mechanisms, simplifying some markets and focusing their analysis on others.

The models to determine the nominal exchange rate can be divided into two broad groups: the monetary models and the portfolio diversification models. The monetary models in Chapters 6 and 7 have some facts in common. They assume (i) that the assets from different countries are perfect substitutes; (ii) that the agents are neutral to exchange rate risk; (iii) that there is perfect capital mobility between countries. These assumptions cause the domestic and foreign asset markets to be seen as one, single market, where the uncovered interest rate parity, defined in Eq. (3.12), must be satisfied.

Chapter 6 studies the exchange movement in the long run, by taking the prices of goods as being perfectly flexible. The model developed in that chapter shows how monetary policy affects the exchange rate, abstracting from considerations regarding the real side of the economy. The real effects appear in Chapter 7, where prices slowly adjust. The models presented there are useful to analyze the short-run dynamics, when prices have not yet completely adjusted to shocks in the economy.

The monetary models with their hypothesis of perfect substitutability between assets from different countries are not able to explain the gross capital flows—the simultaneous international purchases and sales assets. The dizzying increase of the gross capital flows as of the 2000s makes the analysis of its effect on the economy necessary, which is only possible by relaxing the hypothesis that assets are perfect substitutes. This is done in Chapter 8, where we discuss the implications of the gross capital flows and analyze the economic adjustment to shocks when assets from different countries are not perfect substitutes.

# 6

# Money and Exchange Rate in the Long Run

## CHAPTER OUTLINE

We begin by investigating the relationship between monetary policy and the exchange rate in the long run, a period defined as that which allows the complete adjustment of goods prices to economic shocks. Therefore, we assume that the prices of goods are completely flexible. The main consequence of price flexibility is that the relative prices are at their equilibrium level. More specifically, the current account is always at its optimum level, as described in Chapter 4, when the real exchange rate is equal to 1, if all goods are traded at zero cost, or, in the presence of nontradable goods, equal to its equilibrium value as studied in Chapter 5. The model developed here abstracts from these issues, simply assuming that the real economic variables, such as the product level or trade balance, are exogenous, that is, they are taken as given, being determined outside of the model.

**The focus of this model is the money market and the analysis of the impact of monetary shocks**. An open economy can be seen as the interaction of six markets: the domestic and foreign money markets, the domestic and foreign assets markets, and the domestic and foreign goods markets. We begin in Section 6.1 with a description of how each one works according to the monetary model. Section 6.2 analyzes the nominal exchange trajectory as a function of the announced monetary policy and Section 6.3 discusses applications of the model with its extensions, as well as its limitations.

# 6.1 Money, Assets, and Goods Markets

## 6.1.1 Money Market

The domestic money market is in equilibrium when the supply of money is equal to its demand. Since money supply is a government decision, more precisely, that of the central bank, we will take it as an exogenous variable. The demand for money, however, is a decision made by private agents. Given that these individuals need money to carry out their daily activities, it is an increasing function of the aggregate income of the economy. However, money in the wallet does not yield the interest that would be earned if the amount were placed into some interest-bearing bank account. In other words, the interest rate is the cost paid for retaining money. Let us assume that the demand for money is a positive function of income and a negative function of interest rate.[1]

The money market equilibrium can be represented by the equation:

$$m(t) - p(t) = \phi y(t) - \eta i(t), \tag{6.1}$$

where $m(t)$ is the logarithm of money supply[2] and $p(t)$ the logarithm of the price level, so that $m(t) - p(t)$ is the real money supply. The right side of the equation represents the demand for money, where $\phi$ and $\eta$ are parameters that indicate how much income and interest, respectively, affect the demand for money. $y(t)$ is the logarithm of income and $i(t) \equiv \ln(1 + i(t))$.

Monetary models, in general, abstract from the foreign money market. They take the domestic country as a small, open economy. This means that the domestic variables do not have an influence on foreign variables. Therefore, the variables referent to other countries are taken as givens, and the functioning of their economy is not modeled.

## 6.1.2 Assets Market

Assume that the assets from different countries are perfect substitutes, that investors are neutral to exchange rate risk and that there is perfect capital mobility. In equilibrium, the yield expected from domestic assets and foreign assets should be the same, that is, the

---

[1] In this model, we define the demand function in an *ad hoc* way, that is, we use intuitive arguments to characterize it without developing a model where the demand for money is derived based on decisions by individuals. There are important articles in the literature that deal with the microfoundation of money demand, such as Samuelson (1958), who uses a model of overlapping generations to derive an endogenous demand for money, Sidrausky (1967) and Brock (1974), who analyze an environment where individuals derive utility from carrying money, Clover (1967), who introduces models where the agents are subject to *cash-in-advance* constraints, where there are certain goods in the economy that can only be acquired by using money, and Kiyotaki and Wright (1989), who use a general equilibrium model where agents are simultaneously producers and consumers, who meet by chance and use money to make trades.

[2] In monetary models, it is customary to denote the variables in terms of their natural logarithms. This transformation does not in any way change the content of the economic equations, but makes it much easier to manipulate the model.

uncovered interest rate parity must be true. Rewriting the uncovered interest rate parity from Eq. (3.13), in Chapter 3, in continuous time, we have that:

$$E\left(\frac{ds(t)}{dt}\right) = i(t) - i^*(t),\tag{6.2}$$

where $E\left(\frac{ds(t)}{dt}\right)$ represents the expected exchange rate variation rate for period $t$, which is the derivative of the exchange rate with respect to time.[3] When the uncovered interest rate parity is respected, there is no opportunity for arbitrage. The economic agents are indifferent between either the domestic or foreign assets and the capital flow will be exactly what is necessary to cover eventual deficits or surpluses in current account.

## 6.1.3 Goods Market

The two large groups of monetary models differ in relation to the hypotheses regarding how the goods market works. The long-run model, studied in this chapter, assumes that the prices of goods are totally flexible and that there are no barriers to international trade. With these hypotheses, there cannot be a difference in the prices between countries. In other words, the purchasing power parity is valid, as defined by Eq. (3.5), in Chapter 3. The goods market is always in equilibrium, with income being at the level compatible with full employment. Hence, the level of income is an exogenous variable when prices are flexible. The purchasing power parity is true in its absolute version, and can be written, in log, as:

$$s(t) + p^*(t) - p(t) = 0.\tag{6.3}$$

Notice that, in the fixed price models, in Chapter 7, prices can differ between countries, given that, in those models, the trade of goods does not cause an instant arbitrage in prices. The real exchange rate can vary over time (even when there are no nontradable goods), and real exchange changes have an impact on the level of production in the economy. The argument is that there would be slack capacity in the economy, that is, production capability is not totally used due to lack of demand. A depreciation of the real exchange causes domestic products to be relatively cheaper, which increases net exports. There is, then, an increase in total demand for domestic goods that can be met by greater production, given that there is idle production capability. Therefore, exchange rate depreciation would lead to an increase in production. The aggregate income becomes, therefore, an endogenous variable.

As to the market for foreign goods, they are not explicitly modeled, as in the case of the foreign money market. It is simply assumed that the level of foreign prices is at a given level $p^*(t)$.

---

[3] Notice that now we take time as a continuous variable. In the models from the previous chapters, time was discreet, that is, it could be counted in natural numbers, while here time belongs to the set of real numbers. In terms of notation, the convention is that time is denoted as a subscript of the variable in question when it is discreet (e.g., $X_t$), while, when it is continuous, the variable is defined as a function of time (as in $X(t)$).

The flexible price model represents a long-term situation where prices, which can be rigid short term, have already had time to adjust to eventual economic shocks. They serve as a good guide for the future direction of the variables.

## 6.2 Exchange Rate Fundamentals

Equilibrium in the economy is determined by three equations: the money market equilibrium Eq. (6.1), the interest parity condition Eq. (6.2), and the purchasing power parity Eq. (6.3). These three equations define the equilibrium paths of domestic interest rates, domestic prices, and the exchange rate, as a function of the variables exogenous to the model.

To solve the model, the equations of purchasing power parity (6.3) and interest parity condition (6.2) are substituted into the money market equilibrium Eq. (6.1) to obtain:

$$m(t) - s(t) - p^*(t) = \phi y(t) - \eta \left[ E\left(\frac{ds(t)}{dt}\right) + i^*(t) \right]$$

which can be written as:

$$s(t) = m(t) - p^*(t) - \phi y(t) + \eta i^*(t) + \eta E\left(\frac{ds(t)}{dt}\right). \tag{6.4}$$

According to Eq. (6.4), the exchange rate is a function of the exogenous variables of the economy and the expected change in the exchange rate. Let us take a look at the intuition for the impact of each of the exogenous variables on the exchange rate.

- *Money Supply*: An increase in the money supply $m(t)$ would lead to an increase in domestic prices $p(t)$ to rebalance the money market, as can be seen in Eq. (6.1). If domestic prices were higher than foreign prices $p^*(t)$, when measured in the same currency, consumers would buy foreign instead of domestic goods, which would increase demand for foreign currency, raising its price, namely, there would be an exchange depreciation to maintain purchasing power parity, as established by Eq. (6.3).
- *International Prices*: An increase in international prices, $p^*(t)$, would lead consumers to purchase only domestic goods, increasing the demand for domestic money and leading to the fall in price of the foreign money, $s(t)$. There would be an exchange evaluation for the purchasing power parity (6.3) to be respected. The foreign economy is not modeled, but we can imagine that the increase in international prices could have been caused by an expansionist monetary policy in the foreign country. Therefore, we see that monetary expansion in the foreign country leads to an evaluation of the domestic money, while, in a symmetric form, a monetary expansionist policy leads to an exchange depreciation.
- *Income Level*: A higher income level, $y(t)$, raises the demand for money, according to the right side of Eq. (6.1). Domestic prices, $p(t)$, fall in order to increase the real money supply, and, thereby, rebalance the money market. Lower domestic prices stimulate

consumers to purchase domestic goods, which leads to a smaller demand for foreign currency, reducing its price, $s(t)$. Hence, the exchange appreciates to maintain the purchasing power parity.

- *International Interest Rates*: An increase in international interest rates, $i^*(t)$, causes foreign assets to be relatively more attractive. The free mobility of capital leads investors to purchase foreign assets, increasing demand for foreign currency, and, consequently, its price, $s(t)$. The exchange depreciates, which leads to an increase in domestic prices, $p(t)$, to satisfy the purchasing power parity in Eq. (6.3). The increase of prices, in turn, reduces the real supply of money, which causes an increase in domestic interest rates, $i(t)$, to rebalance the money market, according to Eq. (6.1).

We can say that the exogenous variables that explain the exchange rate level in Eq. (6.4) correspond to the *economic fundamentals*, $f(t)$, defined as:

$$f(t) \equiv m(t) - p^*(t) - \phi y(t) + \eta i^*(t). \tag{6.5}$$

Therefore, Eq. (6.4) can be written as:

$$s(t) = f(t) + \eta E\left(\frac{\mathrm{d}s(t)}{\mathrm{d}t}\right). \tag{6.6}$$

For a given path of the fundamentals, $f(t)$, differential Eq. (6.6) determines how the nominal exchange rate $s(t)$ evolves over time. To understand the logic of the equation, remember that the nominal exchange rate is the price of one asset: foreign currency. The price of an asset is always determined by an equation of the type:

asset price = fundamentals + expected price change

Let us take, for example, the case of stock traded on the stock market. Its price depends on the profit earned by the company that issued it, which corresponds to the *fundamentals* of the stock. Moreover, the expectation of a future increase in the price of the stock raises its current demand, which causes the price to rise at once. In equilibrium, the expectation of stock price changes in the future should correspond to changes in the company's future profits. Therefore, the presence of the price variation term means that the stock price depends not only on the company's current profit, but also on the expected trajectory of its future profits.

Equation (6.6) establishes the same principle to determine the exchange rate. The exchange rate depends not only on the current level of economic fundamentals, but also on expected changes in the very exchange rate. What would you do if you knew the dollar would depreciate tomorrow? You would certainly trade your available dollars for euros so that tomorrow, when the euro appreciates with respect to the dollar, you could convert back to dollars and gain from the transaction. The problem is that you would not be the only one doing this. For this reason, the expected exchange rate depreciation, namely, $E\left(\frac{\mathrm{d}s(t)}{\mathrm{d}t}\right) > 0$, increases the demand for foreign currency in the present, which causes an immediate depreciation of the exchange rate.

If we knew the trajectory of the fundamentals for all the future, or if we had at least an expectation as to their trajectory, we could find the equilibrium level of the nominal exchange rate by solving Eq. (6.6). Each family of differential equations has a rule of thumb, which if followed, makes finding the solution possible. We start by rewriting it so as to have the proper format to apply the respective rule of thumb. As shown in the Mathematical Appendix at the end of this chapter, the solution to Eq. (6.6) is:

$$s(t) = E\left[\int_t^\infty \frac{f(\tau)}{\eta} \exp\left(\frac{-(\tau - t)}{\eta}\right) d\tau\right] + E\left[\lim_{T \to \infty} s(T) \exp\left(\frac{-(T - t)}{\eta}\right)\right]. \qquad (6.7)$$

Equation (6.7) states that the current exchange rate is equal to what we can call the present value of fundamentals for all the future, added to a term that corresponds to the present value of the exchange in the future, in a future that tends to infinity. Now, the entire trajectory of fundamentals for all the future is taken into account in the first term on the right side of the equation. The exchange rate should then be equal to this first term only.

If the second term is different from zero, this means the exchange rate is governed by something more, beyond the fundamentals, which cannot be an equilibrium solution. In this case, there would be a speculative bubble. Therefore, the condition to not have speculative bubbles is that:

$$E\left[\lim_{T \to \infty} s(T) \exp\left(\frac{-(T - t)}{\eta}\right)\right] = 0, \qquad (6.8)$$

and the exchange rate is determined by:

$$s(t) = E\left[\int_t^\infty \frac{f(\tau)}{\eta} \exp\left(\frac{-(\tau - t)}{\eta}\right) d\tau\right]. \qquad (6.9)$$

Equation (6.9) is the solution for differential Eq. (6.6), for the case where there is no speculative bubble, namely, when Eq. (6.8) is valid. Notice that Eq. (6.9) is always true, for any exchange rate regime. Actually, the equation shows that **an exchange rate regime corresponds to a fundamentals regime**. More specifically, among the fundamentals there is a policy variable, which is the monetary policy. **When a government commits itself to a determined exchange regime it is, actually, committing itself to follow a monetary policy that is consistent with the announced exchange rate regime**, given that the exchange is determined by Eq. (6.9).

In general, if we knew the expected fundamentals path, we could use Eq. (6.9) to compute the value of the exchange rate. We will do this for some interesting examples of fundamentals path.

## 6.2.1 Constant Fundamentals

In our first example, we use a constant value for the fundamentals, that is,

$$f(t) = \bar{f} \quad \forall\, t \geq t_1. \qquad (6.10)$$

Substituting the fundamentals trajectory in Eq. (6.9), we have:

$$s(t) = \int_t^\infty \frac{\bar{f}}{\eta} \exp\left(\frac{-(\tau - t)}{\eta}\right) d\tau$$

$$= \frac{\bar{f}}{\eta} \int_t^\infty \exp\left(\frac{-(\tau - t)}{\eta}\right) d\tau$$

$$= -\bar{f} \exp\left(\frac{-(\tau - t)}{\eta}\right) \Big|_t^\infty$$

$$= \bar{f}$$

As with the fundamentals, the exchange rate will always be constant and equal to $\bar{f}$. The solution is quite intuitive and can be understood in terms of Eq. (6.6). According to it, the exchange rate is equal to the current value of the fundamentals added to the expected exchange rate variation. If the fundamentals do not change over time and there is no uncertainty in relation to such, there is no reason for expectations of changes in the exchange rate in equilibrium. Therefore, the exchange rate is equal in value to the fundamentals at all times.

In practical terms, **with an announced fixed exchange rate regime, the government commits itself to follow a monetary policy to maintain the fundamentals fixed**. An increase in international interest rates, for example, caused by a contractionist monetary policy in a foreign government, represents an increase in the fundamentals, if there were no government intervention, leading to exchange rate depreciation.[4] The government should therefore reduce the domestic monetary supply, selling international reserves, to maintain the fundamentals fixed. Therefore, **a monetary contraction in a foreign country should be accompanied by a domestic monetary contraction to maintain the exchange rate fixed**.

There is also the possibility of uncertainty in relation to the maintenance of the fixed exchange rate regime. The fixed exchange rate regime demands strict monetary discipline by the government. The government, actually, gives up its freedom of choice in monetary policy, which is the only option that becomes the one necessary to maintain the exchange rate fixed. Specifically, it cannot use an expansionist monetary policy to stimulate the economy when unemployment is high, for example.[5]

In a country with high unemployment that follows a fixed exchange rate regime, people may begin to wonder whether the government will not abandon the fixed exchange rate regime in order to use their monetary policy to stimulate the economy, or not. In terms of our model, this means attributing a positive probability to an increase in the future

[4] Given that the exchange is defined as the domestic currency in terms of the foreign currency, as in praxis, an increase in exchange rate represents exchange rate depreciation.

[5] Actually, in the context of this model, monetary policy has no effect whatsoever on income since it assumes that prices are flexible, so that changes in money supply are immediately absorbed by prices and the economy remains under full employment at all times. In the real world, prices are not perfectly flexible, as in the model, allowing an expansionist monetary policy to have a positive impact on aggregate output if there is unemployment in the economy.

fundamentals, which translates in an expectation of exchange rate depreciation. Therefore, the expectation of exchange depreciation can exist even in a fixed exchange rate regime. This is denoted as the *Peso Problem*, which we saw in Chapter 3, Section 3.3.

To maintain a fixed exchange rate even amid the expectation of exchange rate depreciation, the government must practice an even more restrictive monetary policy. As we saw in Eq. (6.6), the higher the expectation of exchange rate depreciation, the lower the fundamentals levels should be and, consequently, more contractionist the monetary policy to maintain the exchange fixed at a given level. This means that the **cost of maintaining the exchange rate fixed is higher the greater the lack of confidence in relation to the regime**. We will pick up this topic again when we study the exchange rate crises in Chapter 9.

## 6.2.2 Fundamentals Increasing at a Constant Rate

Another interesting case is when fundamentals increase at a constant rate, such as in:

$$f(t) = \theta t, \quad \forall \, t \geq \tilde{t}, \tag{6.11}$$

where $\theta$ is a positive constant. This fundamentals trajectory can represent the case of an economy with an inflation rate equal to $\theta$, fed by monetary expansion at the same rate. Notice that an increase in the fundamentals, as defined by Eq. (6.5), causes an increase in the exchange rate, that is, exchange rate depreciation. An increase in the fundamentals is generally interpreted as their deterioration since it can mean either a monetary expansion (which can lead to a higher inflation rate), a reduction in international prices (which makes domestic products less competitive), a reduction in domestic output (which need not be explained), or an increase in international interest rates (which makes domestic assets less attractive).

Substituting the fundamentals path in Eq. (6.11), the exchange rate is given by:[6]

$$s(t) = \int_t^\infty \frac{\theta \tau}{\eta} \exp\left( \frac{-(\tau - t)}{\eta} \right) \mathrm{d}\tau$$
$$= \theta t + \theta \eta \tag{6.12}$$

which is quite intuitive, when comparing it to the differential Eq. (6.6). That differential equation states that the exchange is equal to the fundamentals, in this case $f(t) = \theta t$, plus the expected exchange rate depreciation, which here is $\theta$, multiplied by $\eta$. Therefore, the rate of change of the exchange rate is identical to that of the fundamentals, with a difference in level that corresponds to the constant expected exchange rate depreciation, as seen in Figure 6.1, that depicts the fundamentals and exchange paths over time. It is important to note that **the exchange rate value depends only on the present and future values of the fundamentals, namely, what happened to the fundamentals or exchange rate in the past does not affect the current exchange rate value**.

---

[6] The derivation of this solution is in the Mathematical Appendix at the end of this chapter.

In this example, it is not difficult to solve the integral from Eq. (6.9), but the next example will be more complex. I will give an alternative form to find the exchange rate path for the fundamentals trajectory established by Eq. (6.11), based on the differential Eq. (6.6), which simplifies the solution for some more complex cases.

Equation (6.11) establishes fundamentals as an injective function of time; namely, each fundamentals value corresponds to a unique moment in time $t$. Therefore, knowing the value of the fundamentals, $f$, one can discern the moment in question. We can therefore make a change of variable in Eq. (6.6) and write the exchange rate as a function of the fundamentals, which, in turn, are a function of time. We will then define a new function, $G(f)$, which defines the exchange rate as a function of the fundamental. Based on Eq. (6.6), function $G(f)$ can be written as:

$$G(f) = f + \eta E \left( \frac{dG(f)}{df} \frac{df}{dt} \right), \tag{6.13}$$

where we use the chain rule to write the second term on the right side of Eq. (6.13): the derivative of the exchange rate with respect to time is equal to the derivative with respect to the fundamentals, in our new definition of the exchange rate function, multiplied by the fundamentals derivative with respect to time.

According to the fundamentals trajectory in Eq. (6.11), we have that $\frac{df}{dt} = \theta$. The equation for the exchange path is now the following differential equation:

$$G(f) = f + \eta \theta \frac{dG(f)}{df}, \tag{6.14}$$

whose general solution is given by:

$$G(f) = f + \eta \theta + C \exp \left( \frac{f}{\eta \theta} \right), \tag{6.15}$$

where $C$ is a constant.

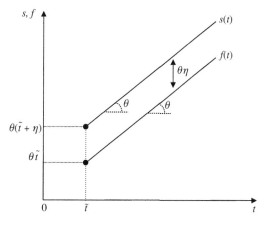

**Figure 6.1** Exchange and fundamentals paths: fundamentals increasing at a constant rate.

Mathematically, Eq. (6.15) is a possible solution for Eq. (6.14) for any value of $C$. In economic terms, however, there is only one value for the constant $C$ that is compatible with the economy equilibrium. In this case, the economic constraint that defines the value of $C$ is the condition of not having a speculative bubble as established in Eq. (6.8), which, by the way, was also used to find Eq. (6.9) as a solution for differential Eq. (6.6). Rewriting the general solution (6.15), now having the exchange as a function of time, we have that:

$$s(t) = \theta t + \eta \theta + C \, exp\left(\frac{t}{\eta}\right). \tag{6.16}$$

Substituting the exchange value defined in Eq. (6.16) on the condition of not having a speculative bubble (Eq. (6.8)), we obtain:

$$E\left[\lim_{t \to \infty}\left[\theta T + \eta \theta + C \, \exp\left(\frac{T}{\eta}\right)\right]\exp\left(\frac{-(T-t)}{\eta}\right)\right] = 0.$$

Using the fundamentals path from Eq. (6.11), we can write the previous equation as:

$$\lim_{t \to \infty} \theta T \exp\left(\frac{-(T-t)}{\eta}\right) + \lim_{t \to \infty} \eta \theta \, \exp\left(\frac{-(T-t)}{\eta}\right) + \lim_{t \to \infty} C \exp\left(\frac{T}{\eta}\right)\exp\left(\frac{-(T-t)}{\eta}\right) = 0$$

$$\Downarrow$$

$$\lim_{t \to \infty} C \exp\left(\frac{t}{\eta}\right) = 0$$

$$\Updownarrow$$

$$C = 0 \tag{6.17}$$

Let us see how we arrived at the conclusion that $C = 0$. The first term of Eq. (6.17) is the multiplication of one term that tends to infinity when $T$ tends to the infinity, $\theta T$, and of a term that tends to zero when $T$ tends to the infinity, $\exp\left(\frac{-(T-t)}{\eta}\right)$. Using the l'Hôpital rule, we see that this product tends to zero.[7] The second term also tends to zero, given that it deals with the multiplication of a constant term, $\eta \theta$, and a term that tends to zero, $\exp\left(\frac{-(T-t)}{\eta}\right)$. Finally, the last term is a constant. It will be equal to zero if, and only if, $C$ is equal to zero.

Substituting $C = 0$ in Eq. (6.16), we have that:

$$s(t) = \theta t + \eta \theta$$

as in the solution found previously (Eq. (6.12)).

Figure 6.2 shows how the exchange path distances more and more from the fundamentals path when $C$ is other than zero. For positive values of $C$, the exchange rate grows more rapidly than the fundamentals and the distance between them increases exponentially. When $C$ is negative, the rate of growth for the exchange rate is lower than that of the

---

[7] Intuitively, $\theta T$ tends toward infinity linearly, while $\exp\left(\frac{-(T-t)}{\eta}\right)$ tends toward zero exponentially. Hence, the product of both terms tends to zero.

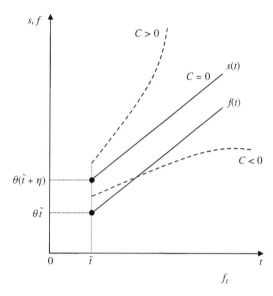

**Figure 6.2** Exchange and fundamentals paths: different values of C.

fundamentals. After a certain point the exchange rate decreases, while the fundamentals increase. The distance between the fundamentals and exchange rate is constant only when $C = 0$.

## 6.2.3 Fundamentals That Increase and Then Remain Constant

The previous case, of fundamentals increasing at a constant rate, can represent an economy under a constant inflation rate. We have seen that there would be constant exchange rate depreciation equal to the rate of inflation, where the exchange rate value would be superior to the fundamentals, and this difference would be proportional to the expected exchange rate depreciation. What would happen if, in this scenario of constant inflation, the government announced a price stabilization policy to be introduced at a certain point in time in the future? This question is answered with this third example of fundamentals path.

We now assume that the fundamentals increase at a constant rate up until a given period, and as of that time, their value is maintained constant. The trajectory is represented by:

$$f(t) = \begin{cases} \theta t \ \text{ for } \ t \le \dfrac{\bar{f}}{\theta} \\[2mm] \bar{f} \ \text{ otherwise} \end{cases}$$

The full line on Figure 6.3 represents the trajectory of the fundamentals.

We can find the path of the exchange rate by substituting the fundamentals path into Eq. (6.9) and solving the integral, but the process is quite complicated. There is another, much easier method to do this, using the results of the two previous examples. Notice that, as of period $t = \frac{\bar{f}}{\theta}$, the fundamentals remain constant, as in the first example in the previously considered item, Constant Fundamentals. Given that the exchange depends on present and future fundamentals, it will follow, from that time forward, the same path as in that example, that is:

$$s(t) = \bar{f} \quad \forall\, t \geq \frac{\bar{f}}{\theta}. \tag{6.18}$$

For periods $0 \leq t \leq \frac{\bar{f}}{\theta}$, the solution is analogous to the second example, where the fundamentals grow at a constant rate. Considering that in this time interval the fundamentals are an injective function of time, we can make a change of variable, as in the previous case, and arrive at the following nominal exchange rate path:

$$G(f) = f + \eta\theta + C \exp\left(\frac{f}{\eta\theta}\right). \tag{6.19}$$

As always, only one value for $C$ will correspond to the equilibrium trajectory. In the previous example, the economic restriction that determined the value of constant $C$ was that of not having a speculative bubble. Here, this condition is already guaranteed in Eq. (6.18), which is the equation that established the exchange value until the end of time.

The condition that determines the constant $C$ is associated with the moment of transition between the two fundamentals regimes. In this example, there is no uncertainty with respect to the future. Everyone knows that at exactly $t = \frac{\bar{f}}{\theta}$, the fundamentals path will become constant after the initial period of growth. At that moment, there cannot be a discontinuity of the exchange rate path, that is, there cannot be a discreet jump in the exchange rate value.

What would you do if you were in this economy and knew that at moment $t = \frac{\bar{f}}{\theta}$ the exchange rate would jump, for example, from $s_1$ to $s_2$, with $s_2 > s_1$? I bet you would trade your dollars for euros before the change in regime, and profit from reselling the euros soon after.

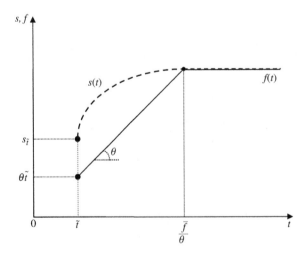

**Figure 6.3** Exchange and fundamentals paths: fundamentals increase and then remain constant.

Given that you are not the only one with this idea, the possibility of arbitrage would generate excess in demand for the foreign currency before the change in regime, which would increase its price. In equilibrium there is no discreet exchange rate change. This is, actually, a general rule: when there is no unexpected event, there cannot be a discreet jump in the price of assets.

In terms of our model, this means that, when arriving at moment $t = \frac{\bar{f}}{\theta}$, the exchange defined by the trajectory in motion should be equal to its value by the trajectory that leads to the future. In mathematical terms, this means that:

$$\lim_{\tau \uparrow \frac{\bar{f}}{\theta}} s(\tau) = \lim_{\tau \downarrow \frac{\bar{f}}{\theta}} s(\tau), \tag{6.20}$$

that is, the lateral limit of the exchange rate to the left of $t = \frac{\bar{f}}{\theta}$ should be equal to its lateral limit to the right of $t = \frac{\bar{f}}{\theta}$. The exchange rate trajectory for periods preceding moment $t = \frac{\bar{f}}{\theta}$ is defined by Eq. (6.19), while for periods following moment $t = \frac{\bar{f}}{\theta}$, it is given by Eq. (6.18). Equation (6.20) can be rewritten as:

$$\lim_{t \uparrow \frac{\bar{f}}{\theta}} \left( \theta t + \eta \theta + C \exp\left(\frac{t}{\eta}\right) \right) = \lim_{t \downarrow \frac{\bar{f}}{\theta}} \bar{f},$$

which results in:

$$\bar{f} + \eta \theta + C \exp\left(\frac{\bar{f}}{\eta \theta}\right) = \bar{f},$$

$$\Updownarrow$$

$$C = -\eta \theta \exp\left(\frac{-\bar{f}}{\eta \theta}\right).$$

The exchange rate path can therefore be written as:

$$s(t) = \begin{cases} \theta t + \eta \theta - \eta \theta \exp\left(\dfrac{\theta t - \bar{f}}{\eta \theta}\right) & \text{for } t \leq \dfrac{\bar{f}}{\theta} \\ \bar{f} & \text{otherwise} \end{cases} \tag{6.21}$$

and is represented by the dotted line in Figure 6.3, where we can see that the value of constant $C$ is that which causes the dotted line to be continuous, namely, at moment $\tau = \frac{\bar{f}}{\theta}$ the exchange rate will be exactly equal to $\bar{f}$ on the exchange rate path prior to this moment.

It is interesting to note that, before the transition of regime, the fundamentals increased at rate $\theta$, while the exchange depreciated at a rate smaller than $\theta$, more precisely, at the rate $\frac{ds(t)}{dt} = \theta\left(1 - \exp\left(\frac{\theta t - \bar{f}}{\eta \theta}\right)\right)$. The intuition for this result is that, despite the fundamentals growing at the rate of $\theta$ in this period, at some time in the future they will cease to grow. Given that the growth of fundamentals at the rate of $\theta$ is not permanent, it is not completely incorporated into the depreciation expectation. Actually, the depreciation expectation decreases as the time approaches when the fundamentals cease to grow. At the transition moment, we have that $\frac{ds(\bar{f}/\theta)}{dt} = 0$, and the expected exchange rate depreciation continues to be zero from this point forward.

# 6.3 Applications, Extensions, and Limits of the Model

The monetary model with flexible prices allows study of the impact of fundamentals on the nominal exchange rate. It shows how monetary policy affects the exchange rate and how it should be used to attain exchange rate goals. The model also explains the role of future expectations on the current exchange rate.

With it we can analyze the use of monetary policy under different exchange regimes. In particular, the flexible price monetary model was quite useful to understand the effects of instituting a regime of exchange rate target zones, where the government commits to maintain the exchange rate within previously established limits (Box 6.1).

In his 1991 seminal article, Paul Krugman shows that exchange rate target zones had a stabilizing effect known as the *honeymoon effect*. According to this effect, the impact of fundamentals variables on the exchange rate reduced as it neared the pre-established limits of the exchange rate band. This honeymoon effect is generated by the impact of the expectations on the exchange rate path, as in our last case studied, where the fundamentals initially increased and then remained constant. We have seen that exchange rate depreciation caused by the growth of fundamentals gradually decreased as the fundamentals neared the time when they ceased to grow, for it is expected that the increase in fundamentals would not continue indefinitely. Analogously, in an exchange rate target zone regime, the economic agents know that, when the exchange rate reaches its limits, the government will intervene in the market to prevent that limit from being bypassed. In the same way, it is expected that the fundamentals variation that leads toward the limit will not continue indefinitely.[8]

Even though the flexible price monetary model allows one to identify the implications of alternate exchange regimes on the economic fundamentals path and, in particular, the use of monetary policy, it does not help in understanding of the relation between the exchange rate and the real side of the economy. The hypothesis of complete price flexibility causes prices to adjust immediately to any movement in the nominal exchange rate, so that the real exchange rate is always constant. This means that changes in the nominal exchange rate affect neither the output level nor the trade balance. From this point of view, any analysis of

---

**BOX 6.1 BRETTON WOODS SYSTEM**

The Bretton Woods Agreement, signed by the main industrial economies after the Second World War, established a set of rules to regulate the international monetary system with the intention of assuring monetary stability. The Agreement, which was in force between 1944 and 1971, reckoned a fixed parity of other currencies to the dollar, and a fixed parity of the dollar to gold. After the end of the Bretton Woods regime in 1971 and before the introduction of the single currency in the region, the European countries widely used the target zone exchange rate regime.

---

[8] Duarte et al. (2010) present a review of the vast literature regarding exchange rate bands that developed after Krugman (1991).

exchange rate regimes and the relation between fundamentals and exchange rate made by the model have no importance whatsoever, if we take them literally.

This, as with any model, is due to the simplifying hypotheses that, by definition, do not correspond to reality. One only need to open the newspaper and notice the change in mood by exporters in face of exchange rate variations to see that the nominal exchange rate has real effects on the economy. According to what has already been stated, this model should be seen as a long-term representation, where prices have had time to adjust to exchange variations. It is this that we will investigate in the next chapter regarding versions of the monetary model with rigid prices.

## Mathematical Appendix

### Solution for Eq. (6.6)

First, Eq. (6.6) should be rewritten as:

$$\frac{s(\tau)}{\eta} - \frac{ds(\tau)}{d\tau} = \frac{f(\tau)}{\eta},$$

where $\tau$ is a period of time. Multiplying both sides by $\exp\left(\frac{-(\tau-t)}{\eta}\right)$, we obtain:

$$\frac{s(\tau)}{\eta}\exp\left(\frac{-(\tau-t)}{\eta}\right) - \frac{ds(\tau)}{d\tau}\exp\left(\frac{-(\tau-t)}{\eta}\right) = \frac{f(\tau)}{\eta}\exp\left(\frac{-(\tau-t)}{\eta}\right).$$

This new equation is valid for any time $\tau$. In particular, it is true for the whole period in the interval $\tau = [t, T]$, where $t$ is the present period and $T$ is a period in the future. We can then add them over all periods in this interval to obtain:

$$E\left[\int_t^T \left(\frac{s(\tau)}{\eta} - \frac{ds(\tau)}{d\tau}\right)\exp\left(\frac{-(\tau-t)}{\eta}\right)d\tau\right] = E\left[\int_t^T \frac{f(\tau)}{\eta}\exp\left(\frac{-(\tau-t)}{\eta}\right)d\tau\right]. \tag{6.22}$$

Notice that now I added the hope operator $E[\cdot]$, given that there could be uncertainty in relation to the future fundamentals.

Solving the left side of Eq. (6.22), we have:

$$E\left[\int_t^T \left(\frac{s(\tau)}{\eta} - \frac{ds(\tau)}{d\tau}\right)\exp\left(\frac{-(\tau-t)}{\eta}\right)d\tau\right] = E\left[-s(\tau)\exp\left(\frac{-(\tau-t)}{\eta}\right)\bigg|_t^T\right]$$

$$= -E\left[s(T)\exp\left(\frac{-(T-t)}{\eta}\right)\right] + s(t) \tag{6.23}$$

Substituting Eq. (6.23) into Eq. (6.22), we arrive at:

$$s(t) = E\left[\int_t^T \frac{f(\tau)}{\eta} \exp\left(\frac{-(\tau - t)}{\eta}\right) d\tau\right] + E\left[s(T)\exp\left(\frac{-(T - t)}{\eta}\right)\right].$$

Finally, we take the limit of this new equation when the last period considered tends to the infinity, that is, $T \rightarrow \infty$:

$$s(t) = E\left[\int_t^\infty \frac{f(\tau)}{\eta} \exp\left(\frac{-(\tau - t)}{\eta}\right) d\tau\right] + E\left[\lim_{T \to \infty} s(T)\exp\left(\frac{-(T - t)}{\eta}\right)\right]. \tag{6.24}$$

## Solution for Eq. (6.12)

We can say that:

$$\begin{aligned}
s(t) &= \int_t^\infty \frac{\theta\tau}{\eta} \exp\left(\frac{-(\tau - t)}{\eta}\right) d\tau \\
&= -\theta \int_t^\infty \tau \left(-\frac{\exp(-(\tau - t)/\eta)}{\eta}\right) d\tau
\end{aligned} \tag{6.25}$$

To solve the integral in Eq. (6.25), we will use fundamental theorem of calculus. Let $a = \tau$ and $b = \exp\left(\frac{-(\tau - t)}{\eta}\right)$. We then have that $da = d\tau$ and $db = -\frac{\exp(-(\tau - t)/\eta)}{\eta} d\tau$. Equation (6.25) can be rewritten as:

$$s(t) = -\theta \int a\, db.$$

Fundamental theorem of calculus says that:

$$\int a\, db = ab - \int b\, da.$$

Using the definitions of $a$ and $b$ provided in the previous paragraph, we then have that:

$$\begin{aligned}
s(t) &= -\theta[ab - \int b\, da] \\
&= -\theta\left[\tau \exp\left(\frac{-(\tau - t)}{\eta}\right)\Big|_t^\infty - \int_t^\infty \exp\left(\frac{-(\tau - t)}{\eta}\right) d\tau\right] \\
&= -\theta\left[-t\left(-\eta \exp\left(\frac{-(\tau - t)}{\eta}\right)\Big|_t^\infty\right)\right] \\
&= \theta[t + \eta] = \theta t + \theta\eta
\end{aligned}$$

## 6.4 Exercises

### Exercise 1

Let there be two economies: domestic and foreign. The money market equilibrium is given by the two following equations:

$$m_t - p_t = \phi y_t - \lambda i_t$$
$$m_t^* - p_t^* = \phi y_t^* - \lambda i_t^*$$

where $y_t$, $p_t$, $m_t$, and $i_t$ represent the product, price index, nominal money supply, and nominal interest rate, respectively. All variables are in logarithm, and the $*$ superscript refers to the foreign economy. The parameters $\phi > 0$ and $\lambda > 0$ represent demand elasticity per money in relation to income and interest, respectively. The international capital market equilibrium is given by the uncovered interest rate parity condition:

$$i_t - i_t^* = E_t(s_{t+1}) - s_t,$$

where $s_t$ represents the nominal exchange rate and $E_t$ represents the operator of conditional hope to the set of available information in $t$. In this model, time is defined in discreet terms. The relationship between price levels and the nominal exchange rate is given by the following purchasing power parity relationship:

$$s_t = p_t - p_t^*.$$

Define the variable $f_t = (m_t - m_t^*) - \phi(y_t - y_t^*)$ as the fundamentals of the economy.

a. Derive the equation that governs the nominal exchange rate behavior, where the exchange rate is a function of the fundamentals as previously defined. Interpret this equation.
b. Present and justify, with economic arguments, the hypothesis of absence of speculative bubbles. Find a solution to the equation in the previous item under this hypothesis.
c. Denote $\Delta f_t = f_t - f_{t-1}$ and assume that the economic fundamentals follow the following stochastic process: $\Delta f_t = \rho \Delta f_{t-1} + z_t$, where $z_t$ is a shock with mean zero and $\rho \in (0.1)$. Using your answer to item (b), calculate the equilibrium exchange rate when the fundamentals follow this process.
d. Show that this model is able to explain the following stylized fact for the exchange rate: $\text{var}(s_t) > \text{var}(\Delta f_t)$, where $\text{var}(\cdot)$ represents the variance operator. Interpret the result.
e. Assume the government establishes a fixed exchange rate policy, simultaneous with an expansionist credit policy. What does the government need to do to maintain the fixed exchange rate? What happens when the government no longer has international reserves?

## Exercise 2

At $t = 0$, a foreign exporter sells you their merchandise. However, you will make the payment (in foreign currency) for this product in time $t = \frac{\bar{f}/\theta}{2}$. To guarantee the rate, the exporter offers you, at $t = 0$, a future sales contract of foreign currency. The contract states the following: at time $t = \frac{\bar{f}/\theta}{2}$, the exporter commits to sell you foreign currency at the exchange rate $s(t) = \theta\eta + \frac{f(t)}{2} + k$, where $\theta > 0$, $\eta > 0$, and $k > 0$. Your answer if you accept, or not, the proposed contract, occurs in time $t = 0$. Possessing extensive knowledge regarding economics, you know (for sure) that the fundamentals will grow at a rate of $\theta$, that is, $f(t) = \theta t$ until the end of time.

**a.** What is the exchange rate trajectory? Present its equation and illustrate your answer by means of a graph.
**b.** If $k = 0$, do you accept, reject, or remain indifferent to the contract? How does your answer depend on the value of $k$?

## Exercise 3

Consider an economy with flexible prices as presented in this chapter. By hypothesis, assume that there is free mobility of goods with no transaction costs, so that purchasing power parity is true, and that there is free mobility of capital that, together with the hypothesis of absence of exchange risk premium, yields the uncovered interest rate parity. Assume also that the money market equilibrium is given by the following equation, where all variables are expressed in logarithmic terms:

$$m(t) - p(t) = \phi y(t) - \eta i(t), \tag{6.26}$$

where the variables have the usual meaning. The foreign economy variables possess analogous annotation, however identified by the symbol *. In this model, time is expressed in continuous terms.

**a.** Show that, by combining the presented hypotheses in the presentation with the Eq. (6.26), we can obtain the following equation $s(t) = f(t) + \eta E_t\left\{\frac{ds(t)}{dt}\right\}$, where $f(t) = m(t) - p^*(t) - \phi y(t) + \eta i^*(t)$ is economic fundamentals, $s(t)$ represents the nominal exchange rate, and $E_t\{\cdot\}$ represents the hope operator conditional.
**b.** Assume that the fundamentals of this economy have the following trajectory:

$$f(t) = \begin{cases} \theta t & \text{if } t < \frac{f_1}{\theta} \\ \eta\beta \ln(f_2 - f_1) + \beta t & \text{otherwise} \end{cases}$$

where $f_2 > f_1$ and $\beta > \theta + 1$. Draw a graph of the fundamentals path. By means of the monetary model, intuitively explain the behavior of the economic fundamentals.

**c.** Assume that all economic agents know the fundamentals path described in item (b). What is the exchange rate path? (*Tip: the general solution for the differential equation* $G(f) = f + \eta\theta \frac{dG(f)}{df}$ *is given by* $G(f) = f + \eta\theta + C\,e^{\frac{f}{\eta\theta}}$, *where C is a constant.*)

**d.** Draw a graph of the exchange rate path along with the fundamentals path. Compare between the two paths, analyzing them based on the intuition proposed by the economic theory present throughout this chapter.

## Exercise 4

In the monetary model to determine the exchange rate studied throughout this chapter, the nominal exchange rate trajectory is given by the equation:

$$s(t) = f(t) + \eta E_t\left\{\frac{ds(t)}{dt}\right\},$$

where $s(t)$ is the nominal exchange rate, $f(t)$ represents the economic fundamentals trajectory, $\eta > 0$ is a sensitivity parameter, and $E_t\{\cdot\}$ is the hope operator conditional for the set of information available in $t$. In this model, time is considered in continuous terms and the variables are expressed in logarithmic terms.

**a.** What are the basic hypotheses of this model? Explain the economic intuition of these hypotheses and their influence on the results of the model.

**b.** Assume that the economic fundamentals follow the following path:

$$f t = \text{if } t < f\theta$$

$$f(t) = \begin{cases} \theta t & \text{if } t < \dfrac{\bar{f}}{\theta} \\ \theta t + J & \text{otherwise} \end{cases}$$

where $\bar{f} > 0$ and $J > 0$. Draw a graph with the fundamentals path. Give an economic interpretation for this path.

**c.** Assume that the fundamentals path in the previous item is common knowledge and there are credibility problems. Derive the exchange rate path. Compare the exchange rate path with that of the fundamentals. Represent them on a graph and present an economic interpretation. (*Tip: The general solution for an equation of the type* $y(x) = x + a\frac{dy(x)}{dx}$ *is given by* $y(x) = x + a + C\,e^{\frac{x}{a}}$, *for a value of C.*)

## Exercise 5

Throughout 2012, the euro suffered significant depreciation in relation to the American dollar. Consider a monetary model to determine the nominal exchange rate as described in this chapter, where demand for money is a positive function of product and negative for domestic exchange rate, and the uncovered interest rate and purchasing power parity conditions are valid. Assume the supply of the money grows at a constant rate.

Based on this model, judge if the following described situations can explain the depreciation of the euro. Justify your answers.

**a.** There was an increase in the US product in relation to the Eurozone.

**b.** There was an increase in supply for the US money in relation to the supply of Eurozone money.

**c.** The nominal interest rate in the United States is less than that of Europe.

**d.** A greater growth rate was expected in the supply of the US money in relation to the Eurozone.

## Exercise 6

Consider a version of the monetary model seen throughout this chapter, composed by the following equations:

$$\text{LM:} \quad m_t - p_t = \bar{y} - \alpha i_t$$
$$\text{UIP:} \quad i_t = i_t^* + E\{s_{t+1} - s_t\}$$
$$\text{PPP:} \quad s_t = p_t - p_t^*$$
$$\text{MG:} \quad m_{t+1} - m_t = \mu$$

where $p_t$ is the level of domestic prices, $s_t$ is the nominal exchange rate, $m_t$ is the nominal money supply, and $i_t$ is the nominal interest rate. The variables identified with * represent variables analogous to the international economy and are taken as constant. The parameters $\mu$, which represents the rate of growth of money supply, and $\bar{y}$, which represents full employment, are strictly positive. The operator $E_t\{\cdot\}$ represents the hope conditional for the set of available information in $t$. To simplify, assume that $i^*, \bar{y}, p^*$, and $m_t$ are equal to zero. In this model, all variables are expressed in logarithmic terms.

**a.** Assume that in $t = 1$ the government fixes the money supply growth rate at $\mu = 0.2$ and that the agents expect this policy to be maintained indefinitely. Obtain the equilibrium trajectory of $s_t$ and of $p_t$ for $t \geq 1$.

**b.** Assume that in the period $t = 1$ the government announces that it will freeze the exchange rate at $\bar{s} = 2$ from the period $t = 2$ forward. The government also announces that it will adjust the money supply for the period $t = 2$ and forward in order to maintain the fixed exchange rate established. Assume that the agents believe the government announcement and that the government in fact will implement the referred measures. Obtain the equilibrium trajectory of $s_t$ and of $p_t$ for $t \geq 1$ and the equilibrium trajectory of the money supply of period $t = 2$ forward.

## Exercise 7

Consider the monetary model seen throughout this chapter, where the behavior of the nominal exchange rate is reproduced by the following equation:

$$s_t = (m_t - m_t^*) - (y_t - y_t^*) + 0.5(E_t\{s_{t+1}\} - s_t)$$

where $s_t$ represents the nominal exchange rate, $y_t$ represents the product level, and $E_t\{\cdot\}$ is the hope operator conditional based on the set of information available for period $t$. The variables identified with * represent international economy variables. In this model, all variables are expressed in logarithmic terms. Assume that the agents possess a perfect forecast of the future, so that $E_t\{s_{t+1}\} = s_{t+1}$. To simplify, assume that $m_t^* = y_t^* = 0$ and it is hoped that these levels are maintained for all future periods. Determine the nominal exchange rate trajectory, before and after the policy changes.

**a.** Assume that the supply of money growth rate has been 10% to date and that the agents hope that this level will be maintained in the future. Then, the following policy changes occurred:

**1.** On date $t$, the central bank announced it would reduce the rate of growth for the supply of money by half from $t$ forward and the agents hope that this new rate will maintain its new level indefinitely.

**2.** On date $t$, the central bank announces that it will reduce the money supply growth rate by half from $t$ forward, but the agents believe that, with probability 1, actually the bank will double the supply of money and will remain at this new level indefinitely.

**3.** On date $t$, the central bank announces it will reduce the money supply growth rate by half from $t$ forward, but the agents believe this may occur with a probability of only 50%, attributing the remainder of the probability to the scenario where the money supply will not be altered, but remain indefinitely at the initial level.

**b.** Assume that the money supply has been constant in $m_j = 10$, until date $j \leq t - 1$. On date $t$, the central bank established the money supply at $m_j = 5$, for $j \geq t$. The agents, however, believe that the money supply will be increased to $m_j = 20$, for the date $j \geq t$.

# 7

# Macroeconomic Policies and Exchange Rate in the Short Run

## CHAPTER OUTLINE

In general, prices do not adjust instantly to economic shocks. There are different explanations for this, such as the presence of costs associated with the alteration in price itself, known as *menu costs*; contracts that do not allow an immediate price adjustment; or asymmetrical information problems that can delay the transfer of shocks to prices. This means that in the short run, or when relative prices have not had time to adjust to economic shocks, relative prices can differ from their equilibrium value, as studied in Chapter 5, causing the current account and the aggregate output to also differ from their long-run equilibrium level.

In this chapter, we will study two sticky price models. In the first, known as the Mundell–Fleming model, prices are maintained fixed. It represents the very short run where no economic shocks are transferred to prices. In the second, named the Mundell–Fleming–Dornbusch model, prices adjust, however slowly, according to the convergence rule for their long-run value. It allows the analysis of the real impacts of a monetary shock in the transition period after an economic shock. Finally, the last section of this chapter provides a critical analysis of the models.

# 7.1 Rigid Prices: The Mundell–Fleming Model

The Mundell–Fleming model, developed at the beginning of the 1960s by Robert Mundell and Marcus Fleming, also known as the IS–LM–BP model,[1] studies the impact of monetary and fiscal policies on the nominal exchange rate and output level. As prices are accepted as being totally rigid, all variations in the nominal exchange rate are translated into real exchange rate variations, as per Eq. (3.2). The real exchange rate variations, in turn, impact the aggregate product of the economy, as we will see further ahead. Therefore, monetary shocks generate real effects based on their impact on the nominal exchange rate. The focus of the model is to study the impact of monetary and fiscal policies on different exchange rate regimes.

## 7.1.1 Money, Assets, and Goods Markets

The assumption in relation to the operation of the money and assets market is identical to the long-run monetary model considered in the previous chapter. We will begin with the money market.

### 7.1.1.1 The Money Market

We assume the demand for money to be a linear function, positive in income and negative in interest rate, so that the equilibrium of this market is that which is defined by Eq. (6.1), which we will repeat here[2]:

$$m_t - p_t = \phi y_t - \eta i_t. \tag{7.1}$$

**In Keynesian models, this equation for the money market equilibrium is known as LM function.**

---

[1] The name IS–LM–BP comes from adding the external sector, represented by the balance of payments (BP), to the equations for equilibrium in the goods and money markets, which are identified as IS and LM functions, respectively, in Keynesian models.

[2] Notice that here we have the equation in discreet time as indicated with time as a subscript of the variables.

### 7.1.1.2 The Assets Market

As to the assets market, we assume that domestic and foreign assets are perfect substitutes and that there is perfect mobility of capital, so that the uncovered interest rate parity is satisfied, as in Eq. (6.2), reproduced here:

$$E(s_{t+1}) - s_t = i_t - i_t^*. \tag{7.2}$$

### 7.1.1.3 The Goods Market

The novelty appears in the goods market. In the flexible price model, nothing interesting happens in the goods market. The free trade of goods between countries, along with price flexibility, causes purchasing power parity to always be satisfied and the aggregate output is exogenous and constant at the full employment level in the economy. Actually, in all models seen until now, the economy is always at full employment. In the model to determine current account presented in Chapter 4, the level of aggregate production can vary over time, depending on the investments made, but all labor and available capital stock are always used in production. The same happens in the model to determine the real exchange rate in Chapter 5. In that model, relative prices affect the allocation of resources between sectors in the economy, with no slack capacity. More precisely, production is always on the production possibility frontier, which represents the production possibilities where all economic resources are used efficiently, with no waste and using all available production factors.

The Mundell–Fleming model assumes that there is slack capacity in the economy: that there are available production factors not being used, such that the amount produced cannot increase without new investments in capital or an increase in labor supply. The level of production is, therefore, restricted by the aggregate demand of the economy and responds to increases in demand. This is the main characteristic of the Keynesian models (Box 7.1).

Summarizing, we assume the goods market works in the following way. Price rigidity causes variations in the nominal exchange rate to also affect the real exchange rate, which is associated to the trade balance. Consumption and investment decisions in the economy, in turn, are affected by the interest rate. Therefore, the combination of the exchange rate and interest rate levels determines aggregate demand, to which production should respond to generate equilibrium in the goods market.

More precisely, the behavioral assumptions of the model can be incorporated into the national accounts identity, according to Eq. (2.2), which can be rewritten as[3]

$$Y_t = C(i_t, Y_t) + I(i_t) + G + \text{TB}(S_t), \tag{7.3}$$

---

[3] Notice that we wrote the output in logarithm in Eq. (7.1), while here we wrote it in level. Also notice that we wrote consumption and investment as functions of the nominal interest rate, when these two variables are actually functions of the real interest rate. In this model, however, this makes no difference: the real interest rate is always equal to the nominal, given that prices are constant.

---

**BOX 7.1 KEYNESIAN THEORY**

Keynesian theory is based on the ideas of economist John Maynard Keynes (1883–1946) presented in his book *A General Theory of Employment, Interest and Money*, published in 1936. In the midst of the 1929 economic crisis, Keynes advocated that an increase in public spending would raise aggregate production in the economy. The underlying idea is that, with the crisis, firms did not use all production factors available in the economy, for there was not enough demand for their products. An increase in public spending would increase consumption in the economy, stimulating an increase in production. Keynesian theory, which fell into disuse during the decades of strong world economic growth, came back into vogue with world economic crisis of 2008.

---

where aggregate consumption is taken as a negative function of interest rates, $\frac{\partial C(i,Y)}{\partial i} < 0$ and a positive function of income, $\frac{\partial C(i,Y)}{\partial Y} > 0$; investment is a negative function of interest rates, $\frac{\partial I(i)}{\partial i} < 0$, and the trade balance is a positive function of the exchange rate, $\frac{\partial TB(S)}{\partial S} > 0$. **The equilibrium equation in the goods market is known as the IS function in Keynesian models.**

The hypotheses contained in Eq. (7.3) can be justified based on the models described in Chapters 4 and 5. We begin with consumption. The Mundell–Fleming model assumes that aggregate consumption in the economy is a negative function of interest rates and a positive function of income level. The intuition for this effect is found in Section 4.2, which analyzes the individual's decisions to consume and save. The Euler equation (4.6) indicates that, as per the substitution effect, an increase in interest rates stimulates smaller present consumption in relation to future consumption, given that a higher interest rate makes current consumption relatively more expensive. Due to this effect, the individual tends to save more when faced with higher interest rates. Based on this motivation, the model assumes that aggregate consumption in the economy is a negative function of interest rates.[4]

As to the relationship between consumption and income, Section 4.2 shows that a temporary increase in income raises aggregate savings in the economy, given that individuals save a part of their extra income to consume more, not only in the present but also in the future. Therefore, the Mundell–Fleming model assumes that an increase in income has a positive impact on consumption and savings, namely the increase in consumption is smaller than the increase in income.

It is worth remembering that a permanent increase in income would have no impact on savings. In this case, all income increase would be used for consumption and, as income remains higher in the future, consumption can also be higher in the future, but without the

---

[4] Observe that, in the complete solution to the consumer problem in Section 4.1, the income effect is added to the interest rate substitution effect. The income effect speaks to the impact of interest rates on economic wealth, which depends if the country is an international lender or borrower. We saw by means of Eq. (4.17) that, actually, the impact of interest rates on consumption is positive if the country is a net creditor and negative if the country is a debtor. The Mundell–Fleming model only takes into consideration the substitution effect of interest on consumption.

need to save more. Given that the Mundell–Fleming model studies short-run adjustments to economic shocks, it is reasonable to assume the income variations are considered temporary.

Investment, in turn, is assumed to be a negative function of interest rate. In the model to determine the current account with production and investment described in Section 4.4, Eq. (4.29) indicates that the optimum investment choice is that which causes the marginal productivity of capital to be equal to the interest rate. Given that the marginal productivity of capital is a decreasing function, a higher interest rate is associated with a lower stock of capital and, consequently, a lower level of investment.

Finally, the model assumes a positive relation between the trade balance and the real exchange rate. Given that prices are fixed, nominal exchange rate changes automatically translates into changes of the real exchange rate. Chapter 5 shows that a more depreciated real exchange rate is associated with a larger trade balance, while an exchange rate appreciation leads to a reduction in the trade balance. Intuitively, a depreciated exchange rate makes the nontradable good relatively cheaper, stimulating an increase in the production of the tradable good and consumption of the nontradable good. The result is an increase in exports and a reduction in imports (Box 7.2).

---

### BOX 7.2 REAL EXCHANGE RATE AND TRADE BALANCE: A DOSE OF REALITY

Equation (5.26) establishes the trade balance as a function of the relative price of tradable goods and shows that exchange rate depreciation leads to an increase in the trade balance. The mechanism comes about by means of the impact of relative price changes on production and consumption decisions. More specifically, exchange rate depreciation renders tradable goods relatively more expensive, which stimulates their production and softens consumption. The result is a greater surplus to export in the tradable goods sector.

There is, however, a negative effect of exchange rate depreciation on the trade balance, by means of import prices, that is not captured by Eq. (5.26), due to the underlying hypotheses, namely, there is only one tradable good that can be imported and exported and the price of which is determined abroad. Let us see what happens when these hypotheses are relaxed. We now assume that there are two types of tradable goods: one exportable, which is produced in the home country, and an exportable good, this produced only abroad. There is no nontradable good. We take the exportable good as a numeraire, such that the relative price of the importable good is represented by $Sp_M^*$, where $p_M^*$ is the international price of the importable good, denominated in foreign currency.

The trade balance is now written as

$$\text{TB}(Sp_M^*) = X(Sp_M^*) - Sp_M^* M(Sp_M^*),$$

where $X(Sp_M^*)$ represents the exports and $M(Sp_M^*)$ the imports. The exports correspond to the foreign demand for domestic exportable goods, which is a positive function of the relative price of importable goods, $\frac{dX(\cdot)}{dSp_M^*} > 0$: the more expensive the foreign goods, the greater will be the foreign demand for domestic products that become relatively cheaper. Analogously, the domestic demand

(*Continued*)

**BOX 7.2 (CONTINUED)**

for imported products is a negative function of their relative price, $\frac{dM(\cdot)}{dSp_M^*} < 0$, since, with imported goods being more expensive, the domestic consumers will consume less imported goods and more national goods.

Within this context, what is the impact on the trade balance when there is exchange rate depreciation, namely, an increase in S? Taking the derivative of the trade balance equation in relation to S, we have that

$$\frac{\partial TB(\cdot)}{\partial S} = \left( \frac{\partial X(\cdot)}{\partial S} - Sp_M^* \frac{\partial M(\cdot)}{\partial S} \right) - p_M^* M(\cdot).$$

The term in parenthesis is positive, that is, exchange rate depreciation increases the trade balance by its effect on the amounts exported and imported. There is, however, a second term that is negative, and that corresponds to the fact that exchange rate depreciation causes imports to be more expensive, reducing the trade balance. In principle, this effect on the price of imports could have a greater magnitude than the effect on the amounts exported and imported in the term in parenthesis.

**THE MARSHALL–LERNER CONDITION**

To understand under what conditions exchange rate depreciation improves the trade balance, we will need to manipulate the previous equation a little. Multiplying both sides of the equation by $\frac{S}{X}$, we obtain

$$\frac{S}{X} \frac{\partial TB(\cdot)}{\partial S} = \left( \frac{S}{X} \frac{\partial X(\cdot)}{\partial S} - \frac{S}{X} Sp_M^* \frac{\partial M(\cdot)}{\partial S} \right) - \frac{Sp_M^* M(\cdot)}{X},$$

which, beginning with a trade balance in equilibrium, namely, $TB = X - Sp_M^* M = 0$, can be written as

$$\frac{S}{X} \frac{\partial TB(\cdot)}{\partial S} = \eta_{XS} - \eta_{MS} - 1.$$

$\eta_{XS} \equiv \frac{S}{X} \frac{\partial X(\cdot)}{\partial S} > 0$ and $\eta_{MS} \equiv \frac{S}{M} \frac{\partial M(\cdot)}{\partial S} < 0$ are the exchange rate elasticity of the exports and imports, respectively.

Therefore, **the trade balance increases with exchange rate depreciation when the sum of the exchange rate elasticity of exports and imports, in absolute value, is greater than one**, to wit

$$|\eta_{XS}| + |\eta_{MS}| > 1,$$

which is known as the **Marshall–Lerner condition.**

**J-CURVE**

Even if the Marshall–Lerner condition is satisfied, the impact of exchange rate depreciation on the amounts exported and imported is generally not immediate. The initial result of exchange rate depreciation is, actually, a deterioration of the trade balance due to its direct and immediate effect on the price of imports. The positive effect appears later, after the export and import decisions respond to the incentive given by the depreciated exchange rate. The trade adjustment forms, therefore, a curve in the form of a J.

## 7.1.2 Graphic Representation and Equilibrium

The economy is in equilibrium when the money, assets, and goods markets are in equilibrium. In terms of the model, when Eqs. (7.1)–(7.3) are simultaneously satisfied. The choice variables for government economic policy are the amount of money supply and public spending, whereas the interest rate, output level, and exchange rate are endogenously determined in the model. The economy equilibrium is represented in Figure 7.1. The graph represents two quadrants, where the vertical axis, common to both, represents the domestic interest rates. The horizontal axis of the left quadrant represents the exchange rate, while the output level is represented on the horizontal axis of the right quadrant. The origins of both horizontal axes meet each other where they cross with the vertical axis.

The right quadrant of the graph represents equilibrium in the goods and money markets. The goods market equilibrium is represented by the IS curve, from Eq. (7.3), which establishes a negative relation between interest rates and output level. The intuition for this negative relation is the following: an increase in interest rates reduces both the investment, captured by function $I(i_t)$, and consumption, by function $C(i_t, Y_t)$. Therefore, a higher interest rate has a negative impact on aggregate demand, represented by the right side of the IS equation (7.3). Given that output is constrained by demand, it also decreases. Notice that the reduction in output leads to a supplementary fall in consumption, given that this is also a function of output.[5]

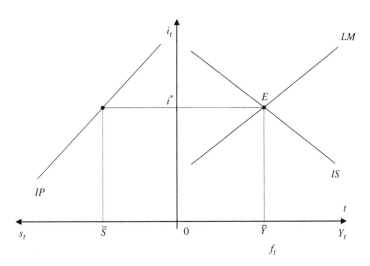

**Figure 7.1** Equilibrium in the Mundell–Fleming model.

[5] It is important to notice that equilibrium is guaranteed by the fact that consumption falls at a lower rate than output reduces, given that, as we have seen, savings decreases in the face of a temporary reduction in output. Otherwise, that is, if the reduction in consumption was equal to or greater than that of output, the product would fall indefinitely.

The position of the curve on the graph depends on the level of government spending and by the trade balance. The greater the value of these two variables, the more distant from the origin the curve will be. Intuitively, greater spending or greater net exports mean a greater aggregate demand, which should then be accompanied by a greater output level, for a given interest rate.

The LM curve on the graph, in turn, represents equilibrium in the money market from Eq. (7.1). It establishes a positive relation between the interest rate and output level. For a constant given real money supply, the demand for money should also be constant. Intuitively, since it reduces the demand for money, an increase in interest rates should be counterbalanced by an increase in output to maintain the demand for money constant. The position of the LM curve on the graph depends on the level of real money supply: the higher the real supply of money, more to the right the curve will position itself. A higher money supply should be accompanied by higher demand, which is attained with a higher income level, for a given interest rate.

Finally, the asset market equilibrium is represented by the IP curve in the left quadrant of the graph, which pictures the interest rate parity equation (7.2). The equation establishes a negative relation between the interest rate and the current exchange rate. Intuitively, a higher interest rate causes domestic assets to be more attractive in comparison to foreign assets. To reduce their attractiveness and reestablish equilibrium in the asset market, there should be an expectation of exchange rate depreciation. For a given expected exchange rate for the next period, $E(s_{t+1})$, a depreciation expectation occurs with a more appreciated exchange rate today. Therefore, a higher interest rate is associated with a lower exchange rate.

Notice that the position of the curve on the graph depends on the exchange rate expectation for the next period: the greater $E(s_{t+1})$ is, the more distant from the origin the curve is. For a given current value of the exchange rate, a higher expected depreciation of exchange rate demands a higher interest rate today so investors remain indifferent between buying domestic or foreign assets. The stationary equilibrium is represented by point $E$ in Figure 7.1. The expected exchange rate in the future should be equal to the exchange rate today $E(s_{t+1}) = s_t = \bar{s}$, if there is no expectation of changes in the future, which implies that the domestic interest rate is equal to the international, $i = i^*$. The IS and LM curves cross at the international interest rate level, $i^*$, and the corresponding output is given by $\overline{Y}$ on the graph. The equilibrium trade balance is that which results from the equilibrium level exchange rate $\bar{s}$. Once equilibrium is established, we analyze how it changes in face of change in government fiscal and monetary policies under two alternative exchange regimes: floating exchange rate and fixed exchange rate.

## 7.1.3 Monetary and Fiscal Policies Under Fixed and Floating Exchange Rate Regimes

The basic difference between the fixed and floating exchange rate regimes resides in government monetary policy. In a fixed regime, the government commits to intervene in the exchange rate market to set its price. A deficit in the balance of payments, for example, represents excess in demand for foreign currency and can cause an exchange rate deprecia-tion. To avoid depreciation, the government should sell its international reserves to rebal-ance the money market without altering the exchange rate, which decreases the money supply. Hence, money supply decreases in the face of pressure to depreciate, and, analo-gously, it increases when there is a pressure for exchange rate appreciation. In this case, we say that the monetary policy has become passive in the sense that it is used to maintain the nominal exchange rate at a given level.

In a floating exchange rate regime, there is no commitment to defend an exchange rate parity, and, therefore, the government can buy and sell its bonds on the open market in order to adjust the money supply in a completely exogenous way.

We will now see how a small, open economy with free capital mobility reacts to changes in monetary and fiscal policies under fixed and floating exchange rate regimes. Before begin-ning the analysis, a warning is in order: The Mundell–Fleming model does not allow the analysis of the transition between different short-run equilibria. I propose an intuition for the economic mechanisms that lead the economy to a new equilibrium after a change in economic policy, even though the model does not allow an analysis of the dynamics.

### 7.1.3.1 Floating Exchange Rate Regime
#### 7.1.3.1.1 PERMANENT FISCAL EXPANSION
Initially, the economy is at a steady-state equilibrium represented by point $E_0$ on Figure 7.2. An increase in government spending represents higher aggregate demand in the economy, shifting curve IS to the right, represented on the figure by the movement of $IS_0$ to $IS_1$. With the new demand structure, the goods and money markets balance at a higher interest rate: the LM and $IS_1$ curves cross at a higher interest rate level, $i_1 > i^*$. A domestic interest rate that is higher than the international attracts foreign capital, leading to an appreciation of the

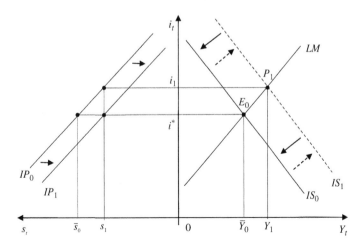

**Figure 7.2** Permanent fiscal expansion under a floating exchange rate regime.

exchange rate. The interest rate parity is then satisfied with a more appreciated exchange rate, as shown in the left quadrant of Figure 7.2, with the exchange rate moving from $\bar{s}_0$ to $s_1$.

Due to the exchange rate appreciation, exports decrease and imports increase, reducing aggregate domestic demand and moving curve IS to the left, in direction of its original position. In this movement, the equilibrium domestic interest rate, where curves IS and LM cross, decreases. The new short-run stationary equilibrium is only attained when the interest rate is again equal to the international.

At the same time, the expected exchange rate adjusts to a more appreciated value (or rather, smaller), which dislocates the interest parity curve to closer to the origin on the left quadrant of the graph. The final exchange rate level is that which takes IS back to its original position, so that both curves cross at the interest rate level equal to that of international interest rate.[6] In the new short-run equilibrium, curve IS coincides with its initial position, producing the same initial output level and interest rate. It is important to draw attention to the fact that, in spite of the output level not changing with the increase in public spending, the composition of the aggregate demand is different from the original: public spending is greater and the trade balance, smaller.

In summary, **in a floating exchange rate regime, an increase in public spending is counterbalanced by a reduction in net exports to the same extent, so that the output level remains unaltered**. A reduction in public spending would have an inverse effect: exchange rate depreciation would cause an increase in the trade balance, which would compensate the initial reduction in expenditures, maintaining the output unaltered.

### 7.1.3.1.2 PERMANENT MONETARY EXPANSION

Monetary expansion causes a shift of the LM curve to the right, which goes from being $LM_0$ to $LM_1$ as shown in Figure 7.3. The equilibrium in goods and money markets is then achieved at an interest rate inferior to international interest rates, $i_1 < i^*$. The less attractive domestic assets cause an exit of capital, which, under the flexible exchange rate regime, causes a depreciation of the home currency, which increases from $\bar{s}_0$ to $s_1$.

Exchange rate depreciation, in turn, leads to a trade balance increase, which means an increase in the aggregate demand of the economy, shifting the IS curve to the right, from $IS_0$ to $IS_1$, which causes an increase in interest rates. Simultaneously, the exchange rate expectation adjusts, leading to an outward shift of the IP curve on the left quadrant of the graph. Analogously to the case of fiscal expansion, the exchange rate variation will be that which leads the IS curve to cross with the LM at the interest rate level equal to the international rate.

In summary, **monetary expansion in a floating exchange rate regime causes an increase in output level due to the increase of aggregate demand induced by the rise in net exports**. The interest rate, as always is the case in equilibrium, is equal to the international rate, while the exchange rate is more depreciated in relation to its initial level.

---

[6] We know that the exchange rate is more appreciated in relation to its initial level, but, in principle, could be higher or smaller than the fictitious intermediary level $s_1$.

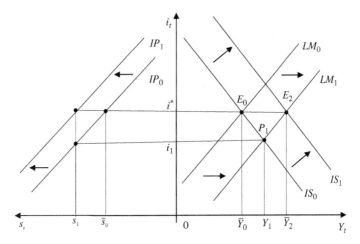

**Figure 7.3** Permanent monetary expansion under a floating exchange rate regime.

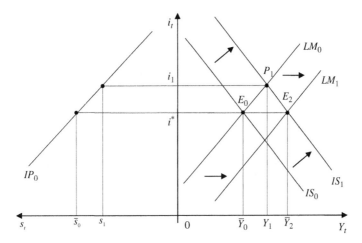

**Figure 7.4** Permanent fiscal expansion under the fixed exchange rate regime.

## 7.1.3.2 Fixed Exchange Rate Regime
### 7.1.3.2.1 PERMANENT FISCAL EXPANSION

As in the case of floating exchange rate, an increase in government spending shifts the IS curve to the right, from $IS_0$ to $IS_1$, which causes increase in the interest rate level that balances the money and goods market. The inflow of capital caused by the increase in interest rate pressures for an exchange rate appreciation. To maintain the exchange rate fixed, the government must purchase the excess foreign currency. The government's international reserves increase, as well as the supply of money. The LM curve then shifts to the right, from $LM_0$ to $LM_1$, as shown in Figure 7.4. The purchase of international reserves occurs until the

---

### BOX 7.3 STERILIZED INTERVENTIONS

The government could use open market operations to offset the change in money supply caused by the intervention in the foreign exchange market. In particular, it could sell government bonds (denominated in domestic currency) in open market operations at the same time it buys foreign currency, so that the monetary base remains constant. Clearly, the same operation could be used in the opposite direction, namely, to sell foreign currency and buy domestic currency securities simultaneously. This double operation is known as *sterilized intervention*.

When domestic and foreign assets are perfect substitutes, as assumed in the models studied so far, sterilized interventions have no impact on exchange rates. The reason is clear from Figure 7.4: if the money supply remains constant, the LM curve does not shift and the intervention is not capable of altering the domestic interest rate. Hence, capital inflow continues, as in the case depicted in the figure, as does its appreciating pressure on the exchange rate.

Although, the empirical literature has found that sterilized interventions have limited effectiveness,[a] some recent empirical studies on emerging markets have unveiled evidence of sterilized interventions affecting exchange rates.[b] Imperfect asset substitutability seems to be a crucial ingredient for sterilized interventions to be effective.[c]

---

[a]Sarno and Taylor (2001) present a review on these findings and theoretical underpinnings.
[b]See, for instance, Domac and Mendoza (2004), Guimarães and Karacadag (2004), Gersl and Holub (2006), Egert (2007), and Kamil (2008).
[c]As shown by Kumhof (2010).

---

domestic interest rate is again equal to the international. At the end of the process, **fiscal expansion is accompanied by monetary expansion to maintain the exchange rate fixed, which causes an expansion of the output level in the economy** (Box 7.3).

### 7.1.3.2.2 PERMANENT MONETARY EXPANSION

Monetary expansion shifts the LM curve to the right, from $LM_0$ to $LM_1$, as shown in Figure 7.5, which causes domestic interest rates to be inferior to international interest rates. Less attractive domestic assets cause an outflow of capital, raising the demand for foreign currency and reducing the demand for domestic currency. By committing to nominal exchange rate parity, the central bank must cover this excess in demand for foreign currency by selling its international reserves and buying domestic currency. The reduction in the supply of money shifts the LM curve back to the left, as shown in the figure. The initial expansionist credit policy is accompanied by a reduction in reserves at the same level, so that the output, interest rate, and exchange rate remain unaltered. Actually, **monetary policy becomes endogenous when a fixed exchange rate is adopted. By choosing a fixed exchange rate regime, the government gives up this economic policy instrument** (Box 7.4).

### 7.1.3.3 Summary

Table 7.1 summarizes the expansionist fiscal and monetary policies under the fixed and floating exchange rate regimes. We see that expansionist fiscal and monetary policies have

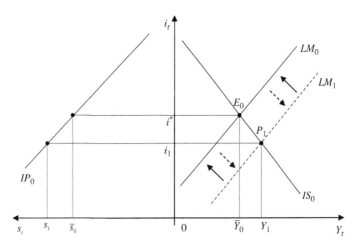

**Figure 7.5** Permanent monetary expansion under a fixed exchange rate regime.

### BOX 7.4 IMPOSSIBLE TRINITY

The Mundell–Fleming model shows that, in a fixed exchange rate regime and with free capital mobility, the government loses monetary policy as an economic policy instrument. The institution of the fixed exchange rate regime indicates the government's commitment to use its monetary policy to stabilize the exchange rate. As we have seen, when the government attempts to expand money supply seeking to stimulate economic activity, the resulting reduction in interest rates causes domestic assets to be less attractive, leading to an exit of capital. To avoid an exchange rate depreciation, the government must sell international reserves, which reduces the money supply. Finally, the money supply returns to its original level, and the interest rate remains equal to the international interest rate. The conclusion is that **it is impossible to simultaneously have free capital mobility, a fixed exchange rate regime, and an independent monetary policy. This is known as the *Impossible Trinity* or the *International Finance Trilemma*.** In general, when there is free capital mobility, the government must opt between stabilizing the exchange rate or having monetary policy autonomy.

Several empirical studies have sought to verify if this trinity is indeed impossible. A means of doing this is to analyze the relation between domestic and international interest rates: these two rates should be correlated under a fixed exchange rate regime. Domestic interest rates should be compared with the interest rates of the country to which the exchange rate parity is established or, in the case of a floating exchange rate regime, in relation to the country to which exchange rate would be tied where a fixed exchange rate regime to be instituted.

Shambaugh (2004) and Obstfeld et al. (2004) examine the validity of the impossible trinity from a global perspective. They found that the correlation between interest rates is strongest in fixed exchange rate regimes than when the exchange rate is floating. In other words, in general, the degree of monetary autonomy under the floating exchange rate regime is greater than in an exchange rate parity regime. However, there is still some monetary autonomy when the exchange rate is fixed, given that the correlation between the interest rates, even though higher, is not perfect. Likewise, even in a floating exchange rate regime, the domestic monetary policy does not vary much from the base country policy, indicating that the exchange rate is never totally floating.

**Table 7.1** Summary of the Mundell–Fleming Model Results

| Exchange Rate Regime | Expansionist Monetary Policy | Expansionist Fiscal Policy |
| --- | --- | --- |
| Floating exchange rate | Output increase | Output level unaltered |
| | Exchange rate depreciation | Exchange rate appreciation |
| | Trade balance increase | Trade balance reduction |
| Fixed exchange rate | Output unaltered | Increase in output |
| | Lower international reserves | Higher international reserves |

opposite impacts on the balance of payments since they have opposite impacts on interest rates. The flow of capital, mobilized by changes in interest rate, leads to an increase in the balance of payments after an increase in government spending, and a deterioration in the balance with an expansionist monetary policy. Changes in the balance of payments balance translate into exchange rate variations when the exchange rate is floating, while there is a change in reserves when the exchange is fixed.

The impact of the policies on the output depends on the exchange rate regime. An expansionist fiscal policy increases output in a fixed regime, while when the exchange rate is floating, only the composition of the output is altered, but without altering its level. More precisely, the increase in aggregate demand caused by an increase in spending is counterbalanced by a reduction in net exports due to exchange rate depreciation. Monetary policy, in turn, only can be used to stimulate the output under a floating exchange rate regime (Box 7.5).

# 7.2 Sticky Prices: The Mundell–Fleming–Dornbusch Model

The Mundell–Fleming model is useful to analyze very short-run situations, when prices have not yet adjusted to shocks or policy changes. However, as prices are always fixed in that model, it is not possible to analyze the evolution of the economy over time. In his 1976 article, Rüdiger Dornbusch added the dynamic of prices to the model, making it more realistic. It is an elegant model that offers a simple structure to analyze the impact of nominal and real shocks on the exchange rate. The main prediction of the model is that the exchange rate responds excessively to permanent monetary shocks, known as *exchange rate overshooting*. This result explains the fact that the nominal exchange rate is more volatile than prices, that is, its variation is greater than that predicted by the flexible price monetary model seen in Chapter 6.

## 7.2.1 Money, Assets, and Goods Markets

As in the Mundell–Fleming model on which it is based, the Dornbusch model is also based on the *ad hoc* hypothesis of the functioning of the economy, with no microfoundations. The hypotheses made in relation to the money and assets markets are exactly the same as the Mundell–Fleming model: money market equilibrium is given by the LM equation (7.1) and for the assets market, the uncovered interest rate parity described in Eq. (7.2) is valid.

## BOX 7.5 EUROPEAN CRISIS

The results of the model suggest that, with the proper mix of fiscal and monetary policies, it would be possible to achieve any desired combination between variations in output and balance of payments. Consider, for example, an economy with a fixed exchange rate regime that suffers simultaneously from unemployment and a deficit in the balance of payments. By increasing spending, the government stimulates domestic production, while the increase in interest rates resulting from this policy would attract international capital, solving the balance of payments problem.[a]

This is, actually, the dilemma countries such as Spain, Portugal, and Greece faced after the 2008 international financial crisis. With the recession that followed the crisis and the difficulty in financing their sovereign foreign debt, these countries came to face balance of payments problems together with high unemployment rates. From the point of view of the model, one can consider these counties, members of the Economic and Monetary Union of the European Union (EMU), as following a fixed exchange rate. As presented in Figure 7.4, fiscal expansion would stimulate economic activity as well as the inflow of foreign capital into the country, solving, thereby, the two main problems in these economies. However, a source of these countries' problems was their elevated fiscal deficit, which led to excessive government debt. Fiscal expansion, therefore, was not an economic policy option.

If these countries had not been tied to the EMU and had their own currencies, they could have promoted monetary expansion and allowed their exchange rates to float. The result would have been a stimulus to production, as illustrated in Figure 7.3. The problem is that, in the EMU, this solution cannot be unilaterally implemented given that monetary policy is decided by the European Central Bank Governing Council, composed of the six members of the Executive Board and the governors of the national central banks of the 18 euro-area countries. If, on the one hand, an expansionist monetary policy would help these countries in recession it would, on the other, create inflationary pressure on EMU countries that did not have an unemployment problem. The monetary policy actually chosen is that which would be adequate for the set of countries that compose the EMU. It will be more distant from the optimum policy for each country individually, the greater the disparities between the countries. In terms of unemployment, the disparities are quite large: while the unemployment rate in the Eurozone in December 2014 was 11.4%, it was less than 6% in Luxembourg and Germany, and over 23% in Greece and Spain.

---

[a]Remember that interest rates always return to their original level, always equal to the international interest rate, when there is perfect capital mobility. The inflow of capital resulting from the higher interest rate generates an excess supply of foreign currency at the current exchange rate, which the government must buy in order to prevent exchange rate appreciation.

---

The novelty appears in the goods market. In the IS equation (7.3) in the Mundell–Fleming model, the trade balance was merely a function of the nominal exchange rate. Prices did not appear in that equation: with fixed prices, as assumed in that model, real exchange rate and nominal exchange rate move together. In the variation of the model proposed by Dornbusch, prices change over time, so that the real exchange rate comes to figure explicitly in the equation.

The basic idea regarding the goods market is the same, in the sense that there is slack capability in the economy so that output is determined by aggregate demand. The latter, in turn, is assumed to have two components. One constant component, which in the IS equation (7.3) of the previous model, corresponds to the sum of consumption, investment, and government spending, and a component that changes with the real exchange rate, which corresponds to the trade balance.

Aggregate demand $y_t^d$ is then described as

$$y_t^d = \bar{y} + \delta(q_t - \bar{q}),\tag{7.4}$$

where $\bar{y}$ is the logarithm of the natural rate of output, defined as the level of production sustainable in the long run, without generating bottlenecks or inflationary pressure. $q_t$ is the logarithm for the real exchange rate which, from Eq. (3.2), can be written as

$$q_t \equiv s_t + p^* - p_t.\tag{7.5}$$

$\bar{q}$ is defined as the level (in logarithm) of the real exchange rate compatible with the long-run equilibrium of the economy. When the current exchange rate is equal to the long-run equilibrium, $q_t = \bar{q}$, aggregate demand is equal to the natural rate of output. Finally, $\delta$ is the parameter that measures the impact of deviations of the real exchange rate from its equilibrium value on the aggregate demand. Intuitively, a more depreciated real exchange rate in relation to its equilibrium level implies relatively cheaper domestic goods, which leads to an increase in net exports. These, in turn, represent an increase in aggregate demand in the economy.

The international price, $p^*$, is taken as a constant, while the domestic price, $p_t$, is predetermined and adjusts sluggishly, according to the following equation:

$$p_{t+1} - p_t = \psi(y_t^d - \bar{y}) + (s_{t+1} - s_t).\tag{7.6}$$

There are two forces that determine price adjustment. The first is that an excess of aggregate demand in relation to the natural rate of output causes inflationary pressure, and $\psi$ measures the impact of excessive demand on prices. The second is that variations in nominal exchange rate are passed on to the price.

## 7.2.2 Real Exchange Rate Dynamic

Substituting the aggregate demand equation (7.4) into the price adjustment equation (7.6) and rearranging the terms, we get

$$\underbrace{s_{t+1} - p_{t+1} + p^*}_{q_{t+1}} - \underbrace{(s_t - p_t + p^*)}_{q_t} = -\psi[\bar{y} + \delta(q_t - \bar{q}) - \bar{y}],$$

which can be rewritten as

$$q_{t+1} - q_t = -\psi\delta(q_t - \bar{q}).\tag{7.7}$$

Equation (7.7) defines the real exchange rate dynamics that guarantees the goods market equilibrium, given the price dynamics.

## 7.2.3 Nominal Exchange Rate Dynamics

Substituting interest rate parity (Eq. (7.2)) in the money market equilibrium equation (Eq. (7.1)), we have that

$$m_t - p_t = -\eta(i^* + s_{t+1} - s_t) + \phi[\bar{y} + \delta(q_t - \bar{q})],$$

which, by rearranging and using the real exchange rate definition (Eq. (7.5)), leads to

$$m_t - s_t + q_t = -\eta(s_{t+1} - s_t) + \phi\delta(q_t - \bar{q}),$$

where we can assume that, to simplify the equation, $p^* = i^* = \bar{y} = 0$.[7] The equation can then be rewritten as

$$s_{t+1} - s_t = \frac{s_t}{\eta} - \frac{(1 - \phi\delta)q_t}{\eta} - \frac{\phi\delta\bar{q} + m_t}{\eta}. \tag{7.8}$$

Equation (7.8) establishes the nominal exchange rate dynamics that guarantees money market equilibrium, satisfying uncovered interest rate parity.

## 7.2.4 Dynamic Equilibrium

Equations (7.7) and (7.8) determine the equilibrium dynamics of the economy, which is depicted in Figure 7.6. According to Eq. (7.7), the real exchange rate is stationary when it is equal to its long-run equilibrium value, i.e.,

$$\Delta q_t = 0 \Leftrightarrow q_t = \bar{q}. \tag{7.9}$$

The vertical line on the graph, identified by $\Delta q_t = 0$, represents the set of points where $\Delta q_t \equiv q_{t+1} - q_t = 0$. As indicated by the small, horizontal arrows on the graph, for all points to the right of the line, i.e., when $q_t > \bar{q}$, the real exchange rate is decreasing, while it is increasing to the left, when $q_t < \bar{q}$.

As to the nominal exchange rate, according to Eq. (7.8) it is stationary, i.e., $\Delta s_t \equiv s_{t+1} - s_t = 0$, when

$$\Delta s_t = 0 \Leftrightarrow s_t = (1 - \phi\delta)q_t + \phi\delta\bar{q} + m_t. \tag{7.10}$$

In the dynamics represented on the graph, it is assumed that $\phi\delta < 1$, so that Eq. (7.10) is represented by line $\Delta s_t = 0$ with a positive slope in Figure 7.6. $\delta$ and $\phi$ are two exogenous

---

[7] The international price levels, the international interest rates, and the natural rate of output are exogenous and constant. We assume, then, that units of measure are such that the level of each of these variables is equal to 1, which makes its logarithm equal to 0.

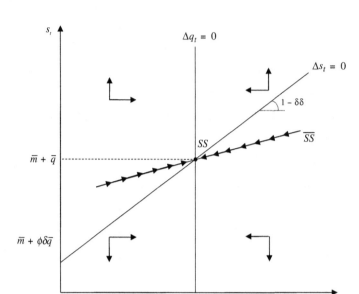

**Figure 7.6** Equilibrium in the Mundell–Fleming–Dornbusch model.

economic parameters: $\delta$ measures the impact of the real exchange rate on output (from Eq. (7.4)), while $\phi$ measures the impact of output on money demand (from Eq. (7.1)). The hypothesis that $\phi\delta < 1$ means, then, that an exchange rate variation has a reduced final impact on the demand for money.

The small vertical arrows indicate the nominal exchange rate dynamics. For points above the line, the right side of Eq. (7.8) is positive, hence the exchange rate depreciates (i.e., increases) over time. The inverse is true for points below the line.

The economy is in the steady state when both the nominal exchange rate and the real exchange rate are such that Eqs. (7.9) and (7.10) are simultaneously satisfied. In terms of Figure 7.6, this situation corresponds to the crossing point of the two lines, represented by point SS. Substituting Eq. (7.9) in Eq. (7.10), we have that

$$\bar{s} = (1 - \phi\delta)\bar{q} + \phi\delta\bar{q} + \overline{m}$$
$$\Downarrow \qquad\qquad (7.11)$$
$$\bar{s} = \bar{q} + \overline{m}$$

where $\overline{m}$ is the (constant) level of money supply. Using the definition of the real exchange rate (Eq. (7.5)), we also have that

$$\bar{p} = \overline{m}. \qquad\qquad (7.12)$$

If an economy finds itself in the steady state, it will remain in this state if there are no economic shocks. What lacks to be defined is where the economy is when it is not in the steady state. Equations (7.7) and (7.8) govern the movement of the two rates and should be satisfied

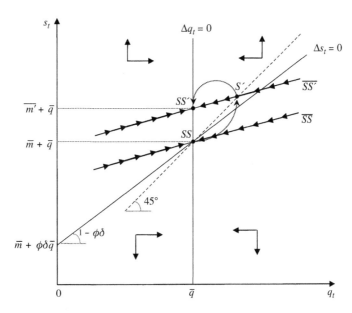

**Figure 7.7** Expansionist monetary policy in the Mundell–Fleming–Dornbusch model.

at all times. Intuitively, it is as if the quadrant on the graph was a sink with a distorted bottom, and these two equations defined its curvature. If a drop of water is spilled, it follows the infinite grooves defined by the two movement equations. The economy is on an equilibrium path when it follows the groove that leads to the steady state. There are two of these grooves: one that leads the economy to the steady state from its right side, and the other that leads to it from its left side, and they are represented on the graph in Figure 7.6 by two lines with arrows in the direction of long-run equilibrium, forming the segment of line $\overline{SS}'$. Therefore, the economy is always on one of these two equilibrium paths or in the steady state.

## 7.2.5 Impact of an Expansionist Monetary Policy

In order to understand the effect of an expansionist monetary policy, suppose that the economy is at the steady state $SS$ when the government unexpectedly promotes a permanent increase in money supply, which jumps from $\overline{m}$ to $\overline{m}'$, for $\overline{m}' > \overline{m}$. In face of the new money supply, the position on the graph of the line $\Delta s_t = 0$ on which the nominal exchange rate is stationary, defined by Eq. (7.10), is not the same: it shifts upwards.

In the new steady state, represented on the graph by point $SS'$ on Figure 7.7, the real exchange rate in the steady state is always equal to its equilibrium level $\overline{q}$, which is determined exogenously of the model.

As to the nominal exchange rate, Eq. (7.11) shows that it will be equal to

$$\overline{s}' = \overline{q} + \overline{m}', \tag{7.13}$$

while the price, according to Eq. (7.12), will be given by

$$\bar{p}' = \bar{m}'. \tag{7.14}$$

Comparing Eqs. (7.12) and (7.14) to Eqs. (7.11) and (7.13), we see that the exchange rate depreciation and the price increase are equal to the increase in money supply, i.e.,

$$\bar{s}' - \bar{s} = \bar{p}' - \bar{p} = \bar{m}' - \bar{m}. \tag{7.15}$$

The economy, however, cannot jump from an steady-state equilibrium to another since prices adjust slowly, according to the rule defined by Eq. (7.6). At the moment the monetary shock occurs, the price is at the original steady-state level, $\bar{p}$, and the definition of real exchange rate (Eq. (7.5)) establishes that the real and nominal exchange rates move together, for a given price level. Therefore, the exchange rates jump to point $s'$ on the new equilibrium path, respecting relation (7.5), namely, along a 45° ray passing through the original steady-state point, as indicated in Figure 7.7. As of that time, the two rates follow the equilibrium path until the new steady state, indicated by point $SS'$ on the graph.

An important result of the model is that, compared to the initial equilibrium, **the exchange rate depreciation in the short run is larger than the depreciation corresponding to the new steady state. Restating, the response of the nominal exchange rate to a monetary expansion is magnified in the short run. This is the famous nominal exchange rate *overshooting* effect.** After this *overshooting*, the nominal exchange rate gradually appreciates along the equilibrium path until the new steady state. The *overshooting* of the exchange rate means that the nominal exchange rate is more volatile than the monetary policy and prices. The same occurs with the real exchange rate: it depreciates at the moment of shock, and then gradually appreciates until attaining its long-run equilibrium value.

What is the intuition for nominal exchange rate *overshooting*? Given that prices are predetermined, an increase in the money supply represents an increase in its real supply, that is, the left side of Eq. (7.1) increases. The demand for money, represented on the right side of the equation, should then increase to balance the money market. The real exchange rate depreciation, caused by the nominal depreciation under rigid prices, increases the aggregate demand, according to Eq. (7.4). The increase in output is proportional to $\delta$, and the impact of the increase of output on money demand is proportional to $\phi$. When $\phi\delta < 1$, the final effect of the real exchange depreciation on money demand is not strong enough to meet the increase in money supply. Consequently, the interest rate should also decrease to further increase money demand and, thereby, balance the money market. However, the interest rate parity equation (7.2) indicates that the domestic interest rate can be smaller than the international one only when there is an expected appreciation of the exchange rate. Therefore, the initial exchange rate depreciation should be sufficiently high for it to appreciate and the domestic interest rates to be lower than the international interest rates on the equilibrium path to the new steady state.

Notice that the model only generates exchange rate *overshooting* when line $\Delta s = 0$, which unites the points where the nominal exchange rate is stationary, has a positive slope. As we saw previously, the slope is positive when $\phi\delta < 1$, which is exactly the condition shown in the previous paragraph for a reduction in interest rates to be necessary to balance the money market before reaching the new steady state.

In the Mundell−Fleming model, where prices are fixed, monetary expansion in a fixed exchange regime leads to the expansion of output and exchange depreciation. With the dynamics introduced by Dornbusch, we learned that the output, after the initial expansion, returns to its full employment rate at the pace that prices adjust and the economy attains its steady state. Therefore, **monetary expansion increased output, but only temporarily**.

# 7.3 Monetary Models with Price Rigidity: Their Uses and Limitations

The rigid price monetary models allow the investigation of the real effect of monetary policy. In these models, the nominal exchange rate adjusts automatically to shocks, while price adjustments are gradual. It is easy to see that the nominal exchange seems to be indeed more flexible than the prices of goods: we read in the paper that the exchange rate is different from day to day, while prices at the supermarket tend to not change much from 1 week to the next, when the inflation rate is not high.[8]

These monetary models with rigid prices are built with heroic simplifying assumptions not found in current economic models, which tend to be much more sophisticated. Yet, every economist learns them, not as a curiosity of history of economic thought, but by the fact that they offer a very good intuition to analyze the effects of government policies in the short run under different exchange regimes, that is, before prices react to the changes in policy.

In the eyes of contemporary economic theory, the main source of discomfort from the rigid price models presented in this chapter resides in the fact that the model is based on an *ad hoc* hypothesis in relation to how the economy works. In other words, the models are not based on microfoundations, where the relations between the economic variables are derived based on the behavior of individuals, be they consumers, businesses, or government, that make decisions in such a way as to maximize their objective function, subject to budget or technological constraints, as be the case, and taking into account the information that is available to them.

Even if the *ad hoc* assumptions were able to describe the economic relations in a reasonable, realistic way, the fact that they are not microfounded means that they do not capture the possible changes in individual behavior after a change in economic policy, for example.[9]

---

[8] For those who live under very high inflation, the story is a little different. With monthly inflation reaching double-digit levels, prices change daily. One cannot go out with exact change for the bus fare since we never know how much the fare will be. But, that is another story...

[9] This is known as the *Lucas Critique*, proposed by the economist Robert Lucas, Jr., from the University of Chicago. He claims that individuals make decisions based on their expectations in relation to the future. Therefore, the relationships between macroeconomic variables observed in the past do not serve to make inferences on the impact of economic policy changes, given that individual behavior would change in response to these changes. The development and application of the hypothesis of rational expectations won Robert Lucas, Jr., the 1995 Nobel Prize in Economics.

It is fact, however, that a model with microfoundations is much more complex than models with *ad hoc* assumptions. One only needs compare the models presented in Chapters 4 and 5, which have microfoundations, to those presented in this chapter.

Furthermore, the models in this chapter do not incorporate the intertemporal consequences of public policy. In the Mundell–Fleming model, we studied the effect of an increase in public spending. The policy represents an increase in the current public deficit, which should have an impact on future public finance. The economic agents should, then, when deciding what to consume, take into consideration the expectation of future governmental action to satisfy its intertemporal budgetary constraint. Private agents could, for example, decide to save more when there is an increase in government spending in order to deal with higher taxes in the future when the budget needs to be balanced.[10] However, these considerations are not incorporated into the model. The increase in public spending translates into an increase in aggregate consumption, with no impact on private consumption.

The intertemporal budget constraint for the country is also not taken into consideration. In the short-run dynamics of the Mundell–Fleming–Dornbusch model, the real exchange rate differs from its equilibrium level. This means the current account balance differs from its optimum level over the transition period. A revision would be then expected of the optimum current-account path for the future, which should be reflected in the equilibrium real exchange rate level. If, for example, a country accumulates credit with the rest of the world along the transition, its wealth increases. The increase in wealth should impact the decision to consume and save. The model does not capture this wealth effect.

Finally, we are not able to use these models to do welfare analysis, since they are not based on microfoundations. The flexible price model studied in Chapter 6 allows for the study of the impact of the fundamentals on the nominal exchange rate, but the real side of the economy is completely exogenous. Allowing for rigid prices as presented in this chapter, we have action on the real side of the economy as well. We saw how monetary policy affects not only the nominal exchange rate but also the real exchange rate and output level in the economy. However, in the end, we would like to be able to say what policy is best for the economy, and that this "best" should be qualified in terms of welfare. With a model based on microfoundations, such as those in Chapters 4 and 5, we have the utility function of the representative consumer, for example, that we can use as a welfare function. Therefore, we are able to analyze the impact of different political policies on economic welfare, taking into consideration the intertemporal aspects.

Actually, this model exits. Obstfeld and Rogoff (1995) propose an intertemporal model of the open economy based on microfoundations and with rigid prices. They make a bridge between the intertemporal current-account adjustment model in Chapter 4 with the Mundell–Fleming–Dornbusch model with sluggish prices. The demand for money is derived

---

[10] Actually, if there were no imperfections in the credit market and the government were to meet its intertemporal budget constraint, such as in the models in Chapters 4 and 5, an increase in public spending should not have any effect on the aggregate demand. The private agents internalize the government budget constraint and every government expense is counterbalanced by a reduction in private consumption. This is known as the *Ricardian Equivalence*.

endogenously in the model, assuming that the representative consumer derives utility from holding money, which is a hypothesis commonly made in the literature to generate demand for money. It is also assumed that there is an infinity of differentiated goods and that each country produces a portion of them. Therefore, there can be variations in the terms of trade between countries. On the other hand, the law of one price, defined in Eq. (3.4), and purchasing power parity, as defined by Eq. (3.5), is valid. Prices are assumedly predetermined, or rather, are fixed for a period, which generates the real effects of the monetary policy.

The results of the Obstfeld and Rogoff (1995) model show the importance of taking into account intertemporal effects. An interesting result of the model is that the income effect causes monetary expansion to have a permanent impact on output, while, in the Mundell—Fleming—Dornbusch model, the output returns to its original level in the long run. More interesting yet is the result of an expansionist monetary policy to increase welfare both for the country that puts it into practice and for the rest of the world. In principle, it was believed that the rest of the world would be harmed by domestic monetary expansion due to the fact that it causes exchange depreciation and a consequent deviation of consumption in favor of domestic goods. This model shows that this effect, even though existent, is of lesser importance in comparison to the positive effect on aggregate world demand in a situation where world production is lower than its optimum level due to the monopoly power of producers.

Even though the model offers a more rigorous treatment of the relationships between variables and allow analyses that were not possible in models with no microeconomic foundations, it is much more complex than the models presented here. The original article by Obstfeld and Rogoff (1995) has no less than 70 equations! Actually, it is not possible to solve the model analytically, nor to perform a graphic analysis as we have done here. Finally, the extensive literature that was developed based on the model shows that the results are, actually, quite sensitive as to the hypotheses used in relation to the nature of price rigidity, the specification of preferences and the financial structure, as pointed out by Lane (2001). In summary, for practical purposes, the Mundell—Fleming and Mundell—Fleming—Dornbusch models remain as relatively simple and efficient alternatives for us to study the main effects of monetary and fiscal policies on exchange rate and income.

# 7.4 Exercises

## Exercise 1

At the beginning of the 1980s, the president of the United States Federal Reserve decided to adopt a strong contractionist monetary policy, seeking to contain the advance of domestic inflation rates. The result was an expressive increase in American interest rates. Consider a small and open foreign country. Using the Mundell—Fleming model, analyze the effect of the American contractionist monetary policy on this foreign country in the following settings:

**a.** The economy of the foreign country operates on a flexible exchange rate regime.

**b.** The economy of the foreign country operates on a fixed exchange rate regime.

## Exercise 2

Decide if the following statements are true, false or if the veracity is uncertain. Explain your answers.

**a.** An economy subject to shocks should adopt a floating exchange rate regime to stabilize the output level.

**b.** With exchange rate depreciation, the domestic interest rates can be maintained lower than the international, given that with foreign currency a foreign investor can purchase more domestic currency.

**c.** In a fixed exchange rate regime, a country can follow an independent monetary policy by using sterilized interventions on the foreign exchange market.

## Exercise 3

Consider the Mundell–Fleming model to determine the nominal exchange rate. Imagine now that the aggregate demand of the domestic and foreign economies obeys the following quantitative equation:

$$M^d = kPY$$
$$M^{d*} = k^*P^*Y^*$$

where $M^d$ represents the demand for money, $k > 0$ is a constant associated to the velocity of money, $P$ is the level of prices, and $Y$ is the output level, in real terms. The variables signed with $*$ represent the foreign economy and have an identical definition.

**a.** Using purchasing power parity, find the nominal exchange rate as a function of the exogenous variables of the model.

**b.** Assume now that a positive, exogenous shock in productivity increases the real, long-run output in the domestic and in the foreign markets alike, namely, $Y_f^* - Y^* = Y_f - Y$. How does the nominal exchange rate in the domestic economy react to this shock?

**c.** Now assume that the shock from the previous item affects the domestic and foreign economies in distinct ways. How does the nominal exchange rate in the domestic economy react to this shock if $Y_f^* - Y^* > Y_f - Y$? How does the nominal exchange rate react to this shock if $Y_f^* - Y^* < Y_f - Y$?

## Exercise 4

Based on the Mundell–Fleming model, answer the following items:

**a.** How does a fall in international interest rates affect the real output in a small, open economy under a flexible exchange rate? What happens to the output in the case of a fixed exchange rate? Graphically illustrate both cases. Explain how your answer depends on the degree of capital mobility in the economy.

**b.** Assume there is perfect capital mobility and that this small, open economy operates on a fixed exchange rate regime. Assume that the government permanently raises its spending level. What are the impacts of this change in fiscal policy on the real output and on the current account for this economy? How does your answer to this item compare with the results that would be obtained in an intertemporal model similar to that seen in Chapter 4?

## Exercise 5

Assume an integration mechanism similar to the European Monetary System (EMS),[11] however, with only two countries: Germany and France. Assume that Germany has an independent monetary policy while that of France is dedicated to maintaining the exchange rate francs/marks fixed at level $S_0$. Answer the following questions, which deal with the impact of the German reunification on this reduced version of the EMS.

**a.** If the uncovered interest rate parity is valid and if the French exchange policy is credible, what would be the relation between the French and German interest rates?
**b.** The reunification of Germany resulted in a substantial increase in public spending and private investments. What is the impact of this shock on the IS curve for the German economy? What is the effect on the IS curve for the French economy?
**c.** Assume there is no change in money supply in Germany. Use your answers to the previous items to determine the postunification interest rate and real output in France. Assuming that the French central bank defends the exchange rate of $S_0$, is it possible to determine if the German unification will increase or decrease the French output? Illustrate your answer by means of graphs for the IS and LM curves for both countries.
**d.** In 1992, the German central bank adopted a more contractionist monetary policy due to inflationary pressure. What would be the impact of this policy on the real output and interest rate in France if the French central bank intends to defend the exchange rate of $S_0$? Illustrate your answer with a graph.

## Exercise 6

Consider a simplified version of the Dornbusch model seen in this chapter, described by the following equations:

$$\text{IS: } y_t = \bar{y} + \eta(s_t + p_t^* - p_t)$$
$$\text{LM: } m_t - p_t = y_t - i_t$$
$$\text{UIP: } i_t = i_t^* + E\{s_{t+1} - s_t\}$$
$$\text{MG: } m_{t+1} - m_t = \mu$$

where $y_t$ represents the domestic economy output, $p_t$ is the domestic prices level, $s_t$ is the nominal exchange rate, $m_t$ is the supply of money, and $i_t$ is the nominal interest rate, all

---

[11] For a description of the EMS, see Box 9.1.

variables are in logarithm. The variables identified with * represent those in the international economy and they are taken as constant. The parameters, $\mu$, which represents the rate of growth of money supply, $\eta$, which represents the elasticity of the aggregate demand with respect to the real exchange rate, and $\bar{y}$, which represents the output under full employment, are strictly positive. The operator $E_t\{.\}$ represents the expected value operator, conditional to the set of information available in $t$. Assume that prices are rigid in the first period ($p_1 = \bar{p}$) and perfectly flexible from the second period forward, a period in which the output is compatible with the level of full employment. All variables in the model are described in logarithmic terms. Derive the nominal and real exchange rate paths in response to the following shocks:

**a.** There is a permanent increase in the rate of growth of money supply $\mu$.
**b.** There is a permanent increase in the full employment output level $\bar{y}$. Make a distinction between the following cases:
   **1.** $\eta = 1$.
   **2.** $\eta \in (0, 1)$.
   To simplify, now assume that $p^*, \bar{p}, i^*$ and $\bar{y}$ are equal to zero. Keeping the same structure presented previously, answer the following items:
**c.** Assume that $\bar{y}$ and $m_t$ are equal to zero, and that agents expect them to indefinitely remain at these levels. Determine the equilibrium values for $y_t$, $p_t$, and $s_t$ from the first period and forward.
**d.** Assume that in period $t = 1$ the level of international prices permanently goes up to $p^* = 1$. Determine the equilibrium values for $y_t$, $p_t$, and $s_t$ from the first period forward. Does nominal exchange rate $s_t$ *overshooting* occur in relation to its long-run level? Explain your answer.
**e.** Assume that the level of international prices is once again equal to $p^* = 0$, however, in period $t = 1$, the international interest rate goes up permanently to $i^* = 1$. Determine the equilibrium values for $y_t$, $p_t$, and $s_t$ from the first period forward. Does nominal exchange rate $s_t$ *overshooting* occur in relation to its long-run level? Explain your answer.

# 8

# Portfolio Diversification and Capital Flows

Between the end of the 1990s and the beginning of the 2000s, the international markets environment was puzzling: growing deficits in the North American current account were financed in large part by surpluses in emerging countries, especially that of China. According to the intertemporal current-account models we studied in Chapter 4, capital should flow from the more developed countries to developing ones. The intertemporal model predicts that less developed countries, but with high-return investment opportunities, such as China, should borrow from developed countries with relatively lower growth expectations, such as the United States. Albeit, this was exactly contrary to what happened in the 2000s.[1]

Due to inconsistencies between the predictions by theoretical models and the financial/-trade relations observed in the international markets, the current-account deficits and surpluses of the 2000s became known as **global imbalances**. It is said that the world was living a Wile E. Coyote moment, referring to the Roadrunner cartoon. In the cartoon, Wile E.

---

[1] See the discussion on global imbalances in the 2000s in Chapter 4, Section 4.7.3.

Coyote, in his frustrated attempts to catch the Roadrunner, at times went over a cliff. Even though no longer over solid ground, Wile E. continued to run without falling. Only when he noticed that he was running in thin air did the law of gravity take over and cause the inevitable fall. Analogously, the American current-account deficit would be unsustainable, and when international investors finally realized it, a difficult reckoning would occur.

The prediction was that the adjustment mechanism would unfold in a relatively simple way: agents would notice the growing risk of insolvency of American papers and deny financing American debt at low rates. There would then be an increase in the average return paid by American assets, resulting in an increase of financing costs for the economy, which would lead to a decrease in consumption and investments and, ultimately, recession. The reduction in capital flows, in turn, would lead to a depreciation of the dollar. The fall in domestic absorption as a result of the economic slowdown, along with the exchange rate depreciation, would result, finally, in a reduction in the current-account deficit.

The end of the first decade of the 2000s was marked by what many considered as the greatest global economic crisis since the Great Depression of 1929.[2] This crisis of grand proportions began in the United States in 2007 and spread worldwide, but not exactly as described in the previous paragraph. Global imbalances were not the factor that directly caused the crisis, even though it was responsible for the increase in financial fragility that unleashed it.[3]

How does one explain that the so-called *global imbalances* were in fact *imbalances*, given they lasted 10 years, and could have lasted longer if not for the 2007 crisis? It does not seem reasonable to believe that international capital flows were motivated mainly by the forces described in the intertemporal model, but with international investors being mistaken the whole time. It is necessary to understand what really generated such flows.

Another noteworthy fact of the 2000s was the increase in gross capital flows between countries. In the 1970s, the average gross capital flow was 9.5% of GDP for rich countries and 7.01% for middle-income countries. In the 2000s, the averages jumped to 32.65% and 15.06% of GDP, respectively.[4]

Given that the intertemporal model assumes that investors are indifferent between domestic and foreign assets, it only explains net capital flows and is unable to explain the simultaneous capital flow in and out of the same country. Given the vertiginous increase in such flow in the last years, this simplifying hypothesis seems to be excluding something important that needs to be explained. In fact, this could be the key to understanding the recent trajectory of net financial flows.

This chapter aims, on one hand, to investigate the implication of the increase of gross capital flow and, on the other, analyze the adjustment of the economy to shocks in a context where assets from different countries are not perfect substitutes. The first section begins with a discussion regarding the imperfect substitutability between assets issued by different

[2] See, for example, Reinhart and Rogoff (2009).
[3] See Caballero (2010) and Obstfeld and Rogoff (2009) regarding the relation between global imbalances and the international financial crisis.
[4] See Broner et al. (2011).

countries. The second section analyzes in detail the accounting implications of the existence of the simultaneous inflow and outflow of capital, possibly in different currencies. Section 8.3 analyzes the net international investment position (NIIP) composition of stocks of debt and credit held in distinct currencies. Finally, Section 8.4 presents a model to analyze economic adjustment in the face of shocks, when assets are not perfect substitutes.

## 8.1 Assets from Different Countries: Imperfect Substitutes

Most of the international macroeconomics literature uses the simplifying assumption that assets issued by different countries are perfect substitutes, as was done in the models covered in the previous chapters. More precisely, it is assumed that the assets have the same characteristics, the same risk associated to them, and, also, that international investors are indifferent to risk. Therefore, when there is free mobility of capital, the return on assets should be the same for all countries. In practical terms, this means that the interest rate paid by the Greek government for foreign loans should be the same as that paid by the Swedish government. This is clearly not the case. International investors do not view Greek sovereign debt as being identical to Swedish, mainly for two reasons. First, the default risk associated to the issuer of the debt is not the same: it is much greater for the Greek government than for the Swedish. Second, the Greek government debt is issued in euros, while the Swedish government bond is issued in Swedish crowns, and the exchange rate between currencies can change between the time of purchase and redemption.

International investors, in turn, are generally not indifferent to risk, but averse to it. Therefore, there should be a difference in yield between the assets that correspond to the difference in risk imputed to each. In other words, the Greek government will only be able to sell its bonds if it pays a higher interest rate than that paid by the Swedish government. By combining Eqs. (3.11) and (3.16) from Chapter 3, we obtain:

$$i_t - i_t^* - [E(s_{t+1}) - s_t] = \phi_t^s + \phi_t^c, \tag{8.1}$$

where $i_t = \ln(1 + i_t)$ and $i_t^* = \ln(1 + i_t^*)$ represent the interest rates paid on foreign debt by the Greek and Swedish governments, respectively, $[E(s_{t+1}) - s_t]$ is the expected depreciation of the euro in relation to the Swedish crown, and $\phi_t^s + \phi_t^c$ is the sum of the sovereign risk premium and exchange rate risk premium between the two countries.

Recognizing that international investors are not indifferent in relation to the risk associated to assets issued by different countries has another important implication on the flow of international capital, in addition to the difference in yield on the assets that has already been described. Due to the different levels of risk attributed to available assets, investors prefer to diversify their assets portfolio. Even if assets had the same expected yield, as in Eq. (8.1), it would be better to have a mixed portfolio of assets in order to diversify the risk. Given that asset risk is not perfectly correlated, when in a given economic state an asset has a smaller yield than expected, another asset may have a higher yield than expected. Therefore, the average yield for a portfolio with a mix of assets will be more certain than the yield from each asset individually.

In the case of international financial capital transactions, foreign investors invest in the domestic country at the same time domestic residents invest in other countries, so that all have a diversified portfolio of assets. A new and growing strand of the international finance literature incorporates the decision for optimal diversification by economic agents in the face of risk in their models.[5] This means that even a country with a balanced financial account will make gross purchase and sales transactions of assets with other countries.

In fact, we observe in the real world simultaneous entry and exit of financial capital. The gross capital flows are much greater than the net financial-account balance.[6] According to data presented by Broner et al. (2011), the average net capital flow, that is, the entry minus the exit of financial capital, between 1970 and 2009 was 0.64% of GDP for rich countries and 1.29% for middle-income countries. In turn, the average gross flow, that is, the entry plus the exit of capital, was 17.67% and 9.31% of GDP, respectively, for both groups of countries.

## 8.2 Gross Capital Flows and Current Account

What is the effect of a greater gross capital flow than a net flow? The gross flow can have an important impact on the current-account balance if the rate of return for the capital that enters the country is different from that of the capital that exits. To understand how this effect occurs, let us take a look at some accounting basics.

We define $B_t$ as the NIIP for period $t$.[7] When $B_t > 0$ the country is a net lender, while the country with foreign debt has $B_t < 0$. When there is simultaneous capital inflow and outflow, $B_t$ is defined as the difference between the gross stock of credit and debt, as in:

$$B_t \equiv F_t - D_t, \tag{8.2}$$

where $F_t$ is the stock of foreign credit for the country and $D_t$ is the gross foreign debt.

As we saw in Chapter 2, Section 2.1.1, the current-account balance is the sum of the trade balance, $\text{TB}_t$, and the sum of primary and secondary income balances, $\text{IB}_t$. We can write it as follows:

$$CA_t = \text{TB}_t + \text{IB}_t, \tag{8.3}$$

To simplify, we remove other incomes besides those associated with the financial capital service from our analysis: we assume that the income balance is composed only of payment and receipt of interest for the debt and credit with other countries.

---

[5] Pavlova and Rigobon (2010) provide a review of this literature.

[6] See, for instance, Broner et al. (2011), Lane and Milesi-Ferretti (2001a), Lane and Milesi-Ferretti (2007), Kraay et al. (2005), Devereux (2007), and Gourinchas and Rey (2007a).

[7] See the definition of the NIIP in Chapter 2.

## 8.2.1 Credit and Debt Denominated in the Same Currency

Let us begin with a very simple case where both credit and debt for a country are denominated in the same currency. This would be the case for developing countries where foreign debt is denominated in dollars. Eichengreen and Hausmann (1999) refer to the fact of developing countries having difficulty acquiring foreign debt in their own currency as **original sin**. For instance, a developing country may use accumulated international reserves to purchase American treasury bonds of value $F_t$, so they have a low-risk return for their dollar-denominated assets. Meanwhile, other international investors lend the amount of $D_t$ to the developing country. The income balance is then equal to:

$$IB_t = i^*_{t-1}F_t - i_{t-1}D_t, \tag{8.4}$$

where $F_t$ and $D_t$ represent the stock of credit and foreign debt in $t$, contracted in $t-1$, both denominated in the same currency. $i_{t-1}$ is the interest rate paid on the foreign debt contracted in $t-1$ for payment in $t$, while $i^*_{t-1}$ corresponds to the interest rate received for loan by the domestic country to foreign countries.[8]

If the interest rate the country pays for its debt is the same as it receives for its credit, the income balance (Eq. (8.4)) can be written as:

$$IB_t = i_{t-1}B_t, \tag{8.5}$$

where $i_{t-1}B_t$ corresponds to the **net investment income**. This is the definition used in prior chapters that assumes a perfect substitutability between domestic and foreign assets, as in Eqs. (2.10), (4.10), and (5.14).

When the interest rates associated with the debt or credit for a country are different, the balance cannot be simplified as in Eq. (8.5). In this case, it may be better to write Eq. (8.4) as:

$$IB_t = i_{t-1}(F_t - D_t) + (i^*_{t-1} - i_{t-1})F_t. \tag{8.6}$$

The first term of the income balance Eq. (8.6) can be interpreted as the net foreign debt payment that would occur if the interest rate received from the stock of credit were equal to the domestic nominal interest rate. The second term corresponds to the impact of the difference between the interest rate received on the credit provided by a country and that which it pays on its debt. This term disappears in the case when the assets are perfect substitutes and, therefore, have the same yield. It also does not exist in the case where a debtor country has no credit extended to other countries. In both cases, the income balance can be represented by Eq. (8.5). Substituting the balance of payments equation (Eq. (8.6)) into the current-account equation (Eq. (8.3)), we have that:

$$CA_t = TB_t + i_{t-1}(F_t - D_t) + (i^*_{t-1} - i_{t-1})F_t. \tag{8.7}$$

---

[8] Notice that we assume that the interest rate to be paid is established when the asset is traded, that is, when the debt or credit is contracted.

A developing economy with a foreign debt and international reserves applied in American bonds, for example, will generally pay a higher interest rate on its debt than what it receives for credit based on American government bonds, so that $i^*_{t-1} - i_{t-1} < 0$. The difference between the two interest rates is associated to the differences in sovereign risk between the two countries, so that, with bonds denominated in the same currency, Eq. (8.1) becomes:[9]

$$i_{t-1} - i^*_{t-1} = \phi^s_t. \tag{8.8}$$

**There is, therefore, an opportunity cost associated with the retention of reserve assets, when they render an interest rate lower than that paid on the country debt.** The greater the stock of reserves, the greater the value of this negative term in the country's current account (Box 8.1).

## 8.2.2 Credit in Foreign Currency and Debt in Domestic Currency

Now, let us look at a case where a country does not suffer from *original sin*, being able to emit debt in its own currency. This could be the case of a European country trading with the United States, for example. The foreign debt is denominated in euros, while credit is denominated in dollars. The income balance (Eq. (8.4)), measured in dollars, is:

$$IB_t = i^*_{t-1} F_t - i_{t-1} \frac{\overline{D}_t}{S_t}$$

where $\overline{D}_t$ is the foreign debt denominated in domestic currency and $S_t$ is the nominal exchange rate for period $t$. We define $D_t$ as the value of the debt measured in dollars at the time it was contracted. Given that $D_t$ corresponds to the stock of contracted debt in $t-1$, it is evaluated according to the exchange rate for that period. Therefore, we have that:

$$D_t \equiv \frac{\overline{D}_t}{S_{t-1}}. \tag{8.9}$$

Substituting into the previous equation, we arrive at:

$$IB_t = i^*_{t-1} F_t - i_{t-1} \frac{S_{t-1}}{S_t} D_t, \tag{8.10}$$

which can then be written as:

$$IB_t = i_{t-1} \frac{S_{t-1}}{S_t} (F_t - D_t) + \left( i^*_{t-1} - i_{t-1} \frac{S_{t-1}}{S_t} \right) F_t. \tag{8.11}$$

---

[9] Here, we assume that foreign debt and credit are denominated in the same currency, so that exchange variations do not affect the relative yield of assets. In the next sections we will cover the case of foreign credit and debt denominated in different currencies.

## BOX 8.1 BRAZIL: A NET CREDITOR WITH A FOREIGN DEBT

Brazil is the case of a country whose accumulation of reserves surpassed its external debt. Figure 8.1 shows that the government became a net foreign creditor as of 2007, when its level of international reserves surpassed the amount of its foreign debt. The Brazilian government pays a higher interest rate on its foreign debt than the income received from its international reserves, which implies that there is a cost in accumulating reserves when there is a gross foreign debt. Moreover, the government maintains a high internal debt, for which it also pays a high interest rate. At the beginning of 2010, the net internal public sector debt was about 50% of GDP, while the international reserves came to almost 10% of GDP.

Merely by accounting logic, it would make no sense for a country to apply its international reserves in assets that have such a low net return. The low availability of low-risk assets with a reasonable return could be used as an argument for those countries, especially emerging countries, to possess a lower level of international reserves. However, the accumulation of international reserves results in positive externalities that are not necessarily accounted for in the return of the country's foreign credit. Among other benefits, the accumulation of reserves can be seen as a mechanism to reduce the country's financial fragility, allowing it to capture foreign resources at a lower cost. Moreover, reserves render the country less vulnerable to abrupt reversals in capital flows. Summarizing, the accumulation of international reserves can be interpreted as an "insurance" to be used in an adverse economic situation. The relevant question to be answered, to which there is not a consensus due to subjective interpretations, is if, in fact, the benefits outweigh the costs of this "insurance."

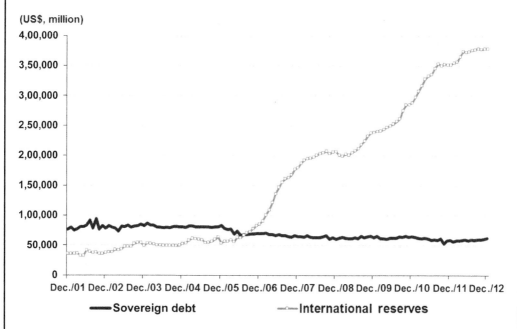

**Figure 8.1** Brazil: sovereign debt and international reserves. Reference (10) on Data List in Appendix.

The difference between this equation for the income balance and that defined in Eq. (8.6) is that, with debt denominated in domestic currency, exchange rate variations will have an impact on the balance of income. The first term in the equation indicates that an exchange rate depreciation, $\frac{S_{t-1}}{S_t} < 1$, reduces the value of the net debt as measured in dollars. This effect does not exist when the debt is also denominated in dollars, as in the case of developing countries, where it is represented by Eq. (8.6). Furthermore, exchange rate depreciation increases the second term in Eq. (8.11), for it reduces the difference between the interest paid on the foreign debt and that received through international credit.

Finally, the current account in this case is represented by:

$$CA_t = TB_t + i_{t-1}\frac{S_{t-1}}{S_t}(F_t - D_t) + \left(i^*_{t-1} - i_{t-1}\frac{S_{t-1}}{S_t}\right)F_t. \tag{8.12}$$

For a country with a net foreign debt, $F_t - D_t < 0$, and that can borrow in its own currency, **exchange rate depreciation has a positive impact on the current-account balance through two channels: first, by its impact on the trade balance**. Exchange rate depreciation causes foreign products to be more expensive, reducing imports, and domestic products are less expensive, stimulating exports. The result is a greater trade balance. **Second, exchange rate depreciation reduces the cost of foreign debt**, given that its average return measured in foreign currency, given as $i_{t-1}(S_{t-1}/S_t)$, also reduces (Box 8.2).

# 8.3 Net International Investment Position

## 8.3.1 Dark Matter

In the 2000s, a mystery began to intrigue economists: even though the United States had become a net debtor as of the end of the 1980s, that is, they presented a **negative NIIP**, they continued to present a **positive net income on international investments**, as can be seen in Figures 8.3A and B. It would be expected that a debtor country *would pay* interest on its debt, and not *receive* a net income related to its international investments. In other words, **for the United States, based on the net income on international investment balance, a greater NIIP is inferred than was effectively observed**.

Hausmann and Sturzenegger (2005) called this discrepancy between the measure of net foreign assets estimated based on the balance of income on international investment and the measure obtained based on official data as **dark matter**. In physics, dark matter is that which is estimated, based on gravitational forces, but that is different than what is measurable by means of direct observation. Analogously, in international finance, **dark matter** corresponds to the stock of assets inferred based on the returns observed. In the American case, it infers a positive NIIP balance, assuming that the country paid on its debt the same interest rate that it received for its credit, namely, computing NIIP based on Eq. (8.5).

Actually, the dark matter found in the American external accounts can essentially be attributed to two motives. First, the United States paid a lower interest rate on its debt than

---

**BOX 8.2 GREEK DEBT CRISIS**

Let us look at the case of Greece. The country has a high foreign debt for which it pays ever-increasing interest rates as a reaction by international investors to the risk of nonpayment. As can be seen in Figure 8.2A, government debt reached extremely high levels in the last years, placing country debt on an apparently unsustainable trajectory. As a direct result of the elevated risk of default by the Greek government, there was a drastic reduction in sources to finance the Greek sovereign debt, which was obliged to sell bonds with increasingly shorter maturity dates at higher and higher interest rates, as can be seen in Figure 8.2B.

A depreciation of the euro would increase the attractiveness of Greek prices for countries outside the Eurozone, but would not have an impact on Greek trade with countries that use the euro as currency. In 2011, total Greek exports were 22.4 billion euros, of which 11.4 billion were from Eurozone countries, while Greek imports totaled 42.1 billion euros in 2011, of which 22.7 came from Eurozone countries. Therefore, in 2011, commerce with the Eurozone was responsible for 52.9% of the total Greek current trade.[a] Therefore, the impact of exchange rate depreciation on the current account by means of its effect on international trade is limited.

However, depreciation of the euro would help Greece due to its effect on the cost of its foreign debt. The foreign Greek debt is denominated in euros, while its credit is denominated partly in euros and partly in other currencies. The income balance (Eq. (8.6)), measured in dollars, can be written as:

$$IB_t = i_{t-1} \frac{S_{t-1}}{S_t}(F_t - D_t) + \left( i_{t-1}^{EUR} - i_{t-1} \right) \frac{S_{t-1}}{S_t} F_t^{EUR} + \left( i_{t-1}^{RDM} - i_{t-1} \frac{S_{t-1}}{S_t} \right) F_t^{RDM}, \qquad (8.13)$$

where the term $i_{t-1}^{EUR}$ represents the average interest rate of Greek assets acquired in the Eurozone ambit, while the term $i_{t-1}^{RDM}$ represents the average interest rate of Greek assets in relation to the rest of the world. $F_t^{RDM}$ represents Greek credit with the rest of the world, which, to simplify, we assume as being denominated in dollars. $\overline{F}_t^{EUR}$ is Greek credit with the member countries of the Eurozone, denominated in euros. In the equation we measure this credit in dollars according to $F_t^{EUR} \equiv \overline{F}_t^{EUR}/S_{t-1}$. Accordingly, $F_t \equiv F_t^{EUR} + F_t^{RDM}$ is the total Greek foreign credit, measured in dollars. The equation shows that a depreciation of the euro would have a positive impact on the current account by means of the balance of income by means of three effects.

First, a depreciation of the euro would reduce the value of service on the net foreign debt measured in dollars, as captured by the first term of Eq. (8.13). Second, the impact (negative) of the interest differential between the Greek debt and the rest of the Eurozone on the current account would be weakened, given that the gross value of credit in euros would have a lesser value in dollars, as indicated in the second term of the equation. Finally, depreciation of the euro would reduce the interest differential between the Greek debt and credit in dollars, as shown in the last term of the equation.

However, depreciation of the euro depends on the monetary policy adopted by the European central bank, and not the Greek government. Therefore, Greece cannot use exchange depreciation as a way of lessening its foreign debt problem. An alternative could be to abandon the euro, create its own currency and transform its contracts in euros into contracts denominated in the new currency. Albeit, it is not as simple as is appears. How are contracts in euros transformed into new contracts in drachmas without breaking them? What would be the extent of the cost of exchange rate depreciation? Is it worth losing European support?

*(Continued)*

BOX 8.2 (CONTINUED)

(A) Evolution of the debt/GDP relation

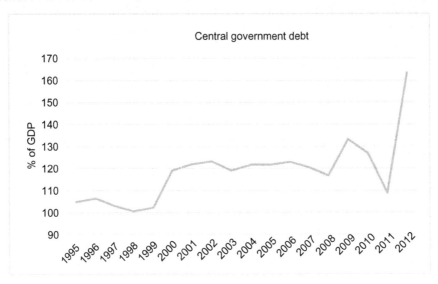

(B) Interest rate on 10-year bonds

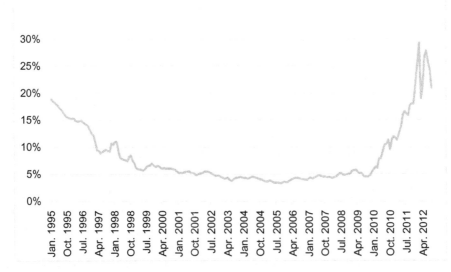

**Figure 8.2** Debt and interest rate in Greece. *Source: European Central Bank—Eurosystem and World Bank, References (3) and (7) on Data List in Appendix.*

[a]Additional information regarding the Greek economic indicators can be obtained from the *Hellenic Statistical Authority.*

(A)

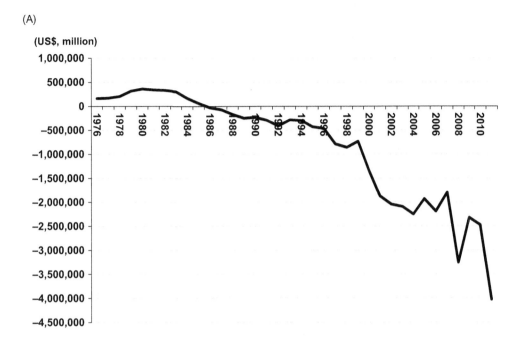

(B)

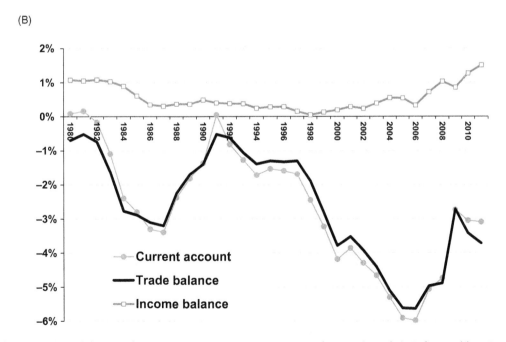

**Figure 8.3** NIIP and the United States current account. *Source: Bureau of Economic Analysis, Reference (7) on Data List in Appendix.*

---

**BOX 8.3 US DEBT CEILING CRISIS**

Due to credibility conquered over time, and the privilege of issuing the currency used as global reference for financial and trade transactions, American government sovereign bonds were always known to be risk-free assets, receiving the best possible credit score by international rating agencies. This image was, however, tarnished in 2011 in an event called the US Debt Ceiling Crisis. On that occasion, in answer to the severe fiscal deterioration seen after the 2007 crisis, the American government passed a bill to reduce the fiscal deficit over the next 10 years. However, the plan to reduce the deficit was below market agent expectations as well as those of the government opposing party. Consequently, there was an impasse in the American congress, which considered the possibility of not raising the debt ceiling for the country, which technically could result in a default of the American debt. Due to uncertainties in relation to American fiscal policy, the Standard & Poor's rating agency lowered the US credit rating for the first time in history, from AAA, the maximum level possible, to AA +, on August 5, 2011.

---

what it received on credit from other countries. This difference can be explained by the privilege of being the issuing country of the main reserve currency used by the rest of the world. This increases the attractiveness of American assets, given that they are issued in dollars, allowing international investors to buy them even at lower interest rates. This American advantage became known as the **exorbitant privilege**, a term coined in 1965 by Valéry Giscard d'Estaing, the French Minister of Finance at the time (Box 8.3).[10]

Second, given that the United States issued debt in its own currency, a depreciation of the dollar implies an increase in the relative return on assets in a foreign currency the country holds. To see how this works, let us write a balance of income equation (Eq. (8.6)) from the American point of view, that is, we compute the income balance measured in dollars, with foreign credit denominated in foreign currency. The exchange rate is defined as the foreign currency in relation to the dollar, that is, the price of the dollar in terms of the foreign currency. We therefore have that:

$$IB_t = i_{t-1}\left(\frac{S_{t-1}}{S_t}F_t - D_t\right) + (i^*_{t-1} - i_{t-1})\frac{S_{t-1}}{S_t}F_t. \tag{8.14}$$

According to the second term of the equation, the American economy exorbitant privilege, $i^*_{t-1} - i_{t-1} > 0$, causes its gross credit with the rest of the world to generate a gain. Also, a depreciation of the dollar, $\frac{S_{t-1}}{S_t} > 1$, has a positive effect on the income balance by increasing the value of American credit in relation to its debt. This effect reduces the net foreign debt for the country, in the first term of the equation, besides increasing the value of the second term.

Notice that not all American credit is in foreign currency. Particularly, credit with developing countries is usually denominated in dollars; therefore, in this case, the effect of

---

[10] Gourinchas and Rey (2007b).

depreciation on the relative value of credit disappears, given that the effect only occurs for the share of credit denominated in foreign currency. Albeit, the interest rate that developing countries pay for their debt is usually even greater: the difference of $i_{t-1}^* - i_{t-1}$ is greater for these countries. Making this division between credit with other developed countries, $F_t^{Dev}$, denominated in foreign currency, and credit with developing economies, $F_t^{Em}$, denominated in dollars, we can write the income balance as:

$$IB_t = i_{t-1}\left(\frac{S_{t-1}}{S_t}F_t^{Dev} + F_t^{Em} - D_t\right) + (i_{t-1}^{Dev} - i_{t-1})\frac{S_{t-1}}{S_t}F_t^{Dev} + (i_{t-1}^{Em} - i_{t-1})F_t^{Em},$$

where $i_{t-1}^{Dev}$ is the interest rate received for credit with other developed countries and $i_{t-1}^{Em}$ is the nominal interest rate that remunerates credit with developing economies.

## 8.3.2 Valuation Effect

A corresponding mystery stalked the American external accounts in the 2000s: the deterioration of the NIIP of the United States was much less than the accumulation of the enormous deficits in current account seen in the country. According to Milesi-Ferretti (2009), the accumulated deficit in current account between 2002 and 2007 was US$ 3.4 trillion, while the NIIP reduction was "only" US$ 400 billion.

Let us take a look. When the balance of payments is in equilibrium, the balance in current account should correspond to the negative financial-account balance, according to what we said in Chapter 2. In the, shall we say, classic world, where we only consider the net transaction of assets between countries, this relation is represented by Eq. (8.11), which we reproduce here:

$$CA_t = -FA_t = B_{t+1} - B_t, \tag{8.15}$$

where, as always, $B_t$ represents the NIIP, or rather, the net stock of assets for a country at the beginning of period $t$. Therefore, the balance in current account should correspond to the variation of the NIIP.

Now consider the situation where there are simultaneous asset purchase and sale transactions, which can be denominated in distinct currencies. Let us look at the case of a developed economy, whose debt is denominated in domestic currency, credit in dollars, and whose exchange rate is defined as the amount of domestic currency necessary to purchase one dollar. The balance of payments equilibrium (Eq. (8.15)) is then represented by:

$$CA_t = -FA_t = \left(F_{t+1} - \frac{\overline{D}_{t+1}}{S_t}\right) - \left(F_t - \frac{\overline{D}_t}{S_t}\right),$$

where $CA_t$ is the balance in current account measured in dollars, $F_t$ is the country's credit, also measured in dollars, and $\overline{F}_t$ is the foreign debt denominated in domestic currency contracted in period $t-1$, such that $\overline{D}_t/S_t$ is its value in dollars in period $t$. We can substitute $D_t$

for its value in dollars at the time it was contracted, as in Eq. (8.9), that is, $S_{t-1}D_t = \overline{D}_t$ and $S_t D_{t+1} = \overline{D}_{t+1}$. We then have that:

$$CA_t = (F_{t+1} - D_{t+1}) - \left(F_t - \frac{S_{t-1}D_t}{S_t}\right) \tag{8.16}$$

which can be written as:

$$CA_t = (F_{t+1} - D_{t+1}) - (F_t - D_t) - \left(1 - \frac{S_{t-1}}{S_t}\right)D_t \tag{8.17}$$

The two first terms of Eq. (8.17) correspond to the NIIP variation between periods $t$ and $t+1$, according to the definition in Eq. (8.2). We then have that:

$$B_{t+1} - B_t = CA_t + \left(1 - \frac{S_{t-1}}{S_t}\right)D_t. \tag{8.18}$$

Notice that the second term of Eq. (8.18) is not present in Eq. (8.15), which does not take into account the gross capital flow.

In a more general way, we can add the balance in current account between periods $t$ and $t+n-1$ to obtain the NIIP variation between $t$ and $t+n$, as in:

$$B_{t+n} - B_t = \sum_{i=0}^{n-1} CA_{t+i} + \sum_{i=0}^{n-1}\left(1 - \frac{S_{t-1+i}}{S_{t+i}}\right)D_{t+i}. \tag{8.19}$$

Equations (8.18) and (8.19) show that when there are simultaneous purchase and sale transactions of international assets, **exchange rate variations cause the change in NIIP to differ from the current-account balance**. The second term of the equation captures the **valuation effect**, which corresponds to changes in the value of assets held by investors. Intuitively, the current-account balance reflects the balance of the purchase and sale of assets with the rest of the world, but does not take into account eventual changes in the value of assets either held or sold by the country. Therefore, changes in the value of assets affect the net indebtedness of the country, or in other words, its NIIP.

According to Eq. (8.18), the value of gross foreign debt varies when there are changes in the exchange rate, given that it is denominated in domestic currency and its value in the equation is measured in dollars. Exchange rate depreciation $\frac{S_{t-1}}{S_t} < 1$, for example, reduces the value in dollars of the debt denominated in domestic currency, which reduces the net indebtedness of the country. This could be the case, for example, of Greece in a depreciation of the euro.

In the American case, we can represent the current account as we did to write its income balance (Eq. (8.14)): we measured the current account in dollars, with its credit denominated in foreign currency, and defined the exchange rate, $S_t^{US}$, as the foreign currency in relation to the dollar. Analogously to what we did to derive Eq. (8.16), the balance of payments equilibrium for the United States can be written as:

$$CA_t = (F_{t+1} - D_{t+1}) - \left( \frac{S_t^{US}}{S_{t-1}^{US}} F_t - D_t \right).$$

Using the above equation, the NIIP variation is:

$$B_{t+1} - B_t = CA_t + \left( \frac{S_t^{US}}{S_{t-1}^{US}} - 1 \right) F_t. \tag{8.20}$$

Hence, through the valuation effect, a depreciation of the dollar, which corresponds to $(S_t^{US}/S_{t-1}^{US}) < 1$, has a positive effect on the NIIP. Returning to the American case in the 2000s, the depreciation of the dollar in the period increased the value in dollars of the American credit denominated in foreign currency, as registered by the second term of Eq. (8.20). The accumulation of debt with the rest of the world was thus less than the deficits in current account accumulated by the country.

### 8.3.2.1 Direct Investment and Stock Market Investment

Up to now we have only considered debt securities transactions, whose face value is always constant in the currency in which they are denominated. Their value can only be changed when measured in a currency different from their denomination due to exchange rate variations. Financial transactions between countries, however, include other assets besides debt. There is direct investment, where the resident of a country assumes control or significant influence over the management of a company established in another country. In this case, the value of the asset is associated with the value of the company, which can change over time. Analogously, the value of equities transacted on the stock market, recorded in the balance of payments under portfolio investment, is also not fixed. Their price can change at any moment, according to negotiations on the stock market. In the case of assets that do not have a fixed face value, the valuation effect can occur independently of exchange rate variations.

To understand the relationship between the NIIP and the current-account balance for assets whose face value changes over time, we consider a case where the assets and current account are denominated in the same currency, so as to abstract exchange variations. Let $D_t^T$ be the value of domestic asset stock in the hands of foreign residents, and $F_t^T$ the value of foreign assets retained by domestic residents, where superscript $T$ refers to assets whose price can vary over time, such as company stock transacted on the stock market or debt securities transacted on the secondary market. The NIIP is then represented by:

$$B_t = F_t^T - D_t^T \tag{8.21}$$

The value of the assets can be written as the product of price and quantity. Following the same logic used previously to establish Eq. (8.9), the value of the stock of assets $J_t^T$, $J = F, D$, corresponds to the stock of assets at the end of period $t-1$, being evaluated, therefore, in terms of the price for that period, $p_{t-1}^J$. Thus, we have that:

$$D_t^T \equiv p_{t-1}^D \overline{D}_t^T \quad \text{and} \quad F_t^T \equiv p_{t-1}^F \overline{F}_t^T \tag{8.22}$$

where $\overline{J}_t^T$ represents the amount retained of asset $J$. Notice that $J_t^T$ is the value of a determined stock of assets expressed in current value.

The current-account balance, in turn, corresponds to the change in value of the net stock of assets, measured in current prices. In terms of the notation described above, we then have the current-account equation as given by:

$$CA_t = (p_t^F \overline{F}_{t+1}^T - p_t^D \overline{D}_{t+1}^T) - (p_t^F \overline{F}_t^T - p_t^D \overline{D}_t^T), \tag{8.23}$$

which can be rewritten as:

$$CC_t = (p_t^F \overline{F}_{t+1}^T - p_t^D \overline{D}_{t+1}^T) - (p_{t-1}^F \overline{F}_t^T - p_{t-1}^D \overline{D}_t^T) - (p_t^F - p_{t-1}^F)\overline{F}_t^T + (p_t^D - p_{t-1}^D)\overline{D}_t^T.$$

Using the NIIP definitions in Eq. (8.21) and the assets value in Eq. (8.23), we can rewrite the previous equation as:

$$B_{t+1} - B_t = CA_t + (p_t^F - p_{t-1}^F)\overline{F}_t^T - (p_t^D - p_{t-1}^D)\overline{D}_t^T. \tag{8.24}$$

Equation (8.24) shows that the variation in the NIIP is equal to the current-account balance plus the valuation effect, which corresponds to the two last terms of the equation. If there is no variation in the prices of assets, this effect does not exist and the NIIP variation is exactly equal to the current-account balance.

An increase in the price of foreign assets held by domestic residents represents an increase in the NIIP, as indicated in the next-to-last term of the equation. For example, this is what happens when a French resident is owner of a factory in Germany and the value of this factory goes up. The greater value of the factory corresponds to an increase in the value of French external credit.

Analogously, the last term of the equation indicates that an increase in the price of a domestic asset in the hands of a foreign resident means an increase in the country's foreign liabilities. We can say that when a foreign resident makes a direct investment or purchases stocks on the domestic stock market, their gain depends on the performance of the country. If the country does well and the value of its assets increases, the foreigner who invested in the country earns more. On the other hand, if there is a crisis with a consequent reduction of asset prices, the foreign liability is also lower. Thus, **the foreign investor shares the risk of a country when buying assets where the prices are in some way tied to the economic performance of the country.**

# 8.4 Impact of Shocks on Exchange Rate and Current Account

In previous chapters we looked at the impact of real and nominal shocks on the exchange rate and current account in different contexts, but always assuming that assets issued from different countries were perfect substitutes. These models, however, have neither been very useful to understand the global disequilibria of the 2000s, nor have they taken into account the effect of gross capital flow. Now we will consider an open economy economic model, based on Blanchard et al. (2005), that allows for this hypothesis.

We begin with the evolution of the NIIP. Net foreign credit can be defined as the difference between the wealth of a country and its stock of assets. Defining $W_t$ as the wealth of the domestic country and $A_t$ as the stock of assets for period $t$, both denominated in domestic currency, this equality can be written as:

$$B_t = \frac{W_t}{S_t} - \frac{A_t}{S_t},\tag{8.25}$$

where $B_t$ is the NIIP for the domestic country measured in foreign currency in $t$, with $B_t > 0$ for a lender country. We divide the wealth and the stock of domestic assets by the exchange rate $S_t$ to obtain the value of these variables in foreign currency, remembering that the exchange rate is defined as the amount of domestic currency necessary to purchase one unit of foreign currency.

We assume there are two countries in the world: the home country and the foreign country. Given that there are only two countries, the NIIP of the home country should be equal to the negative NIIP of the foreign country, $B_t^* = -B_t$: a credit for the home country, for example, corresponds to a debt of equal amount for the foreign country. We have equality analogous to Eq. (8.25) for the foreign country:

$$B_t^* = -B_t = W_t^* - A_t^* \tag{8.26}$$

## 8.4.1 Portfolio Balance

We now want to take a look at the investor portfolio allocation. When assets have different characteristics, depending on their issuing country, they no longer are considered perfect substitutes. In practical terms, this means that investors are no longer indifferent in relation to what asset to acquire, even if they offer the same return. Let us especially assume that there are risks associated with the assets, and that these returns are not perfectly correlated. For example, a fall in the price of oil can reduce the return on Venezuelan assets, which performance is closely tied to oil, and not have any effect on Chilean assets. The price of copper, on the other hand, would affect the Chilean economy, but not the Venezuelan. In such a context, the best option for investors is to diversify their asset portfolio. By buying both Chilean and Venezuelan assets simultaneously, the investor is able to reduce the volatility of the average yield in their portfolio.

Finance literature has extensively studied the optimum portfolio allocation decision when assets are risky and the investor is risk averse. We are not going to develop a model of portfolio allocation based on microfoundations. We will simply assume the result of a model of this genre, which predicts that investors allocate part of their wealth in domestic assets and part in foreign, and that the share of wealth allocated for each asset is a function of the relative yield expected for the assets.

We define $\Lambda$ as the share of wealth the home country allocates for its own assets. Analogously, $\Lambda^*$ is the fraction of the foreign wealth allocated for foreign assets. Shares $\Lambda$ and $\Lambda^*$ are affected by the relative yield of the assets, as well as by exogenous variable $v$ which captures shocks that tilt preferences in favor of foreign assets. They can then be represented by the following functions:

$$\Lambda_t = \Lambda(R^e_{t+1}, v_t) \tag{8.27}$$

$$\Lambda^*_t = \Lambda^*(R^e_{t+1}, v_t) \tag{8.28}$$

where:

$$R^e_{t+1} \equiv \left(\frac{1 + i_t}{1 + i^*_t}\right) \frac{S_t}{E(S_{t+1})} \tag{8.29}$$

is the uncovered interest rate differential between the home country and the foreign.[11]

An increase in the relative expected return for the home asset leads investors to increase the share of this asset in their portfolio. Therefore, we have that $((\partial \Lambda(R^e, v))/\partial R^e) > 0$ and $((\partial \Lambda^*(R^e, v))/\partial R^e) < 0$: the share retained of their own assets increases for home investors and decreases for foreign. As to the variable $v$, we have that $((\partial \Lambda(R^e, v))/\partial v) < 0$ and $((\partial \Lambda^*(R^e, v))/\partial v) > 0$, given that we have defined it as a variable that represents bias in favor of foreign assets.

The empirical data shows that investors tend to allocate a relatively larger share of their wealth in assets from their own country. This preference for home assets, called **home bias**, is captured in the model by the following inequality:[12]

$$\Lambda(R^e_{t+1}, v_t) + \Lambda^*(R^e_{t+1}, v_t) > 1, \tag{8.30}$$

that is, the sum of the share of income allocated to assets from their own country is greater than 1.

---

[11] The explanation regarding how to compare the yield from assets from different countries can be found in Chapter 3, Section 3.3.

[12] We observe empirically that investors tend to allocate a greater share of their wealth in assets from their own country, even though higher gains could be obtained by more international diversification of their asset portfolio. As indicated in the seminal article by French and Poterba (1991), at the end of the 1980s, the share of assets owned by residents in their own country was about 92% for the American and English stock markets, 89% for the French market, and 96% for the Japanese. In fact, this theme gained significant importance in the literature, being identified by Obsfeld and Rogoff (2000) as one of the six great *puzzles* in international finance.

The total demand for home assets will be the sum of the domestic and foreign demands, which, in turn, corresponds to the share of the respective wealth allocated in these assets. Using the definition of $\Lambda$ and $\Lambda^*$ in Eqs. (8.27) and (8.28), we have that the demand for home assets, measured in foreign currency, is given by:

$$\Lambda(R_{t+1}^e, v_t)\frac{W_t}{S_t} + (1 - \Lambda^*(R_{t+1}^e, v_t))W_t^*,$$

The equilibrium condition in the assets market requires that the total supply of assets from one country be equal to its global demand in each period. Taking the stock of domestic assets, $A_t$, as an exogenous variable, we have that:

$$\frac{A_t}{S_t} = \Lambda(R_{t+1}^e, v_t)\frac{W_t}{S_t} + (1 - \Lambda^*(R_{t+1}^e, v_t))W_t^*, \tag{8.31}$$

If the domestic assets market is in equilibrium, the foreign assets will also be, therefore not being necessary to write an equilibrium equation.[13] Notice that in the models studied previously, we did not make the asset market equilibrium equations explicit. With the assumption of perfect substitutability between assets, interest rate parity made investors perfectly indifferent regarding assets from different countries, so that the assets market could be treated as a single, global market. The equilibrium of the other markets guaranteed global asset market equilibrium and investors allocated their portfolio according to the need to obtain equilibrium in the asset market for each country.

Using the definitions of Eqs. (8.25) and (8.26), we can rewrite equilibrium Eq. (8.31) as:

$$\frac{A_t}{S_t} = \Lambda(R_{t+1}^e, v_t)\left(\frac{A_t}{S_t} + B_t\right) + (1 - \Lambda^*(R_{t+1}^e, v_t))(A_t^* - B_t). \tag{8.32}$$

Equation (8.32) establishes the relation between exchange rate S and NIIP $B$, which renders the portfolio composition consonant with the asset market equilibrium. We name the relation equation as **Portfolio Balance (PB)**. Notice that the exchange rate affects the value of domestic assets measured in foreign currency, $A_t/S_t$, while the exchange rate variation expectation, by means of the interest differential $R_{t+1}^e$, determines the allocation of the asset portfolio.

It is interesting to analyze the implications of Eq. (8.32) in the extreme case where there is no substitutability whatsoever between assets, namely, when the share of wealth allocated in each type of asset is constant and is not affected by its relative yield. This would be the extreme case in opposition to the hypothesis normally used where assets are perfect substitutes. It is an unreal situation, but one that helps us understand the impact of imperfect substitutability of assets.

---

[13] According to the Walras Law, which establishes an important result of general equilibrium, in an economy that possesses $n$ markets, if $n - 1$ markets are in equilibrium, the $n$th market will also be in equilibrium. In the case we are analyzing, there are two markets. Therefore, is it only necessary to ensure that one is in equilibrium for the other to also be.

**If there were no substitutability whatsoever between assets, the exchange rate would be completely determined by the distribution of world wealth.** More precisely, Eq. (8.32) would imply:

$$S_t = \frac{(1 - \Lambda)A_t}{(1 - \Lambda^*)A_t^* + (\Lambda^* + \Lambda - 1)B_t}. \tag{8.33}$$

**Any shock in the economy, such as, for example, an improvement in the terms of trade, would be absorbed by variations in the current account**, given that the exchange rate would be predetermined according to Eq. (8.33). How does this result compare with the case of perfect substitutability between assets, which is the hypothesis used in models presented in previous chapters? In the real exchange rate equilibrium model described in Chapter 5, the impact of an improvement in the terms of trade would be exactly opposite, that is, there would be an exchange rate appreciation with no alteration to the current-account balance. We have seen that, on one hand, given that the shock is permanent, it does not alter relative income between the present and the future, hence the decision for optimum savings does not change, which, in turn, determines the current-account balance. On the other hand, the improvement in the terms of trade changes the relation between the current account and the exchange rate: the current-account balance increases for any given exchange rate level. Therefore, if the assets were perfect substitutes, a permanent improvement in the terms of trade would cause an exchange rate appreciation, while the current account would remain unchanged.

Returning to the case where there is no substitutability between assets, in spite of the exchange rate being predetermined as shown in Eq. (8.33), it follows variations in the NIIP over time. To see this effect, we take the derivative of Eq. (8.33) with respect to $B_t$, from which we obtain:

$$\frac{\partial S_t}{\partial B_t} \frac{1}{S_t} = -\frac{(\Lambda + \Lambda^* - 1)}{(1 - \Lambda)\frac{A_t}{S_t}} < 0, \tag{8.34}$$

Given the home bias represented in Eq. (8.30), the derivative in Eq. (8.34) has a negative sign, that is, an increase in net credit for a country causes an appreciation of the exchange rate. The intuition for this effect is as follows: An increase in foreign credit means a transfer of wealth in favor of domestic investors, who have a biased preference in favor of domestic assets. There is, therefore, an increase in relative demand for domestic assets, captured by an increase on the right side of Eq. (8.32). The resulting increase in relative demand for domestic currency causes exchange rate appreciation, which, in turn, increases the value of the stock of domestic assets as measured in foreign currency $A_t/S_t$. Thereby, equilibrium in the assets market is guaranteed, that is, the equation continues to be valid. The intensity of this effect is greater, the greater the home bias, $\Lambda + \Lambda^* - 1$, and the smaller the stock of domestic assets, $A_t$.

## 8.4.2 External Balance

The next step is to establish the relationship between the NIIP evolution and the exchange rate. The trade balance is a positive function of the exchange rate, that is, exchange rate depreciations increase the trade balance. In Chapter 5, we saw how a more depreciated real exchange rate is associated with a greater trade balance. A depreciation of the nominal exchange rate, in turn, represents a depreciation of the real exchange rate, as shown in Chapter 3, Eq. (3.2), when prices remain constant or fluctuate less than the exchange rate, which is an assumption we make here.

We also assume that other economic variables affecting the trade balance are synthesized by term $z_t$. Variable $z$ is related to a set of factors that affect international trade, so that an increase in $z$ results in an increase in the trade balance. It can represent, for example, changes in foreign consumer preferences in favor of domestic products or simply an improvement in the terms of trade. The trade balance can therefore be written as:

$$TB_t = TB(S_t, z_t),\tag{8.35}$$

where $((d\,TB(S, z))/dS_t) > 0$ and $((d\,TB(S, z))/dz_t) > 0$.

The income balance, in turn, can be represented by Eq. (8.10), given that we are considering the case of a country whose debt is denominated in domestic currency and credit in foreign currency. Therefore, the current account is equal to:

$$CA_t = TB_t + IB_t = TB(S_t, z_t) + i^*_{t-1}F_t - i_{t-1}\frac{S_{t-1}}{S_t}D_t.\tag{8.36}$$

Equation (8.18) establishes the relation between the net accumulation of foreign assets and the current account, which we repeat here:

$$B_{t+1} - B_t = CA_t + \left(1 - \frac{S_{t-1}}{S_t}\right)D_t.\tag{8.37}$$

Substituting the current account represented by Eq. (8.36) into Eq. (8.37), and rearranging the terms, as shown in the Mathematical Appendix at the end of the chapter, we have that the net foreign credit for country is equal to:

$$B_{t+1} = TB(S_t, z_t) + (1 + i^*_{t-1})B_t + (1 + i^*_{t-1})\left(1 - \left(\frac{1 + i_{t-1}}{1 + i^*_{t-1}}\right)\frac{S_{t-1}}{S_t}\right)D_t.\tag{8.38}$$

Given the assumption regarding portfolio allocation, the domestic gross foreign debt is the share of foreign wealth allocated in domestic assets, that is, $(1 - \Lambda^*(R^e_{t+1}, v))W^*_t$. We can then say that:

$$\frac{\overline{D_t}}{S_{t-1}} = D_t = (1 - \Lambda^*(R^e_{t+1}, v))W^*_t.\tag{8.39}$$

Remember that here we assume assets are always denominated in the currency of the emitting country, so that the home country credit is denominated in foreign currency, while its foreign debt in domestic currency. Previously we used Eq. (8.9), which defines $D_t$ as the amount of foreign debt measured in foreign currency.

Foreign wealth, in turn, corresponds to the sum of the stock of foreign assets with its NIIP, according to Eq. (8.26): $W_t^* = A_t^* - B_t$. Equation (8.38) can therefore be written as:

$$B_{t+1} = TB(S_t, z_t) + (1 + i_{t-1}^*)B_t + (1 - \Lambda^*(R_{t+1}^e, v))(1 + i_{t-1}^*)(A_t^* - B_t)(1 - R_t) \qquad (8.40)$$

where $R_t \equiv ((1 + i_{t-1})/(1 + i_{t-1}^*))(S_{t-1}/S_t)$ is the yield obtained from the domestic asset in relation to the foreign. Equation (8.40) establishes the relation between the exchange rate and the NIIP compatible with the evolution of current and financial accounts, being therefore denominated as the relation of **External Balance (EB)**.

The first two terms of this equation correspond to the international accounts equilibria without considering the gross capital flow and the difference in monetary denomination of the foreign debt and credit. The last term captures the effect of the gross capital flow associated with the dark matter and the valuation effect discussed in Section 8.3. The difference in yield between domestic and foreign assets, in the last term between parentheses, is the source of the dark matter. The valuation effect, in turn, arises when there are exchange rate variations. An exchange rate appreciation $((S_{t-1}/S_t) > 1)$, for example, increases the value of the net foreign debt measured in foreign currency, which has a negative effect on the NIIP. This effect adds itself to the traditional effect by means of the trade balance, captured by the first term of the equation, according to which an exchange rate appreciation reduces the trade balance, also having a negative effect on the NIIP.

### 8.4.3 Steady-State Equilibrium

To understand the impact of shocks on the economy, we will begin with the economy in the steady-state equilibrium, which is defined as a situation where the variables exogenous to the model are constant and the economy is in long-run equilibrium. The stock of domestic and foreign assets, $A$ and $A^*$, are constant, as well as the variables that affect asset portfolio allocation, $v$, and the trade balance, $z$. We assume the interest rate is constant and equal in both countries: $i^* = i$. In steady-state equilibrium, the exchange rate is constant, $(S_{t-1}/S_t) = 1$, in such that $R_t^e = 1$. The relation of portfolio equilibrium (Eq. (8.32)), is then:

$$\frac{A_t}{S_t} = \Lambda(1, v_t)\left(\frac{A_t}{S_t} + B_t\right) + (1 - \Lambda^*(1, v_t))(A_t^* - B_t). \qquad (8.41)$$

**The PB in steady-state establishes a negative relation between the exchange rate and the NIIP**: an appreciated exchange rate is associated with a greater net credit of the country with the rest of the world. This relation is equivalent to that established by Eq. (8.34). An increase in net external credit represents a transfer of foreign investor wealth to domestic investors. Given that domestic investors allocate a greater share of their wealth in domestic

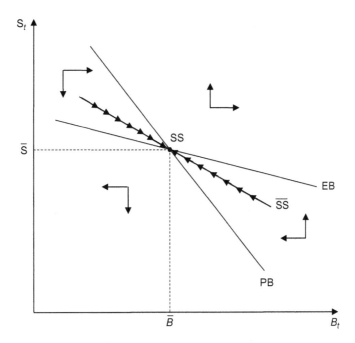

**Figure 8.4** Exchange rate and NIIP in equilibrium.

assets than foreign investors, the result is an increase in demand for domestic assets. Exchange rate appreciation (a reduction in the exchange rate) increases the value of domestic assets as measured in foreign currency, in such a way as to rebalance the economy.

As to the relation of external balance (Eq. (8.40)), its last term disappears, given that interest rates are equal in both countries and the exchange rate is stationary. We also have that $B_{t+1} - B_t = 0$, resulting in:

$$0 = \text{TB}(S_t, z_t) + i^*_{t-1}B_t. \tag{8.42}$$

Notice that Eq. (8.42) corresponds to a balanced current account, remembering that, when the interest rate in both countries is equal, there is no exchange rate variation. **The EB relation in steady-state equilibrium establishes a negative relation between exchange rate and NIIP.** A greater NIIP increases the receipt of interest by net credit (or reduces the payment on the net debt, in the case of a net borrower country). The exchange rate then appreciates to reduce the trade balance and maintain the external equilibrium of the economy.

The NIIP and the exchange rate in the stationary equilibrium should simultaneously satisfy Eqs. (8.41) and (8.42), and are represented by point $\text{SS} = (\overline{B}, \overline{S})$ in Figure 8.4.[14] The

---

[14] Notice that the point at which the vertical axis intersects the horizontal axis is not necessarily the point where $B = 0$. In the case of a net debtor country, that is, with $B < 0$, this point where both axes intersect corresponds to a negative value for $B$.

portfolio balance relation in a stationary state (Eq. (8.41)) is represented by line PB. For points above line PB, the exchange rate value is higher (more depreciated) than what would be necessary to obtain stationary equilibrium in the domestic assets market. The value of the domestic assets is then lower than their demand, and an expectation of exchange rate depreciation is necessary to render domestic assets less attractive, as can be seen by Eq. (8.32). Therefore, the exchange rate increases at points above line PB to maintain the portfolio balance.

The relation of external balance in stationary state (Eq. (8.42)) is represented by line EB. For points to the right of line EB, the net foreign credit is higher than that suitable with a constant NIIP. By Eq. (8.40), we see that this implies a higher balance in primary income, which increases the current-account balance and causes an increase in the NIIP. Therefore, the NIIP grows in points to the right of line EB.

The arrows in Figure 8.4 show the dynamics of the variables, as explained in the two previous paragraphs. **Equilibrium is stable when the PB is steeper than the EB, as drawn on the graph**. This happens when, for a given NIIP increase, the exchange rate appreciation necessary to maintain stationary portfolio balance is greater than that necessary to reestablish the stationary external balance. The intuition is as follows: As of the stationary equilibrium point SS, assume that there is an increase of the country NIIP. On one hand, the greater external credit means a greater receipt of income (or lower expenses with debt service, in the case of a net debtor country), which would increase the current-account balance and promote an even greater increase in the NIIP. On the other hand, the increase in the NIIP would cause an increase in the demand for domestic assets (due to home bias), which results in exchange rate appreciation to maintain portfolio balance. When PB is steeper than EB, this exchange rate appreciation will be greater than that which would maintain the net credit stationary. Therefore, net external credit decreases while the exchange rate gradually depreciates until the economy eventually returns to its original situation of stationary equilibrium. The thick line represents the equilibrium adjustment path, where the relations of portfolio balance (Eq. (8.32)) and external balance (Eq. (8.40)) are simultaneously satisfied.

## 8.4.4 The Impact of Shocks on the Goods Market

Assume that the domestic economy is at first in the steady-state equilibrium, such as point SS in Figure 8.4, when there is a positive shock on the trade balance. This shock could be, for example, an improvement in the terms of trade: An increase in the international price of exported goods in relation to imported goods has a positive impact on the trade balance, as what happened with commodities exporters in the 2000s. In terms of the model, this means an increase in variable $z$, which, as defined in Eq. (8.35), causes an increase in the trade balance. Point SS ceases to be the equilibrium point, for the EB curve, which established external balance in a stationary state, shifts downward, represented by curve EB′ in Figure 8.5. At the new long-term steady-state equilibrium point, point SS′ on Figure 8.5, the exchange rate is more appreciated (is smaller) and the NIIP is higher in comparison with the original equilibrium position. How do we get there?

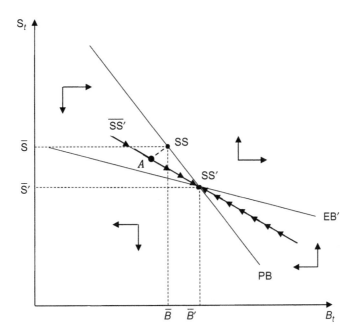

**Figure 8.5** Positive shock on trade balance.

At first, there is an exchange rate appreciation leading to a point over the equilibrium path, such as point A in Figure 8.5. Given that the foreign debt for this country is denominated in domestic currency, the exchange rate appreciation increases its value when measured in foreign currency. As such, the valuation effect, as explained in the last term of the foreign equilibrium equation (Eq. (8.40)), causes a fall in the NIIP. The impact of the exchange rate appreciation on the NIIP will be greater, the greater the gross foreign debt for the country.

After the initial exchange rate appreciation accompanied by the reduction in the NIIP, the exchange rate continues to gradually appreciate until reaching its final value in the new stationary state, SS'. The NIIP, in turn, increases over the equilibrium path, reaching, in the new steady-state, an even greater value than at first. Intuitively, the initial fall of the NIIP was due to the valuation effect caused by the jump in exchange rate. Along the equilibrium path the higher current-account balance due to the trade balance shock $z$ causes the increase of the NIIP. Note, however, the nominal exchange rate appreciation along the equilibrium path has a negative impact on the NIIP, but since it is gradual, of smaller magnitude compared to the positive impact of the trade shock.

How does this result compare to the traditional model that assumes perfect substitutability between assets? Shock $z$ corresponds to a terms of trade shock that, as we saw in the real exchange rate equilibrium model presented in Chapter 5, would cause the exchange rate appreciation necessary to maintain the current account unaltered. In terms of Figure 8.5, the economy would jump from point SS to the point above the EB′ curve at the same level as the initial NIIP, $\overline{B}$, and remain there forever. When assets are perfect substitutes, the PB relation ceases to exist and $R^e_{t+1}$ is always equal to 1. Every permanent shock of $z$ is absorbed by exchange rate appreciation, without a variation of the net foreign credit.

Let us take a look at another extreme case where there is no substitutability whatsoever between assets, that is, shares $\Lambda$ and $\Lambda^*$ are constants. In this case, the portfolio balance is represented by Eq. (8.33), which shows that the exchange rate cannot change if there is no change in $B_t$. Notice that $B_t$ is the net foreign credit that was contracted in period $t-1$, therefore, when a shock occurs in period $t$, $B_t$ is predetermined. The economy is always on curve PB in Figure 8.5, and the exchange rate appreciates at the rate that the NIIP increases until reaching point SS′.

With imperfect substitutability between assets, the relation between $B_t$ and $S_t$ is not predetermined as in Eq. (8.33), given that changes in the expected interest rate differential $R^e_{t+1}$ alters the decision of portfolio allocation. A smaller immediate exchange appreciation in the face of the shock generates an expectation of greater exchange appreciation in the future, which causes a reallocation in the portfolio in favor of domestic assets. The portfolio equilibrium condition (Eq. (8.40)) can then be satisfied for a different combination of exchange rate, $S_t$, and expected interest differential, $R^e_{t+1}$, given the NIIP, $B_t$.

**The imperfect substitutability of assets causes a nonmonotonic trajectory of the NIIP: it initially goes down, to later go up. Moreover, the exchange rate appreciation is larger initially, and progressively continues over time until the new equilibrium.** The greater the substitutability between assets, the greater the initial exchange rate appreciation.

## 8.4.5 The Impact of Shocks on the Asset Market

Assume now that a shock occurs on investor preference in favor of foreign assets. This shock could be generated, for example, by countries subject to exchange rate crises to guard against new crises by accumulating foreign credit, as in the case of the Asian economies at the end of the 1990s. In the model, this shock is represented by an increase in variable $v_t$. Notice that this type of exercise would not be possible in the models presented in the previous chapters, where we assume the perfect substitutability of assets between countries.

The stationary external balance in Eq. (8.42) is not affected by this variable; therefore curve EB does not change due to this preferences shock. As to the portfolio allocation, a bias in preferences in favor of foreign assets causes a reduction in demand for domestic assets, reducing the left side of Eq. (8.42), which determines portfolio balance in a stationary state. Given the NIIP, $B_t$, exchange rate depreciation (greater $S_t$) reduces the value of domestic assets as measured in foreign currency, which rebalances the assets market. The PB curve,

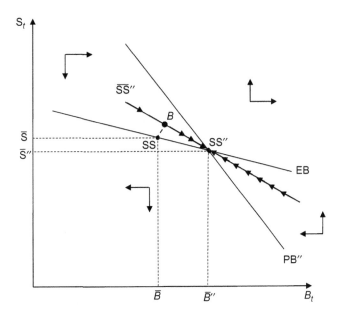

**Figure 8.6** Preferences shock in favor of foreign assets.

therefore, shifts upward, with the new portfolio balance curve in stationary state represented by curve PB″ in Figure 8.6.

The increase in preference for foreign assets, at first, causes exchange rate depreciation, leading the economy to a point over the new equilibrium path, point B in Figure 8.6. Per the valuation effect, exchange depreciation reduces the value the domestic foreign debt measured in foreign currency. Therefore, there is an increase in the NIIP. As in the case of the shock in the goods market, here also the effect is proportional to the size of the gross foreign debt of the domestic country.

On the path to the new steady-state equilibrium SS″, there is a gradual appreciation of the exchange rate. The effect of the gradual exchange rate appreciation is small in relation to the positive impact of the initial depreciation on the trade balance, so that the current account is in surplus, causing an increase in the NIIP. The exchange rate appreciation expectation in the transition period guarantees portfolio balance. Line PB″ represents the points where there is stationary portfolio balance, in other words, with an expected interest differential $R^e_{t+1}$ equal to 1. Given that the economy is below line PB″, there would be an excess in demand for domestic assets if there were not an expectation of exchange rate variation. The expectation of exchange rate appreciation causes domestic assets to be less attractive, balancing this market.

Summarizing, **a shock in preferences in favor of foreign assets causes initial exchange rate depreciation, followed by a gradual appreciation until the new equilibrium where the exchange is more appreciated in relation to the initial point. The NIIP, as would be expected, increases** (Box 8.4).

---

**BOX 8.4 PORTFOLIO DIVERSIFICATION AND GLOBAL IMBALANCES**

The global imbalances of the 2000s can be understood in light of the model presented in this chapter.

For different reasons, a group of countries increased their long-term savings. Countries that went through exchange crises in the 1990s, such as Thailand or South Korea, opted to accumulate international reserves as security against other crises. Countries that exported oil and raw materials experienced a significant increase in terms of trade, and saved a share of their gains. Finally, in countries with high growth and insufficient social security networks, families began to save more. The best example is China, which grew rapidly, has an aging population and a precarious public retirement system. These three motives for long-term saving resulted in higher demand for low-risk financial products and services with a greater degree of sophistication, which in general are not available in emerging or developing economies. The deficits in current account in the United States would then be the counterpoint of the excess demand for secure American assets due to the phenomenon known as the global savings glut. The underlying reason would be associated with differences between the types of financial assets available for savings in each country.

Let us look at the mechanism according to the model of portfolio diversification. Figure 8.5 shows that a positive shock to the trade balance, such as an improvement in the terms of trade for commodity exporters, would cause exchange rate depreciation coupled with an increase in its NIIP. The United States can be seen as a country living on the other side of this situation, that is, a country that has suffered a negative shock to its balance of trade, given that it is a net importer of primary goods. By analogy, the United States should have undergone exchange depreciation combined with a reduction in its NIIP.

It is important to emphasize that portfolio diversification causes a trade shock to exercise an impact on the current account even if it is permanent, while in the intertemporal models seen in Chapters 4 and 5 the current account is only affected by shocks considered temporary.

The increase in long-term saving in emerging countries can, in turn, be captured in the model by an increase in the relative demand for American assets, considered a low-risk investment and, therefore, appropriate for this end. Figure 8.6 shows that a shock in asset preference in favor of foreign assets causes exchange depreciation in the short run, with a more appreciated exchange rate in the long run, while the NIIP increases. The United States, which is on the opposite side of this story, would undergo an initial exchange rate appreciation followed by depreciation over time, at the same time its NIIP goes down.

**Therefore, the model forecasts surpluses in current account, and, consequently, an increase in NIIP, for commodity exporters and countries with an increase in long-term savings, counterbalanced by a deficient current account in the United States, the country to which this saving is directed.** The result is a growing American indebtedness.

# Mathematical Appendix

**Development of** Eq. (8.38):

We repeat Eqs. (8.36) and (8.37) here:

$$CA_t = TB(S_t, z_t) + i^*_{t-1}F_t - i_{t-1}\frac{S_{t-1}}{S_t}D_t$$

$$B_{t+1} - B_t = CA_t + \left(1 - \frac{S_{t-1}}{S_t}\right)D_t$$

Substituting Eq. (3.36) into Eq. (3.37), both in Chapter 3, and simplifying the trade balance notation, we obtain:

$$B_{t+1} = B_t + TB_t + i^*_{t-1}F_t - i_{t-1}\frac{S_{t-1}}{S_t}D_t + \left(1 - \frac{S_{t-1}}{S_t}\right)D_t$$

Adding and subtracting $i^*_{t-1}D_t$ in the previous equation, we get:

$$B_{t+1} = B_t + TB_t + i^*_{t-1}(F_t - D_t) + \left(i^*_{t-1} - i_{t-1}\frac{S_{t-1}}{S_t}\right)D_t + \left(1 - \frac{S_{t-1}}{S_t}\right)D_t$$

Using the definition of Eq. (8.2), we arrive at:

$$B_{t+1} = TB_t + B_t + (B_t + D_t - D_t)i^*_{t-1} + (1 + i^*_{t-1})D_t + \left(1 + i_{t-1}\frac{S_{t-1}}{S_t}\right)D_t$$

$$= TB_t + (1 + i^*_{t-1})B_t + \left(1 + i^*_{t-1} - (1 + i_{t-1})\frac{S_{t-1}}{S_t}\right)D_t$$

$$= TB_t + (1 + i^*_{t-1})B_t + (1 + i^*_{t-1})\left(1 - \left(\frac{1 + i_{t-1}}{1 + i^*_{t-1}}\right)\frac{S_{t-1}}{S_t}\right)D_t$$

# 8.5 Exercises

## Exercise 1

If a country has problems borrowing resources in its own currency, economists say that this country suffers from *original sin*.

**a.** Why do emerging economies, in general, suffer from *original sin*? What are the consequences in practical terms?

**b.** What are the alternatives for an emerging economy suffering from *original sin* to deal with the problem? What are the associated advantages and disadvantages?

c. In this item you will have the opportunity to analyze empirical data with the goal of measuring *original sin* based on real data for assets issued abroad by several countries. Based on data available on the BIS Internet page (Bank of International Settlements), create two distinct groups of countries. The first should be composed of advanced economies, such as the United States, Canada, Japan, the United Kingdom, and member countries of the Eurozone. The second should be composed of emerging economies, such as Brazil, India, China, Russia, and others. What was the total value of debt issued by each group of countries in 2012 and the value issued in their own currency? What conclusions can you draw based on an analysis of this information?

d. Continuing within the context of the previous item, consolidate and organize the information collected for three distinct periods of time, being the first from 1993 to 1998, the second from 1999 to 2006, and the third from 2007 to 2012. What conclusions can you draw based on the consolidated results for these three periods, for each group of countries? Can you find a change in the standard of indebtedness for these economies? Explain your answer.

## Exercise 2

After the 2007/2008 economic crisis, an important debate was revived that questioned the role of the dollar as the world reserve currency, the so-called *exorbitant privilege*. Respected economists remember that, just as the pound lost its position to the dollar at the beginning of the twentieth century, we could be facing a period of transition when the dollar will be substituted by another currency as the world currency reserve value.

a. Based on data obtained from the IMF, prepare a historical series measuring the percentage of world reserves measured in the American dollar, euro, yen, and yuan (or renmimbi). What conclusion can you draw based on the analysis of this data?

b. What characteristics are desirable for a currency to be used as an international reserve value? Explain. What are the advantages and disadvantages of having an international reserve currency? Explain your answer.

c. Would it be plausible to believe that the dollar could be substituted as the global reserve currency in the next years? What currencies would be the natural candidates in this succession? Explain your answer.

## Exercise 3

Consider an economy with external credit in a foreign currency and external debt in local currency.

a. Obtain a mathematical expression to measure the NIIP variation of this economy as a percent of GDP. Consider that the GDP in period $t$ is denoted by $Y_t$.

b. Assume that this country has a current-account surplus of 1% of GDP, that its GDP growth rate is 2%, and that the NIIP of this economy is equal to 3% of GDP. What would be the necessary variation in exchange rate, measured as the amount of domestic currency necessary to purchase one unit of foreign currency, for the NIIP to be stable for next period? Can you measure the valuation effect in this case? How does the exchange rate change affect the NIIP in this economy? Explain your answer.

c. Using the parameters presented in the previous item, now consider a case where the economy has external credit denominated in local currency and external debt denominated in foreign currency. What should be the necessary exchange rate variation for the NIIP to be stable for next period? Would you be able to measure the valuation effect in this case? Compare your answer with the result obtained in the previous item.

d. Consider the case of the American economy. What would be the impact of a change in the price of American assets on the United States NIIP if these assets were positively correlated with price of European and Chinese assets? What would be the impact in the situation if the price of these assets were negatively correlated? Explain your answer.

## Exercise 4

Consider an economic environment where there are only two economies, a domestic and a foreign, and where assets are perfect substitutes. Assume that the accumulation of net foreign assets by the domestic economy follows the dynamics given by the following equation in differences:

$$B_{t+1} = (1 + r)B_t + \text{TB}(q_t, z_t)$$

where $B_t$ represents the NIIP in period $t$, $r$ represents the real domestic exchange rate, TB($\cdot$) is a function that measures the trade balance of the domestic economy, $q_t$ represents the real exchange rate, in terms of units of foreign economy goods necessary to acquire one unit of domestic economic good, and $z_t$ is a variable that synthesizes all other factors that influence the trade deficit, such as preferences for domestic and foreign goods, among others. Assume that the trade balance function is given by $\text{TB}(q_t, z_t) = \theta q_t + z_t$, that the domestic interest rate is equal to the foreign rate, that is, $r = r^*$, both constant, and that goods prices are constant. In this economic environment, the uncovered interest rate parity is given by:

$$(1 + r) = (1 + r^*)\frac{S_t}{E_t[S_{t+1}]}$$

a. Based on the hypotheses presented in the problem, what could you say regarding the evolution of the real exchange rate over time? Explain your answer.

b. Solving the equation in differences from the NIIP forward, and imposing a condition that the net debt does not grow at a rate superior to the interest rate (the transversality condition), obtain the value of the real exchange rate. Present an economic interpretation for your answer.

c. Based on your answer to the previous item, find an expression that determines the evolution of $B_t - B_{t-1}$. Present an economic interpretation for your answer.

**d.** Now consider that a permanent and unexpected shock occurs in $z_t$. What would be the impact of this shock on the real exchange rate and on the net external debt for the domestic economy? Present an economic explanation for the shock, for the exchange rate evolution and the NIIP.

**e.** Could the results obtained in the previous item be used to explain the current-account dynamics for the American economy up to 2007? Explain your answer. What is the role of perfect substitutability among assets on the explicatory power of this model in light of the behavior of the empirical data?

## Exercise 5

Consider an economic environment identical to that developed in Section 8.4. What conditions must be met for the system formed by the portfolio balance relation and the external balance relation to be locally stable? Present an economic interpretation for this result.

## Exercise 6

In the previous chapters, where we considered domestic and foreign assets as perfect substitutes, the uncovered interest rate parity captured this hypothesis in the models developed. However, as has been argued throughout this chapter, international assets are not necessarily perfect substitutes. Present economic reasons that justify the diversification of investor portfolios. What factors, besides the rate of return, can influence the behavior of asset demand?

## Exercise 7

Based on the economic model developed in Section 8.4:

**a.** Compare the behavior of the exchange rate when facing shocks on the current account when assets are perfect substitutes and when there is no substitutability whatsoever between them. Explain your answer.

**b.** Based on the relation of external balance (EB), presented in Section 8.4, explain how exchange rate depreciation affects the NIIP of the domestic economy. How would your answer change if the domestic economy had foreign liabilities denominated in foreign currency? Explain.

**c.** Consider the case where the assets are imperfect substitutes. Assuming that the economy was initially in steady-state equilibrium, what is the impact of a permanent negative shock on the terms of trade? Explain your answer. On a graph, present the old and new equilibrium, including a graph with the NIIP trajectory immediately after the shock for the case when $\Lambda_R \equiv ((\partial\Lambda(R^e, v))/\partial R^e)$ is large and for the case when $\Lambda_R$ is small.

**d.** Considering the case of assets that are imperfect substitutes in an economy initially in steady-state equilibrium, what is the impact of a permanent shock on the preferences of the domestic economy residents that leads them to increase their demand for domestic assets? Construct a graph with the NIIP trajectory and the exchange rate immediately after the shock for the case where $\Lambda_R$ is large and for the case where $\Lambda_R$ is small.

# Crises and Exchange Rate Policy

Based on the analytical framework developed throughout the first three parts of the book, this last is dedicated to the practical topics related to exchange rate policy. We begin in Chapter 9 with a study of the currency crises, presenting the theoretical frameworks used to capture the main characteristics of such crises. Chapter 10, in turn, describes the different exchange rate regimes and analyzes the factors that influence the best choice of exchange rate regime to be adopted by an economy. Finally, Chapter 11 investigates the political motives for a government choosing a particular exchange rate policy.

# 9

# Currency Crises

## CHAPTER OUTLINE

The 1980s had the external debt crisis with its tough consequences for the Latin American economy and society. The Mexican, Asian, and Russian currency crises marked the 1990s. Since 2008, the world has gone through economic turbulence since the American financial system crisis was amplified and disseminated around the world due to the financial connections between countries. Currency crises usually have strong impacts on economies, with serious consequences for families, firms, and government.

In the models studied in the preceding chapters, we saw how the optimum current-account level is determined, which variables affect the real exchange rate, as well as the relation between the nominal exchange rate and other economic variables, such as fiscal and monetary policies. However, at times excessive exchange rate variations or pressure on the exchange rate are observed that do not seem to be explained by the state of the underlying economic variables that determine the exchange rate value. These are the currency crises, or balance of payment crises, that are the objects of our study in this chapter.

**The explanations for the currency crises are divided into three *generations* of models. Each generation was developed with the intention of explaining elements that arose in new currency crises but that were either not present or not important in preceding ones.** Therefore, the models are divided into *generations* according to the chronological order they appear. They are not exclusionary among themselves, that is, each currency crisis can have elements of more than one generation or explanations.

Principles of International Finance and Open Economy Macroeconomics.
English translation © 2015 Elsevier Inc.

---

**BOX 9.1 EUROPEAN MONETARY SYSTEM**

The European Monetary System (EMS) is the result of an agreement signed in 1979 by which most European Economic Community member countries agreed to coordinate their monetary policies so as to avoid large fluctuations in the exchange rate among them. In preparation for the monetary union, the EMS created the European Currency Unit (ECU), which was a basket of currencies containing fixed amounts of most currencies of European Community. The ECU was a virtual currency which served as unit of account and as reference currency for exchange rate policy, being replaced by the euro in 1999 at a 1:1 conversion rate.

One important pillar of the EMS was the European Exchange Rate Mechanism (ERM), according to which governments agreed to intervene in the foreign exchange market to maintain their exchange rates within a narrow band of fluctuation with respect to the ECU. This band was established at 2.25% around a central rate, with the exception of Italy, Portugal, and Spain, for whom the band was established at $\pm 6\%$. In face of speculative attacks, these bands were widened to 15% between 1993 and 1996.

---

The first generation of models was developed in the 1980s. In this first explanation for currency crises, the crisis had its origin in a government fiscal policy incompatible with the fixed exchange rate regime, which led to a continuous loss of reserves to maintain the exchange rate parity. The emphasis of these models is the role of the speculative attack as an arbitrage of asset prices.

The second generation of models, in turn, was developed based on the 1991−1993 European Monetary System (EMS) crisis (Box 9.1). The main element of this crisis was the choice of governments to defend or not to defend exchange rate parity, where the cost to defend depended on the expectations of exchange rate depreciation. The focus came to be the role of expectations as a trigger to set off a currency crisis.

Finally, the financial sector, which is not analyzed in the first- and second-generation models, had a central role in the Asia crisis at the end of the 1990s. The emphasis of the third-generation models is the fragility of firms and bank balance sheets. We will take a look at each of these generations of models.[1]

# 9.1 The Speculative Attack as Asset Price Arbitrage

A speculative attack occurs when there is a massive purchase of an asset by a group of speculators, who are those individuals who operate in the markets by exploiting short-run price movements with the goal of obtaining profits. *Grosso modo*, we say that the asset market suffered a speculative attack when speculators force a trajectory for the price of this asset, a trajectory that usually differs from that which would be generated by the variables that give value to the asset.

---

[1] Lorenzoni (2015) has a thorough recent review of this literature.

In the foreign exchange market, a speculative attack is characterized by a massive sale of domestic currency by both domestic and foreign investors. When speaking of a speculative attack, in general one imagines the occurrence of some event that generates panic or some type of irrational behavior on the part of market participants. The first-generation currency crises model shows that is not necessarily the case: a speculative attack can happen even in an economy where there is no uncertainty and where the private agents are perfectly rational. It emphasizes the speculative attack as resulting from asset price arbitrage. According to Krugman (1979), the seminal article for this literature, the origin would be in the fact of the government following policies that are unsustainable in the medium or long run.

More specifically, the government commits to a fixed exchange rate regime at the same time it implements an expansionist credit policy. As we saw in Chapter 6, to maintain a fixed exchange rate, the fundamentals should also be maintained constant. In particular, the money supply cannot vary when there are no other changes in the economy. A credit expansion policy tends to increase the money supply, which should then be controlled by the sale of international reserves. Economic agents anticipate that when the government reserves run out, the fixed exchange rate regime will have to be abandoned. In anticipating the abandoning of the fixed exchange rate regime, speculators abruptly increase the demand for foreign currency since they believe that soon the exchange rate will depreciate, setting off a speculative attack. This is also an arbitrage operation, given that these operators purchase foreign currency at a current price inferior to that expected to be in force after the exchange rate fluctuation. Notice that the exchange rate market speculation, by means of the purchase of foreign currency, creates pressure for depreciation of the domestic currency. This pressure increases as the stock of international reserves in the central bank decreases.

We will look at a case where there is no uncertainty: the economic agents know exactly the current and future policy to be followed by the government, and there are no economic shocks. With these assumptions, we emphasize the aspect of price arbitrage in the speculative attack. The model is based on the flexible price monetary model, studied in Chapter 6. According to that model, the exchange rate level depends on a set of economic variables that affect the supply and demand for foreign currency, named economic *fundamentals*, as well as the expected variation of the very exchange rate. The exchange rate trajectory is then determined by Eq. (6.4), reproduced here:

$$s(t) = m(t) - p^*(t) - \phi y(t) + \eta i^*(t) + \eta E\left(\frac{ds(t)}{dt}\right),$$

where $s(t)$, $m(t)$, $p^*(t)$, and $y(t)$ represent the nominal exchange rate, the stock of money, international prices, and output, respectively, all in logarithm. $i^*(t) \equiv \ln(1 + i^*)$ is the international interest rate.

According to the previous equation, **being committed to a fixed exchange rate is equivalent to being committed to maintain the fundamentals constant**. However, any variation in the exogenous variables that compose the fundamentals should be counterbalanced by an adequate monetary policy to maintain the fundamentals unaltered. Assume, for the sake of simplicity, that all exogenous variables, except the money supply, are constant and that the units of measure are chosen in such a way that $p^* = i^* = y = 0$.[2] Therefore, the money supply is the only source of variation in the fundamentals, and the exchange rate trajectory can be written as

$$s(t) = m(t) + \eta E\left(\frac{ds(t)}{dt}\right). \tag{9.1}$$

The money supply, in turn, depends on the government credit and exchange rate policies. On the central bank balance sheet, the monetary base corresponds to the bank liability, while the stocks of domestic assets and international reserves constitute its assets. The central bank balance sheet can be represented by

| Assets | Liabilities |
|---|---|
| $A(t)$ | $M(t)$ |
| $S(t)R(t)$ | |

where $A$ are domestic assets, $S$ is the exchange rate, and $R$ are international reserves measured in foreign currency. According to the balance sheet, we have that

$$M(t) = A(t) + S(t)R(t). \tag{9.2}$$

Equation (9.2) is an accounting identity: it is always true whatever the central bank credit or exchange rate policies are, and it does not indicate any causality relationship between the variables.

Assume that the government adopts an expansionist credit policy. More specifically, assume that domestic credit grows at constant rate $\theta$. In terms of the model variables, we have that

$$a(t) = a_0 + \theta t,$$

where $a(t) = \ln A(t)$, which implies that

$$\frac{\dot{A}}{A} = \frac{d(\ln A(t))}{dt} = \dot{a} = \theta. \tag{9.3}$$

At the same time, the government commits itself to a fixed exchange rate where $s(t) = \bar{s}$ for all $t$. According to Eq. (9.1), to maintain the fixed exchange rate, the government must maintain the money supply fixed. The central bank balance sheet equation (Eq. (9.2)), in turn, tells us that, in the face of an expansionist credit policy, the monetary authority should sell international reserves to maintain the money supply fixed. To better understand this mechanism, we can totally differentiate Eq. (9.2), obtaining

$$dM = dA + \bar{s}dR. \tag{9.4}$$

---

[2] Remember that for a variable $x$, we define $x \equiv \ln X$. Hence, we have that $x = 0$ corresponds to $X = 1$.

Hence, when the exchange is fixed:

$$dM = 0 \Leftrightarrow \bar{s}dR = -dA$$

should be true. **To maintain foreign exchange parity, the government should continually sell international reserves at the same rate as the credit expansion.**

Intuitively, the expansionist credit policy would increase the money supply in the case sufficient reserves were not sold to compensate for it. In that case, at the current exchange rate, there would be an excess supply of domestic currency, which counterpoint is excess in demand for foreign currency. To avoid exchange rate depreciation, the government should supply this excess in demand of foreign currency by selling international reserves. However, the situation is not sustainable given that government reserves are finite, and, therefore, will eventually be exhausted. **What would happen if there were not a speculative attack before the government exhausted its reserves?**

While there were reserves, the exchange rate would be fixed, given by

$$s(t) = \overline{m} = \bar{s}. \tag{9.5}$$

When there were no more reserves, the regime would become a floating exchange rate. The money supply would be equal to the stock of assets, given that there were no more reserves, and that the stock of assets would grow at a constant rate, as indicated in Eq. (9.3). According to what we saw by means of Eq. (6.12), the expected change in exchange rate would be equal to the rate of credit growth, and the exchange rate path would be given by

$$s(t) = m(t) + \eta\theta. \tag{9.6}$$

Figure 9.1A represents the exchange rate path and Figure 9.1B the evolution of the fundamentals over time in this hypothetical exercise. Remember that here the fundamentals correspond to the money supply. We see that, at the moment the government reserves run out, let us say in period $t_1$, the nominal exchange rate would jump, going from $\bar{s}$ to $\bar{s} + \eta\theta$. Remember that there is no uncertainty in this economy. If you were there, what would you do the day before the reserves ran out, knowing that on the next day the exchange rate would depreciate? I'm sure that you would use all the money you had or could borrow to buy foreign currency at fixed exchange rate $\bar{S}$, and the next day sell it at the price of $\exp[\bar{s} + \eta\theta]$. Well, not only you, but everyone and their brother would do the same thing. Clearly, the combination of collective behavior with the common knowledge would cause the international reserves to run out one day earlier. Knowing this, you would then want to buy your dollars a day earlier than that, but, unfortunately, all the others would do the same. Continuing this rationale, we see that, in equilibrium, the economic agents buy all government reserves at the exact moment when the fall in fundamentals caused by the sale of the remaining reserves is such that there is no jump in the exchange rate. This movement occurs in period $T < t_1$, when there remains a stock of reserves in the central bank.

The graphs in Figure 9.2 describe how to obtain an equilibrium exchange rate and fundamental paths. In Figure 9.2A, the horizontal dashed line indicates the fixed exchange rate

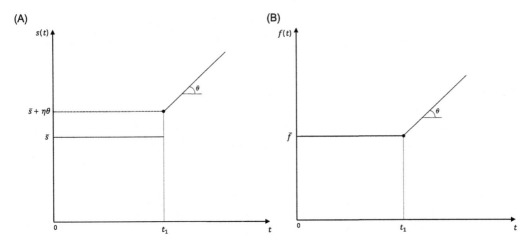

**Figure 9.1** Exchange rate (A) and fundamental paths (B).

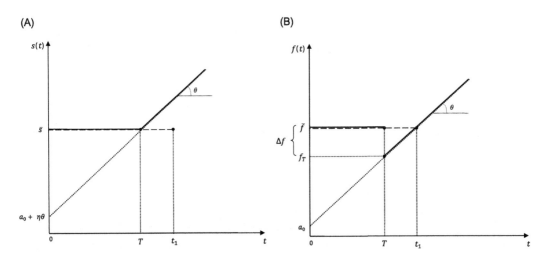

**Figure 9.2** Equilibrium exchange rate (A) and fundamental paths (B).

level, as in Eq. (9.5), while the dotted line with slope $\theta$ shows the floating exchange path when there are no reserves in the central bank, given by Eq. (9.6) with $m(t) = a(t)$. Figure 9.2B, in turn, the dotted line represents the fundamentals path when there are no reserves, i.e., $m(t) = a(t)$, which grows at constant rate $\theta$, and the dashed line, the level of fundamentals fixed in $\bar{f}$. So that there is no discontinuity in the exchange rate trajectory, it is necessary that exactly in period $T$, when the two exchange rate paths cross, the agents make a speculative attack on the central bank reserves. At this moment, the economic agents purchase all central bank foreign currency, which leads the government, now with no reserves to defend the exchange rate parity, to abandon the fixed exchange rate regime. In equilibrium, the exchange rate and the fundamentals follow the dashed line trajectory up to period $T$, and as of that point, continue as per the dotted line, as indicated by the full line in both figures.

What is period $T$? We know that before the speculative attack, the exchange rate is $\bar{s} = \bar{m}$. At moment $T$, when there is a speculative attack, the reserves run out and the money supply becomes identical to the stock of assets in the central bank, i.e., $f(T) = m(T) = a(T) = a_o + \theta T$. Then, at the time of the speculative attack, the exchange rate becomes floating and, according to Eq. (9.6), equal to

$$\hat{s} = f(T) + \eta\theta = a_o + \theta T + \eta\theta.$$

So that there is no discontinuity in the exchange path, it is necessary that $\bar{s} = \hat{s}$, which results in

$$a_o + \theta T + \eta\theta = \bar{s}.$$

Therefore, we know that the moment of the speculative attack will be when

$$T = \frac{\bar{s} - a_o - \eta\theta}{\theta}.$$

Notice that at the moment of the attack, $\bar{s} = \bar{m} = \ln(A(T) + \bar{S}R(T))$. Given that the money supply is constant for the period the fixed exchange rate regime is in force, we have that $\bar{m} = \ln(A(T) + \bar{S}R(T))$ for all of $t < T$, in particular, $\bar{m} = \ln(A(0) + \bar{S}R(0))$. Substituting it in the previous equation, the moment of the speculative attack can be written as

$$T = \frac{\ln(A(0) + \bar{S}R(0)) - a_o - \eta\theta}{\theta}.$$

The previous equation shows that, the greater the initial stock of reserves, the longer it will take before a speculative attack occurs.

At the moment of the speculative attack, the money supply falls, represented by the jump in fundamentals $\Delta f$ in Figure 9.2B. This jump is proportional to the amount of international reserves remaining in the central bank that are bought by speculators, given by

$$\Delta f = \ln(A(T)) - \ln(A(T) + \bar{S}R(T)).$$

In summary, **in a model where there is no uncertainty and with perfectly rational agents, a speculative attack occurs if the government credit policy is inconsistent with the fixed exchange rate regime**. The speculative attack is the result of arbitrage of the price of foreign currency. If there were no attack, there would be an expected exchange rate jump. The agents arbitrate in the market in such a way that, in equilibrium, the exchange rate follows a continuous path, that is, with no jumps. **In general, there cannot be any expected jumps in economic asset prices, for these would open the possibility for arbitrage**.

It is clear that the model presented here is quite simple and excludes any sources of economic uncertainty. In the real world, this is far from the truth. The model can be perfectly extended to include uncertainty, as it is in fact done in the literature. There can be uncertainty, for example, with respect to the amount of reserves the government is willing to use to defend the currency, and the moment chosen for the speculative attack would then be based on agent expectations. If the government uses less reserves than expected to defend the currency, that is, if it sells less foreign currency to speculators, the fall in fundamentals will be less than expected and there will be a discreet depreciation in the exchange rate at the moment of the attack. If the agents knew the government would use fewer reserves, they clearly would have attacked the currency before and there would not be an exchange rate jump. On the other hand, if the government sells more reserves than expected, there will be an exchange rate appreciation, which implies a loss for speculators. In the face of uncertainty, they arbitrate according to the available information and do not always choose the right time to do it. They are right only part of the time, and with each event can either gain or lose, depending on the event that effectively occurs.

## 9.1.1 Model Limitations

The main criticism of the first-generation currency crisis model resides in the hypothesis that, while the private agents are rational and act based on their own interests (such as praxis, otherwise, in the economic models), the government is an automaton, following internal policies that are inconsistent among themselves and that are devoid of any rationale. To defend the model, it can be argued that the government is indeed not a monolithic block where economic policy decisions are made with the rationale of a single entity. Actually, the government is formed by a set of organs directed by different agents, each responsible for different political spheres. This can result in a set of conflicting policies, which can appear somewhat schizophrenic. In the first-generation speculative attack models, the government is neither explicitly modeled, nor is the way it makes decisions, due to the same inconsistency in internal policies. The government objectives are not explicit. The model simply assumes that it follows such inconsistent policies, given that, in fact, this is what has been observed in many actual cases of economies that ended up in currency crises.

One quite uncomfortable characteristic of the model is its prediction that the exchange rate should not jump at the moment of crisis, which appears counterfactual. Some more elaborate models are able, however, to generate discreet exchange rate depreciation in a first-generation model, by adding uncertainty and private information.[3]

Another criticism that can be made regarding the model is that it does not take into consideration other options to defend the currency, those that do not use international reserves under the control of the central bank. There are, however, alternative policies that can be used. If it does not have sufficient international reserves, the government can, for example,

[3] See, for example, Broner (2008) and Rochon (2006).

acquire foreign loans to defend the exchange rate. There is also the option of imposing capital controls or restrictions on imports. Each of these results in different costs to the economy, leading the government to consider if it is worth the effort to continue defending the currency. Well, into this scenario enter the second-generation currency crisis models.

Finally, the model does not consider the potential real effects of the currency crises. Given that it is based on the flexible price monetary model, the real side of the economy is completely exogenous to the model. What happens to the money supply or the exchange rate has no impact on production, the real exchange rate or any other real variable in the economy. Nevertheless, the main concern regarding the currency crises is precisely their negative effect on the activity level of the economy. What can be said regarding the model in this aspect is that it simply is not adequate to cover these questions since its role is to identify the speculative attack as a rational movement of asset price arbitrage.

## 9.2  Crises as Self-Fulfilling Prophecies

The EMS crisis in the early 1990s brought new situations that are hard to be reconciled using the first-generation models. First, the European countries that suffered speculative attacks did not follow clearly inconsistent economic policies, as presupposed in those models. Second, they were developed countries whose governments had easy access to international credit. It is difficult to believe that the governments in those countries did not defend their currencies due to lack of international reserves. Furthermore, those countries had other options to stabilize the exchange rate, such as, for example, adopting contractionist credit policies to increase the interest rate and, thereby, attracting international capital. Finally, the speculative attacks occurred without there being a significant worsening in the economic fundamentals.

The currency crisis model proposed by Obstfeld (1986) was able to explain this type of situation, giving origin to the second-generation currency crisis models. **This generation of models is characterized by two elements. First, they consider that the abandoning of the fixed exchange rate regime or exchange rate bands is not inevitable, but, rather, the result of a political decision.** However, the actions taken to defend the exchange rate are costly, which leads the government to compare the costs of maintaining the regime in relation to other objectives.

**Second, the speculative action by the agents affects the cost to maintain the exchange rate parity, so that there can be self-fulfilling currency crises.** In other words, if on the one hand the agents believe that there will be a speculative attack on the currency, they will speculate, because no one wants to be the last in line. The cost of maintaining the fixed exchange rate then increases, which precipitates a currency crisis. If, on the other hand, the speculators believe the currency will remain stable, they will not speculate against it and exchange rate parity will be maintained.

Let us take a look at a simple model, based on Krugman (1996), which represents the analysis provided in second-generation currency crisis models. The model presented here can be seen as a caricature of the second-generation models, where only the main elements are delineated to capture its essence.[4]

The government decides to either defend exchange rate parity or allow the exchange rate to float so as to optimize an objective function. The objective function tries to capture the trade-off between the cost to defend the exchange rate and the benefit of maintaining its parity. This trade-off is represented by a loss function that the government minimizes when choosing how to respond to a speculative attack. We will look at each of the elements of the government loss function.

**The first element of the loss function is the degree of exchange rate overvaluation.** Clearly, it is only worth attacking the currency, i.e., buying foreign currency, if it is believed it will depreciate when parity is abandoned. Therefore, cases of currency crises only occur when the current fixed exchange rate, $\bar{s}$, is more appreciated than its equilibrium level, $\hat{s}$, i.e., when $\hat{s} - \bar{s} > 0$. And what is the exchange rate equilibrium level? It would be best not get into that discussion at this time—just assume that there is equilibrium exchange rate, exogenously determined. One can use, for example, the model developed in Chapter 5 to identify which variables can affect the equilibrium real exchange rate. Intuitively, the equilibrium exchange rate is that which generates the current-account balance that maximizes the intertemporal welfare of the country. When the exchange rate is more appreciated than its equilibrium value, the current-account balance will be less than its optimum level. This means that the country goes more into debt than what is desirable (or lends less, in the case of the country being a net lender). Therefore, the cost of exchange rate overvaluation is associated with the cost of excessive indebtedness (or of credit with the rest of the world that is lower than optimum).

One important detail is that the second-generation model deals with the nominal exchange rate, but the idea of equilibrium is associated with the real exchange rate, that is, the relationship between the nominal exchange rate and the ratio between international and domestic prices, as per Eq. (3.2). Therefore, an underlying hypothesis of the model is that there is price rigidity in the economy.[5] As discussed in Chapter 7, empirical observation tells us that prices do not adjust immediately to shocks, but the theoretical modeling of price rigidity is not simple. In the models presented in Section 7.1, the prices were fixed, while in Section 7.2, they followed an adjustment rule completely *ad hoc*. Here, we won't even mention prices. A defense of this approach is that the model intends to only analyze the government choice in relation to defending the exchange rate in the face of a speculative attack. It can be seen as a model for the very short run, where prices are fixed, as in the Mundell–Fleming model in Section 7.1. With fixed prices, the nominal exchange rate reflects what happens with the real exchange rate.

---

[4] Alternatively, Obstfeld (1994) presents an excellent description of a basic second-generation model, with a little more structure than the model presented here.

[5] Actually, as it will become clear during the exposé, there are many underlying hypotheses and ideas in the model. Since it is a very simplified version of the second-generation models, many relations are not modeled and interactions are omitted.

**The second term of the government loss function captures the cost associated with defending the exchange rate, which depends on the expectation of exchange rate depreciation** $(E(s) - \bar{s})$. The expected exchange rate depreciation reduces the expected return from domestic assets in relation to foreign assets. The government should, then, increase the domestic interest rates to maintain the domestic assets attractive and avoid an outflow of capital. In the extreme case, where there is free capital mobility and the domestic and foreign assets are perfect substitutes, the difference between the domestic interest rate and the international should correspond exactly to the expected exchange rate depreciation, given that interest rate parity should be satisfied (see Eq. (3.13)). Therefore, the greater the expected exchange rate depreciation, the greater the domestic interest should be to defend parity. A high interest rate, in turn, generates costs for the economy. From the government point of view, the cost of its debt increases. For the private sector, the higher interest rate dampens investment in the economy, besides increasing the cost of indebtedness for companies and families. The result is a reduction in economic activity and an increase in unemployment. If parity is abandoned, there will no longer be the expectation of depreciation, given that the exchange rate will be, effectively, depreciated. The interest rate can then fall to international levels. Well, this story is not in the model, but it is the underlying motivation, once again, to include the expectation of exchange rate depreciation as a cost to maintain exchange rate parity.

**Finally, it is assumed that government incurs a cost in abandoning exchange rate parity.** There are several interpretations for this cost. It could refer to the loss of government credibility, for example, for ceasing to follow the fixed exchange rate regime previously announced. The cost could also be associated to the motive that led the government to adopt the fixed exchange rate regime. In principle the government fixes the exchange rate while seeking some benefit, which it loses when the exchange rate returns to float. The fixed exchange rate can, for example, facilitate international trade. In general, there is a great amount of time between the contracting and fulfilling of an international trade transaction, and exchange rate variations between the two moments affect the relative gains for the parts involved. Therefore, the greater the exchange volatility, the greater the associated risks will be for the transaction, and, consequently, the greater the cost.

Countries with high inflation rates, on the other hand, adopt a fixed exchange rate as a nominal anchor to maintain inflation low. As will be discussed in Chapter 10, a fixed exchange rate is a way of adhering to a stable monetary policy, which leads to the stabilization of the general level of prices. In the case of the EMS, the exchange rate bands regime, with narrow bands, was a form of harmonizing the monetary policy between the countries in preparation for the institution of the single currency. In this case, allowing the exchange rate to float beyond the bands could threaten the whole project of regional monetary unification.

Given the motivations previously discussed, the government loss function, denoted as $L$, is represented by

$$L = b_1(\hat{s} - \bar{s})^2 + b_2(E(s) - \bar{s})^2 + c,\qquad(9.7)$$

where $b_1$ and $b_2$ are parameters associated to the weight given to the exchange rate misalignment and to the expectation of exchange rate depreciation, respectively, while $c$ represents the cost of abandoning exchange rate parity.[6] We use the quadratic form for the first two terms of the equation to indicate that exchange rate misalignments and exchange rate variation expectations are undesirable, be they positive or negative.

The government decides if it defends the exchange rate or not by comparing the loss in the case where it maintains the exchange rate fixed with the loss if it abandons parity. If the exchange rate is maintained fixed, the government loss (Eq. (9.7)) will be

$$L^{\text{FIX}} = b_1(\hat{s}-\bar{s})^2 + b_2(E(s)-\bar{s})^2. \tag{9.8}$$

If the government allows the exchange rate to depreciate, it is expected that the exchange rate will jump to its equilibrium value, $\hat{s}$, and remain at that level. Consequently, the government loss for abandoning parity will be

$$L^{\text{FLEX}} = c.$$

The government will allow the exchange rate to float if

$$L^{\text{FIX}} > L^{\text{FLEX}}$$
$$\Updownarrow \tag{9.9}$$
$$b_1(\hat{s}-\bar{s})^2 + b_2(E(s)-\bar{s})^2 > c$$

and parity will be maintained, if on the contrary.

**According to the inequality (9.9), the government will abandon exchange rate parity if, when comparing the cost of allowing the exchange rate to float, the current exchange rate is very misaligned in relation to its equilibrium value and/or if the depreciation expectation is high.** Expectations have a very important role in the second-generation models, for they can sway the abandon of exchange rate parity. If the agents have an elevated expectation of depreciation, it becomes more expensive for the government to maintain the parity, which results in its abandon. If the agents believe that the regime will be maintained, the cost to maintain it is lower and it can be maintained. Therefore, **there can be multiple equilibria: equilibrium with bad expectations and a currency crisis, or equilibrium with good expectations and the maintenance of the fixed exchange rate regime.**

What does one mean by *good* or *bad* expectations? We can infer what the lower and upper limits of the exchange rate depreciation will be. It is reasonable to assume that if parity is abandoned, the exchange rate will go to its equilibrium value of $\hat{s}$. Additionally assume

---

[6] Some versions of the model assume that cost $c$ depends on the size and the sign of exchange rate variation. In these models, as in Obstfeld (1994), there are shocks that can lead to either exchange rate depreciation or appreciation when it becomes floating. With price rigidity, a change in the nominal exchange rate translates into a change of the real exchange rate, which in turn has real effects on the economy: on the allocation of resources and, possibly, the level of output. For this reason, the cost of exchange rate variation will depend on its magnitude. Here, we simplify, assuming a constant cost for abandoning the parity, which is in accord with the motivation presented in the previous paragraph.

that the agents attribute a probability of $\lambda$ to the maintenance of the fixed exchange rate regime. Therefore, the expectation for the future exchange rate is given by[7]

$$E(s) = \lambda \hat{s} + (1 - \lambda)\bar{s}. \tag{9.10}$$

The expectations are *good* or *bad* depending on the probability, $\lambda$, attributed to the maintenance of parity. The *best* expectation is that where this probability is equal to 1. In this case, $E(s) = \bar{s}$, and the expectation of exchange rate depreciation is equal to zero, $\lambda = 0$:

$$E(s) - \bar{s} = 0. \tag{9.11}$$

In the *worst* expectation, a probability of zero is attributed to the maintenance of exchange rate parity, such that $E(s) = \hat{s}$, and then the expected exchange rate depreciation reaches its maximum value, $\lambda = 1$:

$$E(s) - \bar{s} = \hat{s} - \bar{s}. \tag{9.12}$$

In terms of the government loss function described previously, we can separate the comparison between exchange rate misalignment, $\bar{s} - \hat{s}$, and the cost of abandoning the parity, $c$, into three cases:

**Case I** $(b_1 + b_2)(\hat{s}-\bar{s})^2 < c$: The cost of allowing the exchange rate to float is so high in relation to the exchange rate misalignment that, even if it is expected that the parity will be abandoned, as in Eq. (9.12), the inequality (9.9) will not hold true and exchange rate parity is maintained.

**Case II** $c < b_1(\hat{s}-\bar{s})^2$: This is the opposite of Case I. The cost of abandoning the parity is so low in relation to the exchange rate misalignment that, even if no one expects depreciation, i.e., that Eq. (9.11) is true, inequality (9.9) is satisfied and the government abandons the parity.

**Case III** $b_1(\hat{s}-\bar{s})^2 < c < (b_1 + b_2)(\hat{s}-\bar{s})^2$: This is the most interesting case, for in it, to abandon the parity or not depends on expectations. The higher the expected exchange rate depreciation, the closer to $(b_1 + b_2)(\hat{s}-\bar{s})^2$ is the government loss to maintain the parity given by Eq. (9.8). On the one hand, for a sufficiently high depreciation expectation, condition (9.9) is satisfied so that parity is abandoned. On the other hand, for a low depreciation expectation, the loss to maintain the parity (Eq. (9.8)) nears $b_1(\hat{s}-\bar{s})^2$, the condition of Eq. (9.9) is not satisfied and the government maintains the fixed exchange rate.

The exchange rate misalignment, or the degree of exchange rate overvaluation, can be seen as a measure of the quality of the economic fundamentals. Consider the case of a country that institutes a fixed exchange rate regime, setting the exchange rate at its equilibrium level. The economy would be, then, a Case I, since $(b_1 + b_2)(\hat{s}-\bar{s})^2 = 0 < c$. External or

---

[7] This function for exchange rate expectation was presented in Eq. (3.19), when we discussed the peso problem.

domestic shocks can misalign the nominal exchange rate. For example, if the domestic prices increase, the nominal exchange rate should depreciate (i.e., increase) to maintain the real exchange rate constant, according to the real exchange rate definition in Eq. (3.2). As per the current nominal exchange rate, domestic goods become relatively more expensive, causing trade balance deterioration. To maintain the exchange rate fixed, the government should either increase interest rates to attract foreign capital or sell reserves to balance the balance of payments at the fixed exchange rate level.

Exchange rate misalignment can also be caused by a reduction in prices by trade partners, by a negative domestic production shock, or by an increase in international interest rates.[8] Whatever the source of fundamentals deterioration, exchange rate misalignment will cause both a deterioration of the country's external accounts and a greater cost to maintain exchange rate parity as consequence. In the terms of our model, the deterioration of fundamentals is represented by exchange rate depreciation, i.e., an increase in $\hat{s}$. Therefore, the $\hat{s} - \bar{s}$ exchange misalignment increases, and the economy can go in the direction from Case I to Cases II or III. If the fundamentals deterioration is very large, there can be a direct jump from Case I to Case II, but for a less dramatic deterioration, the economy could find itself in Case III (Box 9.2 and Box 9.3).

**In Case III, there will be a currency crisis if the expectations of a currency crisis are sufficiently high, i.e., there can be self-fulfilling currency crisis prophecies.** There are two possible equilibria. In one of them, the expectation of abandoning parity is low,

---

### BOX 9.2 ARGENTINE PESO MISALIGNMENT

When the Argentine government instituted the currency board regime in 1990, the 1:1 parity of the peso against the dollar seemed to yield the equilibrium real exchange rate. Average GDP growth between 1991 and 1994 was over 9%, unemployment was low, and there was no pressure on the exchange rate. Problems started to appear with the Tequila crisis in December 1994, in which the Mexican peso depreciated about 50% after a capital flight due to an attempt by the Mexican government to devalue its exchange rate. International investors also became skeptical about Argentina, but the Argentine government responded with a rise in interest rates and a reform of the domestic financial market that seemed to put the economy back on track. After a recession in 1995, the economy resumed growth between 1996 and 1998. However, the currency crises in Russia and Brazil dealt the fatal blow. In particular, the depreciation of over 60% of the Brazilian real against the dollar meant a depreciation of equal magnitude against the Argentine peso, given the fixed parity between the peso and the dollar. The appreciation of the peso with respect to the Brazilian real led to a deterioration of the Argentinian trade balance with Brazil and, since Brazil is a major trading partner of Argentina, was an important factor in the balance of payments crisis that followed. Hence, the 1:1 parity between the peso and the dollar, which was the equilibrium rate in 1990, in 1999 represented an overvalued real exchange rate. Argentina experienced negative growth between 1999 and 2002, when it finally abandoned the currency board regime.

---

[8] Chapter 5 shows how variations in production and interest rates affect the equilibrium real exchange rate.

## BOX 9.3 EUROPEAN MONETARY SYSTEM CRISIS

In the case of the European Monetary System (EMS) crisis, the deterioration of member country fundamentals began with the 1990 German reunification. There was a significant increase in German government spending to integrate East Germany, causing an increase in the fiscal deficit, which expanded from less than 1% in 1989 to 3.1% in 1991. With this rapid acceleration, the debt/GDP relation went from about 39% in 1989 to about 56% in 1995. The increase in aggregate demand resulting from the higher fiscal deficit caused an increase in both the activity level and interest rates, as we saw in the Mundell–Fleming model in Chapter 6. Higher economic activity, in turn, pressured prices up. To avoid an inflationary spiral, the German central bank adopted a contractionist monetary policy, which increased the interest rate even more. Consequently, international investors directed their investments toward Germany, in detriment to the other European countries. As a result, the increase in German interest rates represented a deterioration in fundamentals for the other 10 member countries of the EMS. In the model, this deterioration is represented by an increase in exchange rate misalignment, $\hat{s} - \bar{s}$.

To maintain the exchange rate within the band, these countries had to maintain a contractionist monetary policy. As they did not have fiscal expansion equal to that of Germany, the monetary contraction had a recessive effect on the economy. The cost to defend the exchange rate is represented in the model by $b_1(\bar{s} - \hat{s})^2$ in the government loss function (Eq. (9.8)). The interpretation made for the period is that the countries entered into a Case III scenario: they were *ripe* to have their currency attacked. When agents believe the regime will be maintained, it is maintained, for the cost to defend the exchange is relatively low. The government is willing to pay the cost resulting from monetary contraction in order to face exchange rate misalignment. However, if agents believe the government will abandon the parity, monetary contraction will be greater, making its cost excessive. This was the case for the United Kingdom and Italy, two countries with high unemployment rates. In September 1992, they abandoned the exchange rate bands, established by the European exchange rate mechanism, after intense speculation on their currencies. It is reported that George Soros earned more than US$1 billion speculating against the sterling pound.

which makes it less costly to maintain the fixed exchange rate, and the exchange rate remains effectively fixed. In the other, the expectation of depreciation is high, making it costly to maintain the fixed exchange rate, and the government therefore allows the exchange rate to depreciate. We can say that the exchange rate is *ripe* for being attacked. If attacked, it does not resist, but with no attack it continues fixed. What happens, therefore, for there to be or not to be a speculative attack? In other words, what leads investors to reevaluate their expectations?

We can provide an analogy of this situation with banks and other financial institutions in relation to bank runs. There is a difference between *liquidity* and *solvency*. Banks are illiquid, for if all account holders decided to withdraw their money at the same time, the banks could not honor all their obligations. But, this does not mean they are insolvent. The bank has sufficient resources to pay account holders who, under normal circumstances, withdraw their resources. However, a series of negative events can set off a crisis of confidence, leading to a run on the bank and, consequently, a liquidity and solvency problem. According to the second-generation currency crisis models, the same can happen with countries: a series of negative reports can set off a speculative attack. Actually, **any mechanism that coordinates negative expectations, as, for example, currency crises in other countries with similar characteristics to the country in question, can set off a speculative attack in a country that is ripe for being attacked**.

## 9.2.1 First-Generation Models Versus Second-Generation Models

The first- and second-generation models differ in regards to the role of fundamentals in currency crises. **In first-generation models, the crisis has its origin in the continued deterioration of the fundamentals.** In essence, the government economic policy is not compatible with maintaining the exchange rate indefinitely fixed. **The second-generation models, in turn, emphasize the role of expectations.** In these models, the fundamentals are not the best possible, but they are also not bad enough to the point of rendering the exchange rate parity clearly unsustainable. They are in a gray zone, where the additional costs to maintain parity, caused by the high depreciation expectation, actually render the exchange rate parity unsustainable.

These two crises diagnostics have different implications as to the trajectory of macroeconomic variables before and after the crisis. According to the first-generation models, the fiscal policy would be expansionist before and after the speculative attack, with a continuous deterioration of the fundamentals. In other words, an increase in exchange rate overvaluation and loss of reserves up to the moment when there is a speculative attack. For second-generation models, there is no specific standard for credit, monetary or fiscal policies before the speculative attack. However, there will be expansionist fiscal and monetary policies after the attack. The idea is that, in the second-generation model the government follows a prescription of policies to maintain the exchange rate regime, even when pressured by domestic costs, such as a high unemployment rate. After the speculative attack followed by exchange rate flexibility, the government is free to follow the necessary expansionist policies to stimulate the economy (Box 9.4).

---

**BOX 9.4 EMS CRISIS: FIRST OR SECOND GENERATION?**

Eichengreen et al. (1995) analyze the trajectory of several economic variables before and after currency crises for a group of 20 industrial countries between 1959 and 1993. Currency crises are defined by a speculative pressure index, measured by a weighted average of changes in exchange rates, interest rates, and international reserves. They show that for the group of countries in the EMS, there is no significant difference before and after the crisis in the fiscal deficit trajectory, the differential between domestic and international inflation, the trade balance, domestic credit growth, and others. This result corroborates the explanation provided by the second-generation models to explain the EMS crisis in the early 1990s.

# 9.3 The Role of Banks and Foreign Debt

The currency crises that ravaged the Southeast Asia economies between 1997 and 1998 triggered a new generation of currency crisis models. The governments of these economies, in general, did not present fiscal deficits or policies inconsistent with exchange rate stability, which would be the precursors for a speculative attack in the molds of the first-generation models. These economies grew at accelerated rates in the years that preceded the crisis. Thailand, Malaysia, Indonesia, Singapore, and South Korea grew at rates of between 8% and 12% of GDP between the end of the 1980s and the beginning of the 1990s. There did not appear to be, therefore, pressure for expansionist policies, which would be a subjacent condition for a second-generation crisis. Additionally, a characteristic of the East Asia crises was the strong contraction of these economies after the crisis. In 1998, GDP fell by 5.6% in South Korea, 7.3% in Malaysia, 10.5% in Thailand, and 13.1% in Indonesia. According to the first- and second-generation models, there should not have been a recession after the crisis. Actually, the second-generation models forecast an increase in the level of activity after the crisis, when the government is no longer restricted by exchange rate policy and can adopt expansionist policies. This is what happened, for example, in the United Kingdom, which economy had been in recession since 1990 and began to grow after the 1992 currency crisis.

The exchange rate overvaluation in East Asia countries explains, in part, the crisis. These economies tied their currencies to the dollar at a time when the dollar was appreciating in relation to the Japanese yen and Chinese yuan. The result was an appreciation of the real exchange rate in the region in relation to the Japanese and Chinese currencies, which are their main trade partners, leading to a deterioration of the trade balance.

An important element in the Asia crisis is in the relation between the financial fragility of these economies and exchange rate instability. There was fragility in the regional banking systems attributed to the excessive risk taken by banks due to government guarantee incentives, whether explicit or not. Moreover, banks and corporations were indebted in foreign currency, which exposed them to exchange rate risk since their revenues were in local currency and they did not hedge against the mismatch of the monetary denomination of their assets and liabilities. This was also the case in Argentina at the time of the 2002 currency crisis. During the 10 years of the currency board regime in the country, private agents indebted themselves in foreign currency, attracted by the low international interest rates and the guarantee given by the government that the exchange rate would remain constant.

**The third-generation currency crisis models analyze the relation between the currency crisis and the fragility of the banking sector, on one side, and the indebtedness of banks and companies in foreign currency on the other.** There is no standard third-generation model, as in the case of the previous generations, for each model emphasizes different aspects, without there being a single model that includes all the main elements involved in the relation between the financial sector and currency crises. **The models of this generation can be divided into two groups: those that emphasize the relation between banking crises and currency crises, where the source of fragility is in the illiquidity of**

**the banking sector; and those that focus on the indebtedness of firms and banks in foreign currency, placing in scene the mismatch of the monetary denomination between assets and liabilities.**

## 9.3.1 Banking Crises and Currency Crises

Even though it was the Asia crisis that motivated the interest of researchers in the relation between bank and currency crises, this relation was already present in previous crises. Several currency crises occurred during the 1970s, but very few banking crises, which can be explained by the high level of regulation in the financial sector at the time. Banking crises proliferated as of the 1980s, with exchange rate and bank crises occurring simultaneously, a phenomenon known as *twin crises*. **On the one hand, there are mechanisms that cause a currency crisis to lead to a banking crisis, and, on the other, a bank crisis can lead to a currency crisis. There is also the possibility that a common factor leads to both a bank and a currency crisis at the same time.** Let us take a look at these mechanisms.[9]

We begin with how a currency crisis can lead to a banking crisis. In an economy that adopts a fixed exchange rate regime, a currency crisis can be set off, for example, by an external shock, such as an increase in international interest rates. Service on the foreign debt becomes more expensive with the increase in interest rates and, if there is no extra capital inflow to compensate the increase in current-account deficit, a deficit in the balance of payments will result. To maintain exchange rate parity, the government should sell international reserves, which leads to monetary contraction. The resulting reduction in credit can lead to a banking crisis.

The very expectation of abandoning the parity can lead to a banking crisis. If individuals attribute a high probability to domestic currency depreciation, they will want to trade their local currency for foreign. At the rate they withdraw their money from the bank to buy foreign currency, banking sector fragility increases. Therefore, the currency crisis can lead to a banking crisis.[10] This is what happened, for example, in Argentina when the currency board system was abandoned, and in Greece in 2012, when the population attributed a high probability to the country abandoning (or be abandoned by) the euro.

It is interesting to note that when banks are indebted in foreign currency, it can be quite costly to abandon parity and allow the exchange rate to depreciate. Exchange rate depreciation increases the value of the debt when measured in domestic currency. Explicit, or even implicit, guarantees by the government can induce banks to take loans in foreign currency without hedging against exchange rate risk. The result is an increase in the vulnerability of the economy to a speculative attack.[11]

Banking crises, in turn, can also lead to currency crises. Banks are, by their very nature, illiquid. They receive short-term deposits in cash and use them to concede mid- and long-term loans. This does not mean they are insolvent. Banks know how much liquidity they

---

[9] For a description of the mechanisms, see, for example, Corsetti et al. (1999) and McKinnon and Pill (1998).

[10] Chang and Velasco (2000) investigate the relation between currency crises and financial fragility under different monetary regimes in a model where banks receive short-term deposits and have long-term investments.

[11] More details regarding this can be found in Burnside et al. (2001) and Burnside et al. (2004).

> ### BOX 9.5 TWIN CRISIS
>
> Kaminsky and Reinhart (1999) analyze the relationship between banking and currency crises in 20 small, open economies, with either a fixed exchange rate or exchange rate target zone regime with a narrow floating band, between 1970 and 1995. They concluded that banking crises precede currency crises, which in turn intensify the banking crises. Both banking and currency crises are preceded by a deterioration of the fundamentals. In the case of the Asian economies, this deterioration began with financial liberalization, both international and domestic, in a deficient regulatory and supervisory environment. Finally, the twin crises are more harmful to the economy than isolated banking or currency crises.

need, on average, and can program their flow of loans in order to attend the demand for cash by their clients. We know that, even then, they are subject to runs. If all depositors, or a large number of them, believe there will be a run, they will withdraw their deposits and the bank can go bankrupt. To avoid bank runs, the central bank offers some guarantees to depositors in all institutions. Nevertheless, in principle, banks are always vulnerable to runs.

Also, they take risks by making loans, for there is always the possibility the borrower will not honor their debt. Deficient banking regulations or excessive guarantees offered by the government can lead banks to offer credit at a high risk. If depositor confidence is shaken, they can withdraw their deposits fearing the bank will fail, which can lead to effective bankruptcy, as in a self-fulfilling prophecy. Inter-bank relations can cause the bankruptcy of one bank to lead to a crisis of confidence in the banking system, triggering a generalized crisis. To avoid this, the government can decide to save the banks in trouble by injecting liquidity into the system. We can, therefore, have a currency crisis case similar to the first-generation models, when the expansion of credit leads to a speculative attack.[12]

Exchange rate and banking crises can be even more intricate when the banks have short-term debt in foreign currency, that is, when they are internationally illiquid. In this case, bank runs can interact with crises of confidence by external creditors, causing the economy to be more susceptible to crises. A bank run can lead international creditors to not roll over short-term debt, increasing the problem of bank liquidity. On the other hand, an external shock that reduces the capital inflow can make depositors apprehensive regarding the solidity of domestic banks, leading to a run. Financial liberalization and capital inflow, above all short-term, can, therefore, render the economy more vulnerable (Box 9.5).[13]

## 9.3.2 Firm Indebtedness in Foreign Currency

Another strand of third-generation currency crisis models emphasizes the role of private sector foreign debt. The basic idea is that, for a firm in debt in a foreign currency, exchange rate depreciation due to a balance of payments crisis can increase the value of the firm debt

---

[12] See, for example, Corsetti et al. (1999) and McKinnon and Pill (1998).
[13] See Chang and Velasco (2001).

when measured in domestic currency. With a smaller profit, companies invest less, reducing their future production, which leads to an even greater exchange rate depreciation. Therefore, a vicious circle of depreciation and recession would begin.[14]

Aghion et al. (2000) develop a model, which we will describe shortly, that shows how the financial fragility of an economy can lead to a currency crisis, with an emphasis on its effect on the level of economic activity. Specifically, they investigate the best monetary policy to be used in the face of a currency crisis, taking into account firms' indebtedness in a foreign currency. Two effects are considered. On the one hand, the increase in interest rate due to a contractionist monetary policy attracts foreign capital, causing exchange rate appreciation, which, in terms of domestic currency, reduces the cost of the foreign debt denominated in foreign currency. With greater profit, companies can invest more, which increases their level of economic activity. On the other hand, the increase in interest rate has the side effect of tightening credit for companies, restricting the possibility of new investments. Consequently, **a contractionist monetary policy may not be the best answer to a currency crisis when the provision of domestic credit is very sensitive to interest rates and the proportion of foreign debt is relatively low.** Let us see how their model works.

### 9.3.2.1 Model with Credit Constraint

Consider a small, open economy, with only two periods. The prices are determined at the beginning of each period and remain constant until the next period. Both the nominal exchange rate and the interest rate can be adjusted at any moment.

We begin with the nonarbitrage conditions in the goods and assets markets. There is only one good in this economy and purchasing power parity is verified *ex-ante*, i.e., prices are determined at the beginning of the period in such a way as to satisfy the parity in expected value, as in

$$P_t = E(S_t), \quad for\ t = 1, 2, \tag{9.13}$$

where $E(S_t)$ is the expected exchange rate at the beginning of period $t$, and assuming $P^* = 1$. Notice that if there are unexpected shocks, the purchasing power parity may not hold true at the end of the period, that is, with the actual value of the nominal exchange rate.

As to the asset market, we assume that there is perfect mobility of capital and that domestic and foreign assets are perfect substitutes. Therefore, the uncovered interest rate parity is verified as in Eq. (3.12), which we repeat here:

$$\frac{1 + i_t}{1 + i_t^*} = \frac{E(S_{t+1})}{S_t}. \tag{9.14}$$

We can divide the analysis of this economy between the monetary and real sectors. The interest rate parity and the money market equilibrium equation determine equilibrium conditions in the monetary sector of the economy, while the decision to invest determines the real sector equilibrium. Let us begin with the real sector.

[14] See, for example, Krugman (1999).

### 9.3.2.2 Real Sector

The unfolding of events is as follows: at the beginning of the first period, business owners establish a price for their product and the level of investment. Next, there is an unexpected shock and a monetary adjustment that determines exchange rate, $S_1$, and interest rate, $i_t$. The firm's owners produce and, with the profit generated, pay their debt. The remaining profit is used for consumption and to invest in second period production.

Assume that the business owners faced a credit constraint. There is a vast amount of literature that studies the causes of credit constraints in the economy, which will not be discussed here. Let us simply assume the constraint exists and translates by the fact that there is an upper limit to the total amount of credit available to business owners, which is assumed to correspond to a proportion of their wealth, as in

$$D_t \le \mu_{t-1} W_{t-1}, \tag{9.15}$$

where $D_t$ is the debt acquired in period $t-1$, which will be paid in period $t$. $W_{t-1}$ is the real wealth available for investment, which is the profit remaining after paying previous debts and the portion set aside for consumption by the business owner. The debt and wealth in Eq. (9.15) are measured in real terms, that is, in units of the (only) good in this economy.

We assume that the credit constraint will be greater the higher the interest rates are. The motivation for this hypothesis is the following: on the one hand, a higher interest rate causes credit to be unviable for investors with low return investment projects, even if the risk is also low. On the other hand, investors with high return projects, but that are also high risk, remain interested in acquiring credit. Consequently, the higher the interest rate, the greater the risk factor is, on average, for those who remain willing to go into debt. Given that banks do not have access to all information regarding investment project risk, the *adverse selection* of investors leads banks to supply less credit in order to reduce their exposure to risk (Box 9.6). We therefore have that

$$\mu_t = \mu(i_t), \quad with \ \mu'(.) < 0, \tag{9.16}$$

that is, the higher the interest rates, the less credit will be available for the business owner.

---

**BOX 9.6 ADVERSE SELECTION**

*Adverse selection* is a term attributed to a situation where one agent does not have information regarding characteristics of another agent, characteristics that can affect the transaction gains. The informed agent may self-select in a way that is prejudicial to the uninformed agent. In the case in question, the characteristic is the risk involved in the investment project of a businessperson who wishes to obtain credit. The *adverse selection* resides in the fact that, when interest rates are too high, individuals with low return investment projects have little interest in acquiring credit. Therefore, with a high interest rate, the proportion of business owners with riskier projects increases. The seminal article by Akerlof (1970) uses the combination of asymmetric information and uncertainty to explain *adverse selection* in the used car market.

Credit is obtained both from domestic and foreign creditors. Let us also assume that there is limit $D^c$ for debt contracted in domestic currency, and the business owner acquires a foreign loan after reaching their domestic debt limit.

The investment for next period production is the sum of wealth available and the credit acquired by the business owner:

$$I_t = W_t + D_{t+1},$$

and for each period the stock of capital is equal to the investment made in the previous period, for we assume that there is complete capital depreciation each period. We therefore have that

$$K_t = I_{t-1} = W_{t-1} + D_t. \tag{9.17}$$

Capital is the only input in production, with a linear production function, so that:

$$Y_t = \sigma K_t, \tag{9.18}$$

where $\sigma$ is a constant parameter that indicates capital productivity. Notice that investment $I$, capital $K$, and output $Y$ are defined in real terms, as was done with debt and wealth.

Combining Eqs. (9.15), (9.17), and (9.18), we have that the production for period $t$ is given by

$$Y_t = \sigma(1 + \mu_{t-1})W_{t-1}. \tag{9.19}$$

To exactly determine the output level, we must know the level of wealth available. Assume that, of the total profit, the business owner consumes share $\bar{\alpha}$ of their profits, while the fraction $(1 - \bar{\alpha})$ corresponds to the wealth saved. Therefore:

$$W_t = (1 - \bar{\alpha})\frac{\pi_t}{P_t}, \tag{9.20}$$

where $\pi_t$ is the profit in nominal terms, which we divide by price $P_t$ to obtain its real value.

Profit, in turn, is the difference between revenue and payments on the debt contracted in the previous period. It is determined by equation:

$$\pi_t = P_t Y_t - (1 + i_{t-1})P_{t-1}D^c - (1 + i^*)\frac{S_t}{S_{t-1}}P_{t-1}(D_t - D^c). \tag{9.21}$$

Note that the debt is accounted in real terms. Therefore, to arrive at the nominal value of the debt, it should be multiplied by the price of the good at the moment it was contracted. The value of the domestic debt contracted in period $t - 1$ is given by $P_{t-1}D^c$, while the foreign debt has a value of $\frac{P_{t-1}}{S_{t-1}}(D_t - D^c)$, measured in foreign currency at the moment it was acquired. To arrive at its current value in domestic currency, we multiply this value by the current exchange rate. Its value in domestic currency is, therefore, $\frac{S_t}{S_{t-1}}P_{t-1}(D_t - D^c)$.

Substituting Eq. (9.21) into (9.20), and the result into (9.19), we have that the second period output is given by

$$Y_2 = \sigma(1 + \mu_1)(1 - \overline{\alpha}) \left[ Y_1 - (1 + r_0)D^c - (1 + i^*)\frac{S_1}{P_1}(D_1 - D^c) \right], \tag{9.22}$$

where $(1 + r_0) = (1 + i_1)\frac{P_0}{P_1}$ is the real interest rate, defined as the nominal interest rate adjusted by the price variation. Given that, by assumption, there are no shocks in period zero, the purchasing power parity is true for that period: $S_0 = P_0$. We therefore have that $\frac{S_1}{P_1} = \frac{S_1}{S_0}\frac{P_0}{P_1}$, which we use in the last term of the expression between brackets in the equation.

Equation (9.22) summarizes the equilibrium conditions in the real sector of the economy. On the one hand, a contractionist monetary policy in the first period has a negative impact on the second period output through the credit constraint captured by variable $\mu_1$. On the other hand, exchange rate depreciation can also result in a smaller output level in the second period through its impact on the cost of the firm external debt.

Line $W$ in Figure 9.3A represents the set of pairs $(Y_2, S_1)$ that satisfy Eq. (9.22), namely, the set of second period output and exchange rate compatible with equilibrium in the real sector of the economy. The negative slope of the line indicates the negative impact of exchange rate depreciation on the second period output. Notice that the slope depends on the share of foreign debt $(D_2 - D^c)$. The greater the foreign debt, the smaller the slope of the curve and the greater the fall in output generated by exchange rate depreciation. If there had not been any foreign debt, $D_2 = D^c$, the line would be vertical: the exchange rate would not have had any impact on output.

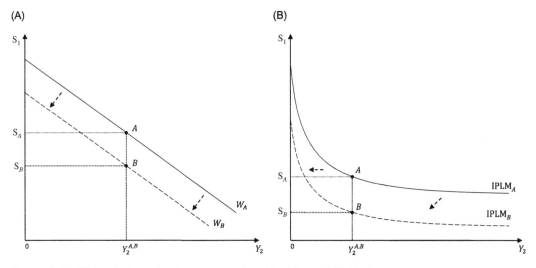

**Figure 9.3** Equilibrium in the real and monetary sectors: (A) W line and (B) IPLM curve.

A monetary contraction in the first period causes a downward shift of line $W$, as can been seen in Figure 9.3A. As we will see in the monetary sector, monetary contraction causes a fall in interest rates, which, in the real sector, leads to a tightening of credit constraint in the economy, namely, a reduction of $\mu_1$, as shown in Eq. (9.16). With less available credit, the firm cannot borrow as much and, consequently, invests less. Therefore, there will be less capital for production in the second period, leading to a contraction in output. Line $W_B$ represents equilibrium in the real sector with a smaller money supply in comparison with line $W_A$. To obtain the same level of output in the second period, $Y_2^{A,B}$, the exchange rate should be appreciated (smaller) when the money supply is lower: $S_B < S_A$.

### 9.3.2.3 Monetary Sector

The way the money market works is the same as in the monetary models in Chapters 6 and 7: demand for money is a positive function of output and a negative function of interest rate. Money market equilibrium is represented by the equation:

$$M_t = P_t m^d(Y_t, i_t), \tag{9.23}$$

where $m^d(\cdot)$ represents the money demand function, with $\frac{\partial m^d(Y_t, i_t)}{\partial Y_t} > 0$ and $\frac{\partial m^d(Y_t, i_t)}{\partial i_t} < 0$.[15] Each period, goods prices and output levels are determined before the money supply decision, so that, to maintain the money market in equilibrium, the interest rate should adjust in response to changes in monetary policy.

According to Eq. (9.13), the level of prices is equal to the expected exchange rate. The price and exchange rate will be different *ex-post* if there are shocks in the economy that cause the exchange rate to be other than its expected value. Assume that there are no shocks in the second period, such that in that the period, price is equal to the exchange rate, namely, that the purchasing power parity is also valid *ex-post*: $P_2 = S_2$. Substituting this equality into the money market equilibrium equation (Eq. (9.23)) for the second period, we have that

$$S_2 = \frac{M_2}{m^d(Y_2, i_2)}.$$

Finally, substituting the previous equation into the interest rate parity equation (Eq. (9.14)), we arrive at the relation between the exchange rate in the first period and the output in the second period, which guarantees equilibrium in the money market:

$$S_1 = \frac{1 + i^*}{1 + i_1} \frac{M_2}{m^d(Y_2, i_2)}. \tag{9.24}$$

---

[15] In Eq. (6.1), Chapter 6, also used in Chapter 7, we assume the specific functional form for function $m^d(Y_t, i_t)$: a linear function in the variables logarithm. Here, we allow a generic function.

Equation (9.24) can be represented by a negatively sloped curve in space $(Y_2, S_1)$, as represented by curve IPLM in Figure 9.3B. The intuition for the negative slope of the curve is as follows: a greater output level in the second period would lead to a greater demand for money in that period. According to Eq. (9.23), goods prices would be lower to balance the money market, resulting in a more appreciated exchange rate, given that purchasing power parity is valid in the second period under no uncertainty, as discussed previously. The appreciation of the exchange rate in the second period would make the domestic currency more attractive already in the first period, causing exchange rate appreciation.

A monetary contraction in the first period leads to a downward shift of the IPLM curve, as can be seen in Figure 9.3B: curve $IPLM_B$ represents the monetary equilibrium with a smaller money supply when compared to curve $IPLM_A$. Monetary contraction causes a shortage of liquidity, and the money demand should reduce in order to maintain the money market in equilibrium. The price of the good is predetermined, by assumption, and output is given by the investment in the previous period, therefore, also constant. Consequently, interest rate $i_A$ rises to balance the money market. To satisfy the uncovered interest rate parity (9.14), the increase of domestic interest rates causes an appreciation of the first period exchange rate, in other words, a reduction of $S_A$. For the same output level in the second period, $Y_2^{A,B}$, the money market equilibrium is obtained with a more appreciated (smaller) exchange when the money supply is smaller: $S_B < S_A$. Notice that this is the rationale behind the prescription of a contractionist monetary policy to avoid exchange rate depreciation.

### 9.3.2.4 Equilibrium

The economy is in equilibrium when the monetary and real sectors of the economy are simultaneously in equilibrium. In terms of the graph, equilibrium in the economy corresponds to the point where curves IPLM and W intercept. There are three possible cases for the relative positioning of the two curves, represented by Figures 9.4A–C. The first case, in Figure 9.4A, would be the good equilibrium. There is only one interception point between the two curves, determining a positive output level and a low exchange rate, that is, appreciated. In the second, Figure 9.4B, there is only one equilibrium, albeit, not a good one: the exchange rate depreciation in the first period is so great that the firm will go bankrupt while paying its debt in foreign currency. In the third, Figure 9.4C, there are multiple equilibria: equilibrium A, which is equivalent to the first case, and equilibrium B, which is equivalent to the second case. In equilibrium B, the economic agents expect greater exchange rate depreciation in the second period, which leads to less demand for money, depreciating the currency in the first period.

A currency crisis can occur in two ways. The economy can be in equilibrium A from Figure 9.4C, and a shock in expectations leads the economy to equilibrium B. Alternately, the economy can be at first in equilibrium A, Figure 9.4A, when there is a shock, such as in a fall in productivity, $\sigma$, that causes the economy to go to equilibrium B as in the case illustrated in Figure 9.4C, or even slip to the only, and bad, equilibrium presented in Figure 9.4B.

What then should be the monetary policy of a government facing a currency crisis? The usual economic prescription is for the government to adopt a contractionist monetary policy,

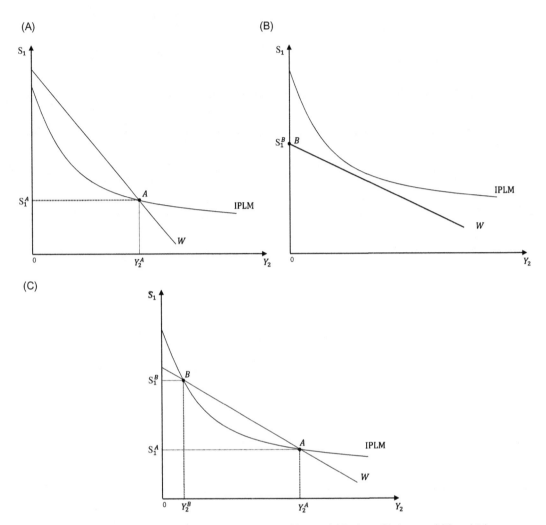

**Figure 9.4** Economic equilibrium possibilities: (A) unique equilibrium, (B) bad equilibrium, and (C) multiple equilibria.

elevating the domestic interest rate. As per the monetary sector in the economy, monetary contraction would lead to exchange rate appreciation, as shown by the downward shift of the IPLM curve in Figure 9.3B. Per the real side, however, monetary contraction would also shift down the W curve on Figure 9.3A. **The effect of monetary policy on the exchange rate and output will depend on its relative impact on the real and monetary sectors of the economy.**

If the W curve shift is greater than that of the IPLM curve, the economy can move towards the Figure 9.4B case, the bad equilibrium, where exchange rate depreciation is large and output, lower. In this case, monetary contraction leads to such a large tightening of credit that it causes a great reduction in second period output, according to Eq. (9.22). Per

Eq. (9.24), which represents the monetary sector equilibrium, a smaller second period output is associated with a more depreciated exchange rate in the first period.

When the IPLM curve shift is greater than that of curve W, the economy can come to have a Figure 9.4A configuration, where there is only one possible equilibrium: a good one. The increase in interest rates attracts foreign capital, leading to exchange rate appreciation by the direct effect of interest rates on the exchange rate in Eq. (9.24). The indirect effect on the credit constraint, which would cause exchange rate depreciation, is relatively smaller. In this case, monetary contraction has the desired effect of avoiding a currency crisis.

It is evident that the monetary policy prescription depends on its relative impact on the shift of the two curves. We can measure the vertical shift of the curves by computing the value of the derivative $\frac{dS_1}{di_1}$ for each of them. For curve IPLM, we have that

$$\frac{dS_1}{di_1}\Big|_{\text{IPLM}} = \frac{d\left(\frac{1+i^*}{1+i_1} \frac{M_2}{m^d(Y_2, i_2)}\right)}{di_1} = -\frac{S_1}{1+i_1}.$$

For curve W, we use the implicit function theorem to compute

$$\frac{dS_1}{di_1}\Big|_{\text{W}} = -\frac{\frac{dW}{di_1}}{\frac{dW}{dS_1}} = \frac{\mu'(i_1)P_1\left[Y' - (1+r_0)D^c - (1+i^*)\frac{S_1}{P_1}(D_1 - D^c)\right]}{(1+\mu'(i_1))(1+i^*)(D_2 - D^c)}.$$

The two shifts are negative: an increase in interest rates causes a fall in the exchange rate, *ceteris paribus*. The shift of the IPLM curve will be greater than that of the W curve when

$$-\frac{\mu'(i_1)P_1\left[Y' - (1+r_0)D^c - (1+i^*)\frac{S_1}{P_1}(D_1 - D^c)\right]}{(1+\mu'(i_1))(1+i^*)(D_1 - D^c)} < \frac{S_1}{1+i_1}. \tag{9.25}$$

Notice that $\mu'(i_1) < 0$, therefore the two sides of the previous inequality are positive.

**When inequality (9.25) is satisfied, a monetary contraction, leading to an increase in interest rates, is the proper policy to avoid a currency crisis.** The equation is satisfied when the impact of interest rates on credit is small, that is, when $\mu'(i_1)$ is sufficiently small. If the increase in interest rates causes a large contraction in domestic credit, there will be a reduction in second period output, leading to exchange rate depreciation in the first period. Inequality is also satisfied when the share of foreign debt is sufficiently high. In this case, exchange rate depreciation would have such a negative impact on production investment in the following period that it would be better to use a contractionist monetary policy to avoid exchange rate depreciation, even if this policy causes a contraction in domestic credit.

It is interesting to investigate the role of financial development in what should be the optimum response to a currency crisis. First, the greater the financial development, the less credit constraint there is. In the model, less credit constraint is represented by a greater value of $\mu$, which increases the value of the denominator on the left side of inequality (9.25).

Therefore, inequality tends to be satisfied, so that monetary contraction is the best response to the currency crisis. Second, both in the economy with no credit and the economy with a perfect credit market, credit constraint does not depend on interest rates, i.e., $\mu'(i_1) \to 0$. In these two extreme cases, the condition of Eq. (9.25) is satisfied, for the left side tends toward zero. In an intermediate economy, with some credit, but with an imperfect credit market, credit constraint can be very sensitive to interest rates. It is in this intermediate case that monetary expansion can be the best answer to a currency crisis.

Finally, financial development has an ambiguous effect on the share of foreign debt, for both the total indebtedness of the agents and the supply of domestic credit increase. In this model, it is impossible to analyze the choice of individuals between domestic and foreign debt. For such, it is necessary to investigate the impact of financial development on the financing structure of businesses.

## 9.4 Contagion

The Asian and Russian crises at the end of the 1990s had a profound impact on Latin American economies, leading to a discussion regarding contagion in the propagation of shocks between economies. In the literature, there are many definitions regarding what contagion is. **One definition simply considers if the probability of having a crisis in a determined country is affected by the fact of there being a crisis in another.** The contagion could occur due to interdependence between the economies, namely, if there is intense trade between them, or if one economy has made a direct investment in another. **In another definition, some authors define contagion as being the change in the propagation of shocks in times of crisis, compared to normal times.** According to this definition, contagion would not be related to the interdependence between economies, but to the factors associated with multiple equilibria, as a reversal in expectations or herd behavior. Some of the factors that can lead to contagion are discussed next.

When two countries have a great deal of trade flow between them, the currency depreciation in one economy makes its more costly for the other to maintain its exchange rate parity. This was the case between Argentina and Brazil in 1999, as explained in Box 9.2.

Financial assets can also have an important role in contagion between countries. There are at least three possible channels. First, if there is difficulty in obtaining information regarding a country, a herd behavior can be created where investors follow the behavior of the agent that is considered better informed. Second, investors can hedge between markets, diversifying their portfolios by purchasing assets in different countries. When a crisis hits a country, investors reallocate their assets portfolios, selling the riskier assets with the intent of maintaining their exposure to risk under control. This behavior can propagate the crisis to other countries that are also considered risky, even when their economies have not suffered negative shocks. Finally, a crisis in one country can generate a problem of liquidity for investors who sense the need to sell their assets in other countries where prices have not fallen. This movement ends by causing a fall in asset prices in other markets.

> ### BOX 9.7 CONTAGION IN LATIN AMERICA
>
> Do Latin America countries suffer from contagion? Forbes and Rigobon (2001) investigate contagion in the region that is not caused by real connections between economies. They compare the propagation of shocks in normal periods with propagation in crisis periods. If there is contagion, the propagation of shocks in crisis periods should be greater. The authors did not find evidence that the transmission diverges over time. They conclude that there are quite strong ties between economies, albeit, they are equal in both normal and crisis periods. Notwithstanding the important role played by trade channels and changes in relative prices, transmission by financial panic, and other factors connected to multiple equilibria, does not appear to be significant.
>
> Latin America presents episodes of lending *booms* followed by currency crises. Comparing the Latin American experience with the rest of the world, Gourinchas and Landerretche (2001) observed that, while in the rest of the world lending *booms*, in general, do not lead to currency crises, in Latin America they do. The authors conjecture that the most probable cause of the crises is the combined financial liberalization effect combined with a deficiency in its regulation and supervision. The results obtained indicate that an economic instrument that limits the taking of loans to avoid lending *booms* in the region could be beneficial.

Why does financial contagion occur in some cases and not others? Kaminsky et al. (2003) identified three determining elements for which contagion occurs, which they named **the *unholy trinity*, which are: an abrupt reversal in capital flow (known as *sudden stop*); unexpected announcements; and a common creditor with leveraged assets**. Contagion situations in general occur after a period of increased capital flow that experiences a sudden stop due to a shock or unexpected (bad) news. The announcement or event that triggers the sudden stop is unexpected, so that it is not part of investor expectations when they made past decisions to buy and sell assets. Finally, creditors with leveraged assets suffer losses with the crisis, which propagates to other countries that issued assets that compose the investor's asset portfolios (Box 9.7).

## 9.5 Exercises

### Exercise 1

Consider a small, open economy inhabited by a large number of individuals who live for an infinite number of periods and who can perfectly forecast the future. In this economy there is only one good, tradable at no cost, such that its domestic price is determined by the *Law of One Price*, $P(t) = S(t)P^F$, where $P(t)$ is the domestic price of the good and $P^F$ is the foreign price of the good, which we will assume is equal to 1. Time is continuous and the economy is endowed with a constant and exogenous flow of the consumption good. There is perfect mobility of capital in the sense that agents can lend or borrow at the international interest rate of $i^* > 0$, which we assume as constant. The real money supply is defined as $m(t) = \frac{M(t)}{P(t)}$, where $M(t)$ is the nominal money supply. This economy finances an exogenous fiscal deficit, denoted by $d > 0$, by issuing money. The rate of growth of the nominal money supply is defined by $\mu(t) \equiv \frac{\dot{M}(t)}{M(t)}$, and the money supply is given by

$$M(t) = P(t)d + S(t)R(t),$$

where $R_t$ represents the level of international reserves.

The demand for money is given by

$$L(i(t)) = \frac{\lambda}{1 + i(t)},$$

where $i(t)$ is the nominal interest rate and $\lambda > 0$ is a constant. Inflation is defined as the percentage change of price: $\pi(t) \equiv \frac{\dot{P}(t)}{P(t)}$. The relation between the nominal and real interest rates is given by the Fisher relation, $i(t) = r(t) + \pi(t)$.

**a.** Show that the rate of growth of the real stock of money is equal to the difference between the rate of growth of money supply and inflation.

**b.** Assume that the government of this country decides to fix the nominal exchange rate at level $\bar{S}$, i.e., $S(t) = \bar{S}$. Show that, if $R(0)$ is sufficiently large, it is possible to temporarily maintain this exchange rate. Also show that, while the nominal exchange rate $S(t)$ remains fixed, the money supply will be constant. Calculate the real money supply.

**c.** What happens with the international reserves while the nominal exchange rate remains constant? Based on the fiscal policy adopted by the government, explain why the fixed exchange rate regime is not sustainable.

**d.** Assume that, when the fixed exchange rate regime ends, the international reserves will be null, i.e., $R(t) = 0$. Show that after the end of the regime there is equilibrium with constant inflation and a constant real money supply. Compute inflation and the real money supply in this equilibrium.

**e.** Considering that the fixed exchange rate regime is unsustainable, calculate the period $T$ in which the regime is abandoned. Show that in period $T$ the trajectory of price levels remains continuous, however, the real demand for money decreases abruptly. What happens with the level of international reserves in period $T$? What is the economic intuition for the result?

**f.** Present illustrative graphs containing the trajectory of the stock of international reserves, the nominal money supply and the nominal exchange rate, both before and after period $T$. Explain each of these graphs.

## Exercise 2

Answer what the following items request.

**a.** Currency crises are normally followed by a sharp fall in economic activity, which results in recession. Based on the first-generation currency crises model and the Mundell–Fleming model, seen in Section 7.1, explain why this happens.

**b.** Consider two distinct countries that decided to adopt a fixed exchange rate regime. The first country operates with a fiscal deficit, while the second operates with a surplus. How can the difference in the fiscal situation of each of these two countries affect the credibility of monetary regime adopted?

**c.** Exposure to speculative attacks is a disadvantage of a fixed exchange rate regime. Explain why speculative attacks are costly for policymakers.

**d.** Using the Mundell–Fleming model seen in Section 7.1, explain why the lack of credibility in a fixed exchange rate regime increases the cost of maintaining a determined exchange rate parity.

## Exercise 3

Consider a second-generation currency crisis model. Assume the gain of maintaining a fixed interest rate is equivalent to 3% of GDP.

**a.** Consider the following situation: If the central bank defends the exchange rate parity, counting on the trust of the economic agents, the GDP will fall 1%. If there is no credibility in the regime, the fall in GDP will be 2%. Will market participants trust the exchange rate parity? In this case, will the central bank defend parity?

**b.** Consider the following situation: If the central bank defends the exchange rate parity, counting on the trust of the economic agents, the GDP will fall 2%. Without trust, the product fall will be 5%. Will the market participants trust the exchange rate parity? In this case, will the central bank defend the parity?

## Exercise 4

Answer what the following items request.

**a.** Explain the break of the Bretton Woods regime under the perspective of the first-generation currency crisis model seen throughout this chapter. (Review the description of the regime in Box 6.1.)

**b.** With a graph, present the evolution of the yen/dollar exchange rate, of international reserves and the balance sheet of the Bank of Japan, before and after the end of Bretton Woods. Do the trajectories follow the pattern predicted by the theory? Explain your answer.

**c.** Explain the break of the Argentine currency board regime in 2001 using the exchange rate crisis models seen in this chapter.

**d.** With a graph, present the evolution of the peso/dollar exchange rate, of international reserves and the balance sheet for the Banco Central de la República Argentina before and after the end of currency board regime. Do the trajectories follow the pattern predicted by the theory? Are trajectories similar to those in item (b) seen? Explain your answer.

## Exercise 5

Consider an economy that adopts a fixed exchange rate regime and that possesses the volume of reserves $R>0$, administered by the central bank with the objective of defending exchange rate parity. Assume that the central bank assets, denoted in the currency to which the parity was established, are represented by $W^{CB}$ and the liabilities are denoted by $B^{CB}$. Also assume that $W^{CB}<B^{CB}$. There are $J$ investors, being $M$ small investors, each of which possesses one unit of domestic currency, and a large investor who alone possesses $N$ units of domestic currency. Consider a noncooperative game in one period when the investors decide whether to speculate against the domestic currency or to maintain their position in this asset, and the central bank decides if it keeps the parity or allows the domestic currency to depreciate. When the investors decide to "attack," selling their domestic currency, they must pay a transaction cost of $c>0$ monetary units for each unit of domestic currency sold. The nominal exchange rate, S, is measured as the price of the foreign currency with which parity was established. This game is represented, in normal form, as follows:

|  |  | Central Bank | |
|---|---|---|---|
|  |  | **Defend ($\Delta S = 0$)** | **Depreciate ($\Delta S > 0$)** |
| Investors | Attack | $-c, -R/(M+N)$ | $\Delta S - c, \Delta S(W^{CB} - B^{CB})$ |
|  | Maintain | $0, 0$ | $-\Delta S, \Delta S(W^{CB} - B^{CB})$ |

**a.** What condition must be met for a speculative attack, in the self-fulfilling prophecy form, for there to be equilibrium of pure strategies for this game?

**b.** Explain under what conditions a speculative attack becomes the optimum answer for any small investor when they observe the large investor sell $N$ units of domestic currency while the other $M-1$ small investors maintain their positions?

**c.** Assume that $N=0$ and that one small investor anticipates that the other small investors intend to hold a speculative attack. What equilibria are possible?

**d.** If you were an economic policymaker in this country, what regulatory instrument would you adopt to reduce the propensity of investors to hold a speculative attack? Explain your answer.

## Exercise 6

Regarding currency crisis models, answer what the following items request.

**a.** Explain what consists in third-generation currency crisis models, highlighting the main characteristics as well as presenting examples of countries that have experienced this type of event.

**b.** Compare the third-generation models with the first- and second-generation models, highlighting the main similarities and differences.

## Exercise 7

Consider a situation where the defense of a fixed exchange rate regime can, at the limit, result in default of the foreign debt for a given country. In this case, international investors who possess assets from this country can decide in one of two ways: panic and sell all assets from this country, or keep the assets while believing the country will not become insolvent. In turn, the government can announce a default of the debt or continue paying its financial obligations. In the case of default, the exchange rate begins to float freely. Such interaction between the government and investors can be modeled as a noncooperative game described by the following normal-form representation:

|  |  | Government | |
|---|---|---|---|
|  |  | **Default** | **Payment** |
| Investors | Panic | $-x, -x$ | $-0.75x, -2x$ |
|  | Maintain | $-2x, -0.75x$ | $x, x$ |

The amount $x$ can be interpreted as a financial amount resulting from a given equilibrium.

**a.** Interpret the strategies of each agent and the possible results due to the interaction between the private investors and government.
**b.** Find the possible equilibria for this game.
**c.** What can be said regarding the equilibria found in the previous item? Would it be possible to create a mechanism with the goal of avoiding the bad equilibrium and conduct the economy toward a good equilibrium? Explain your answer, describing the mechanism, if such be the case.

## Exercise 8

In general, currency crises are associated with severe falls in economic activity. However, a good part of the first- and second-generation currency crisis models does not explicitly model the factors that could explain the recession. Consider a small, open economy with a fixed exchange rate regime and in which investors depend both on the real interest rate, $r$, as well as a variable, $\theta$, which can be interpreted as a variable associated with the risk of a currency crisis, according to the perception of the agents. Therefore, the investment function can be written as

$$I = g(r, \theta) = I_0 + g_1 r - g_2 \theta,$$

where $g_1$ and $g_2$ are constant positive parameters. For the sake of simplification, assume that variable $\theta$ possesses binary behavior, as following described:

$$\theta = \begin{cases} 0, & \text{if } \Delta S \leq 0 \\ \varnothing_c (\Delta S)^2, & \text{if } \Delta S \geq 0 \end{cases}$$

where S represents the nominal exchange rate and $\emptyset_c > 0$ measures the sensitivity of $\emptyset$ in relation to changes in S.

**a.** Explain why the perception of a currency crisis negatively affects investments.

**b.** Based on what has been seen in this chapter, especially in what refers to the asset balance sheet currency mismatch of financial institutions, explain how a *proxy* could be created for variable $\theta$.

**c.** Assume that the nominal exchange rate goes from $S_1$ to $S_2$, with $S_2 > S_1$. Calculate the change in investments in this case.

Consider that the aggregate demand in this economy is given by $Y = C + I + G + TB$, and the trade balance in nominal terms is given by $TB = X - M = PT^* - SP^*T$, where $T$ represents the amount imported and $T^*$ the amount exported. Notice that, according to the trade balance equation, exchange rate depreciation impacts import values, making them more expensive. This effect can be interpreted as a short-term response to changes in the exchange rate, while the decisions to import and export have not yet reacted to the new relative price. Equilibrium in the money market is represented by function $\frac{M^S}{P} = \kappa Y - \lambda i$.

**d.** What is the effect of the exchange rate depreciation described in item (c) on the aggregate demand? Explain your answer in a quantitative and intuitive form, based on the elements of economic theory. Illustrate the possible cases on a graph.

**e.** How could you relate the answer given in the previous item with the third-generation currency crisis models, especially in referring to the output dynamics?

## Exercise 9

Consider a small, open economy that has a nominal exchange rate fixed at $S = 5$ pesos/dollar. In this economy, the La Union Bank possesses $200 million pesos in its own capital, receives $800 million in deposits, and lends $1 billion pesos to companies with a good credit rating. Suppose the bank directors decide to access the international capitals market and are able to raise US$ 100 million in credit, which the bank lends in pesos to local residents. The balance sheet for this financial institution is represented as follows:

| Assets | | Liabilities | |
|---|---|---|---|
| Loans: | $1.5 billion | Deposits | $800 million |
| | | Debt | $500 million |
| | | Capital | $200 million |

**a.** Is it good for agents in this economy to acquire loans in dollars? In general, why does external borrowing denoted in foreign currency (the dollar) cost less in terms of interest rate paid than borrowing denoted in domestic currency (the peso)?

**b.** Suppose that, due to domestic difficulties, the nominal exchange rate depreciates to $S = 10$ pesos/dollar. Present the balance sheet for La Union Bank in this new scenario. What are the consequences of this shock for the bank?

**c.** How will La Union Bank clients respond to this shock? What are the consequences for the credit taken by the bank? What are the consequences for economic activity? Explain your answers.

## Exercise 10

Consider a small, open economy that satisfies absolute purchase power parity, assuming, for simplification, that $\ln(P_t^*) = 0$, where $P_t^*$ is the international price index. The loss function for the central planner in this economy is given by $L = (y_t - \tilde{y}_t)^2 + \chi \pi_t^2 + C(\pi_t)$, where $y_t$ represents the logarithm of output, $\tilde{y}_t$ is the logarithm of optimum output level, $C(.)$ is a function that measures the cost to abandon the fixed exchange rate regime, and $\chi > 0$ is a constant parameter. Assume that the output is given by $y_t = \bar{y}_t + (\pi_t - \pi_t^e) - z_t$, where $\bar{y}_t$ is the natural output (in logarithm) and $z_t$ is a supply shock with zero mean and variance $\sigma^2$. Assume that $\tilde{y}_t - \bar{y}_t = \kappa > 0$ and remember that inflation is defined as $\pi_t = \ln(P_t) - \ln(P_{t-1})$.

**a.** The above-described model can be used to analyze which generation of currency crises models? Explain the main ideas associated with this family of models. Would this type of speculative attack model explains attacks that have occurred in economies that have had low unemployment and growing exports? Explain your answer.

**b.** Obtain the loss function for the social planner as a function of variables $\pi_t^e$, $\pi_t$, and $z_t$, only.

**c.** Initially not considering the cost function, $C(.)$, and given that the government minimizes its loss function after knowing the values of $\pi_t^e$ and $z_t$, determine the optimum level of inflation $\pi_t^*$. What happens to the exchange rate in this case? Determine the loss function for optimum inflation $L_{fl}^*$.

**d.** What is the exchange rate regime when inflation is zero? What is the value of the loss function $L_{fx}^*$ in this case?

**e.** How does the supply shock affect the difference between $L_{fl}^*$ and $L_{fx}^*$? Explain your answer.

# Exchange Rate Regimes

The exchange rate regime defines the government exchange rate policy rules. In the fixed exchange rate regime, for example, the government pledges to intervene in the market to impede that the exchange rate vary in relation to the announced parity, while in a floating exchange rate regime, the government declines to intervene, allowing the exchange rate to float according to the supply and demand of economic agents. The exchange rate regime is intimately associated to the central bank monetary policy, as shown in the monetary models discussed in Chapter 6. In particular, Eqs. (6.5) and (6.6) clearly show how exchange rate variations are associated with changes in the money supply. The monetary policy implemented by the government should be consistent with the chosen exchange rate regime.

We will begin this chapter by discussing the classification of the different existing exchange rate regimes. Following that, we will discuss the economic implications for the different regimes, seeking to identify elements that should be taken into consideration when choosing an exchange rate regime.

# 10.1 Classification of Exchange Rate Regimes

There is a large diversity of exchange rate regimes, which can be divided into three large groups: floating regimes, flexible parity regimes, and fixed parity regimes. **Following is a classification of the exchange rate regimes, ordered from the most flexible to the most rigid.**[1]

1. *Floating Exchange Rate Regimes*
   a. *Free Floating*: The exchange rate level is determined by the supply and demand of money, without the government intervening in the market. The government also does not use monetary policy with the objective of affecting the exchange rate.
   b. *Managed* or *Dirty Floating*: In this regime, the exchange rate is, in principle, floating, but the government can eventually intervene to avoid excessive or undesired variations in the exchange rate. This type of regime is, in practice, quite popular. In general, governments that announce a floating exchange rate do not resist intervening in order to avoid excessive fluctuations in the exchange rate. Calvo and Reinhart (2002) show that, as the name of their article suggests (*Fear of Floating*), countries fear exchange rate fluctuation and tend to intervene in that market even when they officially state that it is a floating regime.

2. *Soft Peg Regimes*
   a. *Crawling Bands*: The exchange rate floats within an announced limit and the government intervenes to prevent the exchange rate from crossing the floating band barriers. The bands can be of two types: horizontal or adjustable. In a *horizontal band* regime, the exchange rate floats around a fixed parity. This was the regime used by European countries before the implantation of the euro, for example. In the case of an *adjustable band*, the parity around which the exchange rate can float follows a tendency, which can be either appreciating or depreciating. Adjustable bands were used extensively by countries with high inflation, such as Brazil at certain times in the 1980s and 1990s. When there is inflation, the exchange rate should follow the inflation to avoid appreciation of the real exchange rate.[2]
   b. *Crawling Pegs*: The exchange rate is periodically adjusted according to a previously announced program. The adjustment can be conditioned to selected indicators. This was a regime that was also used by countries experiencing high inflation, where the programmed exchange rate adjustments served as nominal anchors in price stabilization programs. Example countries that adopted this regime are Chile, Colombia, and Israel. More recently, China also adopted this regime.
   c. *Fixed Exchange Rate*: The government pledges to intervene in the foreign currency market and/or use interest rate policy to maintain the exchange rate fixed at a previously announced level. Even though the parity should be maintained for an undetermined

---

[1] See Corden (2002), Frankel (1999), Goldstein (2002), and Tavlas et al. (2008) regarding the classification of exchange rate regimes.

[2] Equation (10.10) shows that the depreciation of the nominal exchange rate should be equal to the difference between domestic and international inflation rates to maintain the real exchange rate unaltered.

amount of time, in practice the government can alter this value if it wishes. This regime is classified as soft peg due to the fact that it does not possess a mechanism to provide strong government commitment to maintain the parity: all that is necessary to alter the parity is to announce it. In the same way governments tend to not allow floating exchange rates to float, they also tend to readjust an announced fixed exchange rate regime. As Obstfeld and Rogoff (1995) observe, cases are rare of countries that have maintained exchange rate parity for a longer period of time. Many times the government has no choice, such as when agent expectations lead to a speculative attack, as was discussed in Chapter 9.

**3.** *Hard Peg Regimes*

   **a.** *Currency Board*: There is a legal obligation to maintain a given exchange rate parity. In order to guarantee this commitment, the central bank should back the monetary base with the foreign currency in relation to which the parity is established,[3] such that all home currency should be able to be converted into the foreign currency at the parity. Therefore, the central bank has no control over the money supply and cannot be a lender of last resort to banks. This was the regime adopted by Argentina in the 1990s.

   **b.** *Dollarization*: The country unilaterally adopts the currency of another country, ceasing to have its own. The country that issues the currency continues to have sovereignty over its emission and the monetary policy to be followed. It is obvious that the country that adopts dollarization ceases to have monetary policy autonomy, simply because it does not have its own currency. This is the case in Panama and Ecuador. Even though the dollar is the currency most commonly adopted, therefore the name dollarization, adopting the dollar, in particular, does not necessarily have to be the case. San Marino and Montenegro, for example, that have adopted the euro as their currency.

   **c.** *Monetary Union*: The members of a monetary union share the same currency and manage it by means of a common accord. The International Monetary Fund (IMF) classifies the exchange rate regime of countries in a monetary union according to the regime adopted for the common currency. In this way, for example, each country in the Eurozone is classified as following a floating exchange rate regime since they adopt the euro, and the euro is free floating.

**Up to the end of the 1990s, the classification of exchange rate regimes was performed according to what countries officially communicated to the IMF, which was registered in the *Annual Report on Exchange Arrangements and Exchange Restrictions.*** This classification is known as the IMF *de jure* exchange rate regime classification. The problem is that the exchange rate regime effectively followed was not that communicated, as can be seen based on the previous comments. There are countries that announce a free-floating regime, but intervene in the market to avoid variations in the value of the foreign currency, practically implementing a dirty float mechanism. Others commit to a fixed exchange rate, while regularly realigning the parity by following a monetary policy inconsistent with the regime announced, such that the regime appears to be more of a floating exchange rate than a fixed.

---

[3] The monetary base is the sum of all currency in circulation and in commercial bank reserves in their accounts in the central bank.

**As of 1998, the IMF began to present a** *de facto* **exchange rate regime classification based on the exchange rate policy effectively implemented by countries.** This new classification is presented in a report called the *De Facto Classification of Exchange Rates Regimes and Monetary Policy Frameworks.*[4] The regimes are ordered based on the degree of exchange rate flexibility and whether there is a commitment with respect to its trajectory. The IMF classification system also presents the monetary policy followed by the country, highlighting the connection between the exchage rate and the monetary policy, as we saw in Chapter 6. Table 10.1 presents the IMF *de facto* classification based on a revision of the 2009 classification for a sample of countries.

Ever since, some authors have begun to develop alternative *de facto* exchange rate regime classifications. It is not as simple as it appears. In his proposal, Shambaugh (2004) provides a two-regime classification system, peg and nonpeg, based on exchange rate behavior. A regime is classified as peg if in the last 2 years its exchange rate variation has not exceeded an oscillation interval of 2% above or below the initial value, and nonpeg when the exchange rate variation exceeds this interval. Seems reasonable, right? But, is it? An exchange rate that does not float may be the result of an active government exchange rate policy in an unstable environment, but it can also be the result of a world in a state of total apathy. If there are no shocks, there is no reason for exchange rate float, even when the government does not have the exchange rate as one of its economic policy objectives.

Levy-Yeyati and Sturzenegger (2005) seek to solve this problem by taking into consideration not only changes in the exchange rate, but in international reserves as well. With this, they are able to identify if the exchange rate has stalled due to a government policy to intervene in the market by buying or selling reserves. They classify regimes into four categories: flexible, dirty float, crawling peg, and fixed. The problem with their classification is that they cannot always classify what they observe. Keeping to the same example, how can a country be classified whose exchange rate never varies, but also where nothing ever happens? There is no way of knowing if the government would intervene in the case of shocks. The authors classify these cases as *Inconclusive...* and there are many cases that fit this category.

Another problem regarding the classification of exchange rate regimes is in relation to the existence of **dual exchange rate markets** or **multiple exchange rate systems**. The dual exchange rate may be official or unofficial (the latter being the parallel exchange rate or the "black market"). The multiple exchange rate markets establish different exchange rates for different types of transactions. Typically, the government establishes exchange rate parity for commercial transactions, while it allows the exchange rate to float for financial transactions. Thus, commercial transactions are protected from the exchange rate volatility caused by the financial market. Latin American countries ravaged by the foreign debt crisis in the 1980s used this type of system extensively. The scarcity of foreign currency resulted in a very depreciated exchange rate that, on the one hand, increased export competitiveness and, on the other, rendered imports more expensive. The government then guaranteed a cheap dollar for the import of essential products, where the definition of "essential"

---

[4] The complete report can be seen at: http://www.imf.org/external/NP/mfd/er/index.aspx.

**Table 10.1**   Exchange Regimes

| Exchange Rate Regime | Monetary Policy Framework | | | | | | |
|---|---|---|---|---|---|---|---|
| | Exchange Rate Anchor | | | | Monetary Aggregate Target | Inflation Target | Others |
| | **US Dollar** | **Euro** | **Composite** | **Other** | | | |
| Dollarization | Ecuador | Montenegro | — | Kiribati | — | — | — |
| | East Timor | San Marino | — | — | — | — | — |
| Currency board | Barbuda | Bosnia | — | Brunei | — | — | — |
| | Hong Kong | Bulgaria | — | — | — | — | — |
| Other fixed peg arrangements | Angola | Cameroon | Fiji | Bhutan | Argentina | — | — |
| | Argentina | Cape Verde | Kuwait | Lesotho | Malawi | — | — |
| | Lebanon | Croatia | Libya | Namibia | Rwanda | — | — |
| | The Netherlands | Denmark | Morocco | Nepal | Serra Leon | — | — |
| | Qatar | Macedonia | Russia | Swaziland | — | — | — |
| | Saudi Arabia | Nigeria | Tunisia | — | — | — | — |
| Crawling peg | Bolivia | — | Botswana | — | — | — | — |
| | China | — | Iran | — | — | — | — |
| | Ethiopia | — | — | — | — | — | — |
| Crawling band | Costa Rica | — | Azerbaijan | — | — | — | — |
| Managed floating | Cambodia | — | Angelia | — | Haiti | Colombia | Egypt |
| | Myanmar | — | Singapore | — | Jamaica | Ghana | India |
| | Ukraine | — | — | — | Kenya | Indonesia | Malaysia |
| | Liberia | — | — | — | Nigeria | Peru | Pakistan |
| | Mauritania | — | — | — | Nova Guinea | Uruguay | Paraguay |
| Free floating | — | — | — | — | Zambia | Australia | Congo |
| | — | — | — | — | — | South Africa | Japan |
| | — | — | — | — | — | Germany | Switzerland |
| | — | — | — | — | — | Brazil | The United States |
| | — | — | — | — | — | Canada | — |
| | — | — | — | — | — | South Korea | — |
| | — | — | — | — | — | Chile | — |
| | — | — | — | — | — | France | — |
| | — | — | — | — | — | Israel | — |
| | — | — | — | — | — | Italy | — |
| | — | — | — | — | — | México | — |
| | — | — | — | — | — | Nova Zealand | — |
| | — | — | — | — | — | The United Kingdom | — |

**Table 10.2**  Percentage of Agreement in Exchange Rate Regime Classification

|  | IMF | Levy-Yeyati and Sturzenegger | Reinhart and Rogoff | Shambaugh |
|---|---|---|---|---|
| IMF | 100% |  |  |  |
| Levy-Yeyati and Sturzenegger | 59% | 100% |  |  |
| Reinhart and Rogoff | 59% | 55% | 100% |  |
| Shambaugh | 68% | 65% | 65% | 100% |

depended on the government objective: they could be basic necessities, which protected the purchasing power of citizens, or raw materials for industry, with the objective of supporting the domestic industrial sector.

In any case, when there are two exchange rates employed, one being fixed and the other floating, the floating should be used to identify the exchange rate regime. This is what Reinhart and Rogoff (2004) do. The authors propose a *de facto* exchange rate regime classification that takes into account exchange rate movement and international reserves, but that uses the parallel and dual markets to measure its flexibility, particularly when it differs significantly from the official market. Their classification is composed of six groups, which are subdivided into a total of 15 categories. One novelty is the creation of the *free falling* category, which identifies episodes of macroeconomic instability associated with periods of very high inflation.

**Summarizing, we have four exchange rate regime classification proposals (IMF; Shambaugh; Levy-Yeyati and Sturzenegger; Reinhart and Rogoff) that seek to identify the exchange rate regime that is in fact implemented by each country. The problem is that there is not always a consensus between these classifications.** Table 10.2 reproduces table 3.3 from the book *Exchange Rate Regimes in the Modern Era*, by Klein and Shambaugh (2010). It shows the percentage of episodes in each pair of classifications that are in agreement as to the exchange rate regime followed. To make their comparison, the authors distill all classifications into only three categories: pegged, intermediate, and floating. As one can see, they are far from being unanimous. Actually, each of the classification systems measures different things, and their usefulness depends on the context in which they will be used.

# 10.2  What Exchange Rate Regime Should Be Chosen?

## 10.2.1  Fixed Versus Flexible Exchange Rate

**A classic discussion relating to exchange rate regimes is the comparison between the two extreme regimes: fixed or floating exchange rates.** In order to compare these two regimes, we will consider the impact of real shocks (changes in terms of trade, fiscal policy, or technology shocks, for example) and nominal shocks (such as variations in money demand or government monetary policy) on the output, balance of payments and the real exchange rate in each of these regimes. What model should be used to help understand the question? In the long-run model presented in Chapter 6, any change in the monetary policy is completely absorbed by prices, maintaining the real exchange rate unaltered, so that the monetary policy has no effect either on the level of economic activity or on the balance of payments. Therefore, this is not an adequate model to analyze the short-run impacts of exchange rate policy on the economy, a period in which not all economic agents possess complete information regarding the shocks that occurred.

The analytical framework used are the sticky price models described in Chapter 7, where delays in price adjustment cause nominal shocks to have real effects. The main result of the model is that **the economy is better protected from real shocks with a floating exchange rate regime, while a fixed regime is a better alternative in the case of nominal shocks.** The intuition is as follows: a real shock, such as a deterioration in the terms of trade, for example, alters the equilibrium real exchange rate.[5] In a floating exchange rate regime, the nominal exchange rate can immediately jump to the level that leads the real exchange rate to its new equilibrium level. If the exchange rate were fixed, the adjustment would be by means of prices, and the economy would go through a process of increased inflation. The real exchange rate would be out of its equilibrium level during the price adjustment period.

Now consider a nominal shock, such as, for example, a reduction in money demand caused by a financial innovation, such as the implantation of a credit card system. With the reduction in demand for domestic currency, there is excess demand for foreign currency and pressure for exchange rate depreciation. If the exchange rate is flexible, the nominal exchange rate depreciates, which also causes a depreciation of the real exchange rate given that prices do not adjust immediately. While prices adjust to the new equilibrium, the current account balance is greater than its optimal level. On the other hand, in a fixed exchange rate regime, the nominal shock is absorbed by the monetary policy, without any other effects on the economy. To maintain the announced exchange rate parity, the government should meet the excess demand for foreign currency by selling its international reserves. In doing this, the domestic money supply decreases, rebalancing the market. In this process there are no changes in interest or relative prices, such that there is no effect on the real side of the economy.

**In summary, countries exposed to real shocks, such as terms of trade or supply shocks, should opt for a floating exchange rate regime, while countries subject to monetary and financial uncertainties should follow a fixed exchange rate regime.** We can think of this advice in terms of the **impossible trinity**, discussed in Box 7.4, according to which the government should opt between stabilizing the exchange rate or maintaining monetary policy independence when there is free mobility of capital between countries. Given that real shocks require exchange rate adjustment, when these are recurring, it is better to allow the exchange rate to float. Nominal shocks, on the other hand, cause undesirable variations in the exchange rate. Therefore, in economies subject to nominal shocks, it is preferable to stabilize the exchange rate, even at the cost of giving up monetary policy independence.

---

[5] Chapter 5 shows the relation between the equilibrium real exchange rate and other economic variables.

However, with the international mobility of capital, it is difficult to maintain exchange rate parity without becoming vulnerable to speculative attacks, as discussed in Chapter 9. As emphasized by Fischer (2001), for countries open to the international flow of capital, exchange rate parity is only possible in a hard peg regime, such as the currency board, dollarization, and monetary union, where there is a greater commitment by the government to maintain parity. The fundamental characteristic of these regimes is that the cost to abandon them is higher, which serves as a credibility guarantee. To abandon a currency board regime, there is high political cost for the government since it must change the law that establishes the regime. The cost to leave is even higher in the cases of dollarization and monetary union, since they involve the creation of a central bank and a new currency to substitute the foreign currency that had been adopted, in the case of dollarization, or common currency, for the monetary union.

### 10.2.1.1 Trade Openness and Exchange Rate Policy
According to McKinnon (1963), the government can be described as having three objectives:

1. Maintain full employment
2. Maintain external balance
3. Maintain price stability.

When there is disequilibrium in the balance of payments, there are two types of possible policies: **expenditure switching and expenditures reducing. Expenditure switching policies** are those that act directly on relative prices, affecting the relative supply and demand between sectors. Exchange rate variation is an expenditure switching policy, for it affects the relative price between tradables and nontradables, changing the demand and relative supply between the two sectors, as we saw in Chapter 5. Exchange rate depreciation, for example, reduces demand and increases supply in the tradable goods sector, increasing the trade balance. **Expenditure reducing policies**, on the other hand, are those that reduce aggregate demand in the country. A contractionist fiscal policy is one that reduces expenditures. In reducing aggregate demand, the demand for tradable goods decreases, which also causes an increase in the trade balance.

Each of these policies, however, can have undesirable collateral effects. Exchange depreciation can generate inflationary pressure, be it by the very increase in the prices of tradables, or by the increase in demand for nontradables, which can cause an excess of demand in that sector. **The greater the relative size of the tradable sector in the economy, greater will be the inflationary pressure caused by exchange rate depreciation.** The impact of nominal depreciation on the inflation rate is called *pass-through* from exchange to inflation.

Contractionist fiscal policy, in turn, reduces the demand for all goods in the economy. In particular, it reduces the demand for tradable goods, leading to equilibrium in the balance of payments. The problem is that the demand for nontradable goods also decreases, which can lead to recession. **The smaller the relative size of the tradable goods sector, the greater the recession due to the use of fiscal policy to balance the balance of payments.**

Therefore, according to the argument presented by McKinnon, **the degree of economic openness is important in the choice of exchange rate regime.** Exchange rate variations as economic policy instruments used to solve balance of payments problems are relatively more efficient than fiscal policies in more closed economies, that is, with a relatively small tradable goods sector. In more open economies, on the other hand, expenditure reducing policies are more efficient than expenditure switching policies.

McKinnon centers his analysis on a small economy, where the function of exchange rate policy is simply to alter the relative domestic prices between tradable and nontradable goods. It is assumed that domestic and foreign goods are perfect substitutes and that purchasing power parity is always valid. If we abandon this hypothesis, there will be another function of exchange rate policy, which is to alter the price of the good produced domestically in relation to that produced in other countries. If the goods are differentiated, exchange rate depreciation will cause the goods produced domestically to become relatively less expensive, causing an increase in their demand by the rest of the world and, consequently, increasing domestic exports. Likewise, the higher relative price of imported products will reduce our demand for imports. Thus, even if all goods in the economy were tradable, exchange rate depreciation would have a positive effect on the balance of payments. We can therefore say that **the more open an economy, the greater impact exchange rate depreciation will have on the balance of payments**.

**This means that, if, on the one hand, a greater openness increases the *pass-through* from exchange rate to inflation, on the other, the level of exchange rate depreciation necessary for external equilibrium is lower in a more open economy.** Consequently, the relation between inflation and trade openness when the exchange rate is used to balance the balance of payments is, in principle ambiguous. Empirical results by Terra (1998) suggest that the effect of openness on the exchange rate depreciation necessary for external adjustment is what prevails. The article shows that, among more indebted countries that experienced the foreign debt crisis in the 1980s, those that were more open presented a lower rate of inflation.

### 10.2.1.2 Monetary Union

In fixed exchange rate or currency board regimes, the exchange rate ceases to vary in relation to the reference currency. In a dollarization regime, there is not really an exchange rate, given that the domestic currency ceases to exist. A country that adopts one of these regimes ceases to have monetary policy autonomy. The country to which the domestic currency is tied, in the case of fixed exchange rate or currency board, or the country that issues the currency used in the case of dollarization, sovereignly decides its monetary policy, with the domestic country being at its mercy. In a monetary union, this does not happen. When a group of countries adopts a common currency, a common central bank is created and decision-making rules are established in such a way as to attend the needs of each member of the union. This is a fundamental difference of the monetary union that deserves separate analysis.

## 10.2.2 Optimum Currency Area

**When a group of countries adopts a common currency, they must follow the same monetary policy. The question that must be posed is if the benefit generated in having a common currency supersedes the cost of also following a common monetary policy.** Mundell (1961) defines the characteristics that should be shared by countries that adopt a common currency. A simple example illustrates the problem. Consider two countries, Germany and France, that produce different goods, Camembert cheese and Mercedes Benz automobiles. At first the economies are in equilibrium: there is full employment of the production factors in both countries and there is equilibrium in the balance of payments between them. Suppose there is a shift of demand from Camembert cheese, produced in France, to Mercedes Benz automobiles, produced in Germany. Due to some exogenous factor, a change in preference causes consumers to eat less cheese and use more cars. In the short run, namely, before the relative prices adjust, there will be unemployment in France, given that at original prices, consumers demand less Camembert, and there will be inflationary pressure in Germany, with consumers purchasing more Mercedes Benz. Simultaneously, there will be a trade deficit in France and a trade surplus in Germany. How does the adjustment occur in these two economies?

In the case where both economies share the same currency, there are, essentially, two paths:

1. There is inflation in Germany, leading to a change in the terms of trade between the two countries: the Mercedes becomes relatively more expensive. Such variation in price causes a relative increase in demand for Camembert. Full employment of production factors is reestablished in France, while the fall in demand for Mercedes ends the inflationary pressure in Germany.
2. There is deflation in France. The price of Camembert falls, altering the relative price and leading to a new equilibrium, as in the mechanism described before.

Prices, however, are not flexible. Actually, they are particularly rigid to the fall. Typically, prices only fall at the cost of recession and unemployment. Central banks, on the other hand, oppose price increases with restrictive monetary policies. Therefore, if the country with a surplus in the balance of payments stymies an increase in prices, there will be a recessive pressure in the other countries with whom their exchange is fixed.

In the case where the two countries have different currencies, a simple variation in the exchange rate between the two currencies would alter the relative prices between goods from the two countries, leading to instant equilibrium in the balance of payments with no transition costs. Notice that this argument presupposes that, in spite of prices and salaries being rigid, the exchange rate can immediately adjust to real shocks.

This example shows that it is not always desirable that the exchange rate between the currencies be fixed. One of the criteria to determine if a group of countries constitutes an optimum currency area is the correlation of the real shocks that affect their economies. Correlated real shocks mean that the countries suffer, in general, the same shocks of supply and demand for goods. In the previously cited example, France and Germany would have real correlated shocks, in general, if whenever there was an increase in demand for Mercedes, there would also be an increase in demand for Camembert. In this case, the equilibrium of the two economies would not involve changes of the relative price between Mercedes and Camembert. We can say that **the lower the correlation between the real shocks in the economies, the lesser the chance they constitute an optimum currency area**.

It is important to note that the same argument applies to the different regions within the same country. In other words, not always does a country constitute an optimum currency area. If the regions of a country produce distinct goods, subject to idiosyncratic real shocks, theoretically a greater welfare could be reached if each region had its own currency, with a flexible exchange rate between them. The next example illustrates this situation.

Consider two countries, Canada and the United States, with two regions in each country, East and West, producing two goods, automobiles and lumber. The production factors are not mobile between countries or regions, namely, Canadian automobile workers cannot work in the lumber sector within their country, nor can they migrate to the United States to work in the auto industry there. In each of the countries, the east region produces cars and the west, lumber. Both economies are initially in equilibrium, with full employment of factors of productions in both countries and in each region, and equilibrium in the balance of payments between the two countries. Assume that there is an increase in total factor productivity in the automotive sector, which affects each country equally, that is, more automobiles are produced with the same quantity of factors. In the short run, there will be an excess supply of automobiles.

Given there are only two goods markets, lumber and automobiles, the excess supply of automobiles has the excess demand for lumber as a counterpart. There will be unemployment in the east and inflationary pressure in the west in both countries. The new equilibrium will be reached with a fall in the relative price of automobiles. A change in the exchange rate between the two countries would not help adjust the economies to reach the new equilibrium since it does not alter the relative price between the two products. In this case, if there were a different currency for each region, an exchange rate variation between the regional currencies would lead to equilibrium, with no unemployment or inflation.

If production factors were mobile between regions, a migration of factors from east to west would lead to equilibrium in the economy. **Therefore, another important factor in determining the suitability of a single currency is the degree of production factor mobility between regions.** Therefore, one of the policies adopted by member countries of the European Monetary Union was the ease of mobility of goods and production factors between countries.

### 10.2.2.1 Monetary Union and Trade

A strong argument for the creation of a monetary union is related to international trade. Sharing the same currency reduces the cost of trade between members of a monetary union, given that the transactions are made in the same currency. Also, uncertainty in relation to trade cost also is reduced. In general, international trade transactions involve a greater amount of time between the order and delivery of the product, namely, between the purchase and payment. For trade between countries using different currencies, there is the additional risk of the exchange rate varying between the time of purchase and that of payment. This risk disappears when countries use the same currency. Therefore, **the greater the trade between countries, the greater the benefit of sharing the same currency**.

Also, the monetary union stimulates trade between its members. Several empirical studies found evidence that participation in monetary unions has a positive impact on trade between its members.[6] Estimates, however, diverge considerable between studies. Rose and Stanley (2005) analyze the results of 34 different studies and conclude that a monetary union can increase trade somewhere between 30% and 90%. Micco et al. (2003) and Nardis et al. (2008), however, present much more modest estimates for the impact of the European Union: something between 4% and 10%.

### 10.2.2.2 Monetary Union and Public Finance

The issue of public finance should also be taken into consideration when analyzing the costs and benefits of instituting a monetary union. When a group of countries forms a monetary union, its members are subject to a single monetary policy, which depends on fiscal policy. As we saw in Chapter 7, fiscal expansion leads to an increase in the money supply in a fixed exchange rate regime. Consequently, to maintain an austere monetary policy, it is necessary that the monetary union member countries follow equally austere fiscal policies. For this reason, the European Monetary Union established the *Stability and Growth Pact* with the objective of monitoring and guaranteeing the fiscal stability of union member countries (Box 10.1). The recent crisis showed that the pact was not as effective as expected, as we will discuss in section 10.2.5.1.

Another element that can be relevant in the choice of monetary policy is the inflation tax it generates, and countries may diverge as to their preferred inflation tax level.[7] Taxes are, in general, distorting, be they on goods, labor, or currency. The optimum tax structure is that which equalizes the marginal disutility for each tax, which can be different for each country or region. In countries where the distortion from taxing goods, labor, and capital is too high, the optimal tax on currency will be relatively greater.

Italy and Germany are examples of countries that clearly have distinct optimum tax structures. Italy has a relatively large informal sector, which cannot be directly taxed. A means to tax this sector is with an inflation tax. Germany, however, does not have this problem. Therefore, the optimum inflation tax for Germany will be lower than that for Italy. **The creation of a single currency zone will be beneficial if the transaction costs for the existence of several currencies exceed the cost for each country to cease**

---

[6] See, for example, Rose (2000), Glick and Rose (2002), and Baldwin and Nino (2006).
[7] See Canzoneri and Diba (1992).

---

**BOX 10.1 STABILITY AND GROWTH PACT**

The monetary policy would be common for all member countries of the Eurozone after the institution of the monetary union. Under the leadership of Germany, it was established that the goal of the European Central Bank in setting monetary policy would be to keep inflation under control. The Stability and Growth Pact was then designed to ensure that Member States would follow fiscal policies compatible with this common, and austere, monetary policy. According to the definition given by the European Commission, "The Stability and Growth Pact is a rule-based framework for the coordination of national fiscal policies in the European Union. It was established to safeguard sound public finances, based on the principle that economic policies are a matter of shared concern for all Member States." In other words, the Pact would ensure fiscal discipline among the Eurozone members. According to it, government budget deficit should not exceed 3% of GDP, while public debt should not be higher than 60% of GDP. The Pact called for the imposition of sanction for noncompliance with its directives. In practice, however, there was much more leniency with noncompliance than provided for by Pact.

---

**following its optimum allocation of taxes.** Moreover, the higher the public spending, the less probable the optimum inflation rate will be the same between countries. Finally, even when coming to an agreement as to the level of inflation tax for the monetary union, another important question related to public finance is how to divide this tax between the union members.[8]

### 10.2.2.3 Monetary Union and the Trade-Off Between Inflation and Unemployment

Maybe the most sensitive issue in a monetary union is related to the use, or not, of an active monetary policy to soften negative shocks to the economy. In an economy with sticky prices, monetary expansion can increase the level of activity in the short run, before prices have time to adjust, as we saw in Chapter 7. The side effect of using monetary policy to stimulate the economy is its effect on inflation. There is, therefore, a trade-off between inflation and unemployment.

The trade-off becomes even more delicate when one takes into consideration the credibility of maintaining an austere monetary policy in the future. The problem of intertemporal inconsistency of monetary policy is well known: governments would like to commit themselves to maintain low inflation, but if the economic agents expect low inflation, governments have an incentive to generate surprise inflation to stimulate economic activity. Given that economic agents foresee this government motivation, they already expect a higher inflation rate. In the end, there is positive inflation, however, with no stimulus to the economy since it is perfectly expected by individuals.[9]

Central bank independence is one way to try to solve this problem, as suggested by Rogoff (1985). An independent central bank with a strong preference for low inflation rates

---

[8] This question is discussed in Casella (1992).

[9] Barro and Gordon (1983) propose a simple model that captures this situation, which is the basis of the model described in this section.

would be immune to government pressure to inflate, generating an expectation of low inflation. The result would be a low equilibrium inflation rate. A classic example is the German central bank, which signaled a strong preference for low inflation as a mechanism to control expectations, before the introduction of the monetary union. What happens when an independent central bank is common in monetary union member countries? That is what we will see next.

Government preferences, that in some way should capture the preferences of the citizens that elected them, are represented by a loss function that considers the losses associated with inflation and unemployment. The preferred government inflation rate would be equal to zero. As to unemployment, there is a *natural rate of unemployment* that corresponds to the unemployment inherent to the function of the economy. It reflects the structure of the labor market and the rate that prevails over the long run, after any necessary adjustments and shocks have taken place. The government, however, prefers the unemployment rate to be less than its natural level. One explanation could be the existence of imperfections in the goods market, such as monopolies or regulations, which cause the natural unemployment rate to be greater than the socially desirable unemployment level.

To capture the situation described in the previous paragraph, let us suppose that the government of country $i$ chooses inflation[10] so as to minimize the loss function, $L_i$, which increases with unemployment, $u$, and with inflation, $\pi$:

$$L_i = (u - \overline{u}_i)^2 + \theta_i \pi^2, \tag{10.1}$$

where $\overline{u}_i$ is the level of unemployment desired by the government.

Unemployment, in turn, is given by

$$u = \tilde{u}_i + \varepsilon_i - (\pi - \pi^e). \tag{10.2}$$

In Eq. (10.2), $\tilde{u}_i$ represents the natural rate of unemployment, which corresponds to the average unemployment in the economy, where there are no surprises in the inflation rate or shocks. We assume that it is greater than the government desired unemployment rate, $\overline{u}_i$, so that: $\tilde{u}_i - \overline{u}_i = k_i > 0$, where $k_i$ corresponds, therefore, to unemployment in *excess* to that which the economy on average presents. Variable $\varepsilon_i$ represents random shocks on unemployment, with a zero mean, i.e., $E[\varepsilon_i] = 0$. Finally, $\pi^e$ is the inflation rate expected by the public, and $(\pi - \pi^e)$ is the surprise inflation.

This last term shows that surprise inflation can reduce the unemployment level in the economy. The impact of unexpected inflation on unemployment can be explained with the existence of fixed wages in the economy. Typically, wages are determined by contracts that establish the periodicity or conditions when they can or should be altered. This means that wages are fixed for a given period. If prices increase during this period, the real wage, that is, the average wage in terms of goods, decreases. Labor becomes relatively cheaper, which

---

[10] We can assume, more precisely, that the government chooses the monetary policy, which, in turn, determines the inflation rate. We take a shortcut in assuming that the government directly chooses the inflation rate.

stimulates the increase of its demand, raising production and reducing unemployment. If inflation were expected, wage contracts would already imbed future price increases. In the terms of our model, the source of this effect is not of interest. We simply suppose that there is a negative relation between surprise inflation and the level of unemployment, as captured by the last term of Eq. (10.2).[11]

Substituting the equation for unemployment (Eq. (10.2)) in the government loss function for country $i$ (Eq. (10.1)), we get

$$L_i = [k_i + \varepsilon_i - (\pi - \pi^e)]^2 + \theta_i \pi^2. \tag{10.3}$$

The government chooses the inflation rate so as to maximize its loss function represented by Eq. (10.3), taking as a given the inflation expected by private agents, $\pi^e$.

Notice that the first term of the loss function, referent to the cost of unemployment, contains the positive constant $k_i$, which captures the average "excess" unemployment in the economy. Even if there are no shocks on unemployment, i.e., when $\varepsilon_i = 0$, this excessive unemployment implies a loss of welfare to the economy. If the public expected an inflation equal to zero, the government would have an incentive to inflate the economy a little, causing a surprise inflation, $(\pi - \pi^e) > 0$, to reduce unemployment. For a sufficiently low inflation rate, this strategy might be worthwhile, for the second term, which represents the cost of inflation, will be low. The public, however, expects this perverse government incentive.

The chosen inflation rate is given by Eq. (10.4), which is developed in more detail in the Mathematical Appendix at the end of this chapter:

$$\pi_i = \frac{k_i + \varepsilon_i + \pi^e}{1 + \theta_i}. \tag{10.4}$$

What would be the inflation rate expected by the public? If the public has rational expectations, it knows that, after forming its expectations, the government will choose the inflation rate according to Eq. (10.4). Therefore, the inflation rate expected by the public is the expected value of inflation rate in Eq. (10.4), as in

$$\pi_i^e = E\left[\frac{k_i + \varepsilon_i + \pi_p^e}{1 + \theta_i}\right] = \frac{k_i + \pi_i^e}{1 + \theta_i},$$

which, solving, allows us to arrive at the expected inflation as a function of the unemployment rate:

$$\pi_i^e = \frac{k_i}{\theta_i}. \tag{10.5}$$

---

[11] A good introduction regarding the relation between wages and prices can be found in Taylor and Woodward (1999), Chapter 15. A more advanced treatment of the theme, presenting the microfoundation of the New Keynesian Phillips Curve, can be found in Galí (2008).

Substituting expected inflation (10.5) into the inflation rate equation (10.4), we have the equilibrium inflation rate in the economy, which is given by

$$\pi_i = \frac{k_i}{\theta_i} + \frac{\varepsilon_i}{1 + \theta_i}. \tag{10.6}$$

Equilibrium inflation is composed of two terms. The first, $\frac{k_i}{\theta_i}$, corresponds to the government attempt to cause surprise inflation to reduce the average unemployment and bring it near the desired rate. However, as can be seen in Eq. (10.5), this portion of inflation is already expected by the public and causes no surprise at all, having no effect whatsoever on unemployment. This would be the "inefficient" part of inflation. The greater the weight given to inflation in the loss function, $\theta$, the smaller this term will be. In other words, the less government likes inflation, the less inflation there will be in the economy, on average. Due to this, Rogoff (1985) proposes that the central bank be independent, being as such, immune to government pressure, besides nominating an institution president who does not like inflation. In the terms of the model, this would be someone with a high $\theta$. Inflation in the economy would then be given by

$$\pi_{cb} = \frac{k_i}{\theta_{cb}} + \frac{\varepsilon_i}{1 + \theta_{cb}}, \tag{10.7}$$

where $\pi_{cb}$ is equilibrium inflation with an independent central bank and whose presidential preference regarding inflation is represented by $\theta_{cb}$.

Having a central bank president who does not like inflation also has its cost, and it can be seen in the second term of the equilibrium inflation rate. This second term, $\frac{\varepsilon_i}{1+\theta_{cb}}$, corresponds to the inflation generated in response to unemployment shocks. As, by definition, these shocks are unexpected, this parcel of inflation is also unexpected, reason for which it can achieve its objective, which is to smooth the effect of the shock. The problem with having a central bank president who does not like inflation is that he uses monetary policy less to counter shocks. Comparing the inflation that would be chosen by the government (Eq. (10.6)) with that chosen by the central bank (Eq. (10.7)), we see that, on average, the inflation chosen by the central bank is lower $\left(\frac{k_i}{\theta_{cb}} < \frac{k_i}{\theta_i}\right)$, but the smoothing of shocks is also lower $\left(\frac{\varepsilon_i}{1+\theta_{cb}} < \frac{\varepsilon_i}{1+\theta_i}\right)$.

So, what happens when there is a monetary union? Well, in this case the monetary policy choice is made by the monetary union central bank. It chooses inflation based on a function such as Eq. (10.7), where the values for unemployment shocks, $\varepsilon$, and excessive unemployment, $k$, are taken as an average of the union members. The preference in relation to inflation, $\Theta$, is that of the central bank president, as in equation:

$$\pi_{mu} = \frac{k}{\Theta} + \frac{\varepsilon}{1 + \Theta}. \tag{10.8}$$

Clearly, the chosen inflation (Eq. (10.8)) is not exactly equal to the inflation that would be chosen by any of the members individually.

We can compare what the expected loss would be for a country, when it is a member of a monetary union, to its loss if it had its own currency. When a country is part of a monetary union, the inflation rate is given by Eq. (10.8). Substituting this value into the loss function for the country, $i$, (Eq. (10.1)), we can calculate the expected loss by the country when it is a member of a monetary union:

$$E[L_i^{\text{mem}}] = E\left[\left(k_i + \varepsilon_i - \frac{\eta}{1+\Theta}\right)^2 + \theta_i\left(\frac{k}{\Theta} + \frac{\eta}{1+\Theta}\right)^2\right].$$

If the country were autonomous, it could choose its own monetary policy. The expected inflation and inflation rate would be analogous to Eqs. (10.5) and (10.6), however with the parameters and variables of the country, contrary to those in force in a monetary union. In this case, the loss function for the country would be

$$E[L_i^{\text{aut}}] = E\left[\left(k_i + \frac{\theta_{\text{cb}}}{1+\theta_{\text{cb}}}\varepsilon_i\right)^2 + \Theta_i\left(\frac{k_i}{\theta_{\text{cb}}} + \frac{\varepsilon_i}{1+\theta_{\text{cb}}}\right)^2\right].$$

We can then calculate the difference between the loss expected when the country is part of a monetary union and the loss expected when it is autonomous:

$$EL_i^{\text{mem}} - EL_i^{\text{aut}} = \theta_i\left[\left(\frac{k}{\Theta}\right)^2 - \left(\frac{k_i}{\theta_{\text{cb}}}\right)^2\right] + \frac{1+2\theta_{\text{bc}}\theta_p}{(1+\theta_{\text{cb}})^2}\sigma_\varepsilon^2 + \frac{1+\theta_i}{(1+\Theta)^2}\sigma_\eta^2 - \frac{2}{1+\Theta}\sigma_{\varepsilon n}, \tag{10.9}$$

where $\sigma_\varepsilon^2$ and $\sigma_\eta^2$ represent the variance of domestic shocks, $\varepsilon_i$, and aggregate shocks, $\eta$, while $\sigma_{\varepsilon n}$ is the covariance between the two shocks.

A negative value for Eq. (10.9) means that the loss when a country is a member of a monetary union is smaller than the loss if the country were not part of the union. There are basically two sources for the difference between these two losses. The first source is related to the so-called "inefficient" portion of inflation, that is, that which is relative to the attempt to inflate in order to increase the level of activity, however, without success since the agents incorporate this portion of inflation into their expectations, as previously explained. Ideally, this parcel should be zero. If the monetary union has the objective of a smaller reduction in unemployment than the country under consideration ($k < k_i$), and/or the central bank president has a greater repulsion to inflation ($\Theta > \theta_i$), then this inefficient portion of inflation will be smaller in the monetary union, and the first term, $\theta_i\left[\left(\frac{k}{\Theta}\right)^2 - \left(\frac{k_i}{\theta_{\text{cb}}}\right)^2\right]$, will be negative. The greater the weight given to the loss function of the country, $\theta_i$, the greater the weight that will be given to this term in Eq. (10.9).

A second source of difference is the random unemployment shocks to which inflation responds, captured by the three last terms of the equation. The higher the variance of domestic shocks, $\sigma_\varepsilon^2$, the greater the relative loss in being a member of the monetary union, given that the common monetary policy does not respond to them. On the other hand, it does respond to common shocks, $\eta$, which is not desirable for the country. Therefore, a high variance of common shocks, $\sigma_\eta^2$, also represents a cost in participating in the union. Nevertheless, when the shocks are correlated, the union monetary policy will respond, in part, to the stability desire of the country. Hence, the greater the covariance between shocks, $\sigma_{\varepsilon\eta}$, the smaller the relative loss of welfare in country $p$ for participating in the monetary union. We can conclude that **countries with more homogeneous objectives and that are subject to more correlated real shocks will have their objectives better met in a monetary union.**

The decision to participate in a monetary union also depends on the influence of the country in union decisions. The parameters of monetary union objective function should be the result of a joint decision by member countries. If influence were determined solely by the size of the country, small countries would probably prefer to not join the monetary union. It would be necessary, therefore, to give relatively more power to smaller countries in order to guarantee their participation.[12]

**Summarizing**, we can list the following factors that determine if a group of countries would form an optimum currency area:

1. The greater the trade volume, the greater the transaction costs when there is more than one currency. Also, the institution of a monetary union causes an increase in trade between its members.
2. Countries that suffer similar real shocks are the most indicated to form an optimum currency area. When economies simultaneously suffer the same real shocks, their optimum monetary policy is the same. Consequently, a single monetary policy satisfies the needs of all.
3. The greater the flexibility of prices and wages, the easier it is to make nominal adjustments without exchange rate variations, making it less costly to give up the exchange rate as an adjustment variable.
4. The greater the mobility of production factors across countries, the smaller the need for exchange rate variation to face real shocks.
5. The sustainability of the monetary union will be more certain if there is a definite leader, or if there is an institutional framework that guarantees that the loss of monetary autonomy will be compensated for by other gains in cooperation.

## 10.2.3 Inflation and Exchange Rate Anchoring

Problems of intertemporal inconsistency of monetary policy are often the root of chronic inflation. As discussed in the previous subsection, with the objective of stimulating the economy, the government has an incentive to cause inflation when the citizen inflation

---

[12] The same type of problem can arise with an inflation tax partition between the countries. Casella (1992) shows that it may be necessary to give small countries a proportionally larger portion of the inflationary payment to guarantee monetary union membership.

expectations are low. Given that individuals are aware of this motivation, they already expect positive inflation. The result is chronic inflation that is unable to stimulate the economy. In the terms of the model previously described, $\frac{k_i}{\theta_i}$ of equilibrium inflation, described by Eq. (10.6) corresponds to this inefficient portion of positive, expected inflation. It would be preferable if government could credibly commit to not concede to this temptation. A way to "tie the hands" of government is to institute a fixed exchange rate regime. Let us see how it works.

In an open economy, domestic prices cannot diverge from international prices when measured in the same currency. In this context, relative purchasing power parity establishes that nominal exchange rate changes should follow the inflation differential between the domestic country and the foreign country, as was established by Eq. (3.7), which we repeat here:

$$\dot{s} = \pi_t - \pi_t^*. \tag{10.10}$$

Accordingly, if the government establishes a fixed exchange rate regime, the domestic inflation should be equal to that of the country to which parity was established. **One way of committing to a lower inflation rate, therefore, is to peg the currency to that of a country with low inflation. This is what is known as** *exchange rate anchoring*: **by maintaining currency parity with a low inflation country, the domestic inflation will also be low.**

The advantage of using the exchange rate as an anchor to maintain low inflation is that it is a visible and easily verifiable instrument, therefore more efficient as a sign of the government commitment to low inflation rates. One disadvantage is that the government loses its monetary policy autonomy. It would be desirable to use monetary policy to smooth temporary shocks to the economy, as captured by the second term of Eq. (10.6). By tying their own hands with a fixed exchange rate, the government eliminates not only the inefficient portion of inflation, referent to chronic inflation, but also the part that would help stabilize the level of activity in the face of shocks.

It is important to emphasize the fact that the policy only works if the government effectively follows a monetary policy compatible with the fixed exchange rate. If it announces a fixed exchange rate but continues to follow a lack of monetary control, domestic prices will increase in relation to international prices, configuring a real exchange rate appreciation. With domestic goods relatively more expensive, imports increase and exports decrease, generating a trade deficit. The excess demand for foreign currency causes a depreciation of domestic currency, unless the government intervenes in the market by selling reserves, thereby meeting the excess demand for foreign currency and eliminating the pressure to depreciate. Clearly, the situation cannot be maintained indefinitely,[13] as testified by the Latin American experience in the 1980s. Several Latin American countries used the exchange rate as a nominal anchor in an attempt to control

---

[13] The speculative attack model in Section 9.1 shows how an incompatible credit policy with exchange rate parity leads to a speculative attack.

---

**BOX 10.2 THE CURRENCY BOARD REGIME IN ARGENTINA**

Argentina tried to solve its recurrent problem with high inflation by adopting a currency board regime, which demands a greater commitment to exchange rate parity. Besides the law establishing the exchange rate regime, it requires all monetary base to be backed foreign currency reserves in the central bank at the established parity. Hence, the monetary policy is directly controlled by the regime, being totally dependent on the variation of reserves in the central bank. If an external shock causes a trade deficit, for example, and the capital inflow through the financial account does not compensate it, the government must sell reserves to cover the resulting balance of payments deficit, causing a monetary contraction. In theory, monetary contraction would lead to a reduction in domestic prices, which would cause domestic goods to be more competitive on the foreign market. The trade balance would increase, rebalancing the balance of payments. There would be, thereby, a natural adjustment mechanism.

In practice, however, the solution is not that simple. Workers rarely accept a reduction in their nominal wage and producers are reticent to permanently reduce the price of their products. The result of monetary contraction is that it ends in recession, with little impact on prices. This is what happened in Argentina. A series of shocks led to expressive trade deficits. Along with this, credibility problems related to the sustainability of the system caused investors to be hesitant in relation to the country, leading the balance of payments to also present growing deficits, which led to monetary contraction. The lack of liquidity was such that barter clubs began to proliferate around the country, where citizens traded goods among themselves. What more, bonds issued by local governments began to be used as a means of payment. The province of Buenos Aires, for example, issued US$ 90 million in low value bonds, known as *patacones*, which were widely used as currency. Even McDonald's launched a combo known as the *Patacombo*: two cheeseburgers, fries and a soft drink, all for one *patacón*: about a five dollar value.

---

the persistently high inflation rates that had ravaged the area after the foreign debt crisis of 1982. Inflation, even though low, was above foreign inflation, which, ultimately, led to the abandon of exchange rate parity and the resurgence of inflation (Box 10.2).

In general, the experience showed that fixed rate regimes produced overvalued real exchange rates, be it due to residual inflation or to external shocks. The result was a deterioration of the trade balance and the nonsustainability of exchange rate parity. The tendency in the 2000s was to adopt a regime of inflation targeting with an independent central bank, allied with a floating exchange rate. The floating exchange rate gives monetary policy autonomy to the central bank, while the inflation targeting regime clearly establishes the monetary policy to be followed, which objective should be the maintenance of inflation within a previously established band.

**Inflation targeting, combined with flexible exchange rates, promotes the monetary austerity necessary to maintain inflation under control, without the risk of causing imbalances as those generated by a fixed exchange rate.** The system requires, however, better quality institutions. First, with the independence of the central bank to conduct its inflation targeting policy, the government cannot use monetary policy for its own political goals, such as, for example, to stimulate economic activity before an election. Second, the central bank should develop technical abilities needed to refine its monetary policy to reach inflation targeting, which involves data processing and the use of econometric models to estimate the proper policy, given the state of the economy. Third, communication instruments should be created to allow its policies to be more transparent to the public. One important aspect of the regime consists in creating low inflation expectation, hence credibility problems in relation to the policy adopted by the central bank should be avoided. Last, but certainly not least, the central bank should build its credibility with the goal of more efficiently combating inflation. In theory, a central bank with greater credibility will have a lower cost, in terms of economic activity, to deflate an economy than a bank central with little credibility.

## 10.2.4 Exchange Rate Regime and Financial Dollarization

**Financial Dollarization** refers both to domestic investors purchasing assets denominated in foreign currency and domestic residents borrowing in foreign currency. We say "dollarization" since, in general, it is the dollar that is the foreign currency under consideration, even though financial dollarization can refer, in principle, to financial assets in any foreign currency. **There are at least three channels by which the adoption of a fixed exchange rate regime can incite financial dollarization.**

**First, a fixed exchange rate regime, especially if it is a hard peg regime, reduces the exchange rate risk of having foreign currency assets.** Consider an investor who must choose the optimum allocation for their portfolio, knowing that the large part of their future expenditures will be in domestic currency. With a floating exchange rate, they would have a biased preference in favor of domestic bonds so as to reduce their exposure to exchange rate risk. This problem is lessened with a hard peg regime. If the investor believes there will not be exchange rate variation when they redeem their investment in foreign currency to consume goods denominated in domestic currency, the foreign assets will not be in disadvantage in relation to domestic.

**Second, a fixed exchange rate regime to which economic agents attribute a certain probability of being abandoned, can generate the *peso problem*,** as discussed in Chapter 3. The exchange rate remains stable while the regime is maintained, even with the expectation of exchange rate depreciation. Therefore, there are persistent errors in depreciation expectation. In this case, the domestic interest rate should be higher than the foreign in order to maintain the attractiveness of domestic assets, as was established by the uncovered interest rate parity (Eq. (3.13)). If the probability of a regime change is small, even if it carries large exchange rate depreciation, some individuals will be tempted to borrow externally to take advantage of relatively lower international interest rates.

**Finally, in the case of an exchange rate crisis, the commitment to defend the exchange rate parity can be taken as an implicit government guarantee to save banks and domestic businesses that are indebted in foreign currency.**[14] The idea is that the government has an incentive to help banks and large businesses when an exchange rate crisis

---

[14] See, for example, Mishkin (1996) and Obstfeld (1998).

---

**BOX 10.3 EXCHANGE PARITY AND FINANCIAL DOLLARIZATION: THE ARGENTINE CASE**

With the currency board regime in force between 1991 and 2001, Argentina was able to reduce the high inflation rates that had desolated the economy during the previous decade. Between 1991 and 1998, the Argentine economy grew over 40%, with 1 peso being equal to 1 dollar, with total convertibility.[a] In this rose-colored scenario, Argentine foreign debt increased substantially: government foreign debt rose about 60%, while that of the private sector grew an impressive 618%.[b] Problems began with a series of foreign shocks at the end of the 1990s, leading, ultimately, to the abandon of the regime, as discussed in Box 9.2. The high level of Argentine private sector debt in dollars had an important role in the deep recession that followed the depreciation of the Argentine peso: in 2002, the real GDP was 28% lower than in 1998.

---

[a]See Galiani et al. (2003).
[b]See Lischinsky (2003).

---

causes massive bankruptcies. Believing they will be bailed out in the case of a crisis, banks and businesses excessively expose themselves to exchange rate risk. Actually, there are many examples that such expectations are unfounded.

The problem of financial dollarization is that it causes a mismatch of the monetary denomination of the assets and liabilities for banks, businesses, or individuals in general who borrow or save abroad. When revenues or income are in domestic currency and the debt in foreign currency, exchange rate depreciation increases the real cost of the debt in relation to the resources available to pay it. On the other hand, when consumption is made in domestic currency, exchange rate appreciation reduces the purchasing power of the individual who has their savings in foreign currency. Consequently, in general, **financial dollarization increases the exchange rate risk for economic agents**, which leads us to our next point.

The two channels previously discussed lead to large foreign debt, which increases the cost of exchange rate depreciation. When businesses and banks have debt in foreign currency and their revenue is in local currency, exchange rate depreciation increases the real cost of their debt. As we saw in Section 9.3, if the foreign debt is substantial, depreciation can lead to bankruptcy, which intensifies the exchange rate crisis.

An exchange rate parity regime can stimulate debt in dollars, which increases the cost of an eventual exchange rate crisis. The Argentine currency board experience is an example, as presented in Box 10.3.

## 10.2.5 Exchange Rate Regime, Sovereign Debt and Crises

**The exchange rate regime should be evaluated not only by the benefits it generates while it is in force but also by its sustainability and the consequences when it cannot be maintained.** More precisely, one should take into consideration the role of the exchange rate regime on the generation and economic cost of crises.

**The impact of private foreign debt is different than that of public foreign debt.** A high level of private foreign debt gives the exchange rate crisis an amplifying effect on the level of economic activity due to bankruptcies and corporate financing problems caused by the exchange rate depreciation, as was previously discussed. When the external debt is public, on the other hand, an exchange rate crisis causes deterioration in public finances, given that exchange rate depreciation increases foreign debt when measured in domestic currency, which is the currency in which government revenue is denominated. The government should increase its revenue to be able to meet the larger financial expenses.

Payment of the sovereign foreign debt requires a double transfer of resources.[15] On the one hand, trade surpluses must be generated to obtain resources for foreign creditor payments, which corresponds to external transfer. On the other hand, the government should raise resources by means of taxes to cover its financial expenses, that is, effectuate an internal transfer. The two transfers are connected by the exchange rate. **The exchange rate depreciation necessary for the foreign transfer increases the amount of internal transfer required to balance the government budget.** It is not for nothing that Latin American indebted countries spent the decade after the 1982 debt crisis fighting fiscal problems and high inflation rates, given that the inflationary tax was one of the resources used to balance government accounts. In the 1980s, the Latin American lost decade, growth rates in the region fell to an average of 2.12% compared to the average of 5.66% in the previous decade (Box 10.4).[16]

### 10.2.5.1 European Debt Crisis

The European experience in the years surrounding 2010 provides us a new version of the Latin American experience 30 years ago. The countries that make up the Eurozone are not perfectly homogenous in relation to their economic policy institutions. Let us look at two extreme examples. First, we have Germany that controls its public finances with an iron hand and defended the German mark at any cost, which was its pre-euro currency. Second, at the other extreme, we have Greece, where tax evasion and corruption are endemic problems and the country had lived with high inflation rates before doing its homework in order to be accepted into the European Monetary Union. The difference between the two countries is reflected in the interest rates they paid on their sovereign debt. At the beginning of the 1990s, Greece paid interest rates of over 20% on its foreign debt, while in Germany the rate was at about 6%.

According to what we saw in Chapter 3, the discrepancy between the interest rates on bonds issued by the two countries can be explained by the expectation of exchange rate depreciation, exchange rate risk and the difference in sovereign risk between the two countries, which can be described by the following equation:

$$i_t^{\text{Gree}} - i_t^{\text{Germ}} = [E(s_{t+1}) - s_t] + \phi_t^c + \phi_t^s,$$

---

[15] See Rodrik (1990) and Terra (1997).

[16] According to data from ECLAC—United Nations Economic Commission for Latin America and the Caribbean.

### BOX 10.4 THE LATIN AMERICAN DEBT CRISIS

The Latin American foreign debt crisis was an important problem in the 1980s. An excess of international liquidity had characterized the previous decade, with oil producing countries seeking financial applications for their petrodollars.[a] Latin American countries, especially Argentina, Brazil, and Mexico, took advantage of low international interest rates to finance their development projects with foreign capital. Being that there were many restrictions on international private finance transactions, the lion's share of foreign debt was sovereign debt. Problems began in 1979 when industrialized countries began to adopt contractionist monetary policies to counter the inflation of prices resulting from the oil shock. Such policies had two disastrous effects on indebted countries. First, international interest rates increased, causing the service on foreign debt contracted under floating interest rates to be more expensive. Second, the recession in industrialized countries resulting from monetary contraction caused deterioration in the terms of trade for developing countries, resulting in a reduction in their trade balance. The crisis came to light with the 1982 Mexican moratorium. The flow of capital dried up and borrower countries were no longer able to roll over their debt, creating the need to generate substantial trade surpluses to meet their foreign obligations.

---

[a]At the beginning of the 1970s, the members of OPEC decided, in cartel, to increase the price of oil. Being that the world economy at the time was totally dependent on oil as an energy source, its demand was inflexible, or rather, did not respond much to the increase in price. The result was a large increase in receipts for oil producing countries. As we saw in Chapter 4, when a country has in increase in income that it knows will not be permanent, it saves a part of this additional income. The international financial liquidity in the 1970s was a result of this. The exchange values that came as a result of oil exports became known as petrodollars.

where $\phi_t^c$ and $\phi_t^s$ refer to the exchange rate and sovereign risk premium, respectively, paid by Greece.[17] Therefore, part of the discrepancy between the interest rates paid by Germany and Greece was explained by the higher and more uncertain inflation in Greece, which was reflected in the evolution of the exchange rate.[18]

After the institution of the euro, expectations of exchange rate depreciation and exchange rate risk ceased to exist. The differences in interest rates among Eurozone member countries reflected, however, only their sovereign risk. Figure 10.1 shows the evolution of interest rates on debt securities with a 10-year maturity issued between 1993 and 2012 for a sample of countries.[19] It is impressive to see how the interest rates for different countries migrated toward the German rates after the institution of the euro. Governments of countries such as Portugal, Spain, and Italy, which historically paid a sovereign risk premium, began to pay less to borrow. The same occurred for countries that later joined the Eurozone, such as

---

[17] Notice that there is an important difference between expectation of exchange rate depreciation, measured by term $E(s_{t+1}) - s_t$, and exchange rate risk $\phi_t^c$. The expectation of exchange rate depreciation takes into consideration the information available up to period $t$ regarding elements that in some way exert influence on the exchange rate trajectory. In turn, exchange rate risk takes into consideration the possibility of unexpected shocks to the exchange rate.

[18] Equation (10.10) shows the relation of the inflation rate to exchange rate evolution.

[19] The figure plots the average interest rate over the reference month for the sovereign bonds of each country, with a maturity of 10 years.

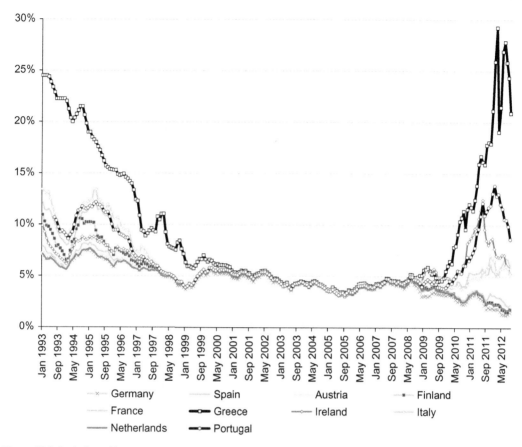

**Figure 10.1** Evolution of interest rates in Europe. *Source: European Central Bank—Eurosystem, Reference (7) on Data List in Appendix.*

Greece, Slovakia, and Slovenia. These countries benefitted from an implicit guarantee for their sovereign debt, borrowing from German credibility.

Presented with lower interest rates, governments and private agents from these countries could borrow at a lower cost, which they promptly did. Private credit increased in the European countries depicted in Figure 10.2, excepted for Germany. In Ireland, Portugal, and Spain, private credit jumped from around 100% of GDP in 1999 to over 200% by 2010. The increase was also significant for Greece and Italy: from 80−90% to over 150% of GDP over the same period. Part of this increase in indebtedness came from external sources, accumulated through current-account deficits. Between 2000 and 2007, Greece and Portugal presented an average deficit in current account of 8.1% and 9.1% of GDP, respectively. For Spain, the average current-account deficit amounted to 5.6% of GDP. Germany, on the other hand, accumulated an average current-account surplus of over 3% of GDP over the same period. To make things worse, a large part of the increased indebtedness was used to build real state, which does not increase future production capacity.

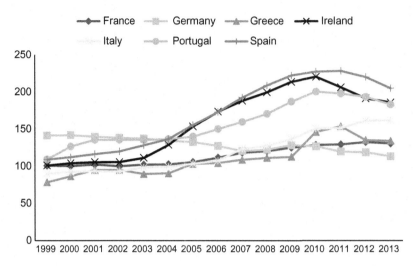

**Figure 10.2** Evolution of private credit provided by financial sector (% of GDP). *Source: World Bank, Database: World Development Indicators, Reference (8) on Data List in Appendix.*

As for the public debt, the *Stability and Growth Pact*[20] was not able to guarantee the fiscal contention of countries in the region. There was complacency in relation to fiscal disequilibria in some cases, while in others reality was other than what the official statistics presented. Greece and Italy, for instance, never met the debt/GDP ratio of 60% imposed by the pact. The final result was the excessive foreign indebtedness of those countries that benefitted from lower interest rates upon joining the euro, that is, those that had historically less credibility in regards to the conduct of their economic policies. The world financial crisis that began in 2008 exposed the fragility of the situation.[21] The scarcity of credit that followed made financing difficult and highlighted the difficulty of the European Union to deal with the crisis of its over-indebted members. In fact, original European Union regulations prohibited the rescue of countries in crisis and the financing of their debt, without there being any alternative mechanisms to deal with the eventual sovereign insolvency of one of its members.

One important difference between the European situation in the 2010 years and the Latin American in the 1980s is that the European states debt was largely denominated in euros, their own currency, while the Latin American debt was denominated in foreign currency. However, the fact of having the debt in the local currency did not help much in the European case since the countries did not have direct control over monetary policy, which is determined by the European Central Bank. One solution for a country with an independent monetary policy would be to adopt an expansionist monetary policy so that the increase in inflation reduces the real value of the government debt, sort of like a disguised *default*. The following exchange depreciation would not increase the value of the debt since it is

---

[20] For the definition of the Stability and Growth Pact, see Box 10.1.

[21] Lane (2012) presents a thorough description and analysis of the European sovereign debt crisis.

denominated in local currency. It would be the "perfect crime"! Well, almost perfect, because as with any *default*, someone must pay. In this case, all creditors would suffer a real loss, and all debtors (not only the government) would be benefitted with a reduction in the real value of their debt. There would also be the cost of inflation itself.

The creditors for Greece, Spain, and Portugal are, for the large part, financial institutions from other European countries, mainly France and Germany. Thus, whatever the solution, the Europeans are those who pay the bill. The bottom line question is if the European creditors will pay the bill in order to save the euro. Restated: Do the benefits of having the euro as the single currency in the region and the transition cost for its abandonment be higher than the cost of bailing out the indebted countries? Here is another difference in relation to Latin American three decades ago: those countries were on their own.

# Mathematical Appendix

## Solution to the Government Problem

The government optimization problem in this economy can be represented as follows:

$$\text{Max}_{\{u,\pi\}} L_i = (u_i - \bar{u}_i)^2 + \theta_i \pi_i^2$$
$$\text{Subject to: } u_i = \tilde{u}_i + \varepsilon_i - (\pi_i - \pi_i^e).$$

To solve this problem, we write the Lagrangian function as

$$\mathcal{L} = (u_i - \bar{u}_i)^2 + \theta \pi_i^2 - \lambda\{\tilde{u}_i + \varepsilon_i - (\pi_i - \pi_i^e) - u_i\}$$

where $\lambda$ is the Lagrange multiplier. The maximum point is that for which the derivatives of the Lagrangian function with respect to the choice variables, $u$ and $\pi$, and to the Lagrange multiplier, $\lambda$, are equal to zero. The first-order conditions for maximization are therefore

$$[u]: \frac{\partial \mathcal{L}}{\partial u} = 0 \Rightarrow 2(u_i - \bar{u}_i) + \lambda = 0 \Rightarrow$$
$$\lambda = -2(u_i - \bar{u}_i) \tag{10.11}$$

$$[\pi]: \frac{\partial \mathcal{L}}{\partial \pi} = 0 \Rightarrow 2\theta_i \pi_i + \lambda = 0 \Rightarrow$$
$$\lambda = -2\theta_i \pi_i \tag{10.12}$$

$$[\lambda]: \frac{\partial \mathcal{L}}{\partial \lambda} = 0 \Rightarrow -\{\tilde{u}_i + \varepsilon_i - (\pi_i - \pi_i^e) - u_i\} = 0 \Rightarrow$$
$$u_i = \tilde{u}_i + \varepsilon_i - (\pi_i - \pi_i^e) \tag{10.13}$$

Substituting Eq. (10.11) into Eq. (10.12), we obtain

$$-2(u_i - \bar{u}_i) = -2\theta_i \pi_i \Rightarrow \pi_i = \frac{u_i - \bar{u}_i}{\theta_i}. \tag{10.14}$$

Substituting Eq. (10.14) into Eq. (10.13), we arrive at $\theta_i \pi_i + u_i - \tilde{u}_i = \varepsilon_i - (\pi_i - \pi_i^e)$, and using the definition presented in the text, $k_i \equiv \tilde{u}_i - \bar{u}_i$, we arrive at Eq. (10.4):

$$\pi_i = \frac{k_i + \varepsilon_i + \pi_i^e}{1 + \theta_i}.$$

# 10.3 Exercises

## Exercise 1

In relation to exchange rate regimes, answer what the following items request:

**a.** List at least five distinct exchange rate regimes, in progressive order, beginning with a totally flexible regime and ending with a totally fixed regime. List the main characteristics of these regimes, providing examples of countries that adopted them. What are the main economic characteristics of these countries?

**b.** Research at least three countries that have changed its exchange rate regime over the last 20 years. What was the economic conjuncture of these countries when the new exchange rate regime was adopted? Compare their economic performance 10 years before and 10 years after the change. What are the main differences you can highlight?

**c.** Assuming that the equilibrium relation in the money market is given by $\frac{M_t}{P_t} = \frac{Y_t^\eta}{i_t^\epsilon}$, and using the relation of purchasing power parity and uncovered interest rate parity, find a mathematical relationship that establishes the relation between the nominal money supply and the nominal exchange rate. Consider that the level of prices and international interest rates are fixed. Use this equation to explain how the adoption of a fixed exchange rate regime affects monetary policy. (Tip: Log-linearize the referred equations.)

**d.** Suppose you are the president of a central bank in an economy that has decided to fix the domestic exchange rate. Using the equation obtained in the previous item, explain how the adoption of a fixed exchange rate regime affects monetary policy. How should the monetary policy be adjusted in response to changes in prices and the domestic output? How should the monetary policy be adjusted in response to changes in prices and international interest?

**e.** Suppose that, similarly the Eurozone, the countries that compose Mercosur decide to form a monetary union. Using the economic arguments seen in this chapter, present the pros and cons of a decision of this nature.

## Exercise 2

Consider the elements of the *impossible trinity*: (i) independent monetary policy, (ii) free capital mobility, and (iii) fixed exchange rate.

**a.** Using the concepts seen throughout this chapter and Chapter 7, explain why only two of these objectives can be simultaneously attained.

**b.** Research on the functioning of the following international monetary systems, explaining their main characteristics and countries that have adopted them:
- Gold Standard
- Bretton Woods System

**c.** How are the international monetary systems related to the impossible trinity? Explain your answer.

**d.** How is your answer to the previous item related to the factors that resulted in the break-up of said exchange rate mechanisms?

## Exercise 3

In relation to the exchange rate regimes presented throughout this chapter, answer what the following items demand:

**a.** What factors should be considered by policymakers in the choice between a fixed exchange rate regime and a floating exchange rate regime? Explain the importance of each factor in detail.

**b.** Explain how a managed exchange rate regime works. Give examples. Why did this regime become popular with industrialized countries after 1973?

**c.** Explain how a currency board works. Why was this regime adopted by some developing economies?

**d.** Explain how a country can dollarize its monetary system. How is the economy of the United States affected when a country adopts dollarization? Why did some countries adopt this regime?

## Exercise 4

This exercise deals with the choice between a fixed exchange rate regime and a floating exchange rate based on a variation of the Dornbusch model seen in Section 7.2. The equilibrium relation in the goods market and the uncovered interest rate parity are given by the following equations, respectively:

$$m_t - p_t = y_t - \lambda i_t + v_t$$
$$i_t = i_t^* + E_t\{s_{t+1} - s_t\} + \varepsilon_t,$$

where $m_t$ is the nominal money supply, $p_t$ is the level of domestic prices, $i_t$ is the nominal interest rate, $v_t$ represents a shock on the money demand, $s_t$ represents the nominal exchange rate, and $\varepsilon_t$ represents the risk premium. Both $v_t$ and $\varepsilon_t$ are shocks i.i.d., such that $E_t[v_t] = 0$ and $E_t[\varepsilon_t] = 0$. All variables used in the model are expressed in logarithmic terms. Let $w_t$ be the nominal wage, which is predetermined (and therefore constant on date $t$), established on $t-1$ in such a way as to be equal to the price level expected for period $t$, based on the set of available information on $t-1$. The aggregate economic demand is given by the following equation:

$$y_t^d = \delta(s_t + p_t^* - p_t) + g_t,$$

where $g_t$ is a shock of demand i.i.d., such that $E_t[g_t] = 0$. The aggregate supply of the economy is given as:

$$y_t^s = \theta(p_t - w_t).$$

a. Under the hypothesis that $m_t$ is fixed and that $s_t$ is floating, calculate the equilibrium values of $s_t$, and $y_t$. Further assume that $i_t^* = p_t^* = 0$.
b. Continuing within the context of the previous item, calculate the variance of output $y_t$, supposing that shocks $v_t$, $\varepsilon_t$, and $g_t$ are orthogonal.
c. Solve the model while now assuming that the exchange rate is fixed, i.e., $s_t = s$.
d. In the context of the previous item, calculate the variance of output $y_t$, assuming that shocks $v_t$, $\varepsilon_t$, and $g_t$ are orthogonal.
e. Define the random variable $\phi_t \equiv v_t - \lambda\varepsilon_t$, which can be interpreted as the financial shock that acts upon the economy. Show that when the variance of financial shocks is zero, the output variance will be lower under a floating regime than under a fixed regime. Show that when the variance of the demand shock is zero, the variance of output is lower under a fixed regime.

## Exercise 5

In 2002, the economic news reported that a group of six countries, formed by Saudi Arabia, Bahrain, the United Arab Emirates, Kuwait, Oman, and Qatar, were considering the creation of a single currency. At that time, all cited countries maintained a parity exchange rate regime with the American dollar. Their economic activity depended mainly on oil exports to the rest of the world, hence the diversification of growth and international trade sources are a recurrent concern among their political leaders. Based on this information, discuss the main criteria that should be considered by these countries to whether they should implement a common currency. What would be the main advantages of a policy of this type? What would be the main disadvantages?

## Exercise 6

Answer what the following items request:

a. Explain what the Bretton Woods system was and the reasons for its collapse.
b. Even after the end of the Bretton Woods system at the beginning of the 1970s, many Asian and Middle East countries continued tying their currencies to the American dollar. Give examples of countries that followed this type of exchange rate policy. What are the costs and benefits that these countries enjoyed by maintaining this exchange rate regime?

## Exercise 7

The incentives for a country to join a monetary union depend on the possible sources of economic shocks and the mechanisms by which such shocks will be absorbed when the country participates in the monetary union. Consider the following situations:

**a.** A country believes it will suffer expressive and frequent shocks in money demand over the next years. With everything else being constant, would this country be more inclined to join a monetary union than any other country whose money demand would be more stable over the same period of time? Explain your answer.

**b.** A country has historically been reluctant regarding the issue of population geographic mobility. With all else being constant, would this country be more inclined to join a monetary union than any other country whose population had a more flexible work force in relation to geographic mobility? Explain your answer.

**c.** How would your answer to item (b) change if the educational system in the country was qualitatively inferior to the educational system in the other countries in the monetary union? Explain.

# 11

# Political Economy of Exchange Rate Policy

**CHAPTER OUTLINE**

Economic policy decisions are guided both by economic constraints and political considerations. They can be divided into two levels. The first is the choice of the economic goal, while the second regards what policies will be used to attain it. Let us look at the first: what is the objective of the economic policy? The resources constraint and the very relation among variables demand the prioritization of some objectives in detriment to others. The government does not, for example, have sufficient administrative or financial resources to simultaneously solve problems related to education, health, or lack of housing in large metropolitan areas, which demand the ordering of priorities. Or yet, a policy to combat poverty may impair attempts to attain fiscal austerity with the goal of reducing inflationary pressure. What determines what the main economic policy objective will be?

When an acute crisis arises in some specific area, that area is automatically chosen as a priority in the formulation of economic policy. Such was the case, for example, in the exchange rate crises that ravaged several countries during the 1990s, which were generated by abrupt reversals in capital flow. In those cases, economic restrictions dictated the choice of policy focus: solving the crisis. In favorable economic situations, where there are neither imminent crises nor growing vulnerabilities, one can say that the choice of objectives is primordially political. The government bases its choices on its own preferences, while taking into consideration the political pressure exerted by groups within society, both by means of lobbies and by the voting power of the voters.

Once the objectives have been determined, the government must decide what economic policy to use in order to attain them. Going back to the example of exchange rate crises, they can, in general, be solved by exchange rate depreciation, which allows adjustment by increasing the trade balance. Alternatively, a high interest rate policy may be used to attract foreign capital, so that the increase in the financial account balances the balance of payments, keeping the exchange rate level unaltered. The impact of these policies on the different economic and social agents is quite distinct. The option for exchange rate depreciation favors, on the one hand, the export sectors and producers who compete with imported products. On the other hand, exchange rate depreciation fuels inflation, especially harming citizens at lower income levels who have less access to indexation mechanisms in the financial market. It is clear that political factors will have a role in this choice, while respecting economic constraints.

The study of the political motivations for exchange rate policy is divided into three parts. First, the distributive aspects of the exchange rate are analyzed, when the choice of exchange rate level is based on the conflicting interests of different sectors of the economy. The second part studies exchange rate policy as signal of the degree of government competence and the resulting electoral cycle. Finally, fiscal policy is the focus. Knowing that fiscal policy impacts the equilibrium real exchange rate, as described in Chapter 5, the political determinants of fiscal policy in a democratic regime are analyzed.

## 11.1 Distributive Impacts of the Real Exchange Rate

Exchange rate policy can have distributive effects either by a direct or indirect channel. The direct channel is due to the fact of the real exchange rate being related to the relative price between tradable and nontradable goods, while the indirect channel is related to the impact of nominal exchange rate variations on the inflation rate, especially in an economy with price indexation mechanisms.

The analysis performed here presupposes that the policymaker possesses instruments to influence the real and nominal exchange rates of the economy, which is true, at least in the short run. Chapters 6 and 7 analyzed the mechanisms by which the monetary and fiscal policies can affect the nominal and real exchange rates. We begin with the nominal exchange rate. The nominal exchange rate is the price of foreign currency. As with any price, its value is determined by the conditions of supply and demand. The government has some economic policy instruments at it disposition that can alter these variables. For example, the sale of foreign currency by the government, based on its stock of international reserves, increases the supply of foreign currency in the domestic market, which leads to a reduction in its price, that is, to the appreciation of the domestic exchange rate. Also, a higher interest rate on public bonds increases the supply of foreign currency in the domestic market, given that it renders domestic bonds more attractive to international investors, who should trade their foreign currency for domestic currency in order to purchase them.

As to the real exchange rate, it is related to the relative price between tradable and nontradable goods, as described in Chapter 5. There are basically two ways for the government to influence it. First, by means of manipulating the variables that affect the relative supply and demand in these two sectors, such as, for example, the level of government spending. An increase in spending in the nontradable goods, such as spending in services, increases relative demand for these goods, leading to an increase in their relative price, that is, an appreciation of the real exchange rate. Second, a policy that alters the nominal exchange rate, as discussed in the paragraph above, can also have an impact on its real level, if prices are sticky. When the nominal exchange rate changes and prices do not automatically adjust, the real exchange rate also changes. In fact, there is strong evidence that the nominal and real exchange rates accompany each other, at least in the short run.

We will begin with the analysis of the impact of the real exchange rate on the relative income in the tradable and nontradable sectors. Following, we will discuss the distributive effect of exchange rate policy by means of its impact on inflation.

## 11.1.1 Producers of Tradable Goods Versus Nontradable Goods

The real exchange rate is a function of the relative price between tradable and nontradable goods, which in turn is associated to the relative income between the production sectors of those two types of goods. A simple model of a small, open economy can represent the conflict of interests between these two sectors in the economy. To simplify, let us assume that, for each period, each citizen in the economy receives an endowment of one type of good, either tradable or nontradable, depending on the sector to which they belong. Citizens then choose their consumption basket, subject to a budget constraint that establishes that total consumption cannot exceed their income. We assume that consumer preference can be represented by a Cobb–Douglas utility function, as in Eq. (5.11), which we use here in logarithm[1]:

$$U(C_T, C_N) \equiv (1 - \alpha)\ln C_T + \alpha \ln C_N, \tag{11.1}$$

where $C_j$ is the amount of good $j$ consumed, for $j \in \{T, N\}$, given that $T$ represents the tradable good and $N$ the nontradable.

The budget constraint for the consumer from the tradable sector is represented by

$$C_T + p_N C_N \leq Y_T,$$

---

[1] A strictly increasing function of a utility function represents the same preferences of the original utility function. Therefore, the logarithm of the Cobb–Douglas utility function also represents preferences where the share of income spent on each of the goods is constant.

while in the other sector, the budget constraint is

$$C_T + p_N C_N \leq p_N Y_N,$$

where we take the price of tradable goods as numeraire, i.e., $p_T = 1$, so that $p_N$ is the relative price between nontradable and tradable goods.

The real exchange rate is inversely related to the relative price of nontradable goods as indicated in Eq. (5.2), which we repeat here:

$$Q = \left( \frac{p_N^*/p_T^*}{p_N/p_T} \right)^\alpha. \tag{11.2}$$

Assuming that the relative price of nontradables is constant in the rest of the world, choosing the unit of measure in such a way that $(p_N^*/p_T^* = 1)$, and given $p_T = 1$, Eq. (11.2) can be written as

$$Q = \left( \frac{1}{p_N} \right)^\alpha. \tag{11.3}$$

Given the prices and endowments, we can find the maximum utility reached by each consumer by substituting their optimum consumption choices in the utility function. We can then obtain their *indirect utility function*, which represents the utility obtained by the consumer as a function of the relative price of nontradables. For citizens in the tradable sector, the indirect utility function has the form of[2]

$$V_T = h_T + \ln Q,$$

and, for the nontradable sector

$$V_N = h_N - \frac{1-\alpha}{\alpha} \ln Q,$$

where $h_j \equiv \alpha \ln \alpha + (1-\alpha)\ln(1-\alpha) + \ln Y_j$, for $j = T,N$.

The two previous indirect utility functions imply

$$\frac{\partial V_T(Q)}{\partial Q} = \frac{1}{Q} > 0 \quad \text{and} \tag{11.4}$$

$$\frac{\partial V_N(Q)}{\partial Q} = -\left( \frac{1-\alpha}{\alpha} \right) \frac{1}{Q} < 0. \tag{11.5}$$

This means that **citizens in the tradable goods sector attain a higher utility with a more depreciated exchange rate, while citizens in the nontradable sector prefer a more**

---

[2] The derivation of the following equations is developed in detail in the Mathematical Appendix for this chapter.

**appreciated exchange rate**. An appreciated exchange rate is associated with a higher relative price for nontradable goods, which implies greater purchasing power for the citizen that produces these goods (or, in the case of our simplified model, the citizen who receives an endowment of these goods). Producers of tradable goods, in turn, have greater purchasing power when the exchange rate is more depreciated.

We now move on to the government choice in relation to the level of the real exchange rate. To simplify the analysis, we will disregard which instruments the government uses to affect the real exchange rate. We assume that the government directly chooses the real exchange rate level, within given limits established by economic restrictions, that is, we assume the government chooses $Q$, $Q \in [\underline{Q}, \overline{Q}]$.[3] If the economic policy, in this case the real exchange rate, were chosen by a benevolent policymaker, in other words, a government whose only objective was the welfare of the citizens, the chosen exchange rate would be that which would maximize social welfare. Social welfare, which aggregates the welfare of all citizens in the economy, is usually measured by an weighted average of the citizens' utility, with the share of each type of citizen in society used as weights, as in

$$W(Q) = \gamma V_N(Q) + V_T(Q), \tag{11.6}$$

where $\gamma \equiv \frac{n}{1-n}$, and $n$ is the share of citizens belonging to the nontradable sector.

Does the government prefer a more appreciated or more depreciated exchange rate? In mathematical terms, the answer is in the derivative of the welfare function with respect to the real exchange rate, i.e.,

$$\frac{\partial W(Q)}{\partial Q} = \gamma \frac{\partial V_N(Q)}{\partial Q} + \frac{\partial V_T(Q)}{\partial Q} = \left[1 - \gamma\left(\frac{1-\alpha}{\alpha}\right)\right]\frac{1}{Q},$$

which implies that

$$\frac{\partial W(Q)}{\partial Q} = \begin{cases} \leq 0 & \text{for } \gamma \geq \dfrac{\alpha}{1-\alpha} \\[2mm] > 0 & \text{for } \gamma < \dfrac{\alpha}{1-\alpha} \end{cases}.$$

Therefore, the answer to this question depends on how society is divided between these two sectors. When the group of citizens belonging to the nontradable sector is sufficiently large, the government will choose a more appreciated exchange rate, $\underline{Q}$, and when this group

---

[3] One should keep in mind that the real exchange rate is always associated to the relative price that balances the tradable and nontradable markets. The government policy instrument should be a variable that affects this equilibrium relative price, that is, that affects the relative supply and demand between tradable and nontradable goods. Bonomo and Terra (2005), for example, suppose that to manipulate the equilibrium real exchange rate, the government taxes the tradable sector and spends on the nontradable goods sector.

is small, the chosen exchange rate will be more depreciated, $\overline{Q}$. Therefore, the exchange rate chosen by benevolent policymaker $Q^b$, will be

$$
Q^b = \begin{cases} \overline{Q} & \text{for } \gamma \leq \dfrac{\alpha}{1-\alpha} \\[2ex] \underline{Q} & \text{for } \gamma > \dfrac{\alpha}{1-\alpha} \end{cases} . \tag{11.7}
$$

**By taking into consideration political issues in selecting policy, policymakers cease being merely benevolent and add other elements to their choice.** Of course, the policymaker continues to be concerned with the well-being of the population, as represented in the welfare function in Eq. (11.6), but additional variables come into consideration. The president, for example, may be concerned with reelection and be aware that economic policies chosen prior to elections may, under certain circumstances, be liable to affect the probability of reelection. Alternatively, a government that does not enjoy a majority in congress should form alliances, and the possibility of forming such alliances may depend on the economic policy chosen. Or, **some sectors of the economy may form *lobbies* and offer benefits to the government for a policy bias in their favor.** Such benefits can be perfectly legal and in keeping with democratic rules, such as campaign contributions, or conversely illicit, such as bribes and other forms of corruption. Given the distributive character of the exchange rate, the elements of economic policy considered will essentially affect the weight given to the nontradables sector in the government choice of policy. Hence, the government chooses the level of real exchange rate so as to maximize the function:

$$
W(Q) = \gamma^p V_N(Q) + V_T(Q),
$$

where $\gamma^p$ is the new relative weight attributed to welfare of citizens in the nontradable sector, now taking the political factors into consideration.

Lobby action can alter the relative weight of sectors in the government's objective function when faced with the offer of private benefits in exchange for an economic policy biased in favor of the lobby group.[4] Benefits received by the government can take various forms. They could be financial contributions to election campaigns, the policymaker could receive future benefits such as, for example, being part of the administrative council for lobby groups when no longer in office, or, simply, the lobby group can make financial transfers to members of the government as a form of corruption.

These agreements tend to be secret and there are no legal instruments to force each of the parts to fulfill what was agreed upon. The success of the agreement depends on factors such as mutual trust between the parts and the nature of the professional and social interaction of the persons involved over time, which serves to discipline the actions of the participants in cases where they cannot rely on legal support. Nevertheless, agreements may be broken, either for lack of compliance from one the parties, or because information leaks to

---

[4] See Bonomo and Terra (2005) and Bonomo and Terra (2010).

the public, at high cost to government popularity. When deciding whether to accept such an agreement, policymakers must contrast the possible gains, when the agreement is fulfilled, with the costs, in the case of failure. When the policymaker attributes a sufficiently high probability of success to it, they enter into agreement, and favor the lobby group with their economic policy.

It is reasonable to assume that lobbyists come from the tradable goods sector, which is composed mainly of the industry and agriculture. In industry, there are oligopolies where it is easier to organize pressure groups, solving the problem of free riders, and where individual gains are sufficiently high to make the lobby effort worth the while. Parts of the agricultural sectors, especially those involved with exports, have analogous characteristics. This leads us to assume that, in our simplified economic model, the tradable goods sector organizes itself to lobby the government.

To further simplify, we assume that there are two types of policymakers: those that are *close* to lobbyists and those that are *distant*. For the policymakers close to lobbyists, the possibility of failure of an agreement between them is very small, due to their tight relation. Hence, there are few if any impediments to forming an agreement. Consequently, this type of policymaker will be co-opted by the lobby group. The *distant* will not accept an agreement with the lobbyist because they do not see a sufficiently high probability of success. In such a situation, $\gamma^{\text{cl}} < \gamma^{\text{dist}}$, where $\gamma^{\text{cl}}$ is the weight attributed to the nontradable sector by policymakers *close* to the lobby group and $\gamma^{\text{dist}}$ is that attributed by policymakers *distant* from the lobbyists.

We also assume that $\gamma^{\text{cl}} > \frac{\alpha}{1-\alpha}$ and $\gamma^{\text{dist}} \leq \frac{\alpha}{1-\alpha}$. According to Eq. (11.7), this means that the policymaker *close* to the lobby group attributes a high weight to the tradable sector welfare, and due to this chooses a more depreciated real exchange rate. On the other hand, policymaker that is *distant* from the lobby favors the nontradable sector, choosing a more appreciated exchange rate.

In a relatively closed economy, such as the Brazilian, the majority of the population belongs to the nontradable sector. This major portion of the population would always like to elect politicians who are *distant* from lobby groups. However, for the general public, it is difficult to identify exactly the degree of proximity between lobby groups and government. **Before election, voters observe the government economic policy and, based on this observation, try to deduce the type a policymaker is: either *close* or *distant* from lobbyists.** Conscious of voter deductions, the government in power will choose an economic policy that favors the probability of their reelection. If the policymaker is *close* to lobbyists, they will choose a policy that does not favor the lobbyists in an attempt to hide their proximity. Analogously, *distant* type policymakers will favor nontradables even more in order to make their distance from lobbyists clear. **The result will be an exchange rate cycle revolving around the elections: the real exchange rate will tend to be more appreciated before elections than after** (Box 11.1).[5]

---

[5] Bonomo and Terra (2010) present an asymmetric information model where the choice of economic policy serves as a sign for the type of policymaker. The model is applied to a variety of contexts, including that of exchange rate policy.

---

**BOX 11.1 EXCHANGE RATE ELECTORAL CYCLES IN PRACTICE**

There are many empirical studies that document exchange rate cycle trends around elections. Frieden et al. (2001) identify an exchange rate electoral cycle in a study based on 26 Latin American and Caribbean countries, and Pascó-Fonte and Ghezzi (2001) do the same for Peru. In a study on Brazil, Bonomo and Terra (1999) analyzed the misalignment of the real exchange rate in relation to its equilibrium value in order to study fluctuations of the real exchange rate that cannot be explained simply by economic variables. Two distinct regimes were observed: one overvalued and another undervalued. Empirical evidence shows that the probability of being in an overvalued regime is higher prior to elections, while the probability of an undervalued regime increases in periods after elections.

Blomberg et al. (2005), in turn, focus on the choice of exchange rate regime. They show that, among the Latin American economies, those possessing a larger tradables sector have a lower probability of maintaining a fixed exchange rate. This result agrees with the idea that the tradables sector can organize into lobbies to pressure government for policies that lead to a more depreciated exchange rate. Given that inflation is usually prevalent in the region, a fixed exchange rate is invariably associated with a tendency toward real exchange rate appreciation. Consequently, a more flexible exchange rate is less subject to overappreciation. When the tradables sector is large, the government can become hostage to the sector's interests, resulting in more flexible exchange rate regimes.

Investigating the situation in East Asian countries, Huang and Terra (2014) encountered evidence of an electoral cycle exchange rate opposite to that found among Latin American economies: in East Asian economies, the exchange rate tends to be more depreciated before elections and appreciated after. They show that electoral cycle of exchange rates, both in Latin America and East Asia, can be explained by a model that includes political preference variables. The difference between the two regions is the identity of the median voter: in Latin America, the median voter is associated with the nontradable sector, while in the more open economies of East Asia, they belong to the tradable sector.

---

## 11.1.2 The Trade-Off Between External Competitiveness and Inflation Fighting

Another important aspect to be taken into consideration in relation to exchange rate policy is its impact on the rate of inflation. Nominal depreciation is responsible for raising the price of tradable goods. If there are indexation mechanisms in the economy, the increase in prices translates, at least partially, into a higher inflation rate. The impact of nominal depreciation on inflation, known as *pass-through*, depends on variables such as the degree of openness of the economy and existing indexation mechanisms.

The previous section established the distributive character of the exchange rate due to its relation to the relative price between tradable and nontradable goods. **This section adds another element to the analysis: the impact of exchange rate policy on inflation, which has its own distributive impact.** Individuals with access to financial markets have a wider array of indexation mechanisms at their disposal. In general, low-income citizens have less access to the financial market and, consequently, sustain greater losses due to inflation.

The previous model showed that citizens from the nontradables sector would prefer a more appreciated exchange rate. Adding the cost of inflation only increases their preference for an appreciated exchange rate. As to citizens from the tradable goods sector, on the one hand they prefer a more depreciated exchange rate due to its impact on the relative price of what they produce. On the other hand, depreciation is also costly due to its perverse effect on inflation. Whether they prefer a more depreciated exchange rate or not depends on which of the two effects is more important. We can represent this situation with some small modifications to the model.

To capture the impact of exchange rate depreciation on inflation, we will, this time, conduct the analysis in a two-period environment. Citizen preferences correspond to those in Eq. (11.1), however in two periods, as in

$$U(C_{T1}, C_{T2}, C_{N1}, C_{N2}) \equiv (1 - \alpha)\ln C_{T1} + \alpha \ln C_{N1} + \beta[(1 - \alpha)\ln C_{T2} + \alpha \ln C_{N2}],$$

where $\beta \in (0, 1)$ is, as always, the intertemporal discount rate.

Budget constraints are also modified to incorporate the impact of inflation on welfare. An important source of cost from inflation for the consumer, that I wish to capture in the model, refers to the fact that they receive their wage at the beginning of the month to make their purchases over that time period. As time goes by, inflation reduces the purchasing power of the income received. In a high inflation period, this represents a substantial loss for the consumer. One solution would be to make all purchases as soon as the wage is received. However, this is not always possible. It is difficult to know exactly what goods will be necessary during the period, besides the need for perishable goods that, by their very nature, cannot be stocked. Another solution would be to resort to the financial market, investing in assets that have a rate of return that accompanies inflation. However, there is no guarantee that assets of this nature are available or even if their supply is sufficient to allow the complete compensation of damages caused by inflation. Whatever the case, it is not possible for the consumer to completely protect their wage purchasing power in an inflationary environment.

To capture this situation, let us assume that individuals each period must sell their endowment before purchasing their consumption basket. They have access to an indexation mechanism, albeit incomplete: their income is readjusted only to a fraction of inflation. To simplify, without compromising our analysis, we also assume that their budget must be balanced for each period, that is, there are no mechanisms to transfer income between periods. The budget constraint for each period, $t \in \{1, 2\}$, can be represented by

$$p_{Tt}C_{Tt} + p_{Nt}C_{Nt} \leq p_{Tt-1}Y_T\pi_t^\delta,$$

for the citizen in the tradable goods sector, and

$$p_{Tt}C_{Tt} + p_{Nt}C_{Nt} \leq p_{Nt-1}Y_N\pi_t^\delta,$$

for the nontradable goods sector. $Y_j$ is the endowment received each period for each individual in sector $j$, $j \in \{T, N\}$, $p_{jt}$ is the price of the sector $j$ good in period $t$, and $\pi_t \equiv \frac{P_t}{P_{t-1}}$ is the inflation rate, that is, the ratio between the price indexes in $t$ and $t - 1$.

Note that the endowment is evaluated at the previous period prices, and $\delta$, $\delta \in (0,1)$ represent the fraction of inflation to which the income is readjusted, which in turn is associated to the fact that the financial market in this economy does not have instruments capable of providing complete protection against inflation. The higher the value of $\delta$, the better the indexation mechanism used by the individual to protect their purchasing power. To simplify, we assume that all individuals have access to the same indexation mechanism, so that $\delta$ is the same for all.

As in the previous model, we calculate the citizen indirect utility function, which shows us their preferences in relation to the policy adopted by the government. The indirect utility function for an individual from the tradables sector is represented by[6]

$$V_T(Q_t, \pi_t) = \overline{h}_T + \ln Q_0 - (1 - \delta)\ln \pi_1 + \beta[\ln Q_1 - (1 - \delta)\ln \pi_2], \qquad (11.8)$$

where $\overline{h}_T \equiv (1 + \beta)[\alpha \ln \alpha + (1 - \alpha)\ln(1 - \alpha) + \ln Y_T]$. Using the real exchange rate definition in Eq. (11.2) and maintaining the assumption that we made in the previous section that international prices are such that $(p_N^*/p_T^*) = 1$, we have that $Q_t = \left(\frac{p_{T_t}}{p_{N_t}}\right)^\alpha$.

Equation (11.8) shows that, **on the one hand, citizens in the tradable sector prefer a more depreciated exchange rate since it means a higher relative price for the tradable good.** On the other hand, they prefer low inflation since inflation reduces their purchasing power. As we will see ahead, a more depreciated exchange rate is associated with higher inflation. Therefore, **by its indirect effect on inflation, exchange rate depreciation also has a negative effect on the welfare of individuals in the tradable goods sector.** Notice that inflation would not have any impact on the welfare of this individual if they had access to a perfect indexation mechanism for their endowment, that is, as with $\delta = 1$.

In the nontradable sector, the indirect utility function is given by

$$V_N(Q_t, \pi_t) = \overline{h}_N - \frac{1 - \alpha}{\alpha}\ln Q_0 - (1 - \delta)\ln \pi_1 - \beta\left[\frac{1 - \alpha}{\alpha}\ln Q_1 + (1 - \delta)\ln \pi_2\right], \qquad (11.9)$$

where $\overline{h}_N \equiv (1 + \beta)[\alpha \ln \alpha + (1 - \alpha)\ln(1 - \alpha) + \ln Y_N]$. According to this function, **a nontradable goods producer prefers a more appreciated exchange rate, both by its direct effect on the value of their output, and by the fact that the appreciated exchange rate implies a lower rate of inflation**, as we will see next.

Two heroic assumptions are made to represent, in a simple way, how exchange rate variations affect inflation. First, we assume that there is constant inflation on the price of nontradable goods: $\frac{p_{N_t}}{p_{N_{t-1}}} = \eta$. Second, we assume that this is a small economy in terms of international markets and that international prices are constant, so that price variation in the

---

[6] The derivation of the following equation can be seen in detail in the Mathematical Appendix at the end of this chapter.

tradables sector is proportional to the nominal exchange rate variation, i.e., $\frac{p_{Tt}}{p_{Tt-1}} = \frac{S_t}{S_{t-1}}$, where $S_t$ is the nominal exchange rate. Given our assumption of Cobb–Douglas preferences, the price index is given in Eq. (5.1):

$$P_t = p_{Nt}^{\alpha} p_{Tt}^{1-\alpha}.$$

Given the price index, the two hypotheses define the following relation between the inflation rate and the real exchange rate variation:[7]

$$\pi_t = \eta \left( \frac{Q_t}{Q_{t-1}} \right)^{\frac{1-\alpha}{\alpha}}. \tag{11.10}$$

Real exchange rate depreciation over time $(Q_t > Q_{t-1})$ is associated with a higher rate of inflation, and the impact of the exchange rate on inflation is proportional to the relative share of the tradable good in consumption.

Seeking to simplify the analysis, we assume that the only choice variable by the government is the current period exchange rate. We then assume that the real exchange rate for the previous period, $t = 0$, is an exogenous variable, that is, we take its value as a given. We also assume that in the following period, $t = 2$, the government will repeat the exchange rate decision for the current period: $Q_2 = Q_1$. With these additional hypotheses, the indirect utility function, in Eqs. (11.8) and (11.9), can be rewritten as[8]

$$V_T(Q_1) = \overline{k}_T + \left[ \frac{\beta}{1-\alpha} - (1-\delta) \right] (1-\alpha) \ln Q_1, \quad \text{and} \tag{11.11}$$

$$V_N(Q_1) = \overline{k}_N - \left[ \frac{\beta}{\alpha} + (1-\delta) \right] (1-\alpha) \ln Q_1, \tag{11.12}$$

where constants $\overline{k}_T$ and $\overline{k}_N$ are functions of the constant model parameters, given by

$$\overline{k}_T \equiv \overline{h}_T - (1+\beta)(1-\delta) \ln \eta + \left[ (1-\delta) + \frac{1}{1-\alpha} \right] (1-\alpha) \ln Q_0, \quad \text{and}$$

$$\overline{k}_N \equiv \overline{h}_N - (1+\beta)(1-\delta) \ln \eta + \left[ (1-\delta) - \frac{1}{\alpha} \right] (1-\alpha) \ln Q_0.$$

Do individuals prefer a more appreciated or more depreciated exchange rate? Well, that depends on the individual. The derivative of the indirect utility functions

---

[7] The derivation of the equation is in the Mathematical Appendix at the end of this chapter.
[8] The derivation of the equation is in the Mathematical Appendix at the end of this chapter.

(Eqs. (11.11) and (11.12)) with respect to the real exchange rate for each type of individual is given by

$$\frac{\partial V_T(Q_1)}{\partial Q_1} = \left[\frac{\beta}{1-\alpha} - (1-\delta)\right]\frac{(1-\alpha)}{Q_1} \quad \text{and} \tag{11.13}$$

$$\frac{\partial V_N(Q_1)}{\partial Q_1} = \left[-\frac{\beta}{\alpha} - (1-\delta)\right]\frac{(1-\alpha)}{Q_1}. \tag{11.14}$$

The first term in the brackets of the two previous derivatives refers to the impact of the real exchange rate on the income of individuals and corresponds to the effect discussed in the previous section, captured by derivatives (11.4) and (11.5). Due to this effect, citizens in the tradable goods sector prefer a more depreciated exchange rate, while, for those in the nontradable, an appreciated exchange rate is better. The second term within the brackets, in turn, regards the effect of the exchange rate by its impact on inflation. Exchange rate depreciation increases inflation, which harms all individuals, independent of what sector they belong to.

The first term in the brackets of the two previous derivatives refers to the impact of the real exchange rate on the income of individuals and corresponds to the effect discussed in the previous section, captured by derivatives (11.4) and (11.5). Due to this effect, citizens in the tradable goods sector prefer a more depreciated exchange rate, while, for those in the nontradable, an appreciated exchange rate is better. The second term within the brackets, in turn, regards the effect of the exchange rate by its impact on inflation. Exchange rate depreciation increases inflation, which harms all individuals, independent of what sector they belong to.

Therefore, individuals in the nontradables sector prefer a more appreciated exchange rate both by its direct effect on income and by its indirect effect on inflation. As to those citizens in the tradables sector, their preference in relation to exchange rate depends on which exchange rate effect is strongest: the effect on income, captured by $\frac{\beta}{Q_1}$, or the indirect effect on inflation, in $-\frac{(1-\delta)(1-\alpha)}{Q_1}$. They will continue to prefer a depreciated exchange rate when $\frac{\beta}{1-\alpha} > 1 - \delta$, that is, when there is sufficiently high protection against inflation, when they give a high value $\beta$ to the future, or when the share of tradable goods in expenditures, $1-\alpha$, is low. We will assume this is the case.

Alternatively, we could have considered a situation where, in the tradables sector, there were two groups of individuals with different levels of access to indexation mechanisms used to protect their income purchasing power. More specifically, the tradables sector would be split into two groups, rich and poor, where the rich would be able, by means of the financial market, to receive protection for their income against inflation, and who continue to prefer a depreciated exchange rate. The poor, in turn, would not have access to the financial market, remaining vulnerable to the nefarious effects of inflation on their purchasing power. They would prefer an appreciated exchange rate accompanied by low inflation.

As we did in the previous model, we assume that the government chooses the real exchange rate, restricted by the limits established by economic conditions, which results in a choice between an interval: $Q_1 \in [\underline{Q}, \overline{Q}]$.[9] The choice is made in such a way as to maximize the government utility function, which weights the welfare of each group according to government political motivations. The government objective function is represented by a weighted average of the welfare for each type of individual, where the weights depend on government preferences, as in

$$W(Q_1) = \gamma^P v_N(Q_1) + v_T(Q_1). \tag{11.15}$$

[9] More precisely, in this model, the government will choose the nominal exchange rate that, given the preestablished price trajectory, results in a given real exchange rate value.

The derivative of the government welfare function (Eq. (11.15)) with respect to the real exchange rate, $Q$, indicates if the government prefers a more appreciated or depreciated exchange rate. It is given by

$$\frac{\partial W(Q_1)}{\partial Q_1} = \gamma^P \frac{\partial v_N(Q_1)}{\partial Q_1} + \frac{\partial v_T(Q_1)}{\partial Q_1} = \left\{ \frac{\beta}{1-\alpha} - \left[ \gamma^P \frac{\beta}{\alpha} + (1+\gamma^P)(1-\delta) \right] \right\} \frac{(1-\alpha)}{Q_1}.$$

If relative weight $\gamma^P$, attributed to citizens in the nontradable goods sector, is sufficiently high, the government will choose the more appreciated exchange rate, $\underline{Q}$. On the contrary, the chosen exchange rate will be more depreciated, $\overline{Q}$. More specifically, we can show that the exchange rate chosen by policymaker type $P$, $Q^P$, is

$$Q_1^P = \begin{cases} \overline{Q} & \text{for } \gamma^P \leq \overline{\gamma} \\ \underline{Q} & \text{for } \gamma^P > \overline{\gamma} \end{cases}, \tag{11.16}$$

where $\overline{\gamma} \equiv \frac{\frac{\beta}{1-\alpha} - (1-\delta)}{\frac{\beta}{\alpha} + (1-\delta)}$ is the cut-off point for the relative weight given to the nontradables sector from which point the government chooses an appreciated exchange rate. This cut-off point is lower in comparison with the cut-off point in Eq. (11.7) from the previous model, where inflation was not considered. It makes sense since the effect of the exchange rate on inflation makes exchange rate depreciation more costly. More specifically, if the weight attributed to the nontradables sector, $\gamma^P$, is situated in the interval $\left( \frac{\frac{\beta}{1-\alpha} - (1-\delta)}{\frac{\beta}{\alpha} + (1-\delta)}, \frac{\alpha}{1-\alpha} \right)$, the government will choose the depreciated exchange rate if the effect of inflation were not considered (Eq. (11.16)), and an appreciated exchange rate when inflation is taken into account (Eq. (11.7)). Notice that if there is perfect indexation, $\delta = 1$, the optimal exchange rate level choice will be according to Eq. (11.16) and will be exactly equal to that established by Eq. (11.7).

With respect to what determines the relative weight attributed to the nontradables sector, $\gamma^P$, let us look at the difference between a democratic and dictatorial regime to understand the important transition that occurred in Latin American countries during the 1980s. In a democratic regime, the government is concerned with pleasing its voter base if it wants to remain in power. In a dictatorship, on the other hand, the government is more concerned with the interests of groups that help maintain them in power.

With a transition to democracy, public opinion certainly came to hold greater weight in government decisions. To be reelected, or to elect your successor, the government needs to count on the support of the population majority. When the larger part of the population belongs to the nontradable sector, it would be expected that more weight would be attributed to the nontradables sector in a democratic regime than in a dictatorship. For the same reason, with democracy, the weight given to the welfare of the less favored portion of the population should also be higher. In general, less favored individuals have less access to indexation mechanisms and are more harmed by inflation. In the terms of our model, this is represented by $\gamma^{\text{dictatorship}} < \gamma^{\text{democracy}}$. **The result would be, on average, a more appreciated real exchange rate in democracy than in dictatorship** (Box 11.2).

## BOX 11.2 BRAZILIAN EXCHANGE RATE POLICY VIEWED BY ITS DISTRIBUTIVE IMPACT

From the beginning of the military dictatorship in Brazil, in 1964, up to the first oil shock, in 1974, the exchange rate was kept, on average, appreciated within the favorable international context. Concomitantly, the implemented wage policy guaranteed low real wages, so as to maintain competiveness in the export sector. Therefore, even with an appreciated exchange rate, domestic industry was the main beneficiary from the set of economic policies.

However, government did not promote the necessary external adjustments when faced with the 1974 oil shock. Instead, taking advantage of the high international liquidity on international financial markets, it increased its foreign debt to counter the deficit in current account resulting from the deterioration in its terms of trade. Bonomo and Terra (2001) argue that the fact of the government not implementing an immediate adjustment in the economy was due to the desire for political legitimacy by those in power. The Armed Forces were divided between a moderate group, to which President Ernesto Geisel (1974–1979) belonged, and a hardline group, associated with his predecessor, Emílio Garrastazu Médici (1969–1974), president during the economic "miracle" period. The desire for political legitimacy would have led the president to prioritize fighting inflation to the detriment of the balance of payments balance.

The exchange rate was depreciated after the second oil shock in 1979, and more intensely depreciated after the 1982 external debt crisis. Between 1981 and 1985, the accumulated exchange rate depreciation reached 100%. Exchange rate depreciation, allied to price indexing mechanisms existent at the time, led to an increase in the inflation rate. With the return of democracy in 1985, the period of inflation fighting began.

Between 1985 and 1994, the exchange rate cycles can be explained by the trade-off between inflation and external competitiveness. The decade was marked by a series of price stabilization plans that, in one way or another, used the exchange rate as a nominal anchor. Since price stabilization did not happen overnight, the policy generated an appreciation of the real exchange rate, deteriorating external competiveness. Eventually, inflation returned, the plan was abandoned, and the exchange rate depreciated. Some of these exchange rate stabilization plan/depreciation cycles coincided with the election period, as what happened with the first of them, the Cruzado Plan (Plano Cruzado). It was launched on February 28, 1986, a few months before the gubernatorial and legislative elections set for November of that year. The plan resulted in an appreciation of the exchange rate before elections, and, just one week after elections, the government kicked off a series of daily exchange rate depreciations that caused a depreciation of the real exchange rate.

It is interesting to note that the electoral cycle of price stabilization with an exchange rate anchor is not a uniquely Brazilian phenomenon. Using data from developing countries, Aisen (2007) shows that, on average, using the exchange rate as nominal anchor is implemented in price stabilization plans when they are adopted in the period prior to elections, while in other periods a monetary anchor is used. As Calvo and Vegh (1999) show, the price stabilization plans with an exchange rate anchor applied in Latin America and Israel during the 1990s caused, in general, an initial growth in GDP and private consumption. The coincidence of price stabilization plans with electoral periods is, therefore, not strange.

Given that the great majority of stabilization plans based on exchange rate anchors failed, we can ask ourselves why, after all, they were repeatedly used. Alfaro (2002) proposes an explanation for the implementation of these short-term plans based on the distributive impacts of the real

(Continued)

BOX 11.2 (CONTINUED)

exchange rate appreciation. According to the author, the benefit generated for nontradable goods producers could support the implementation of the plan, even though temporary.

Another interesting case to be considered in this light is that of the Fernando Collor de Mello government, in Brazil. Immediately after his inauguration, Fernando Collor de Mello instituted a radical stabilization plan that, besides using the exchange rate as a nominal anchor, causing its real appreciation, froze all economic financial assets. In the end, inflation was not controlled and exchange rate policy maintained the exchange rate, on average, appreciated during his government. The result, however, was a combination of policies that did not please any of the economic groups identified in the models presented. Tradable goods producers were dissatisfied with the appreciated exchange rate and even citizens in the nontradable goods sector, those with less resources to protect against inflation, suffered at the hands of the out of control inflation. The president was eventually impeached under allegations of corruption. Clearly, this is a simplification, given that there were also other factors and policies that displeased potential presidential supporters.

Coalition governments have governed Brazil since 1993. The government must maintain the unity of a diverse parliamentary base, and, as such, offers benefits and advantages to those members of the coalition. The more popular the government, the easier it is to convince parliamentarians to support it. Support can then be acquired at a reduced cost. Coalition governments, therefore, are expected to show greater concern in maintaining their popularity high, even in nonelectoral periods. The result is a constant prioritization of interests belonging to the most numerous population groups, which include low-income citizens and nontradable goods producers.

The reaction to the international currency crises that marked the 1990s can be seen as a sign of this prioritization. During the decade, there were the 1994 Mexican, 1997 Asian, 1998 Russian, and 2001 Argentine crises, just to mention the most important. This turbulence in the international markets caused, to a greater or lesser degree, a reduction in financial flow to Brazil. Different than what occurred at the beginning of the 1980s, the answer to exchange rate pressure in the 1990s was a policy of high interest rate policy to attract international capital. With this, exchange rate depreciation was avoided and the stabilization of prices preserved. Such policy favors the poorer citizens and those in the nontradable goods sector, in detriment to those in the tradable goods sector, thereby aiding the government in its constant quest for popularity.

## 11.2 Exchange Rate as an Indicator of Competence

It is argued that the government can use the exchange rate level as an indicator of its competence. The explanation is based on the impact of exchange rate depreciation on the seigniorage tax collected by the government.[10] **The more competent the government, the less the need to collect taxes to offer its services. If, ultimately, exchange rate depreciation translates into tax collection for the government, the more competent government depreciates their currency less.**[11]

---

[10] Seigniorage is government revenue resultant from the emission and maintenance of the stock of currency in circulation.

[11] Stein and Streb (2004) and Stein et al. (2005) explore this channel.

The complete model that shows how the exchange rate can be a sign of competence is quite complex and its explanation deviates from the scope of this chapter. Alternatively, I will present only a part of its basic framework necessary to understand its mechanism. The fundamental element in the model is how exchange rate depreciation affects the government *seigniorage* revenue.

We assume that consumption should be made in cash, so that the value of consumption cannot exceed the amount of money held by the consumer, i.e.,

$$M_t \geq P_t C_t,$$

where $M_t$ is demand for money and $P_t C_t$ is the total expenditure on consumption. This restriction, known as the *cash-in-advance* constraint, is, actually, a commonly used method to justify the demand for money by individuals.

By retaining cash, however, consumers forfeit receiving interest that would result from the purchase of government bonds. From the government point of view, this lost income translates into *seigniorage* revenue, $\Omega_t$:

$$\Omega_t = i_t M_t, \tag{11.17}$$

since it saves on interest that would be paid if the consumer had purchased bonds instead of retaining cash.[12]

The government resources constraint establishes that the change in government debt should be equal to the interest payment on the existing debt added to the resources necessary to supply public goods, minus the seigniorage revenue, as in

$$D_{t+1} - D_t = i_{t-1} D_t + \frac{k G_t}{\theta_t} - \Omega_t, \tag{11.18}$$

where $D_t$ represents government debt in $t$, $G_t$ is public expenditures, and $\theta_t \in [1, k]$, for a constant $k > 1$, is a parameter that represents the government level of competence. The higher the value of $\theta_t$, the less resources are necessary to promote a determined level of public spending, and, therefore, the more efficient government administration is. This parameter seeks to represent the fact that governments differ in their efficiency in generating public resources.

Assume that there is free mobility of capital between countries and that the assets from different countries are perfect substitutes, that is, economic agents are indifferent in relation from which country to purchase assets to save their wealth, when the yield between them is

---

[12] This is one of the ways to measure seigniorage, based on the opportunity cost of retaining currency. There is also the monetary measure, based on the change of the real value of the monetary base, and the fiscal measure, which focuses on receipts obtained by the central bank operations associated, not only with the emission of currency but also its maintenance. Neumann (1992) is an interesting text that covers both the empirical and theoretical aspects of seigniorage.

the same. The uncovered interest rate parity verifies as in Eq. (3.12). Also assume that the international interest rate is constant and equal to 0, we have that

$$\frac{E(S_{t+1})}{S_t} = 1 + i_t. \tag{11.19}$$

It is reasonable to assume that the public does not have complete information regarding the value of all variables chosen by the government. Collecting information is costly, and it is only publicly available to the media with a delay. Specifically, we consider a situation where the public can observe neither the level of government competency nor its level of indebtedness. These variables are observed only with a one-period delay. The level of exchange rate, however, can be observed currently, for it is a variable that affects the consumers purchasing power. The level of public spending is also easily observed for the citizen benefits from this variable.

We now have all elements necessary to understand how exchange rate policy can be a sign of government competence. Let us take the case where there are only two periods, with no initial debt, $D_1 = 0$, and the government should pay all contracted debt at the end of the second period. Based on Eq. (11.18), the government budget constraint can be written as

$$D_2 = \frac{kG_1}{\theta_1} - i_1 M_1,$$

where we use the definition of seigniorage presented in Eq. (11.17). Substituting the interest rate parity condition (Eq. (11.19)) in the previous equation and rearranging the terms, we have that

$$G_1 = \frac{\theta_1}{k} \left[ D_2 + \left( \frac{S_2}{S_1} - 1 \right) M_1 \right]. \tag{11.20}$$

Equation (11.20) shows that there are at least three ways for the government to generate more public spending: being more competent (higher $\theta_1$), increasing its level of debt (higher $D_2$), or generating more seigniorage tax by means of exchange rate depreciation (higher $\left( \frac{S_2}{S_1} - 1 \right)$). Let us consider the case where the public observes simultaneously a high level of public spending and a low exchange rate depreciation. Remembering that the public does not see the government choice variables, the citizen is unable to discern, in principle, if the high expense was reached by greater debt, or by the fact of the government being competent. Here is the exchange rate policy as a sign of government competence: a government that is in fact competent can choose low enough depreciation, given the level of public spending, in such a way that an incompetent government has no interest in emulating it.

Stein and Streb (2004) and Stein et al. (2005) show that, in a context similar to that described, under certain conditions, the **policymaker delays exchange rate depreciation until after elections in order to signal its greater competence. This generates an**

**exchange rate cycle surrounding the elections where the exchange rate remains, on average, more appreciated before the elections and more depreciated after.**

Notice that this same type voter exchange rate cycle is also generated by models based on the distributive impacts of the exchange rate, considered in Section 11.1. It is important to observe that these two alternative suggestions for the cycles are not necessarily conflicting. In fact, they can be seen as complementary when the median voter is a citizen from the nontradable sector. In maintaining the exchange rate appreciated before the elections, the government not only signals its competence but also favors a large part of its electorate in countries where they are of the nontradables sector.

## 11.3 The Economic Policy of Fiscal Policy

Up to now, the analysis was based on the exchange rate policy economic impacts, and political issues derived from them. The focus of this section will be the economic policy of fiscal policy. **The exchange rate now ceases to be the focus of economic policy and becomes only the residual effect of the choice of fiscal policy.**

Based on national accounts, the relation between fiscal policy and the real exchange rate can be identified. We know that the GDP, $Y$, can be divided into private consumption, $C$, investment, $I$, public spending, $G$, and the trade balance, TB, as seen in Eq. (2.2), which we reproduce here:

$$Y = C + I + G + \text{TB}. \tag{11.21}$$

Equation (11.21) is an accounting identity. It does not indicate how the variables behave, what causes their variation, or what the relationship between them is. All that the national accounts tell us is that Eq. (11.21) always verifies. Many economic theories examine the determinants of the variables that compose the equation, seeking to understand individual incentives and how they react to the economic policies implemented.

The model developed in Chapter 4 shows how changes in fiscal policy, $G$, affect the current-account balance, while Chapter 5 enriches the model by incorporating the effects on the real exchange rate. The model shows that an increase in public spending affects the real exchange rate by means of two complementary effects: the intertemporal effect and the composition effect. By means of the intertemporal effect, a temporary increase in spending alters the consumers' disposable income across the periods, affecting their decision to save. As a result, aggregate savings decline, causing a reduction in the trade balance, which is associated to a more appreciated real exchange rate. The composition effect is due to the composition of government spending between tradable and nontradable goods. **When government spends relatively more on nontradable goods than the private sector, an increase in public expenditures implies an increase in the relative price of these goods, which means an appreciation of the real exchange rate.** Hence, both by the intertemporal effect and the composition effect, an increase in public spending generates an appreciation of the real exchange rate.

Let us now analyze the economic policy of the fiscal policy. As always in political economy, we start the analysis with the conflicting interests of different groups in the economy regarding the policy choice. In the case of fiscal policy, the focus is on the hypothesis that individuals with different income levels also differ in their preference regarding fiscal policy. The basic idea is that wealthier individuals pay more taxes and thus prefer less public expenditure than the less wealthy. This effect is captured in a simple fiscal policy model presented by Persson and Tabellini (2000), and reproduced here.

Assume an economy with a continuum of citizens indexed by $i \in [0, 1]$, where each of them receives a different endowment of income in terms of quantity of a determined good, represented by $Y_i$. Except for the value of the received endowment, all individuals in the economy are identical, and derive utility from the consumption of a privately consumed good, $C_i$, and a public good, $G$, provided by the government. The utility function of consumer $U_i$ is represented by

$$U_i = C_i + H(G),$$

where $H(G)$ is an increasing and concave function: $H_g(G) > 0$ and $H_{gg}(G) < 0$, and $G$ is the *per capita* quantity of public good.

The government collects taxes from the citizens and transforms them into public goods with no additional costs. The income tax rate, $\tau$, is the same for all. The government budget constraint is represented by

$$\tau Y = G,$$

where $Y \equiv \int_0^1 Y_i di$ is the average income in the economy.

The consumer, in turn, should also comply with their budget constraint, which establishes that expenditure on consumption should be equal to disposable income:

$$C_i = (1 - \tau)Y_i.$$

Substituting the government and citizen budget constraints into the citizen utility function, we have an indirect utility function that represents citizen preferences in relation to fiscal policy, which is represented by

$$V(G; Y_i) = (Y - G)\frac{Y_i}{Y} + H(G). \tag{11.22}$$

The preferred level of public spending by the citizen $i$, $G^i$, is that which maximizes the function of Eq. (11.22). Taking the derivative of the indirect utility function and making it equal to zero, we have the public spending level that maximizes welfare as given by

$$G^i = H_g^{-1}\left(\frac{Y_i}{Y}\right). \tag{11.23}$$

Given that function $H(G)$ is concave, $H_{gg}(G) < 0$, function $H_g(G)$ is decreasing. Therefore, Eq. (11.23) establishes a negative relation between income and preferred public expenditures: individuals with a higher income prefer a lower level of government spending. In mathematical terms, we can say that, for two individuals, $k$ and $l$, we have that

$$Y_k > Y_l \Leftrightarrow G^k < G^l. \tag{11.24}$$

If public expenditures were chosen by a benevolent policymaker, the level chosen would be that which maximizes the social welfare function of the economy, which is the sum of the welfare of all citizens, given as

$$V(G; Y) = \int_0^1 \left[ (Y - G)\frac{Y_i}{Y} + H(G) \right] di = Y - G + H(G).$$

The chosen level of expenses, $G^*$, would therefore be equal to

$$G^* = H_g^{-1}(1),$$

in other words, it would be the spending level preferred by the average income voter in the economy.

As is always the case in political economy analysis, the chosen policy is not that of a benevolent government. **In choosing the policy that will be implemented, the government takes into consideration its political interests, in addition to population welfare. In this case, it will act in accordance with its electorate's interests.** Assume that there are two candidates running in the same election. They announce their campaign platforms, which consist of the level of expenditures that will be implemented after the election. The voters consider the announced platforms and vote for the candidate of their preference. To simplify the analysis, let us assume that there is no credibility problem with voters in relation to the announced platforms, and that they will be effectively implemented after the election.

Voters will vote for the candidate with the platform closest to their preference. It is easy to show that, **in equilibrium, the two candidates offer the same platform, and this will be that preferred by the median voter.** The median voter in this economy is the one in relation to which half of the voters have a higher income, and the other half a lower income.

To understand this result, assume that there are two candidates, $A$ and $B$. Candidate $A$ chooses the spending level preferred by the median voter, $G^m$, while candidate $B$ announces a lower spending level, $G^B < G^m$. According to inequality (11.24), all voters with an income lower than the median voter will prefer a higher spending level than the median voter. They will vote for candidate $A$, whose announced policy is closer to their preferences than that presented by candidate $B$. The votes of voters with an income between that of the median voter and the income of the voter who prefers $G^B$ will be divided between the two candidates. Hence, candidate $A$, who announces the level of spending preferred by the median voter, has more than 50% of the votes and wins the election. If candidate $B$ was to announce the same level of spending, the voters would be indifferent between the two candidates.

Each candidate therefore has a 50% chance of winning, if the votes are random in the case of indifference. Therefore, the announced policy by the two candidates is

$$G^m = H_g^{-1}\left(\frac{Y_m}{Y}\right),$$

where $Y_m$ is the median voter income.

Economies always present some degree of income concentration: there are less very rich individuals and many with a lower level of income. **With income concentration, the average income in an economy is higher than the income of the median voter: $Y > Y_m$. Given the relation of** Eq. (11.24), **the result is that the level of public spending chosen by the politician with election motivations is higher than that which would be socially optimum.** Adding this result to the analysis of the national accounts done at the beginning of this chapter, it can be concluded that the higher level of spending is also associated with a more appreciated exchange rate (Box 11.3).

---

**BOX 11.3 DEMOCRATIZATION: BRAZIL AND ARGENTINA**

Let us look at the facts. With the end of the military dictatorships in Argentina and Brazil at the end of the 1980s and the resulting democracies, politicians in both countries began to worry over election. According to the model just described, the result would be the implementation of policies more aligned with median voter preferences. In economies with high-income inequality, as in these two countries, the median voter has an income level below the average income of the economy. A more expansionist fiscal policy in a democratic environment would be expected. In fact, public spending jumped as of the beginning of political democratization in these countries.

Figures 2.2 and 2.3 show the path of GDP decomposition between 1970 and 2010 for both Brazil and Argentina, respectively. It can be seen that in these two countries, up to the beginning of the 1980s, public spending corresponded for a constant share of more or less 10% of output. As of the beginning of democracy, in 1983 for Argentina and 1985 for Brazil, public spending rose, reaching 20% of GDP in 1990, and remained at that level. One could argue that the beginning of democracy increased politician electoral concerns, leading them to implement policies more to the liking of the median voter. In Brazil, particularly, the new constitution, approved in 1988, established several expenses as mandatory. The result was an even greater increase in public spending as of that date, as can be seen in Figure 2.2.

The counterpart of the increase in public spending was different for each country. In Argentina, there was a large reduction in private consumption and, to a greater degree, of investment during the 1980s, along with a deficit in current account. In Brazil, in turn, the decrease in private spending was the main counterpart to increased government consumption. In both Argentina and Brazil, there was a partial recovery of private consumption in the 1990s, offset by an increase in current-account deficit. The period characterized the movement predicted by the political economy of public spending and its effect on the exchange rate: the increased level of public spending brought by democracy caused a deficit in current account, validated by an appreciation of the real exchange rate.

It has been discussed regarding if other developing countries should adopt the "Chinese model," which is a policy of maintaining a depreciated exchange rate in order to foster economic growth. Independent of its efficacy to really promote growth, what do political economy studies have to say regarding this policy? One common point in all studies is the identification of an appreciated exchange rate as the preferred policy by the median voter in Latin American countries. Therefore, the depreciated exchange rate of the Chinese model is unpopular. In implementing it, the government must be ready to lose the support of a large part of the electorate, who will have their purchasing power reduced.

There is also the question of how to maintain the exchange rate depreciated. A depreciated exchange rate leads to trade surpluses. According to the national accounts identity, these surpluses should increase output or reduce private consumption, government consumption, or investment as an offset. It is hard to imagine that depreciation could cause a rapid and sufficiently large increase of output for the adjustment to be made without a reduction in consumption or investment. Reductions in consumption are unpopular, while falls in investment hinder growth. In other words, the depreciated exchange rate policy has side effects that go against the interests of a large part of the population or that may be harmful to the country's own growth. Popularity is not a problem for the Chinese government, being that their political system is dictatorial. In democracies, on the other hand, unpopular measures are punished at the voting polls.

# Mathematical Appendix

## Solution to the Consumer Problem—No Inflation

The consumer problem in sector $j$, $j \in \{T, N\}$, who chooses the optimum way to allocate their income between tradable and nontradable goods, with no inflation, is given by

$$\text{Max}(1 - \alpha)\ln C_T + \alpha \ln C_N$$
$$\text{Subject to } p_T C_T + p_N C_N \leq p_j Y_j.$$

To solve the problem, we write the Lagrangian function as

$$\mathcal{L} = (1 - \alpha)\ln C_T + \alpha \ln C_N + \lambda \{p_j Y_j - p_T C_T - p_N C_N\},$$

where $\lambda$ is the Lagrange multiplier associated with the constraint. The maximum point is that for which the derivatives of the Lagrangian function with respect to the variables of choice, $C_T$ and $C_N$, and to the Lagrange multiplier, $\lambda$, are equal to zero. The first-order conditions for maximization are, therefore:

$$[C_T]: \frac{\partial \mathcal{L}}{\partial C_T} = 0 \Rightarrow (1 - \alpha)\frac{1}{C_T} - \lambda p_T = 0 \Rightarrow$$

$$\lambda = (1 - \alpha)\frac{1}{p_T C_T} \tag{11.25}$$

$$[C_N]: \frac{\partial \mathcal{L}}{\partial C_N} = 0 \Rightarrow \alpha \frac{1}{C_N} - \lambda p_N = 0 \Rightarrow$$

$$\lambda = \alpha \frac{1}{p_N C_N} \tag{11.26}$$

$$[\lambda]: \frac{\partial \mathcal{L}}{\partial \lambda} = 0 \Rightarrow$$

$$p_T C_T + p_N C_N = p_j Y_j \tag{11.27}$$

Substituting Eq. (11.25) into Eq. (11.26), we obtain

$$(1 - \alpha) \frac{1}{p_T C_T} = \alpha \frac{1}{p_N C_N}$$

$$\Updownarrow \tag{11.28}$$

$$C_T = \frac{(1 - \alpha) p_N C_N}{\alpha p_T}.$$

Substituting expression (11.28) into Eq. (11.27), we obtain

$$\frac{(1 - \alpha) p_N C_N}{\alpha p_T} p_T + p_N C_N = p_j Y_j$$

$$\Updownarrow$$

$$p_N C_N \left( 1 + \frac{(1 - \alpha)}{\alpha} \right) = p_j Y_j \tag{11.29}$$

$$\Updownarrow$$

$$C_N^{j*} = \frac{\alpha p_j Y_j}{p_N},$$

where $C_N^{j*}$ is the optimal consumption level of nontradables for a consumer from sector $j$.

Substituting Eq. (11.29) into expression (11.28), we arrive at

$$C_N^{j*} = \frac{(1 - \alpha) p_j Y_j}{p_T}. \tag{11.30}$$

When $j = T$, and remembering that $p_T = 1$, the demands for nontradable and tradable goods will be given by

$$C_N^{T*} = \frac{\alpha Y_T}{p_N} \tag{11.31}$$

$$C_T^{T*} = (1 - \alpha) Y_T. \tag{11.32}$$

For the case where $j = N$, the demands will be given by

$$C_N^{N*} = \alpha Y_N \tag{11.33}$$

$$C_T^{N*} = \frac{(1 - \alpha) p_N Y_N}{p_T}. \tag{11.34}$$

## The Indirect Utility Function

We begin with the indirect utility function for a consumer from the tradables sector. Substituting Eqs. (11.31) and (11.32) into Eq. (11.1), we obtain the following function:

$$
\begin{aligned}
V_T &\equiv U(C_T^{T*}, C_N^{T*}) \\
&= (1 - \alpha)\ln C_T^{T*} + \alpha \ln C_N^{T*} \\
&= (1 - \alpha)\ln((1 - \alpha)Y_T) + \alpha \ln\left(\frac{\alpha Y_T}{p_N}\right) \\
&= \alpha \ln \alpha + (1 - \alpha)\ln(1 - \alpha) + \ln Y_T + \alpha \ln Y_T - \alpha \ln Y_T - \alpha \ln p_N.
\end{aligned}
\tag{11.35}
$$

Taking the natural logarithm of Eq. (11.3), which defines the real exchange rate, we obtain

$$
Q = \left(\tfrac{1}{p_N}\right)^{\alpha}
$$

$$
\Downarrow
$$

$$
\begin{aligned}
\ln Q &= \alpha(\ln(1) - \ln(p_N)) \\
q &= -\alpha \ln p_N.
\end{aligned}
\tag{11.36}
$$

Defining $h_T = \alpha \ln \alpha + (1 - \alpha)\ln(1 - \alpha) + \ln Y_T$, and substituting Eq. (11.36) into (11.35), we arrive at the intended expression for the indirect utility function:

$$
\begin{aligned}
V_T &\equiv U(C_T^{T*}, C_N^{T*}) \\
&= h_T - \alpha \ln Q.
\end{aligned}
\tag{11.37}
$$

To obtain the indirect utility function for a consumer from the nontradables sector, one needs to follow an analogous procedure, only this time substituting Eqs. (11.33) and (11.34) into the utility function for the individual. Proceeding as such, we obtain

$$
\begin{aligned}
V_N &\equiv U(C_T^{N*}, C_N^{N*}) \\
&= h_N - \frac{1 - \alpha}{\alpha}\ln Q.
\end{aligned}
\tag{11.38}
$$

## Solution to the Consumer Problem—With Inflation

The problem of the consumer from sector $j$, $j \in \{T, N\}$, who chooses the optimum way to allocate their income between tradable and nontradable goods, and who receives exogenous endowment $Y_j$ each period, when there is inflation, is given by

$$
\text{Max}(1 - \alpha)\ln C_{T1} + \alpha \ln C_{N1} + \beta[(1 - \alpha)\ln C_{T2} + \alpha \ln C_{N2}]
$$

$$
\begin{aligned}
\text{Subject to:} \quad & p_{T1} C_{T1} + p_{N1} C_{N1} \leq p_{j0} Y_j \pi_1^{\delta} \\
& p_{T2} C_{T2} + p_{N2} C_{N2} \leq p_{j1} Y_j \pi_2^{\delta}.
\end{aligned}
$$

To solve this problem, we write the Lagrangian function as

$$\mathcal{L} = (1 - \alpha)\ln C_{T1} + \alpha \ln C_{N1} + \beta[(1 - \alpha)\ln C_{T2} + \alpha \ln C_{N2}]$$
$$+ \lambda_1\{p_{j0}Y_j\pi_1^\delta - p_{T1}C_{T1} - p_{N1}C_{N1}\} + \lambda_2\{p_{j1}Y_j\pi_2^\delta - p_{T2}C_{T2} - p_{N2}C_{N2}\},$$

where $\lambda_t$ is the Lagrange multiplier associated with each constraint. The maximum point is that for which the derivatives of the Lagrangian function with respect to the variables of choice, $C_{T1}, C_{T2}, C_{N1}$, and $C_{N2}$, and with respect to the Lagrange multipliers, $\lambda_t$, with $t \in \{1, 2\}$ are equal to zero. The first-order conditions for maximization are therefore

$$[C_{T1}]: \frac{\partial \mathcal{L}}{\partial C_{T1}} = 0 \Rightarrow (1 - \alpha)\frac{1}{C_{T1}} - \lambda_1 p_{T1} = 0 \Rightarrow$$

$$\lambda_1 = (1 - \alpha)\frac{1}{p_{T1}C_{T1}}, \tag{11.39}$$

$$[C_{N1}]: \frac{\partial \mathcal{L}}{\partial C_{N1}} = 0 \Rightarrow \alpha\frac{1}{C_{N1}} - \lambda_1 p_{N1} = 0 \Rightarrow$$

$$\lambda_1 = \alpha\frac{1}{p_{N1}C_{N1}}\,(2), \tag{11.40}$$

$$[\lambda_1]: \frac{\partial \mathcal{L}}{\partial \lambda_1} = 0 \Rightarrow$$

$$p_{T1}C_{T1} + p_{N1}C_{N1} = p_{j0}Y_j\pi_1^\delta, \tag{11.41}$$

$$[C_{T2}]: \frac{\partial \mathcal{L}}{\partial C_{T2}} = 0 \Rightarrow \beta(1 - \alpha)\frac{1}{C_{T2}} - \lambda_2 p_{T2} = 0 \Rightarrow$$

$$\lambda_2 = (1 - \alpha)\frac{\beta}{p_{T2}C_{T2}}, \tag{11.42}$$

$$[C_{N2}]: \frac{\partial \mathcal{L}}{\partial C_{N2}} = 0 \Rightarrow \beta\,\alpha\frac{1}{C_{N2}} - \lambda_2 p_{N2} = 0 \Rightarrow$$

$$\lambda_2 = \alpha\frac{\beta}{p_{N2}C_{N2}}, \tag{11.43}$$

$$[\lambda_2]: \frac{\partial \mathcal{L}}{\partial \lambda_2} = 0 \Rightarrow$$

$$p_{T2}C_{T2} + p_{N2}C_{N2} = p_{T1}Y_T\pi_2^\delta. \tag{11.44}$$

Combining Eqs. (11.39) and (11.40), we obtain

$$(1 - \alpha)\frac{1}{p_{T1}C_{T1}} = \alpha\frac{1}{p_{N1}C_{N1}} \Rightarrow p_{T1}C_{T1} = \frac{(1 - \alpha)}{\alpha}p_{N1}C_{N1}. \tag{11.45}$$

Substituting expression (11.45) into Eq. (11.41), we get

$$\frac{(1-\alpha)}{\alpha}p_{N1}C_{N1} + p_{N1}C_{N1} = p_{T0}Y_T\pi_1^\delta \Rightarrow p_{N1}C_{N1}\left(1 + \frac{(1-\alpha)}{\alpha}\right) = p_{T0}Y_T\pi_1^\delta$$

$$C_{N1}^* = \alpha Y_j\pi_1^\delta\frac{p_{j0}}{p_{N1}}.$$

(11.46)

Substituting Eq. (11.46) into expression (11.45), we arrive at

$$C_{T1}^* = (1-\alpha)Y_j\pi_1^\delta\frac{p_{j0}}{p_{T1}}.$$

(11.47)

Combining Eqs. (11.42) and (11.43), we obtain

$$(1-\alpha)\frac{\beta}{p_{T2}C_{T2}} = \alpha\frac{\beta}{p_{N2}C_{N2}}$$

$$\Updownarrow$$

$$p_{T2}C_{T2} = \frac{(1-\alpha)}{\alpha}p_{N2}C_{N2}.$$

(11.48)

Substituting expression (11.48) into Eq. (11.44), we obtain

$$\frac{(1-\alpha)}{\alpha}p_{N2}C_{N2} + p_{N2}C_{N2} = p_{T1}Y_T\pi_2^\delta$$

$$\Updownarrow$$

$$p_{N2}C_{N2}\left(1 + \frac{(1-\alpha)}{\alpha}\right) = p_{T1}Y_T\pi_2^\delta$$

(11.49)

$$\Updownarrow$$

$$C_{N2}^* = \alpha Y_j\pi_2^\delta\frac{p_{j1}}{p_{N1}}.$$

Substituting Eq. (11.49) into expression (11.48), we arrive at

$$C_{T2}^* = (1-\alpha)Y_j\pi_2^\delta\frac{p_{j1}}{p_{T2}}.$$

(11.50)

Substituting Eqs. (11.46), (11.47), (11.49), and (11.50) into the original utility function, we have the following expression:

$$V_j \equiv U(C_{T1}^*, C_{T2}^*, C_{N1}^*, C_{N2}^*)$$

$$= (1-\alpha)\ln C_{T1}^* + \alpha\ln C_{N1}^* + \beta[(1-\alpha)\ln C_{T2}^* + \alpha\ln C_{N2}^*]$$

$$= (1-\alpha)\ln\left((1-\alpha)Y_j\pi_1^\delta\frac{p_{j0}}{p_{T1}}\right) + \alpha\ln\left(\alpha Y_j\pi_1^\delta\frac{p_{j0}}{p_{N1}}\right) + \beta\left[(1-\alpha)\ln\left((1-\alpha)Y_j\pi_2^\delta\frac{p_{j1}}{p_{T2}}\right) + \alpha\ln\left(\alpha Y_j\pi_2^\delta\frac{p_{j1}}{p_{N1}}\right)\right].$$

For the citizen in the tradable goods sector, i.e., $j = T$, we have that

$$V_T = (1 - \alpha)\ln(1 - \alpha)Y_T + (1 - \alpha)\ln\left(\frac{p_{T0}}{p_{T1}}\right) + (1 - \alpha)\delta \ln \pi_1 + \alpha \ln \alpha\, Y_T$$

$$+ \alpha \ln\left(\frac{p_{T0}}{p_{N1}}\right) + \alpha\delta \ln \pi_1 + \beta\left[(1 - \alpha)\ln(1 - \alpha)Y_T + (1 - \alpha)\ln\left(\frac{p_{T1}}{p_{T2}}\right)\right.$$

$$\left. + (1 - \alpha)\delta \ln \pi_2 + \alpha \ln \alpha Y_T + \alpha \ln\left(\frac{p_{T1}}{p_{N2}}\right) + \alpha\delta \ln \pi_2\right]$$

$$= \alpha \ln \alpha + (1 - \alpha)\ln(1 - \alpha) + \ln Y_T + \ln\left(\frac{p_{T0}}{p_{T1}}\right)^{1-\alpha}\left(\frac{p_{N0}}{p_{N1}}\right)^{\alpha}\left(\frac{p_{T0}}{p_{N0}}\right)^{\alpha} + \delta \ln \pi_1 \tag{11.51}$$

$$+ \beta\left[\alpha \ln \alpha + (1 - \alpha)\ln(1 - \alpha) + \ln Y_T + \ln\left(\frac{p_{T1}}{p_{T2}}\right)^{1-\alpha}\left(\frac{p_{N1}}{p_{N2}}\right)^{\alpha}\left(\frac{p_{T1}}{p_{N1}}\right)^{\alpha} + \alpha \ln \pi_2\right]$$

$$= (1 + \beta)[\alpha \ln \alpha + (1 - \alpha)\ln(1 - \alpha) + \ln Y_T] + \ln\left(\frac{p_{T0}}{p_{T1}}\right)^{1-\alpha}\left(\frac{p_{N0}}{p_{N1}}\right)^{\alpha} +$$

$$\ln\left(\frac{p_{T0}}{p_{N0}}\right)^{\alpha} + \delta \ln \pi_1 + \beta\left[\ln\left(\frac{p_{T1}}{p_{T2}}\right)^{1-\alpha}\left(\frac{p_{N1}}{p_{N2}}\right)^{\alpha} + \ln\left(\frac{p_{T1}}{p_{N1}}\right)^{\alpha} + \delta \ln \pi_2\right]$$

Notice that $\left(\frac{p_{T0}}{p_{N1}}\right)^{\alpha} = \left(\frac{p_{N0}}{p_{N1}}\right)^{\alpha}\left(\frac{p_{T0}}{p_{N0}}\right)^{\alpha}$. To simplify the expression, according to what was done throughout the main text, let us define the term,

$$\overline{h}_T \equiv (1 + \beta)[\alpha \ln \alpha + (1 - \alpha)\ln(1 - \alpha) + \ln Y_T],$$

and use the fact that, by definition, inflation is given by

$$\pi_t = \frac{P_t}{P_{t-1}} = \frac{p_{Nt}^{\alpha}p_{Tt}^{1-\alpha}}{p_{Nt-1}^{\alpha}p_{Tt-1}^{1-\alpha}}.$$

Moreover, remember that the real exchange rate was defined in Chapter 5 as $Q = \left(\frac{p_N^*/p_T^*}{p_N/p_T}\right)^{\alpha}$. Specifically, if we assume that the ratio between the price of tradable and non-tradable goods is constant in the world economy, we can write the real exchange rate as $Q = \left(\frac{P_T}{P_N}\right)^{\alpha}$. Using the definitions and hypotheses in Eq. (11.51), we obtain

$$V_T = \overline{h}_T + \ln \pi_1 + \ln Q_0 + \delta \ln \pi_1 + \beta[\ln \pi_2 + \ln Q_1 + \delta \ln \pi_2]$$
$$= \overline{h}_T + \ln Q_0 - (1 - \delta)\ln \pi_1 + \beta[\ln Q_1 - (1 - \delta)\ln \pi_2].$$

The development of the expression for $V_N$ is done analogously.

**Derivation of** Eq. (11.10):

Considering the hypothesis that the relative price of nontradable goods in the foreign economy is equal to 1, from Eq. (3.2) we have that the real exchange rate will be defined as $Q = \left(\frac{P_T}{P_N}\right)^{\alpha}$. Moreover, we will also use the hypothesis presented in the text, according to which $\frac{P_{Nt}}{P_{Nt-1}} \equiv \eta$. By definition, inflation is given by the variation in the general price index in the economy, i.e., $\pi_t \equiv \frac{P_t}{P_{t-1}}$. Using the fact that $P_t = p_{Nt}^{\alpha} p_{Tt}^{1-\alpha}$, we then have

$$\pi_t \equiv \frac{P_t}{P_{t-1}} = \frac{p_{Nt}^{\alpha} p_{Tt}^{1-\alpha}}{p_{Nt-1}^{\alpha} p_{Tt-1}^{1-\alpha}}.$$

Multiplying the previous equation by $\frac{P_{Nt}}{P_{Nt-1}} \frac{P_{Nt-1}}{P_{Nt}}$, we have

$$\pi_t \equiv \frac{P_t}{P_{t-1}} = \frac{p_{Nt}^{\alpha} p_{Tt}^{1-\alpha}}{p_{Nt-1}^{\alpha} p_{Tt-1}^{1-\alpha}} \frac{P_{Nt}}{P_{Nt-1}} \frac{P_{Nt-1}}{P_{Nt}} \Rightarrow \pi_t = \frac{p_{Nt}^{\alpha-1} p_{Tt}^{1-\alpha}}{p_{Nt-1}^{\alpha-1} p_{Tt-1}^{1-\alpha}} \eta = \frac{\left(\frac{P_{Tt}}{P_{Nt}}\right)^{1-\alpha}}{\left(\frac{P_{Tt-1}}{P_{Nt-1}}\right)^{1-\alpha}} \Rightarrow$$

$$\pi_t = \eta \left(\frac{Q_t^{\frac{1}{\alpha}}}{Q_{t-1}^{\frac{1}{\alpha}}}\right)^{1-\alpha} \Rightarrow \pi_t = \eta \left(\frac{Q_t}{Q_{t-1}}\right)^{\frac{1-\alpha}{\alpha}}.$$

**Derivation of** Eq. (11.11):

From Eq. (11.8), we saw that the indirect utility function of tradable goods producers is given by

$$V_T(Q_t, \pi_t) = \overline{h}_T + \ln Q_{t-1} - (1 - \delta_T)\ln \pi_t + \beta[\ln Q_t - (1 - \delta_T)\ln \pi_{t+1}].$$

Substituting inflation as a function of the real exchange rate, as defined by Eq. (11.10), we obtain

$$V_T(Q_t) = \overline{h}_T + \ln Q_{t-1} - (1 - \delta_T)\ln \eta \left(\frac{Q_t}{Q_{t-1}}\right)^{1-\alpha} + \beta\left[\ln Q_t - (1 - \delta_T)\ln \eta \left(\frac{Q_t}{Q_t}\right)^{1-\alpha}\right].$$

Rewriting:

$$V_T(Q_t) = \overline{h}_T + \ln Q_{t-1} - (1 - \delta_T)\ln \eta \left(\frac{1}{Q_{t-1}}\right)^{1-\alpha} - (1 - \delta_T)\ln Q_t^{1-\alpha} + \beta[\ln Q_t - (1 - \delta_T)\ln \eta] \Rightarrow$$

$$V_T(Q_t) = \overline{h}_T + \ln Q_{t-1} - (1 - \delta_T)\ln \eta + (1 - \delta_T)(1 - \alpha)\ln Q_{t-1} - (1 - \delta_T)(1 - \alpha)\ln Q_t$$
$$+ \beta[\ln Q_t - (1 - \delta_{Ti})\ln \eta] \Rightarrow$$

$$V_T(Q_t) = \overline{h}_T + [1 + (1 - \delta_T)(1 - \alpha)]\ln Q_{t-1} - (1 + \beta)(1 - \delta_T)\ln \eta - (1 - \delta_T)(1 - \alpha)\ln Q_t + \beta \ln Q_t \Rightarrow$$

$$V_T(Q_t) = \overline{h}_T - (1 + \beta)(1 - \delta_T)\ln \eta + [1 + (1 - \delta_T)(1 - \alpha)]\ln Q_{t-1} - \beta(1 - \delta_T)(1 - \alpha)\ln Q_{t+1}$$
$$+ [\beta - (1 - \delta_T)(1 - \alpha)]\ln Q_t$$

$$V_T(Q_t) = \overline{k}_T + \left[\frac{\beta}{1 - \alpha} - (1 - \delta_T)\right](1 - \alpha)\ln Q_t,$$

where

$$\bar{k}_T \equiv \bar{h}_T - (1+\beta)(1-\delta_T)\ln\eta + [1+(1-\delta_T)(1-\alpha)]\ln Q_{t-1}.$$

**Derivation of** Eq. (11.12):

By Eq. (11.9), we saw that the indirect utility function of nontradable goods producers is given by

$$V_N(Q_t,\pi_t) = \bar{h}_N - \frac{1-\alpha}{\alpha}\ln Q_{t-1} - (1-\delta_N)\ln\pi_t - \beta\left[\frac{1-\alpha}{\alpha}\ln Q_t + (1-\delta_N)\ln\pi_{t+1}\right].$$

Substituting inflation as a function of the real exchange rate

$$V_N(Q_t) = \bar{h}_N - \frac{1-\alpha}{\alpha}\ln Q_{t-1} - (1-\delta_N)\ln\eta\left(\frac{Q_t}{Q_{t-1}}\right)^{1-\alpha} -$$

$$\beta\left[\frac{1-\alpha}{\alpha}\ln Q_t + (1-\delta_N)\ln\eta\left(\frac{Q_t}{Q_t}\right)^{1-\alpha}\right].$$

Rewriting

$$V_N(Q_t) = \bar{h}_N - \frac{1-\alpha}{\alpha}\ln Q_{t-1} - (1-\delta_N)\ln\frac{\eta}{Q_{t-1}^{1-\alpha}} - (1-\delta_N)(1-\alpha)\ln Q_t$$

$$- \beta(1-\delta_N)\ln\eta - \beta\frac{1-\alpha}{\alpha}\ln Q_t \Rightarrow$$

$$V_N(Q_t) = \bar{h}_N - \frac{1-\alpha}{\alpha}\ln Q_{t-1} - (1-\delta_N)\ln\frac{\eta}{Q_{t-1}^{1-\alpha}} - \beta(1-\delta_N)\ln\eta - \left[(1-\delta_N) + \frac{\beta}{\alpha}\right](1-\alpha)\ln Q_t \Rightarrow$$

$$V_N(Q_t) = \bar{h}_N - (1+\beta)(1-\delta_N)\ln\eta + (1-\alpha)\left[(1-\delta_N) - \frac{1}{\alpha}\right]\ln Q_{t-1} - \left[\frac{\beta}{\alpha} + (1-\delta_N)\right](1-\alpha)\ln Q_t \Rightarrow$$

$$V_N(Q_t) = \bar{k}_N - \left[\frac{\beta}{\alpha} + (1-\delta_N)\right](1-\alpha)\ln Q_t \Rightarrow$$

where

$$\bar{k}_N \equiv \bar{h}_N + (1-\alpha)\left[(1-\delta_N) - \frac{1}{\alpha}\right]\ln Q_{t-1} - (1+\beta)(1-\delta_N)\ln\eta.$$

## 11.4 Exercises

### Exercise 1

As has been seen throughout this chapter, political factors, such as government objectives and the weight of sectors affected by exchange rate policy, are important elements that affect the decision in regards to the exchange rate regime adopted by a country. In this context, answer what the following items request.

**a.** Discuss the costs and benefits of a fixed exchange rate system, identifying which groups benefit and which are harmed with the adoption of this type of regime.
**b.** Discuss the costs and benefits of a floating exchange rate system, identifying which groups benefit and which are harmed with the adoption of this type of regime.
**c.** Considering your answers to the previous items, in a country whose elected ruler holds a high degree of influence on economic policy and is committed to growth, what would be the most adequate exchange rate regime? Give examples of countries that possess this type of political structure, associating it with the exchange rate regime adopted.
**d.** Continuing within the context of the previous item, in a country whose elected ruler is committed to democratic institutions and is subject to political pressure that is fairly scattered among the economic sectors, what would be the most adequate exchange rate regime? Give examples of countries that possess this type of political structure, associating it with the adopted exchange rate regime.
**e.** Considering the strict relation between monetary policy and exchange rate policy, what type of institutional rule would you use to reduce political influence on the exchange rate? Explain your answer, presenting, if possible, examples of countries that have implemented institutional reforms of this nature.

## Exercise 2

Just as what happens with the choice of exchange rate regime, the choice of the exchange rate level also has highly important electoral implications. Governments cannot directly choose the real exchange rate for their respective economies, but can affect their short-run tendency. In this context, answer what the following items request.

**a.** What are the trade-offs associated with the exchange rate level, that is, what are the costs and benefits of an excessively appreciated currency? Explain your answers.
**b.** Present the economic impacts of unexpected exchange rate depreciation. What are the distributive impacts between the productive sectors and consumers in an event of this nature?

## Exercise 3

We have seen over the course of the text that the real exchange rate has important distributive effects, which, in turn, make this variable an element of fundamental importance as a political instrument in the hands of the government. Consider the economic model developed in Section 11.1.

**a.** What is the impact of a real exchange rate appreciation on the welfare of individuals who produce tradable and nontradable goods? Using a graph with the budget constraint for individuals in each sector, illustrate the impact of a real exchange rate appreciation on the welfare of these individuals. Explain the economic logic for your answer.

**b.** The relative weight given by the government to two types of citizens can depend on political factors, and this weight can change due to lobby influence. Assume that $\gamma$ is the true share of individuals in the nontradables sector, and that $\gamma \geq \frac{\alpha}{1-\alpha}$. Now assume that $\gamma^p \leq \frac{\alpha}{1-\alpha} \leq \gamma$ is the weight attributed to the sector with the government under lobby influence. What is the impact of lobby action on the welfare of individuals?

## Exercise 4

Exchange rate policy, in general, has an impact on inflation. Consider the economic model developed in Section 11.1, particularly the case that incorporates the distributive effects of inflation on individual welfare.

**a.** Explain how exchange rate depreciation affects domestic prices, generating inflation, and how inflation, in turn, impacts the real exchange rate. Also explain how inflation reduces individual welfare.

**b.** How does the exchange rate in period $t = 0$, i.e., $Q_0$, affect individual welfare? If the government could choose $Q_0$, what would be the chosen value? What is the threshold for the weight attributed to the nontradables sector for the government to prefer a more appreciated exchange rate?

**c.** Now assume that the government only chooses the real exchange rate for period $t = 1$. In this case, how does the intertemporal discount rate for individuals, i.e., $\beta$, affect the cut-off point, $\overline{\gamma}$, which serves as a reference to define the real exchange rate level? Explain your answer, relating it to the economic and political elements that can affect the value of $\beta$.

**d.** Now assume that the government chooses the trajectory for the real exchange rate in all periods, that is, that the government chooses $Q_t$, $t = 1, 2$. Find the exchange rate chosen by the government, assuming that the weight attributed to individuals in the nontradables sector is given by $\gamma^p$. Explain for your answer.

**e.** Compare the results obtained in the previous item with those presented throughout the text of Section 11.1, that is, evaluate the difference between choosing the real exchange rate alone at each point in time and choosing the whole exchange rate trajectory at once. Explain your answer.

## Exercise 5

In this exercise, we will develop a model that analyzes the choice of exchange regime based in a political environment where there are two parties, the right and the left, each with distinct preferences regarding public spending and inflation. Both parties are making an effort either to reach or maintain power. Consider a small, open economy with flexible prices and free capital mobility. The economy is populated by two distinct groups of individuals. The first group is formed by a continuum of consumers, denoted by set $I_C$, and the second composed by politicians, denoted by $I_P$. Individuals from the political group are the only ones who can run for government office. The political group is divided into two subgroups (parties): the right and the left.

The agents in group $I_C$ are both consumers and voters. There is only one consumption good, tradable, that is used as numeraire. Each individual receives a real, exogenous income endowment $y > 0$ in each period and pays a share $\tau \in (0, 1)$ of this income in the form of taxes to the government. In period $t = 2$, besides the receipts and expenses for period $t = 1$, the agent observes the amount of public goods provided by the government, measured in *per capita* terms, denoted by $g$.

Assume that purchasing power parity is valid and that the level of international prices is normalized to 1.

The initial wealth of each agent consists of a real stock, that is, measured in units of domestic goods, of international bonds, $f_0$, and of a nominal stock of money, $M_0$. For each period, the individuals choose how much to consume and how much to allocate of their wealth in international bonds, that pay the holder the return of $1 + r^*$, or in domestic currency. The real stock of international bonds in period $t$ is denoted by $f_t$, and the nominal stock of domestic currency by $M_t$. The nominal domestic interest rate is given by $i_t = r^* + \pi_t$, where $r^*$ is the international interest rate and $\pi_t = \frac{P_t - P_{t-1}}{P_{t-1}}$ is domestic inflation.

Individual $i \in I_C$ has preferences represented by the following utility function:

$$U_i(c_1, c_2, m_0, m_1, g) = v(c_1) + \left(\frac{\varepsilon}{\varepsilon - 1}\right) m_0^{\frac{\varepsilon-1}{\varepsilon}} + \beta \left[ v(c_2) + \left(\frac{\varepsilon}{\varepsilon - 1}\right) m_1^{\frac{\varepsilon-1}{\varepsilon}} + \alpha_i u(g) \right],$$

where $c_t$ represents the consumption of goods in period $t$, $v(.)$ is an increasing and strictly concave function, i.e., $v' > 0$ and $v'' < 0$. $m_1 \equiv \frac{M_t}{P_t}$ is the real stock of money in period $t$, $\varepsilon \in (0, 1)$ is a preference parameter in relation to currency, $\beta$ is the intertemporal discount rate that we assume is equal to the interest rate, $\beta = \frac{1}{1+r}$, $\alpha_i$ is a parameter that captures preference of consumer $i \in I_C$ in relation to public spending, and $u(.)$ is an increasing and concave function.

**a.** Write the budget constraint for individual $j \in I_C$ for each period, as well as their intertemporal budget constraint. Interpret these equations.

**b.** Characterize the solution to the intertemporal optimization problem for this individual. What conclusion can you make based on the relationships found?

The group of politicians in this economy is divided into two political parties, the right and the left, denoted by $I_P = \{R, L\}$. The preferences of both parties in this economy can be represented by the following function:

$$U_i(c_1, c_2, m_0, m_1, g) = v(c_1) + \left(\frac{\varepsilon}{\varepsilon - 1}\right) m_0^{\frac{\varepsilon-1}{\varepsilon}} + \beta \left[ v(c_2) + \left(\frac{\varepsilon}{\varepsilon - 1}\right) m_1^{\frac{\varepsilon-1}{\varepsilon}} + \alpha_j u(g) \right],$$

where the symbols and parameters are analogous to those for the individuals who are purely consumers. What differs between the parties are their preferences in relation to public spending, measured by parameter $\alpha_j$. Nevertheless, it is common knowledge that $\alpha_R < \alpha_L$, which means that individuals from the left assign a higher value to government spending than individuals from the right.

The government in period $t = 1$ has a real stock of foreign debt, denoted by $b_0$ and a money supply denoted by $M_0$, in nominal terms. To pay for public spending in the first period, the government issues debt, denoted by $b_1$, and issues money, represented by $m_t$, in real terms, in addition to seigniorage and the collection of taxes, $\tau y$, as sources of income. In the second period, the only sources of income are the collection of taxes and seigniorage. In $t = 2$, government spending equals $g$. Assume that the government objective, independent of party, is to maximize the utility of the group each party represents, subject to the budget constraint of each period.

**c.** Obtain the government budget constraint for each period, along with its intertemporal resource constraint. Interpret your results.

**d.** Present the aggregate resource constraint for this economy. Based on the results obtained in the item, find the individual consumption for each period.

Assume the government in period $t = 1$ chooses the exchange rate regime. Consider that when the government decides to adopt the fixed exchange rate regime, it fixes inflation for period 1 at zero, i.e., $\pi_1 = 0$, and when it chooses a floating exchange rate regime, it fixes the money supply growth rate at zero, i.e., $\theta \equiv \frac{M_1 - M_0}{M_0} = 0$. In a simplified way, begin with the principle that individual preferences of group $I_C$ can be represented by the preferences of a median voter, whose preference in relation to government spending is represented by $\alpha_M$. Also assume that the following relation is true: $\alpha_R < \alpha_M < \alpha_L$. The timing of events is as follows:

- At the beginning of period 1, the government announces the chosen exchange rate regime.
- In period 1, the median voter makes their choice of $c_1$ and $m_0$.
- The election is at the end of period 1.
- The elected government for period 2 announces the provision of public good ($g$) at the beginning of the period.
- The median voter chooses $c_2$ and $m_1$.
- The government pays all its debts.

**e.** Considering that the government in period 1 knows it will not win the elections, what exchange regime will be chosen in period 1? (*Tip: You can solve the optimum regime choice using backward induction, that is, first solve the problem faced by the period 2 government and then solve the period 1 government problem, taking into consideration the optimum answer of the government for $t = 2$. Also consider possible changes in government, that is, that the period 1 government could be from the right, which will change to one from the left, or the contrary. Also assume that* $\frac{\alpha_M}{\alpha_R} \geq 1 + \frac{1 + 1/r^*}{(1/\varepsilon) - 1}$.)

**f.** Now consider that the period 1 government, be it either from the left or the right, knows it will remain in power. With this in mind, what will be the chosen exchange rate regime for period 1? (*Tip: You can solve the optimum regime choice problem using backward induction, as was done in the previous item. Use the same hypotheses as in the previous item, if necessary.*)

PART

V

# Annexes

## I List of Currencies

**Table 1** List of Currencies

| Country | Code[a] | Currency | Country | Code[a] | Currency |
|---|---|---|---|---|---|
| Afghanistan | AFN | Afghani | Brunei | BND | Brunei Dollar |
| South Africa | ZAR | Rand | Bulgaria | BGN | Bulgarian Lev |
| Albania | ALL | Lek | Cameroon | XAF | CFA Franc |
| Saudi Arabia | SAR | Saudi Riyal | Cambodia | KHR | Riel |
| Algeria | DZD | Dinar | Canada | CAD | Canadian Dollar |
| Germany | EUR | Euro | Kazakhstan | KZT | Tenge |
| Andorra | EUR | Euro | Chile | CLP | Chilean Peso |
| Angola | AOA | Kwanza | China | CNY | Yuan |
| Argentina | ARS | Argentine Peso | Cyprus | EUR | Euro |
| Armenia | AMD | Dram | Colombia | COP | Colombian Peso |
| Aruba | AWG | Guilder | Croatia | HRK | Kuna |
| Australia | AUD | Australian Dollar | Congo | CDF | Congolese Franc |
| Austria | EUR | Euro | South Korea | KRW | Won |
| Azerbaijan | AZN | New Manat | Costa Rica | CRC | Colon |
| Bahamas | BSD | Bahamian Dollar | Cuba | CUP | Cuban Peso |
| Bangladesh | BDT | Taka | Denmark | DKK | Danish Krone |
| Bahrain | BHD | Dinar | Ecuador | USD | American Dollar |
| Barbados | BBD | Barbadian/Bajan Dollar | Egypt | EGP | Egyptian Libra |
| Barbuda | XCD | East Caribbean Dollar | El Salvador | SVC | Colon |
| Belarus | BYR | Belarusian Ruble | Spain | EUR | Euro |
| Belgium | EUR | Euro | United States | USD | Dollar |
| Bhutan | INR | Indian Rupee | Fiji | FJD | Fiji Dollar |
| Bolivia | BOB | Boliviano | Finland | EUR | Euro |
| Bosnia | BAM | Marco | France | EUR | Euro |
| Brazil | BRL | Real | Gabon | XAF | African Franc |
| Ghana | GHS | Cedi | Mozambique | MZN | Metical |
| Greece | EUR | Euro | Nepal | NPR | Nepalese Rupee |
| Guatemala | GTQ | Quetzal | Nicaragua | NIO | Cordoba Gold |
| Guinea-Bissau | GWP | CFA Franc | New Zealand | NZD | New Zealand Dollars |
| Haiti | HTG | Gourde | Norway | NOK | Norse Krone |
| Netherlands | EUR | Euro | Oman | OMR | Rial Omani |
| Honduras | HNL | Lempira | Samoa | USD | Dollar |
| Hong Kong | HKD | Hong Kong Dollar | | | |
| Hungary | HUF | Forint | Pakistan | PKR | Pakistani Rupee |

*(Continued)*

**Table 1**    (Continued)

| Country | Code[a] | Currency | Country | Code[a] | Currency |
|---------|---------|----------|---------|---------|----------|
| Iceland | ISK | Icelandic Krona | Paraguay | PYG | Guarani |
| India | INR | Indian Rupee | Peru | PEN | Novo Sol |
| Indonesia | IDR | Indonesian Rupee | Porto Rico | XPT | Dollar |
| Iran | IRR | Iranian Rial | Portugal | EUR | Euro |
| Iraq | IQD | Dinar | Qatar | QAR | Rial |
| Ireland | EUR | Euro | United Kingdom | GBP | Sterling Pound |
| Israel | ILS | Shekel | Romania | RON | New Leu |
| Italy | EUR | Euro | Russia | RUB | Ruble |
| Jamaica | JMD | Jamaican Dollar | Sweden | SEK | Swedish Krone |
| Japan | JPY | Yen | Switzerland | CHF | Swiss Franc |
| Lebanon | LBP | Lebanese Libra | Taiwan | TWD | Taiwan New Dollars |
| Luxemburg | EUR | Euro | Turkey | TRY | Turkish Lira |
| Madagascar | MGA | Ariary | Uruguay | UYU | Uruguayan Peso |
| Malaysia | MYR | Ringgit | Venezuela | VEF | Bolivar |
| Mexico | MXN | Mexican Peso | Zimbabwe | ZWD | Dollar |
| Morocco | MAD | Dirham | | | |
| Monaco | EUR | Euro | | | |

[a]According to ISO classification 4217, established by the International Organization for Standardization (ISO).

# II  Data List

The following table contains a list of the electronic addresses of the databases used to prepare the figures contained in several chapters. The reference number provided in the figure correlates to the reference numbers below.

**Table 2**    Data Reference List

| Reference | Description | Agency | Internet Address |
|-----------|-------------|--------|------------------|
| (1) | Current Account and Trade Balance | The World Bank | http://data.worldbank.org/indicator/BN.CAB.XOKA.GD.ZS and http://data.worldbank.org/indicator/NE.RSB.GNFS.ZS |
| (2) | National Accounts | International Monetary Fund | http://www.principalglobalindicators.org/default.aspx |
| (3) | Nominal Exchange | World Bank | http://data.worldbank.org/indicator/PA.NUS.FCRF |
| (4) | Nominal Interest Rate | Eurostat | http://epp.eurostat.ec.europa.eu/ |
| (5) | Nominal Interest Rate | Federal Reserve | http://www.federalreserve.gov/econresdata |
| (6) | Nominal Interest Rate | Banco de la Nación Argentina | http://www.bcra.gov.ar/index_i.htm |
| (7) | Nominal Interest Rate | European Central Bank | http://sdw.ecb.europa.eu/home.do |
| (8) | Private Credit | World Bank | http://data.worldbank.org/indicator/FS.AST.DOMS.GD.ZS |
| (9) | CRB Index | Thomson Reuters CRB Index | http://thomsonreuters.com/en/products-services/financial/commodities/commodity-indices.html |
| (10) | Sovereign Debt and International Reserves | Brazilian Central Bank | https://www3.bcb.gov.br/sgspub/localizarseries/ |

# III  List of Mathematical Symbols

The following table contains a summary of the main mathematical symbols used in the text. It is important to emphasize that this list of the symbols is common throughout the whole book. However, each chapter contains other symbols used in specific ways, whose meaning is explained in the text where they are used.

**Table 3**   List of Mathematical Symbols

| Symbol | Description |
| --- | --- |
| $a_j$ | Sector $j$ productivity |
| $\alpha$ | Preference parameter: share of income spent on nontradable goods |
| $B$ | Net international investment position |
| TB | Trade balance |
| IB | Income balance |
| PI, SI | Primary and secondary income balances |
| $\beta$ | Intertemporal discount rate |
| $C$ | Aggregate consumption |
| CA | Balance in current account |
| $D$ | Gross external debt |
| $E(\cdot)$ | Conditional expectation operator |
| $F$ | Gross external credit |
| $G$ | Public expenditures |
| $I$ | Aggregate investment |
| $1 + i^*$, $i^*$ | Nominal international interest rate and its natural logarithm |
| $1 + i$, $i$ | Nominal domestic interest rate and its natural logarithm |
| $K$ | Stock of physical capital |
| $\Lambda$ | Share of wealth allocated in home assets |
| $M$, $m$ | Stock of money and its natural logarithm |
| $P$ | General price index |
| $p_b$ | Price of good $b$ |
| $\pi$ | Inflation rate |
| $Q$, $q$ | Real exchange rate and its natural logarithm |
| $r$ | Real interest rate |
| $\rho$ | Parameter of elasticity of transformation between two goods |
| $S$, $s$ | Nominal exchange rate and its natural logarithm |
| $S$ | Aggregate savings |
| $T$ | Taxes |
| $u(\cdot)$ | Utility function |
| $Y$, $y$ | Gross domestic product and its natural logarithm |

# References

Aghion, P., Bacchetta, P., Banerjee, A., 2000. A simple model of monetary policy and currency crises. Eur. Econ. Rev. 44 (4–6), 728–738.

Aisen, A., 2007. Money-based vs. exchange-rate-based stabilization: is there space for political opportunism? IMF Working Papers, 54, 1–30.

Aitken, B., Harrison, A., 1999. Do domestic firms benefit from direct foreign investment? Evidence from Venezuela. Am. Econ. Rev. 89 (3), 605–618.

Akerlof, G.A., 1970. The market for lemons: quality uncertainty and the market mechanism. Q. J. Econ. 84 (3), 488–500.

Alfaro, L., 2002. On the political economy of temporary stabilization programs. Econ. Polit. 14 (2), 133–161.

Arezki, R., Brückner, M., 2012. Commodity windfalls, polarization, and net foreign assets: panel data evidence on the voracity effect. J. Int. Econ. 86 (2), 318–326.

Bacchetta, P., 2013. Explaining deviations from uncovered interest rate parity. In: Caprio, G. (Ed.), Encyclopedia of Financial Globalization. Elsevier, Amsterdam.

Baldwin, R.E., Nino, V.D., 2006. Euros and zeros: the common currency effect on trade in new goods. NBER Working Papers, National Bureau of Economic Research, 12673.

Barro, R.J., Gordon, D.B., 1983. Rules, discretion and reputation in a model of monetary policy. J. Monet. Econ. 12 (1), 101–121.

Blanchard, O., Giavazzi, F., Sa, F., 2005. International investors, the U.S. current account and the dollar. Brookings Pap. Econ. Act. 1 (1), 1–49.

Blomberg, S.B., Frieden, J., Stein, E., 2005. Sustaining fixed rates: the political economy of currency pegs in Latin America. J. Appl. Econ. 8 (2), 203–225.

Bonomo, M., Terra, C., 1999. The political economy of exchange rate policy in brazil: an empirical assessment. Rev. Bras. Econ. 53 (4), 411–432.

Bonomo, M., Terra, C., 2001. The dilemma of inflation vs balance of payments: crawling pegs in brazil, 1964–98. In: Frieden, J., Stein, E. (Eds.), The Currency Game: Exchange Rate Politics in Latin America. Inter-American Development Bank, Washington, pp. 119–156.

Bonomo, M., Terra, C., 2005. Elections and exchange rate policy cycles. Econ. Polit. 17, 151–176.

Bonomo, M., Terra, C., 2010. Electoral cycles through lobbying. Econ. Polit. 22 (3), 446–470.

Brock, W.A., 1974. Money and growth: the case of long run perfect foresight. Int. Econ. Rev. 15, 750–777.

Broner, F.A., 2008. Discrete devaluations and multiple equilibria in a first generation model of currency crises. J. Monet. Econ. 55 (3), 592–605.

Broner, F.A., Didier, T., Erce, A., Schmukler, S., 2011. Gross capital flows: dynamics and crises. Centre for Economic Policy Research, Discussion Paper, World Bank (8591).

Burnside, C., Eichenbaum, M., Rebelo, S., 2001. Hedging and financial fragility in fixed exchange rate regimes. Eur. Econ. Rev. 45, 1151–1193.

Burnside, C., Eichenbaum, M., Rebelo, S., 2004. Government guarantees and self-fulfilling speculative attacks. J. Econ. Theory. 119 (1), 31–63.

Caballero, R.J., 2010. The "other" imbalance and the financial crisis. NBER Working Papers, 15636.

Caballero, R.J., Farhi, E., Gourinchas, P.-O., 2008. An equilibrium model of "Global Imbalances" and low interest rates. Am. Econ. Rev. 98 (1), 358–393.

Calvo, G., Reinhart, C., 2002. Fear of floating. Q. J. Econ. 117 (2), 379–408.

Calvo, G., Vegh, C.A., 1999. Inflation stabilization and bop crises in developing countries. In: Taylor, J.B., Woodford, M. (Eds.), Handbook of Macroeconomics, first ed., vol. 1, pp. 1531–1614.

Canzoneri, M.B., Diba, B.T., 1992. The inflation discipline of currency substitution. Eur. Econ. Rev. 36 (4), 827–845.

Casella, A., 1992. Participation in a currency union. Am. Econ. Rev. 82 (4), 847–863.

Cassel, G., 1918. Abnormal deviations in international exchanges. Econ. J. 28 (112), 413–415.

Chang, R., Velasco, A., 2000. Financial fragility and the exchange rate regime. J. Econ. Theory. 92 (1), 1–34.

Chang, R., Velasco, A., 2001. A model of financial crises in emerging markets. Q. J. Econ. 116 (2), 489−517.

Clover, R.W., 1967. A reconsideration of the microfoundation of monetary theory. West. Econ. J. 6, 1−8.

Corden, W.M., 2002. Too Sensational: On the Choice of Exchange Rate Regimes. MIT Press, Cambridge, MA.

Corsetti, G., Pesenti, P., Roubini, N., 1999. Paper tigers? A model of the Asian crisis. Eur. Econ. Rev. 43 (7), 1211−1236.

Crespo, N., Fontoura, M.P., 2007. 30 anos de investigação sobre externalidades do ide para as empresas nacionais—que conclusões? Estud. Econ. 37 (4), 849−874.

Devereux, M., 2007. Financial globalization and emerging market portfolios. Monet. Econ. Stud. 25, 101−130.

Domac, I., Mendoza A., 2004. "Is there room for foreign exchange interventions under an inflation targeting framework ? Evidence from Mexico and Turkey," Policy Research Working Paper Series 3288, The World Bank.

Dornbusch, R., 1976. Expectations and exchange rate dynamics. J. Polit. Econ. 84 (6), 1161−1176.

Driver, R.L., Westaway, P.F., 2004. Concepts of equilibrium exchange rates. Bank of England working papers 248, Bank of England.

Duarte, A.P., Andrade, J.S., Duarte, A., 2010. Exchange rate target zones: a survey of the literature. GEMF Working Papers, Faculdade de Economia, Universidade de Coimbra, 2010−14.

Easterly, W., 2001. The lost decades: explaining developing countries stagnation in spite of reform 1980−1998. J. Econ. Growth. 6 (2), 135−157.

Egert, B., 2007. "Central bank interventions, communication and interest rate policy in emerging European economies". J. Comp. Econ., Elsevier 35(2), pages 387−413.

Eichengreen, B., Hausmann, R., 1999. Exchange rates and financial fragility. NBER Working Papers, 7418.

Eichengreen, B., Rose, A.K., Wyplosz, C., 1995. Exchange market mayhem: the antecedents and aftermath of speculative attacks. Econ. Policy. 21, 249−312.

Feldstein, M., Horioka, C., 1980. Domestic saving and international capital flows. Econ. J. 90 (358), 314−329.

Fischer, S., 2001. Exchange rate regimes: is the bipolar view correct? J. Econ. Perspect. 15 (2), 3−24.

Forbes, K., Rigobon, R., 2001. Contagion and Latin America: definitions, measurement, and policy implications. J. LACEA Econ. 1 (2), 1−46.

Frankel, J., 1999. No single currency regime is right for all countries or at all times. Essays in International Finance. Princeton University Press, Princeton, NJ, p. 215.

French, K., Poterba, J., 1991. Investor diversification and international equity markets. Am. Econ. Rev. 81 (2), 222−226.

Frieden, J., Ghezzi, P., Stein, E., 2001. Politics and exchange rates: a cross-country approach. In: Frieden, J., Stein, E. (Eds.), The Currency Game: Exchange Rate Politics in Latin America. Inter-American Development Bank, Washington, pp. 21−64.

Galí, J., 2008. Monetary Policy, Inflation, and the Business Cycle: An Introduction to the New Keynesian Framework. Princeton University Press.

Galiani, S., Heymann, D., Tommasi, 2003. Great expectations and hard times: the argentine convertibility plan. J. Lat. Am. Caribb. Econo. Assoc. 4, 109−160.

Gersl, A., Holub, T., 2006. "Foreign exchange interventions under inflation targeting: the czech experience". Contemp. Econ. Policy West. Econ. Assoc. Int. 24 (4), 475−491.

Glick, R., Rose, A.K., 2002. Does a currency union affect trade? The time-series evidence. Eur. Econ. Rev. 46 (6), 1125−1151.

Goldstein, M., 2002. Managed floating plus. Institute for International Economics, Washington, DC.

Gourinchas, P., Rey, H., 2007a. International financial adjustment. J. Polit. Econ. 115, 665−703.

Gourinchas, P., Rey, H., 2007b. From world banker to world venture capitalist: U.S. external adjustment and the exorbitant privilege. NBER Chapters, in: G7 Current Account Imbalances: Sustainability and Adjustment, pp. 11−66.

Gourinchas, P.-O., Valdes, R., Landerretche, O., 2001. Lending booms: Latin America and the world. Economía. 1 (2), 47−99.

Guimarães R.P., Karacadag, C. "The Empirics of Foreign Exchange Intervention in Emerging Markets". In The Empirics of Foreign Exchange Intervention in Emerging Markets: The Cases of Mexico and Turkey. (USA: INTERNATIONAL MONETARY FUND, 2004). <http://dx.doi.org/10.5089/9781451854640.001>.

Hausmann, R., Sturzenegger, F., 2005. U.S. and global imbalances: can dark matter prevent a big bang? Working Paper, Kennedy School of Government.

Huang, S., Terra, C., 2014. Exchange rate populism. Thema Working Paper n°2014−12, Université de Cergy Pontoise.

Kamil, H., 2008. "Is Central Bank Intervention Effective Under Inflation Targeting Regimes? The Case of Colombia," IMF working paper 08/88.

Kaminsky, G., 1993. Is there a peso problem? evidence from the dollar/pound exchange rate, 1976–1987. Am. Econ. Rev., Am. Econ. Assoc. 83 (3), 450–472.

Kaminsky, G., Reinhart, C., Végh, C., 2003. The unholy trinity of financial contagion. J. Econ. Perspect. 17, 51–74.

Kaminsky, G.L., Reinhart, C.M., 1999. The twin crises: the causes of banking and balance-of-payments problems. Am. Econ. Rev. 89 (3), 473–500.

Khawar, M., 2003. Productivity and FDI—evidence from Mexico. J. Econ. Stud. 30 (1), 66–76.

Kiyotaki, N., Wright, R., 1989. On money as a medium of exchange. J. Polit. Econ. 97, 927–954.

Klein, M.W., Shambaugh, J.C., 2010. Exchange rate regimes in the Modern Era, 1. MIT Press Books, The MIT Press (1).

Kraay, A., Loayza, N., Servén, L., Ventura, J., 2005. Country portfolios. J. Eur. Econ. Assoc. 3, 914–945.

Kraay, A., Ventura, J., 2000. Current accounts in debtor and creditor countries. Q. J. Econ. 115 (4), 1137–1166.

Krugman, P., 1979. A model of balance-of-payments crises. J. Money, Credit Banking. 11 (3), 311–325.

Krugman, P., 1996. Are currency crises self-fulfilling? NBER Macroecon. Annu. 11, 345–407.

Krugman, P., 1999. Balance sheets, the transfer problem, and financial crises. Int. Tax Public Finance. 6 (4), 459–472.

Krugman, P.R., 1991. Target zones and exchange rate dynamics. Q. J. Econ. 106 (3), 669–682.

Kumhof, M., 2010. "On the theory of sterilized foreign exchange intervention". J. Econ. Dyn. Control. 34, 1403–1420.

Lane, P., Milesi-Ferretti, G.M., 2001a. Long-term capital movements. NBER, Macroecon. Annu. 2000, 73–116.

Lane, P.R., 2001. The new open economy macroeconomics: a survey. J. Int. Econ. 54 (2), 235–266.

Lane, P.R., Milesi-Ferretti, G.M., 2001b. The external wealth of nations: Measures of foreign assets and liabilities for industrial and developing countries. J. Int. Econ. 55 (2), 263–294.

Lane, P.R., Milesi-Ferretti, G.M., 2007. The external wealth of nations mark ii: revised and extended estimates of foreign assets and liabilities, 1970–2004. J. Int. Econ. 73 (2), 223–250.

Lane, P.R., 2012. The European sovereign debt crisis. J. Econ. Perspect. 26 (3), 49–68.

Levy-Yeyati, E., Sturzenegger, F., 2005. Classifying exchange rate regimes: deeds vs. words. Eur. Econ. Rev. 49 (6), 1603–1635.

Lischinsky, B., 2003. The puzzle of Argentina debt problem: virtual dollar creation? In: Teunissen, J.J., Akkerman, A. (Eds.), The Crisis That Was Not Prevented: Lessons for Argentina, the IMF and Globalization. FONDAD.

Lorenzoni, G., 2015. International Financial Crises. In: Gopinath, G., Rogoff, K. (Eds.), Handbook of International Economics. Elsevier, pp. 689–740.

MacDonald, R., 2000. Concepts to calculate equilibrium real exchange rates: an overview. Discussion Paper Series 1: Economic Studies, Deutsche Bundesbank, Research Centre.

Markusen, J., Venables, A.J., 1999. Foreign direct investment as a catalyst for industrial development. Eur. Econ. Rev. 43 (2), 335–356.

McKinnon, R., Pill, H., 1998. International overborrowing: a decomposition of credit and currency risks. World Dev. 26 (7), 1267–1282.

McKinnon, R.I., 1963. Optimum currency areas. Am. Econ. Rev. 53 (4), 717–724.

Mendoza, E.G., Quadrini, V., Ríos-Rull, J.-V., 2009. Financial integration, financial development, and global imbalances. J. Polit. Econ. 117 (3), 371–416.

Micco, A., Stein, E., Ordoñez, G., 2003. The currency union effect on trade: early evidence from emu. Econ. Policy. 37, 315–356.

Milesi-Ferreti, G.M., 2009. A 2 trillion question. VOX, pp. 11–66.

Mishkin, F., 1996. Understanding financial crises: a developing country perspective. In: Bruno, Michael, Boris Pleskovic (Eds.), Annual World Bank Conference on Development Economics, Washington, DC. World Bank, pp. 29–62.

Mundell, R.A., 1961. A theory optimum currency areas. Am. Econ. Rev. 51 (4), 657–665.

Nardis, S., De Santis, R., Vicarelli, C., 2008. The euro's effects on trade in a dynamic setting. Eur. J Comp Econ. 5 (1), 73–85.

Neumann, M.J., 1992. Seigniorage in the United States: how much does the U.S. government make from money production? Fed. Reserve Bank St Louis Rev. 74 (2), 29–40.

Obsfeld, M., Rogoff, K., 2000. The six major puzzles in international macroeconomics: is there a common cause? In: Bernanke, B., Rogoff, K. (Eds.), NBER Macroeconomics Annual 2000. The MIT Press, pp. 339–390.

Obstfeld, M., 1986. Rational and self-fulfilling balance-of-payments crises. Am. Econ. Rev. 76 (1), 72−81.

Obstfeld, M., 1994. The logic of currency crises. Cah. Econ. Monetaires. 43, 189−213.

Obstfeld, M., 1998. The global capital market: benefactor or menace? J. Econ. Perspect. 12 (4), 9−30.

Obstfeld, M., Rogoff, K., 1995. Exchange rate dynamics redux. J. Polit. Econ. 103 (3), 624−660.

Obstfeld, M., Rogoff, K., 1996. Foundations of International Macroeconomics. MIT Press, Cambridge, Massachusetts.

Obstfeld, M., Rogoff, K., 2009. Global imbalances and the financial crisis: products of common causes. CEPR Discussion Papers, 7606.

Obstfeld, M., Shambaugh, J.C., Taylor, A.M., 2004. The trilemma in history: tradeoffs among exchange rates, monetary politics, and capital mobility. Rev. Econ. Stat. 87 (3), 423−438.

Pascó-Fonte, A., Ghezzi, P., 2001. Exchange rates and interest groups in Peru, 1950−1996. In: Frieden, J., Stein, E. (Eds.), The Currency Game: Exchange Rate Politics in Latin America. Inter-American Development Bank, Washington, DC, pp. 249−276.

Pavlova, A., Rigobon, R., 2010. International macro-finance. NBER Working Paper Series (16630).

Persson, T., Tabellini, G., 2000. Political economics: Explaining economic policy. MIT Press Books.

Reinhart, C., Rogoff, K., 2009. This Time Is Different: Eight Centuries of Financial Folly. Princeton University Press, Princeton.

Reinhart, C.M., Rogoff, K.S., 2004. The modern history of exchange rate arrangements: a reinterpretation. Q. J. Econ. 119 (1), 1−48.

Rochon, C., 2006. Devaluation without common knowledge. J. Int. Econ. 70, 470−489.

Rodriguez-Clare, A., 1996. Multinationals, linkages and economic development. Am. Econ. Rev. 86 (4), 852−873.

Rodrik, D., 1990. The transfer problem in small open economies: exchange rate and fiscal policies for debt service. Ricer. Econ. XLIV, 231−250.

Rogoff, K., 1977. Rational expectations in the foreign exchange market revisited. Unpublished manuscript, Massachusetts Institute of Technology.

Rogoff, K., 1985. The optimal degree of commitment to an intermediate monetary target. Q. J. Econ. 100 (4), 1169−1189.

Rogoff, K., 1996. The purchasing power parity puzzle. J. Econ. Lit. 34, 647−668.

Rose, A., Stanley, T.D., 2005. A meta-analysis of the effect of common currencies on international trade. J. Econ. Surv. 19, 347−365.

Rose, A.K., 2000. One money, one market? the effects of common currencies on international trade. Econ. Policy. 15 (30), 9−45.

Samuelson, P.A., 1958. An exact consumption-loan model of interest with or without the social contrivance of money. J. Polit. Econ. 66 (4), 467−482.

Sarno, L., Taylor, M.P., 2002. Purchasing power parity and the real exchange rate. IMF Staff Papers, Palgrave Macmillan. 49 (1).

Sarno, L., Taylor, M.P., 2001. "Official intervention in the foreign exchange market: is it effective and, if so, how does it work?". J. Econ. Lit. 39, 839−868.

Shambaugh, J., 2004. The effect of fixed exchange rates on monetary policy. Q. J. Econ. 119 (1), 301−352.

Sidrauski, M., 1967. Rational choice and patterns of growth in a monetary economy. Am. Econ. Rev. 57 (2), 534−544.

Stein, E.H., Streb, J.M., 2004. Elections and the timing of devaluations. J. Int. Econ. 63 (1), 119−145.

Stein, E.H., Streb, J.M., Ghezzi, P., 2005. Real exchange rate cycles around elections. Econ. Polit. 17 (3), 297−330.

Tavlas, G., Dellas, H., Stockman, A., 2008. No single currency regime is right for all countries or at all times. Working Papers, Bank of Greece, 90.

Taylor, A.M., Taylor, M.P., 2004. The purchasing power parity debate. J. Econ. Perspect. 18 (4), 135−158.

Taylor, J.B., Woodford, M., 1999. Staggered price and wage setting in macroeconomics. Handb. Macroecon. 1009−1050.

Terra, C., 1997. Debt crisis and inflation. Rev. Econom. 17 (2), 21−48.

Terra, C., 1998. Openness and inflation: a new assessment. Q. J. Econ. CXIII (2), 641−648.

Terra, C., Vahia, A.L., 2008. A note on purchasing power parity: the choice of price index. Rev. Bras. Econ. 62 (1), 95−102.

Tille, C., van Wincoop, E., 2010. A new perspective on the new rule of the current account. J. Int. Econ. 80 (1), 89−99.

Tornell, A., Lane, P.R., 1999. The voracity effect. Am. Econ. Rev. 89 (1), 22−46.

# Index

*Note*: Page numbers followed by "*f*", "*t*" and "*b*" refer to figures, tables and boxes, respectively.

Printed in the United States
By Bookmasters